# Global Ecology

READINGS TOWARD A RATIONAL STRATEGY FOR MAN

UNDER THE GENERAL EDITORSHIP OF

Peter Collier

# Global Ecology

### READINGS TOWARD
### A RATIONAL STRATEGY FOR MAN

EDITED BY

## John P. Holdren

*University of California,*
*Lawrence Radiation Laboratory*

## Paul R. Ehrlich

*Stanford University*

 Harcourt Brace Jovanovich, Inc.

*New York    Chicago    San Francisco    Atlanta*

To Cheri and Anne

ISBN: 0-15-529622-1

Library of Congress Catalog Number: 70-153748

Printed in the United States of America

Drawings by Graphic Presentation Services, Inc.

Cover photograph by Jerome Hirsch.

# Preface

This collection of essays emphasizes the unified nature of the problems in population, resources, and environment which confront mankind today. The readings are taken from the literature of the physical sciences, technology, sociology, demography, conservation, political commentary, and economics. Together with our commentary at the beginning of each section, they comprise a perspective shaped by two underlying themes: the first is the enormous complexity of the problems we face, embracing a wealth of interconnections among human populations, man-made systems, and the often ill-understood natural systems on which all life depends; the second is the fundamentally radical changes in human institutions and behavior prerequisite to the global ecological strategy we need so desperately.

The addition of yet another volume to the growing shelf of readings on man's predicament needs more specific justification. We are hopeful, in particular, that our contributions to the book as editors reflect a fruitful interaction between our respective technological and biological backgrounds. Such a collaboration greatly simplifies the task of lending cohesiveness to the multifaceted array of problems represented here. It also eliminates many blind spots in the attempt we make—perhaps brashly—to identify and coordinate some elements of the needed solutions.

We hope the audience, too, will be interdisciplinary. The book should be suitable for supplementary reading in courses in both the biological and sociological sciences, and in the many multidisciplinary programs in human ecology now springing up in colleges across the country. The concerned layman with some previous exposure to discussions of population, resources, and environment will also find much of interest here.

*John P. Holdren*
*Paul R. Ehrlich*

# Contents

# Elements of
# an Ecological Revolution

*It is a secret both in nature and states that it is safer to
change many things than one.**

## THE SCOPE OF MAN'S PERIL

The world faces today a multiplicity of crises: explosive political and
ideological conflicts, rampant malnutrition, grinding poverty, and inexorable
erosion of the capacity of the natural environment to support life. These
extant and potential disasters are inextricably entwined with each other and
with a global population size and growth rate unprecedented in the tenure
of *Homo sapiens* on Earth. Together they preclude a humane and fruitful
existence for a considerable fraction of the world's inhabitants, they bid fair
to destroy such worthwhile values as today's civilization may embody, and
in their most sinister aspects they imperil even the habitability of the planet.

These crises cannot be dealt with in isolation; there are no panaceas for
the mess we are in. Neither green revolutions, nor population control, nor all
the technology man can muster will alone salvage the future. What is required
is no less than a revolution in human behavior, one which embodies fundamental reforms in our economic and political institutions, coupled with the
wisest technological enterprises, the necessary ingredient of population control, and a new perception of man's place in nature. Since such a revolution
must embrace all the relationships which bind man to his fellows and to the
living and nonliving environment, it is appropriate to call it "an ecological
revolution."

We use the word "ecological" advisedly, in spite of the prevalent observation that it is in danger of being bludgeoned into meaninglessness. Most of
the participants in the bludgeoning hadn't an inkling of the word's implications in the first place; many of those who deplore its overuse are either
similarly in the dark, or are seeing the light and finding it decidedly threaten-

* Francis Bacon, *Of Regimen of Health.*

ing. We hope this book will offer something to both groups (and to those in between): to the first, a sense of the scope of man's predicament, the inadequacy of the piecemeal measures now being touted as "solutions," and the radical implications of viewing the situation in a unified context; to the second, the demonstration that the revolution we advocate—the anxiety and hazards of rapid change notwithstanding—is preferable by far to the alternatives.

## THE ELEMENTS OF CHANGE

There are three principal elements in a successful response to societal crisis. The first is recognizing the threat and, more specifically, perceiving the consequences of not averting it. This perception provides the impetus for the second element—the changes in attitudes and values which must precede any drastic action. The third element, of course, is the translation of the new consensus into a structure of institutions and programs capable of implementing it. Perhaps the pre-eminent question of our time is whether the threats are not materializing and growing faster than this traditionally time-consuming process of structural change can respond. Indeed, we are far from achieving so much as the first step—a widespread perception of the threats and their consequences—among even the well-educated fraction of the world's population today. For this reason, a good part of the present book is devoted to elucidating the threats (Sections 1-3 and parts of 4 and 7).

Most of the remaining selections in the book deal primarily with the third element—the sorts of changes or innovations in institutions and programs which might have beneficial effects. In most of these cases, the prerequisite changes in values are assumed; in one notable exception (Berelson's paper in Sec. 6), the absence of this assumption serves to classify all constructive proposals examined as infeasible. There is, then, a logical gap in our presentation, which we propose to remedy here. Specifically, we offer some suggestions on a specific set of attitudes, values, and goals commensurate with the threats and conducive to solutions.

## GOALS AND VALUES

It should be understood at the outset that the ideas and attitudes which must be abandoned if the ecological revolution is to materialize are not the exclusive property of American businessmen. Some of the most untenable propositions are shared by members of the SDS and the John Birch Society, Soviet party functionaries, and poor peasants in the People's Republic of China.

As a beginning, we must all relinquish the notion that there are single, monolithic solutions to the multidimensional plight of man. Once *Homo sapiens* faces up to the totality of forces operating on him and on the life support systems of the Earth, several conclusions should follow: it will be futile to control resource utilization if we do not also control population; it is self-defeating to plan agricultural development in a sociological and ecological vacuum; it is myopic to speak of "ecology" in terms of roadside litter and air pollution while ignoring the ecocatastrophe of the ghetto and the ecocide of war.

The euphemistic classification of countries as "developed" or "underdeveloped" reflects another untenable proposition—that it is both desirable and possible for the bulk of mankind to duplicate the behavior of today's industrial nations. Sheer population size in the poor countries and the long history of exploitation of high-grade resources by the industrial nations have probably already made this impossible in principle. Simply the size of the gap to be narrowed and the ability of population growth to erode potential gains will certainly make it operationally impractical in the next 100 years. Finally, the "goal" is itself absurd from both ecological and humanistic standpoints. The global ecosystem shows symptoms of overloading today; to subject it to several times the strain by making our industrial atrocities universal would surely be suicidal. And, by any reasonable criteria—crime rates, incidence of stress-related diseases, quality of both urban and suburban environments—the quality of life has been declining in the "developed" countries for some time. That this decline has for the most part escaped widespread notice is a tribute to the adaptability of man (the same sort of "adaptability" enables a frog to be gradually heated in a pan of water and eventually boiled to death without becoming agitated until the end).

Clearly, the word "overdeveloped" is the best description for the majority of today's industrial nations. But in a neat bit of cultural egotism, we have labelled the attendant destructive behavior "advanced", and persuaded the remainder of the world community to follow suit if they can. Thus, the ironic situation exists in which most leaders in the poor nations would *welcome* a little more environmental deterioration as a sign of progress. In this they cannot be blamed. And the overdeveloped countries (ODC's), having looted the world of its most accessible resources and poisoned the ecosystem with the wastes, may find it unseemly to demand that the others now go slow to preserve what's left.

Only one rational path is open to us—simultaneous de-development of the ODC's and semi-development[1] of the underdeveloped countries (UDC's), in order to approach a decent and ecologically sustainable standard of living for all in between. By de-development we mean lower per-capita energy consumption, fewer gadgets, and the abolition of planned obsolescence. We mean ecologically sound agricultural practices which may make food more expensive and diets among the non-poor less extravagant. We mean transportation systems which cater to efficiency rather than to egos. Under the rubric of semi-development, in turn, we propose to avoid inflicting the likes of Los Angeles, Liverpool, Hamburg, or Tokyo on Ghana, Bolivia, and Indonesia. Indeed, we suspect that any practical (i.e., sustainable) system may find most of today's UDC's developed primarily agriculturally, with the fruits of industrialization provided them through a reformed world trade system.

[1] A more detailed discussion of de-development and semi-development may be found in *Population, Resources, Environment: Issues in Human Ecology* by P. R. and A. H. Ehrlich (W. H. Freeman & Co., San Francisco, 1970).

The rewards of success in such a transformation would be great, and the penalties relatively small. In the present ODC's (by then simply "developed") the air would be cleaner and life more leisurely. The Protestant ethic, immortalized over the gates of Auschwitz in the phrase "Arbeit macht frei", would be dead, and with it the crass hucksterism so visible in today's TV commercials about the whiteness of wash and the freshest mouth in town. There would be fewer but more permanent appliances, and more people employed in repair, recycling, and artistic pursuits; less air conditioning, but better building insulation and less clothes in hot weather; more use of muscle power, but less chance of dying prematurely of a coronary. Citizens of the present UDC's, in turn, would be well-fed, well-housed, and free to pursue cultural goals quite different from those considered suitable by Western thinkers from Adam Smith and Karl Marx (who thought non-Western culture nonexistent) to Milton Friedman. Presumably, with the salutory example of more rational behavior in the former ODC's, the remainder of humanity would not feel deprived without skylines like that of Gary, Indiana.

We do not overestimate, of course, the likelihood of this utopian vision coming to pass (an alternative scenario concludes this book). It presupposes an unprecedented change in values, particularly the willingness of individuals to weigh long-term consequences against short term "gains". But it has the merit, at least, that the greatest changes must occur in the ODC's, where the educability is presumably greatest. For while continued population growth must be recognized as untenable everywhere, we in the ODC's must renounce our overdevelopment as well as our overpopulation. The judicious rechanneling of our technological extravagance is essential both to the preservation of the world's ecosystems in working condition and to the hope of drastic improvement in living conditions for the bulk of humanity.

## THE GREEN REVOLUTION: A CASE STUDY

Both the potential and the pitfalls of approaches to narrowing the gap between the ODC's and the UDC's are visible today in the Green Revolution, a phenomenon which is touched upon in several of the selections in this book. As an attempt to increase dramatically the agricultural production of the UDC's, the Green Revolution is fundamentally sound. The focus is on improving yields on land already under cultivation by using new varieties of traditional crops, thus averting the huge expense and ecological damage inevitably involved in bringing marginal land under cultivation. The impetus and the initial infusions of capital have come from the ODC's (the new seeds were developed under the auspices of the Ford and Rockefeller Foundations). And initial successes have been impressive, although characteristically exaggerated in the reporting. (It is worth noting, for example, that in India—a major target of the Green Revolution—widely hailed crop increases in 1967 and 1968 barely restored the inadequate *1964* per capita diet level, after monsoon failures produced nutritional disaster in 1965 and 1966.) It must be remembered that in the race to feed the hungry, we are starting out far behind. Simply "keeping pace with population growth," as the popular magazines so often put it, is far from sufficient performance.

To continue to do much better than this through the Green Revolution will take much greater amounts of technical assistance and capital from the ODC's than have been forthcoming so far. Seeds alone are far from enough for the new grain varieties thrive only with abundant water and with large doses of fertilizer. Much of the existing irrigated land in the target UDC's is already planted with the new grains; if the dramatic improvements are to continue, then, the expensive and elaborate task of constructing vast new irrigation systems must proceed apace. These and related points are treated in detail in the first two papers in Section 1, and we will not belabor them further here. The significant conclusion is that absolutely massive contributions from the ODC's—perhaps 15 per cent of their gross national products—will be required to extend and generalize the Green Revolution to fill the needs of the UDC's in the next two decades. Such a transfer of funds would itself represent the beginning of the de-development/semi-development revolution we advocate.

Unfortunately, the Green Revolution as presently constituted is tinged with precisely the "development mentality" which we have argued against above. To too great a degree, it is an attempt to transfer Western agricultural technology directly to the UDC's. In other words, its sponsors propose to inflict on the UDC's the same ecological blunders which have long been perpetrated in Western agriculture—for example, an overdependence on inorganic fertilizers (which has polluted groundwater and contributed to the eutrophication of lakes and streams) and extensive use of persistent pesticides with attendant threats throughout the biosphere. The tendency to repeat these blunders in the UDC's is due in part to the characteristics of the new grain varieties themselves; they produce their higher yields only under heavy fertilization, and the need to protect them from pests motivates heavy use of ecologically dangerous pesticides. Moreover, planting enormous areas to a relatively few new crop varieties to achieve high yields now may ultimately prove a disastrous gamble—such large monocultures are notoriously vulnerable to plant diseases.

Another bit of conventional wisdom from the development ethic that the UDC's are adopting is the notion that efficient agriculture must be mechanized agriculture. Already the Green Revolution has driven Indians by the thousands off the land, exacerbating an unemployment problem which may cause social disintegration before famine does. It has become clear that the tractors and combines on which Western agri-business thrives are precisely what the UDC's do *not* need; instead, heavily labor-intensive approaches to the needed high yields must be developed and implemented if sociological disaster is to be avoided.

Even if all the pitfalls are averted, of course, neither the Green Revolution nor any imaginable variation on the theme can cope with present population growth rates for long. Even the most impassioned advocates of improvements in agricultural technology (a few economists and journalists excepted) concede that such measures, at best, offer a means of buying time. If the time we buy is not put to good use in bringing world population growth to zero, the entire enterprise will have been futile. To restate a point made earlier, there are no monolithic solutions to man's predicament; to neglect any component of the spectrum of crises will guarantee failure in all of them.

## THE INTRICATE DEFENSIVE

There are many who are not prepared to admit that man's problems are as severe as we have argued here. It seems particularly offensive to some that so fundamental a phenomenon as human reproduction could be implicated in our plight; these individuals have occupied themselves in the construction of an endless stream of preposterous arguments to rationalize continued inaction. C. P. Snow got to the nub of this phenomenon when he described "the excessive unsimplicity (which) crops up whenever anyone makes a proposal which opens up a prospect, however distant, of new action. It involves a skill which all conservative functionaries are masters of, as they ingeniously protect the status quo; it is called the 'technique of the intricate defensive.'"

The reader will be familiar with some of the techniques employed in this aptly-named procedure, for example, changing basic assumptions in mid-argument, and proof by vigorous assertion. Among the most discouraging, of course, is the continued revival of bedraggled arguments which already have been repeatedly and resoundingly refuted ("The world could not possibly be overpopulated because I just flew around it in a jet plane and saw lots of empty space," or "There's no population problem; just a distribution problem.") We hope the papers and commentary assembled here enable the reader to deal with such nonsense, because the eager defenders of the status quo can be relied upon to continue to generate it.

It may fairly be said that the collection which follows this introduction presents a pessimistic picture. We and many of the authors represented are calling for drastic changes in human behavior and institutions—indeed, for an ecological revolution—and the likelihood of that coming to pass in time seems slim. In this connection, we have been warned by our more cautious colleagues that those who discuss threats of sociological and ecological disaster run the risk of being "discredited" if those threats fail to materialize on schedule. So we do, but technological optimists with projections of utopia-around-the-corner have long been running the same sort of risk—unabashedly and, we would note, attended by far fewer outraged accusations of "irresponsibility." The principal difference, perhaps, is this: we pessimists *hope* to be discredited, and, more specifically, to be discredited by the fruits of the concerted action which we hope our considered pessimism will stimulate.

# PART ONE

# Resource Realities

*Unless the rate of population increase can be sharply diminished, all the efforts to augment agricultural production will merely postpone the time of mass starvation and increase the agony when it inevitably occurs.**

When a population of organisms grows in a finite environment, sooner or later it will encounter a resource limit. This phenomenon, described by ecologists as reaching the "carrying capacity" of the environment, applies to bacteria on a culture dish, to fruit flies in a jar of agar, and to buffalo on a prairie. It must also apply to man on this finite planet.

The classical mechanism by which a resource limit brings population growth to a halt is most unpleasant: insufficiency of the limiting requisite of life—for example, food, mineral nutrients or water—initiates a dramatic increase in the death rate. In localized animal populations severely over-stressing a food resource, as in the case of deer over-browsing their winter range, the increase in deaths may drive the population nearly or completely to extinction. Fortunately, the depleted resource in such cases is usually "renewable," that is, it is replenished by natural processes once the stress is removed. Thus the animal population may ultimately recover or, if it had actually become extinct, be re-established by migrants.

In nature, population growth is rarely controlled by resource limits alone; predators, parasites, disease, or other kinds of rapid environmental change may act in concert with each other or with resource limitations in determining population size. All these factors in some form are relevant to the special case of human population growth. Although the present section deals specifically with the resource aspect, it is useful to enumerate here some similarities and differences in the operation of all of the factors on humans, as compared with that on other species.

First, the global growth of the human population has for some centuries displayed the growth pattern observed locally and temporarily in many other animals. At the present time, our numbers are doubling every thirty-five years

* President's Science Advisory Committee Panel on the World Food Supplies. Vol. I, 1967 (U.S. Govt. Printing Office).

—little more than a generation. Such resource limits as have loomed in the past as obstacles to this growth have been evaded by expanding frontiers and an aggressive, consumptive technology. Today the frontiers are gone, and the evidence is mounting that technology cannot hold the law of diminishing returns at bay much longer. Resources being stressed today are often being stressed globally; they will not be replenished from outside the "system." Moreover, many of these resources are not renewable. It is clear, for example, that the present 3.6 billion human beings are sustainable only by the consumption on a time scale of centuries of fossil fuels which were accumulated on a time scale of millions of years. Fission and fusion reactors may buy more time (if we learn to handle the wastes of the former, and if the latter can be made to work at all); of course, even an infinite amount of energy could not solve *all* our resource problems. And if man should misstep badly— as with a thermonuclear war—no energy-intensive civilization can be expected to rise from the ashes; the easily mined and harnessed fossil fuels will be gone, the pure metals dispersed beyond recovery, and our descendants, if any, shall not be building nuclear reactors from scratch.

Man's only significant predator is other men—we are speaking again of war. The probability that this particular death-rate "solution" to population growth will come to pass is not independent of resource problems. The obvious connection is the politics of access to high-grade mineral and fuel deposits, rich ocean fisheries, and fertile river basins. Those who doubt this should attempt to define for themselves the "vital interests" of the United States in Southeast Asia and the Middle East, so frequently alluded to in Presidential speeches and news conferences.

Nor is the susceptibility of the human population to control by parasitic disease and epidemic independent of resource limits. Populations short of food or specific nutrients have little resistance to disease, shortage of clean water encourages unsanitary conditions, and crowded populations form the ideal breeding ground for viruses (habitable space is in many localities a scarce resource). The ability of the environment to absorb wastes is also a resource, perhaps the first one to be exhausted in the industrial nations. Here emerges a significant quantitative difference between the human population/ resource/environment interaction and that of other animals: the human is capable of altering his environment for the worse on an unprecedented scale. Many animals now extinct were helpless victims of a natural ice age; man may initiate his own.

Having mentioned these complexities for perspective, we will restrict ourselves in the papers of this section to the more elementary resource questions, particularly with respect to food and minerals. The related environmental issues are treated in the following section.

In the introductory paper, "Population and Panaceas," we discuss the contention that the population-food imbalance may be corrected solely by increasing the food supply, and examine related problems with supplies of water and energy in an ever-more crowded world. We show that, even ignoring the serious environmental consequences of population growth, no plan which excludes dramatic and successful attempts at population control can avoid disaster.

In the following article, "Population, Food Supply, and Economic Development," the late Max F. Millikan discusses the agricultural prospects of the underdeveloped countries. He places a commendable emphasis on nutrition, rather than calories alone. (Many people concerned with the world food problem fail to realize that high-quality protein is the central element in the problem, and that it is precisely this constituent which is so expensive to obtain, in both economic and ecological terms.) We could grow enough calories for many times the present population of the world simply by expanding acreage planted in sugar beets and sugar cane. Unfortunately, you can't raise a single child on all the sugar cane grown in Hawaii.

Professor Millikan rightly comments on the need for substantial economic aid in order to improve nutritional standards in the underdeveloped world. We would go even further—without massive aid in agricultural development we see little hope that even the production of calories will keep pace with population growth for more than a few years. Recall that even the most successful imaginable population control programs will not stabilize population in the UDC's until the middle of the next century. One or two decades of agricultural success will not avoid disaster. Professor Millikan's discussion of the economic realities of the Green Revolution is most instructive. To the rather gloomy prognosis for nutrition which emerges from his analysis, we would add only the warning we have issued before: the environmental consequences of spreading ecologically incompetent agricultural technology from the developed countries throughout the UDC's, in the form of the Green Revolution, may ultimately be the downfall of the entire enterprise.

Perhaps the most pervasive and dangerous myth regarding food supply is the idea that the sea can serve as an infinite larder for mankind. Today, the sea provides 3 per cent of the world's calories and 20 per cent of its animal protein. The dream that much larger amounts await only our judicious harvesting is deflated by John H. Ryther in "Photosynthesis and Fish Production in the Sea." His calculations indicate that, *if we do everything right,* avoiding both overfishing and polluting the ocean, and if we are thus able to obtain the maximum potential yield of fish by the year 2000, then at that time the per capita supply of fish will be smaller than it is today (the increase from today's catch to the theoretical maximum is proportionally smaller than the anticipated population growth). Some experts feel that Ryther underestimates the maximum annual sustainable yield of fish, and that it actually is 2–3 times larger than the 100 million metric tons he predicts. If they are right it will make little difference; if, for example, 200 million tons is reached by 2030 the *per capita* yield will also be lower than today's. All these calculations must of course be tempered by the awareness that, in ocean fisheries, we're doing practically nothing right. We are both overfishing and polluting the sea, putting even the inadequate theoretical yield out of reach. At present the most realistic prediction of food from the sea is that within 10 to 15 years the *per capita* yield will enter a steady, probably rapid, decline.[1]

---

[1] Since this was written, the Food and Agriculture Organization of the U.N. has announced the shocking news that in 1969 world fisheries output *fell* by 3 per cent. Overdeveloped nations, in spite of increased efforts, suffered a 1 per cent loss and the catch of the protein-starved UDCs was down 5 per cent. A per capita loss in fisheries production at this early date would have been surprising; the absolute loss actually experienced is ominous.

The study of the availability of mineral resources to meet spiralling demand seems to have been dominated by two positions. The first notes that known world reserves of most essential minerals will be adequate to meet projected "needs" until the year 2000; thus there is nothing to worry about. Of course, most of the "need" is in the U.S. and in the other developed countries. The tacit assumption that the present lopsided consumption patterns will be maintained indefinitely into the future reveals the hollowness of our rhetoric about developing the UDC's. Nor is there any suggestion of what to do for an encore when the year 2000 comes and goes, and discoveries prove not to have kept pace with consumption. The second and more refined position is promoted by those we shall call "cornucopian economists". They contend that increases in demand can always be met by mining more abundant, lower-grade ores, and, indeed, that improvements in technology will keep costs down in spite of the increasing bulk of ore to be processed for each pound of metal. This happy state of affairs has in fact been borne out for *some* minerals over limited periods of time. But there is ample evidence that the cornucopian dream will not survive even the next thirty years for many of the minerals vital to an industrial economy. This crucial issue and its relation to quality of life in an increasingly crowded world is thoroughly explored by Thomas Lovering in his essay "Non-Fuel Mineral Resources in the Next Century." One can only hope the cornucopians can read as well as write, for little of their case survives Lovering's analysis.

This section concludes with excerpts from the introduction to *Resources and Man*, the report of the Committee on Resources and Man of the National Academy of Sciences. This committee, chaired by geologist Preston Cloud and including other distinguished authorities in geology, demography, zoology, agriculture, ocean fisheries, and energy resources, produced a powerfully worded indictment of complacency and unfounded optimism regarding population increase and resource availability. The frank conclusion of this report, that "to delay progress toward full self-regulation of population size is to play 'Russian roulette' with the future of man," is made all the more striking by the stature of its authors, the scope of their investigation and the wealth of data applied to the task. We are accustomed to obtuse and equivocal writing from the distinguished bodies usually appointed to study these matters; this striking exception deserves far more attention than it has received, and we hope the excerpts which so appropriately conclude our own survey of "Resource Realities" will stimulate the reader to seek out the full report.[2]

---

[2] Available in book form, W. H. Freeman & Co., San Francisco, 1969.

# Population and Panaceas:
# A Technological Perspective

PAUL R. EHRLICH AND JOHN P. HOLDREN

Today more than one billion human beings are either undernourished or malnourished, and the human population is growing at a rate of 2% per year. The existing and impending crises in human nutrition and living conditions are well-documented but not widely understood. In particular, there is a tendency among the public, nurtured on Sunday-supplement conceptions of technology, to believe that science has the situation well in hand—that farming the sea and the tropics, irrigating the deserts, and generating cheap nuclear power in abundance hold the key to swift and certain solution of the problem. To espouse this belief is to misjudge the present severity of the situation, the disparate time scales on which technological progress and population growth operate, and the vast complexity of the problems beyond mere food production posed by population pressures. Unfortunately, scientists and engineers have themselves often added to the confusion by failing to distinguish between that which is merely theoretically feasible, and that which is economically and logistically practical.

As we will show here, man's present technology is inadequate to the task of maintaining the world's burgeoning billions, even under the most optimistic assumptions. Furthermore, technology is likely to remain inadequate until such time as the population

Population and Panaceas: A Technological Perspective. From *BioScience*, Vol. 19, No. 12, December 1969, pp. 1065–1071. Reprinted by permission of the authors and the publisher.

growth rate is drastically reduced. This is not to assert that present efforts to "revolutionize" tropical agriculture, increase yields of fisheries, desalt water for irrigation, exploit new power sources, and implement related projects are not worthwhile. They may be. They could also easily produce the ultimate disaster for mankind if they are not applied with careful attention to their effects on the ecological systems necessary for our survival (Woodwell, 1967; Cole, 1968). And even if such projects are initiated with unprecedented levels of staffing and expenditures, without population control they are doomed to fall far short. No effort to expand the carrying capacity of the Earth can keep pace with unbridled population growth.

To support these contentions, we summarize briefly the present lopsided balance sheet in the population/food accounting. We then examine the logistics, economics, and possible consequences of some technological schemes which have been proposed to help restore the balance, or, more ambitiously, to permit the maintenance of human populations much larger than today's. The most pertinent aspects of the balance are:

1. The world population reached 3.5 billion in mid-1968, with an annual increment of approximately 70 million people (itself increasing) and a doubling time on the order of 35 years (Population Reference Bureau, 1968).

2. Of this number of people, at least one-half billion are undernourished (deficient in

calories or, more succinctly, slowly starving), and approximately an additional billion are malnourished (deficient in particular nutrients, mostly protein) (Borgstrom, 1965; Sukhatme, 1966). Estimates of the number actually perishing annually from starvation begin at 4 million and go up (Ehrlich, 1968) and depend in part on official definitions of starvation which conceal the true magnitude of hunger's contribution to the death rate (Lelyveld, 1968).

3. Merely to maintain present inadequate nutrition levels, the food requirements of Asia, Africa, and Latin America will, conservatively, increase by 26% in the 10-year period measured from 1965 to 1975 (Paddock and Paddock, 1967). World food production must double in the period 1965–2000 to stay even; it must triple if nutrition is to be brought up to minimum requirements.

## FOOD PRODUCTION

That there is insufficient additional, good quality agricultural land available in the world to meet these needs is so well documented (Borgstrom, 1965) that we will not belabor the point here. What hope there is must rest with increasing yields on land presently cultivated, bringing marginal land into production, more efficiently exploiting the sea, and bringing less conventional methods of food production to fruition. In all these areas, science and technology play a dominant role. While space does not permit even a cursory look at all the proposals on these topics which have been advanced in recent years, a few representative examples illustrate our points.

**Conventional Agriculture.** Probably the most widely recommended means of increasing agricultural yields is through the more intensive use of fertilizers. Their production is straightforward, and a good deal is known about their effective application, although, as with many technologies we consider here, the environmental consequences of heavy fertilizer use are ill understood and potentially

dangerous[1] (Wadleigh, 1968). But even ignoring such problems, we find staggering difficulties barring the implementation of fertilizer technology on the scale required. In this regard the accomplishments of countries such as Japan and the Netherlands are often cited as offering hope to the underdeveloped world. Some perspective on this point is afforded by noting that if India were to apply fertilizer at the per capita level employed by the Netherlands, her fertilizer needs would be nearly half the present world output (United Nations, 1968).

On a more realistic plane, we note that although the goal for nitrogen fertilizer production in 1971 under India's fourth 5-year plan is 2.4 million metric tons (Anonymous, 1968a), Raymond Ewell (who has served as fertilizer production adviser to the Indian government for the past 12 years) suggests that less than 1.1 million metric tons is a more probable figure for that date.[2] Ewell cites poor plant maintenance, raw materials shortages, and power and transportation breakdowns as contributing to continued low production by existing Indian plants. Moreover, even when fertilizer is available, increases in productivity do not necessarily follow. In parts of the underdeveloped world lack of farm credit is limiting fertilizer distribution; elsewhere, internal transportation systems are inadequate to the task. Nor can the problem of educating farmers on the advantages and techniques of fertilizer use be ignored. A recent study (Parikh et al., 1968) of the Intensive Agriculture District Program in the Surat district of Gujarat, India (in which scientific fertilizer use was to have been a major ingredient) notes that "on the whole, the performance of adjoining districts which have similar climate but did not enjoy relative preference of input supply was as good as, if not better than, the programme district. . . . A particularly disheartening feature is that the farm production plans, as yet, do not carry any educative

[1] Barry Commoner, address to 135th Meeting of the AAAS, Dallas, Texas (28 December 1968).
[2] Raymond Ewell, private communication (1 December 1968).

value and have largely failed to convince farmers to use improved practices in their proper combinations."

As a second example of a panacea in the realm of conventional agriculture, mention must be given to the development of new high-yield or high-protein strains of food crops. That such strains have the potential of making a major contribution to the food supply of the world is beyond doubt, but this potential is limited in contrast to the potential for population growth, and will be realized too slowly to have anything but a small impact on the immediate crisis. There are major difficulties impeding the widespread use of new high-yield grain varieties. Typically, the new grains require high fertilizer inputs to realize their full potential, and thus are subject to all the difficulties mentioned above. Some other problems were identified in a recent address by Lester R. Brown, administrator of the International Agricultural Development Service: the limited amount of irrigated land suitable for the new varieties, the fact that a farmer's willingness to innovate fluctuates with the market prices (which may be driven down by high-yield crops), and the possibility of tieups at market facilities inadequate for handling increased yields.[3]

Perhaps even more important, the new grain varieties are being rushed into production without adequate field testing, so that we are unsure of how resistant they will be to the attacks of insects and plant diseases. William Paddock has presented a plant pathologist's view of the crash programs to shift to new varieties (Paddock, 1967). He describes India's dramatic program of planting improved Mexican wheat, and continues: "Such a rapid switch to a new variety is clearly understandable in a country that tottered on the brink of famine. Yet with such limited testing, one wonders what unknown pathogens await a climatic change which will give the environmental conditions needed for their growth."

Introduction of the new varieties creates enlarged monocultures of plants with essentially unknown levels of resistance to disaster. Clearly, one of the prices that is paid for higher yield is a higher risk of widespread catastrophe. And the risks are far from local: since the new varieties require more "input" of pesticides (with all their deleterious ecological side effects), these crops may ultimately contribute to the defeat of other environment-related panaceas, such as extracting larger amounts of food from the sea.

A final problem must be mentioned in connection with these strains of food crops. In general, the hungriest people in the world are also those with the most conservative food habits. Even rather minor changes, such as that from a rice variety in which the cooked grains stick together to one in which the grains fall apart, may make new foods unacceptable. It seems to be an unhappy fact of human existence that people would rather starve than eat a nutritious substance which they do not recognize as food.[4]

Beyond the economic, ecological, and sociological problems already mentioned in connection with high-yield agriculture, there is the overall problem of time. We need time to breed the desired characteristics of yield and hardiness into a vast array of new strains (a tedious process indeed), time to convince farmers that it is necessary that they change their time-honored ways of cultivation, and time to convince hungry people to change the staples of their diet. The Paddocks give 20 years as the "rule of thumb" for a new technique or plant variety to progress from conception to substantial impact on farming (Paddock and Paddock, 1967). They write: "It is true that a *massive* research attack on the problem could bring some striking results in less than 20 years. But I do not find such an attack remotely contemplated in the thinking of those officials capable of initiating it." Promising as high-yield agriculture may be,

---

[3] Lester R. Brown, address to the Second International Conference on the War on Hunger, Washington, D.C. (February 1968).

[4] For a more detailed discussion of the psychological problems in persuading people to change their dietary habits, see McKenzie, 1968.

the funds, the personnel, the ecological expertise, and the necessary years are unfortunately not at our disposal. Fulfillment of the promise will come too late for many of the world's starving millions, if it comes at all.

**Bringing More Land Under Cultivation.** The most frequently mentioned means of bringing new land into agricultural production are farming the tropics and irrigating arid and semiarid regions. The former, although widely discussed in optimistic terms, has been tried for years with incredibly poor results, and even recent experiments have not been encouraging. One essential difficulty is the unsuitability of tropical soils for supporting typical foodstuffs instead of jungles (McNeil, 1964; Paddock and Paddock, 1964). Also, "the tropics" are a biologically more diverse area than the temperate zones, so that farming technology developed for one area will all too often prove useless in others. We shall see that irrigating the deserts, while more promising, has serious limitations in terms of scale, cost, and lead time.

The feasible approaches to irrigation of arid lands appear to be limited to large-scale water projects involving dams and transport in canals, and desalination of ocean and brackish water. Supplies of usable ground water are already badly depleted in most areas where they are accessible, and natural recharge is low enough in most arid regions that such supplies do not offer a long-term solution in any case. Some recent statistics will give perspective to the discussion of water projects and desalting which follows. In 1966, the United States was using about 300 billion gal of water per day, of which 135 billion gal were consumed by agriculture and 165 billion gal by municipal and industrial users (Sporn, 1966). The bulk of the agricultural water cost the farmer from 5 to 10 cents/1000 gal; the highest price paid for agricultural water was 15 cents/1000 gal. For small industrial and municipal supplies, prices as high as 50 to 70 cents/1000 gal were prevalent in the U.S. arid regions, and some communities in the Southwest were paying on the order

of $1.00/1000 gal for "project" water. The extremely high cost of the latter stems largely from transportation costs, which have been estimated at 5 to 15 cents/1000 gal per 100 miles (International Atomic Energy Agency, 1964).

We now examine briefly the implications of such numbers in considering the irrigation of the deserts. The most ambitious water project yet conceived in this country is the North American Water and Power Alliance, which proposes to distribute water from the great rivers of Canada to thirsty locations all over the United States. Formidable political problems aside (some based on the certainty that in the face of expanding populations, demands for water will eventually arise at the source), this project would involve the expenditure of $100 billion in construction costs over a 20-year completion period. At the end of this time, the yield to the United States would be 69 million acre feet of water annually (Kelly, 1966), or 63 billion gal per day. If past experience with massive water projects is any guide, these figures are overoptimistic, but if we assume they are not, it is instructive to note that this monumental undertaking would provide for an increase of only 21% in the water consumption of the United States, during a period in which the population is expected to increase by between 25 and 43% (U.S. Dept. of Commerce, 1966). To assess the possible contribution to the *world* food situation, we assume that all this water could be devoted to agriculture, although extrapolation of present consumption patterns indicates that only about one-half would be. Then using the rather optimistic figure of 500 gal per day to grow the food to feed one person, we find that this project could feed 126 million additional people. Since this is less than 8% of the projected world population growth during the construction period (say 1970 to 1990), it should be clear that even the most massive water projects can make but a token contribution to the solution of the world food problem in the long term. And in the crucial short term—the years preceding 1980—*no* additional people will be fed by projects still on the drawing board today.

In summary, the cost is staggering, the scale insufficient, and the lead time too long. Nor need we resort to such speculation about the future for proof of the failure of technological "solutions" in the absence of population control. The highly touted and very expensive Aswan Dam project, now nearing completion, will ultimately supply food (at the present miserable diet level) for less than Egypt's population growth during the time of construction (Borgstrom, 1965; Cole, 1968). Furthermore, its effect on the fertility of the Nile Delta may be disastrous, and, as with all water projects of this nature, silting of the reservoir will destroy the gains in the long term (perhaps in 100 years).

Desalting for irrigation suffers somewhat similar limitations. The desalting plants operational in the world today produce water at individual rates of 7.5 million gal/day and less, at a cost of 75 cents/1000 gal and up, the cost increasing as the plant size decreases (Bender, 1969). The most optimistic firm proposal which anyone seems to have made for desalting with present or soon-to-be available technology is a 150 million gal per day nuclear-powered installation studied by the Bechtel Corp. for the Los Angeles Metropolitan Water District. Bechtel's early figures indicated that water from this complex would be available at the site for 27-28 cents/1000 gal (Galstann and Currier, 1967). However, skepticism regarding the economic assumptions leading to these figures (Milliman, 1966) has since proven justified—the project was shelved after spiralling construction cost estimates indicated an actual water cost of 40-50 cents/ 1000 gal. Use of even the original figures, however, bears out our contention that the *most* optimistic assumptions do not alter the verdict that technology is losing the food/ population battle. For 28 cents/1000 gal is still approximately twice the cost which farmers have hitherto been willing or able to pay for irrigation water. If the Bechtel plant had been intended to supply agricultural needs, which it was not, one would have had

to add to an already unacceptable price the very substantial cost of transporting the water inland.

Significantly, studies have shown that the economies of scale in the distillation process are essentially exhausted by a 150 million gal per day plant (International Atomic Energy Agency, 1964). Hence, merely increasing desalting capacity further will not substantially lower the cost of the water. On purely economic grounds, then, it is unlikely that desalting will play a major role in food production by conventional agriculture in the short term.[5] Technological "break-throughs" will presumably improve this outlook with the passage of time, but world population growth will not wait.

Desalting becomes more promising if the high cost of the water can be offset by increased agricultural yields per gallon and, perhaps, use of a single nuclear installation to provide power for both the desalting and profitable on-site industrial processes. This prospect has been investigated in a thorough and well-documented study headed by E. A. Mason (Oak Ridge National Laboratory, 1968). The result is a set of preliminary figures and recommendations regarding nuclear-powered "agro-industrial complexes" for arid and semi-arid regions, in which desalted water and fertilizer would be produced for use on an adjacent, highly efficient farm. In underdeveloped countries incapable of using the full excess power output of the reactor, this energy would be consumed in on-site production of industrial materials for sale on the world market. Both near-term (10 years hence) and far-term (20 years hence) technologies are considered, as are various mixes of farm and industrial products. The representative near-term case for which a detailed cost breakdown is given involves a seaside facility with a desalting capacity of 1 billion gal/day, a farm size of 320,000 acres, and an industrial electric power consumption of 1585 Mw. The initial

---

[5] An identical conclusion was reached in a recent study (Clawson et al., 1969) in which the foregoing points and numerous other aspects of desalting were treated in far more detail than was possible here.

investment for this complex is estimated at $1.8 billion, and annual operating costs at $236 million. If both the food and the industrial materials produced were sold (as opposed to giving the food, at least, to those in need who could not pay),[6] the estimated profit for such a complex, before subtracting financing costs, would be 14.6%

The authors of the study are commendably cautious in outlining the assumptions and uncertainties upon which these figures rest. The key assumption is that 200 gal/day of water will grow the 2500 calories required to feed one person. Water/calorie ratios of this order or less have been achieved by the top 20% of farmers specializing in such crops as wheat, potatoes, and tomatoes; but more water is required for needed protein-rich crops such as peanuts and soybeans. The authors identify the uncertainty that crops usually raised separately can be grown together in tight rotation on the same piece of land. Problems of water storage between periods of peak irrigation demand, optimal patterns of crop rotation, and seasonal acreage variations are also mentioned. These "ifs" and assumptions, and those associated with the other technologies involved, are unfortunately often omitted when the results of such painstaking studies are summarized for more popular consumption (Anonymous, 1968b, 1968c). The result is the perpetuation of the public's tendency to confuse feasible and available, to see panaceas where scientists in the field concerned see only potential, realizable with massive infusions of time and money.

It is instructive, nevertheless, to examine the impact on the world food problem which the Oak Ridge complexes might have if construction were to begin today, and if all the assumptions about technology 10 years hence were valid *now*. At the industrial-agricultural

mix pertinent to the sample case described above, the food produced would be adequate for just under 3 million people. This means that 23 such plants per year, at a cost of $41 billion, would have to be put in operation merely to keep pace with world population growth, to say nothing of improving the substandard diets of between one and two billion members of the present population. (Fertilizer production beyond that required for the on-site farm is of course a contribution in the latter regard, but the substantial additional costs of transporting it to where it is needed must then be accounted for.) Since approximately 5 years from the start of construction would be required to put such a complex into operation, we should commence work on at least 125 units post-haste, and begin at least 25 per year thereafter. If the technology *were* available now, the investment in construction over the next 5 years, prior to operation of the first plants, would be $315 billion—about 20 times the total U.S. foreign aid expenditure during the past 5 years. By the time the technology *is* available the bill will be much higher, if famine has not "solved" the problem for us.

This example again illustrates that scale, time, and cost are all working against technology in the short term. And if population growth is not decelerated, the increasing severity of population-related crises will surely neutralize the technological improvements of the middle and long terms.

**Other Food Panaceas.** "Food from the sea" is the most prevalent "answer" to the world food shortage in the view of the general public. This is not surprising, since estimates of the theoretical fisheries productivity of the sea run up to some 50-100 times current yields (Schmitt, 1965; Christy and Scott, 1965). Many practical and economic difficulties, however, make it clear that such a figure will never be reached, and that it will not even be approached in the foreseeable future. In 1966, the annual fisheries harvest was some 57 million metric tons (United Nations, 1968). A careful analysis (Meseck, 1961) indicates that

[6] Confusing statements often are made about the possibility that food supply will outrun food demand in the future. In these statements, "demand" is used in the economic sense, and in this context many millions of starving people may generate no demand whatsoever. Indeed, one concern of those engaged in increasing food production is to find ways of increasing demand.

this might be increased to a world production of 70 million metric tons by 1980. If this gain were realized, it would represent (assuming no violent change in population growth patterns) a small per capita *loss* in fisheries yield.

Both the short- and long-term outlooks for taking food from the sea are clouded by the problems of overexploitation, pollution (which is generally ignored by those calculating potential yields), and economics. Solving these problems will require more than technological legerdemain; it will also require unprecedented changes in human behavior, especially in the area of international cooperation. The unlikelihood that such cooperation will come about is reflected in the recent news (Anonymous, 1968d) that Norway has dropped out of the whaling industry because overfishing has depleted the stock below the level at which it may economically be harvested. In that industry, international controls were tried —and failed. The sea is, unfortunately, a "commons" (Hardin, 1968), and the resultant management problems exacerbate the biological and technical problems of greatly increasing our "take." One suspects that the return per dollar poured into the sea will be much less than the corresponding return from the land for many years, and the return from the land has already been found wanting.

Synthetic foods, protein culture with petroleum, saline agriculture, and weather modification all may hold promise for the future, but all are at present expensive and available only on an extremely limited scale. The research to improve this situation will also be expensive, and, of course, time-consuming. In the absence of funding, it will not occur at all, a fact which occasionally eludes the public and the Congress.

## DOMESTIC AND INDUSTRIAL WATER SUPPLIES

The world has water problems, even exclusive of the situation in agriculture. Although total precipitation should in theory be adequate in quantity for several further doublings of population, serious shortages arising from problems of quality, irregularity, and distribution already plague much of the world. Underdeveloped countries will find the water needs of industrialization staggering: 240,000 gal of water are required to produce a ton of newsprint; 650,000 gal, to produce a ton of steel (International Atomic Energy Agency, 1964). Since maximum acceptable water costs for domestic and industrial use are higher than for agriculture, those who can afford it are or soon will be using desalination (40-100+ cents/1000 gal) and used-water renovation (54-57 cents/1000 gal [Ennis, 1967]). Those who cannot afford it are faced with allocating existing supplies between industry and agriculture, and as we have seen, they must choose the latter. In this circumstance, the standard of living remains pitifully low. Technology's only present answer is massive externally-financed complexes of the sort considered above, and we have already suggested there the improbability that we are prepared to pay the bill rung up by present population growth.

The widespread use of desalted water by those who *can* afford it brings up another problem only rarely mentioned to date, the disposal of the salts. The product of the distillation processes in present use is a hot brine with salt concentration several times that of seawater. Both the temperature and the salinity of this effluent will prove fatal to local marine life if it is simply exhausted to the ocean. The most optimistic statement we have seen on this problem is that "*smaller plants* (our emphasis) at seaside locations may return the concentrated brine to the ocean if proper attention is paid to the design of the outfall, and to the effect on the local marine ecology" (McIlhenny, 1966). The same writer identifies the major economic uncertainties connected with extracting the salts for sale (to do so is straightforward, but often not profitable). Nor can one simply evaporate the brine and leave the residue in a pile—the 150 million gal/day plant mentioned above would produce brine bearing 90 million lb. of salts daily (based on figures by Parker, 1966). This amount of salt would cover over 15 acres to a depth of one foot. Thus, every year a plant of the billion gallon per day, agro-industrial complex size would produce a pile of salt over 52 ft. deep and covering a square mile. The high winds typical of coastal deserts would seriously aggravate the associated soil contamination problem.

## ENERGY

Man's problems with energy supply are more subtle than those with food and water: we are not yet running out of energy, but we are being forced to use it faster than is probably healthy. The rapacious depletion of our fossil fuels is already forcing us to consider more expensive mining techniques to gain access to lower-grade deposits, such as the oil shales, and even the status of our high-grade uranium ore reserves is not clear-cut (Anonymous, 1968e).

A widely held misconception in this connection is that nuclear power is "dirt cheap," and as such represents a panacea for developed and underdeveloped nations alike. To the contrary, the largest nuclear-generating stations now in operation are just competitive with or marginally superior to modern coal-fired plants of comparable size (where coal is not scarce); at best, both produce power for on the order of 4-5 mills (tenths of a cent) per kilowatt-hour. Smaller nuclear units remain less economical than their fossil-fueled counterparts. Underdeveloped countries can rarely use the power of the larger plants. Simply speaking, there are not enough industries, appliances, and light bulbs to absorb the output, and the cost of industrialization and modernization exceeds the cost of the power required to sustain it by orders of magnitude, regardless of the source of the power. (For example, one study noted that the capital requirement to consume the output of a 70,000 kilowatt plant—about $1.2 million worth of electricity per year at 40% utilization

and 5 mills/kwh—is $111 million per year if the power is consumed by metals industries, $270 million per year for petroleum product industries [E. A. Mason, 1957].) Hence, at least at present, only those underdeveloped countries which are short of fossil fuels or inexpensive means to transport them are in particular need of nuclear power.

Prospects for major reductions in the cost of nuclear power in the future hinge on the long-awaited breeder reactor and the still further distant thermonuclear reactor. In neither case is the time scale or the ultimate cost of energy a matter of any certainty. The breeder reactor, which converts more nonfissile uranium ($^{238}$U) or thorium to fissionable material than it consumes as fuel for itself, effectively extends our nuclear fuel supply by a factor of approximately 400 (Cloud, 1968). It is not expected to become competitive economically with conventional reactors until the 1980's (Bump, 1967). Reductions in the unit energy cost beyond this date are not guaranteed, due both to the probable continued high capital cost of breeder reactors and to increasing costs for the ore which the breeders will convert to fuel. In the latter regard, we mention that although crushing granite for its few parts per million of uranium and thorium is possible in theory, the problems and cost of doing so are far from resolved.[7] It is too soon to predict the costs associated with a fusion reactor (few who work in the field will predict whether such a device will work at all within the next 15-20 years). One guess puts the unit energy cost at something over half that for a coal or fission power station of comparable size (Mills, 1967), but this is pure speculation. Quite possibly the major benefit of controlled fusion will again be to extend the energy supply rather than to cheapen it.

A second misconception about nuclear power is that it can reduce our dependence on fossil fuels to zero as soon as that becomes necessary or desirable. In fact, nuclear power plants contribute only to the electrical portion

[7] A general discussion of extracting metals from common rock is given by Cloud, 1968.

of the energy budget; and in 1960 in the United States, for example, electrical energy comprised only 19% of the total energy consumed (Sporn, 1963). The degree to which nuclear fuels can postpone the exhaustion of our coal and oil depends on the extent to which that 19% is enlarged. The task is far from a trivial one, and will involve transitions to electric or fuel-cell powered transportation, electric heating, and electrically powered industries. It will be extremely expensive.

Nuclear energy, then, is a panacea neither for us nor for the underdeveloped world. It relieves, but does not remove, the pressure on fossil fuel supplies; it provides reasonably-priced power where these fuels are not abundant; it has substantial (but expensive) potential in intelligent applications such as that suggested in the Oak Ridge study discussed above; and it shares the propensity of fast-growing technology to unpleasant side effects (Novick, 1969). We mention in the last connection that, while nuclear power stations do not produce conventional air pollutants, their radioactive waste problems may in the long run prove a poor trade. Although the AEC seems to have made a good case for solidification and storage in salt mines of the bulk of the radioactive fission products (Blanko et al., 1967), a number of radioactive isotopes are released to the environment, and in some areas such isotopes have already turned up in potentially harmful concentrations (Curtis and Hogan, 1969). Projected order of magnitude increases in nuclear power generation will seriously aggravate this situation. Although it has frequently been stated that the eventual advent of fusion reactors will free us from such difficulties, at least one authority, F. L. Parker, takes a more cautious view. He contends that the large inventory of radioactive tritium in early fusion reactors will require new precautions to minimize emissions (Parker, 1968).

A more easily evaluated problem is the tremendous quantity of waste heat generated at nuclear installations (to say nothing of the usable power output, which, as with power from whatever source, must also ultimately be dissipated as heat). Both have potentially disastrous effects on the local and world ecological and climatological balance. There is no simple solution to this problem, for, in general, "cooling" only moves heat; it does not *remove* it from the environment viewed as a whole. Moreover, the Second Law of Thermodynamics puts a ceiling on the efficiency with which we can do even this much, i.e., concentrate and transport heat. In effect, the Second Law condemns us to aggravate the total problem by generating still *more* heat in any machinery we devise for local cooling (consider, for example, refrigerators and air conditioners).

The only heat which actually leaves the whole system, the Earth, is that which can be radiated back into space. This amount steadily is being diminished as combustion of hydrocarbon fuels increases the atmospheric percentage of $CO_2$ which has strong absorption bands in the infrared spectrum of the outbound heat energy. (Hubbert, 1962, puts the increase in the $CO_2$ content of the atmosphere at 10% since 1900.) There is, of course, a competing effect in the Earth's energy balance, which is the increased reflectivity of the upper atmosphere to incoming sunlight due to other forms of air pollution. It has been estimated, ignoring both these effects, that man risks drastic (and perhaps catastrophic) climatological change if the amount of heat he dissipates in the environment on a global scale reaches 1% of the solar energy absorbed and reradiated at the Earth's surface (Rose and Clark, 1961). At the present 5% rate of increase in world energy consumption,[8] this level will be reached in less than a century, and in the immediate future the direct contribution of man's power consumption will create serious local problems. If we may safely rule out circumvention of the Second Law or the divorce of energy requirements from

[8] The rate of growth of world energy consumption fluctuates strongly about some mean on a time scale of only a few years, and the figures are not known with great accuracy in any case. A discussion of predicting the mean and a defense of the figure of 5% are given in Gúeron et al., 1957.

population size, this suggests that, whatever science and technology may accomplish, population growth must be stopped.

## TRANSPORTATION

We would be remiss in our offer of a technological perspective on population problems without some mention of the difficulties associated with transporting large quantities of food, material, or people across the face of the Earth. While our grain exports have not begun to satisfy the hunger of the underdeveloped world, they already have taxed our ability to transport food in bulk over large distances. The total amount of goods of *all* kinds loaded at U.S. ports for external trade was 158 million metric tons in 1965 (United Nations, 1968). This is coincidentally the approximate amount of grain which would have been required to make up the dietary shortages of the underdeveloped world in the same year (Sukhatme, 1966). Thus, if the United States *had* such an amount of grain to ship, it could be handled only by displacing the entirety of our export trade. In a similar vein, the gross weight of the fertilizer, in excess of present consumption, required in the underdeveloped world to feed the additional population there in 1980 will amount to approximately the same figure—150 million metric tons (Sukhatme, 1966). Assuming that a substantial fraction of this fertilizer, should it be available at all, will have to be shipped about, we had best start building freighters! These problems, and the even more discouraging one of internal transportation in the hungry countries, coupled with the complexities of international finance and marketing which have hobbled even present aid programs, complete a dismal picture of the prospects for "external" solutions to ballooning food requirements in much of the world.

Those who envision migration as a solution to problems of food, land, and water distribution not only ignore the fact that the world has no promising place to put more people, they simply have not looked at the numbers of the transportation game. Neglecting the fact that migration and relocation costs would probably amount to a minimum of several thousand dollars per person, we find, for example, that the entire long-range jet transport fleet of the United States (about 600 planes [Molloy, 1968] with an average capacity of 150), averaging two round trips per week, could transport only about 9 million people per year from India to the United States. This amounts to about 75% of that country's annual population *growth* (Population Reference Bureau, 1968). Ocean liners and transports, while larger, are less numerous and much slower, and over long distances could not do as well. Does anyone believe, then, that we are going to compensate for the world's population growth by sending the excess to the planets? If there were a place to go on Earth, financially and logistically we could not send our surplus there.

## CONCLUSION

We have not attempted to be comprehensive in our treatment of population pressures and the prospects of coping with them technologically; rather, we hope simply to have given enough illustrations to make plausible our contention that technology, without population control, cannot meet the challenge. It may be argued that we have shown only that any one technological scheme taken individually is insufficient to the task at hand, whereas *all* such schemes applied in parallel might well be enough. We would reply that neither the commitment nor the resources to implement them all exists, and indeed that many may prove mutually exclusive (e.g., harvesting algae may diminish fish production).

Certainly, an optimum combination of efforts exists in theory, but we assert that no organized attempt to find it is being made, and that our examination of its probable eventual constituents permits little hope that even the optimum will suffice. Indeed, after a far more thorough survey of the prospects than we have attempted here, the President's Science Advisory Committee Panel on the world food supply concluded (PSAC, 1967): "The solution of the problem that will exist after about 1985 *demands* that programs of population control be initiated now." We most emphatically agree, noting that "now" was 2 years ago!

Of the problems arising out of population growth in the short, middle, and long terms, we have emphasized the first group. For mankind must pass the first hurdles—food and water for the next 20 years—to be granted the privilege of confronting such dilemmas as the exhaustion of mineral resources and physical space later.[9] Furthermore, we have not conveyed the extent of our concern for the environmental deterioration which has accompanied the population explosion, and for the catastrophic ecological consequences which would attend many of the proposed technological "solutions" to the population/food crisis. Nor have we treated the point that "development" of the rest of the world to the standards of the West probably would be lethal ecologically (Ehrlich and Ehrlich, 1970). For even if such grim prospects are ignored, it is abundantly clear that in terms of cost, lead time, and implementation on the scale required, technology without population control will be too little and too late.

What hope there is lies not, of course, in abandoning attempts at technological solutions; on the contrary, they must be pursued at unprecedented levels, with unprecedented judgment, and above all with unprecedented attention to their ecological consequences. We need dramatic programs now to find ways of ameliorating the food crisis—to buy time for humanity until the inevitable delay accompanying population control efforts has passed. But it cannot be emphasized enough that if the population control measures are *not* initiated immediately and effectively, all the technology man can bring to bear will not fend off the misery to come.[10] Therefore, confronted as we are with limited resources of time and money, we must consider carefully what fraction of our effort should be applied to the cure of the disease itself instead of to the temporary relief of the symptoms. We should ask, for example, how many vasectomies could be performed by a program funded with the 1.8 billion dollars required to build a single nuclear agro-industrial complex, and what the relative impact on the problem would be in both the short and long terms.

The decision for population control will be opposed by growth-minded economists and businessmen, by nationalistic statesmen, by zealous religious leaders, and by the myopic and well-fed of every description. It is therefore incumbent on all who sense the limitations of technology and the fragility of the environmental balance to make themselves heard above the hollow, optimistic chorus—to convince society and its leaders that there is no alternative but the cessation of our irresponsible, all-demanding, and all-consuming population growth.

## ACKNOWLEDGMENTS

We thank the following individuals for reading and commenting on the manuscript: J. H. Brownell (Stanford University); P. A. Cantor (Aerojet General Corp.); P. E. Cloud (University of California, Santa Barbara); D. J. Eckstrom (Stanford University); R. Ewell (State University of New York at Buffalo); J. L. Fisher (Resources for the Future, Inc.); J. A. Hendrickson, Jr. (Stanford University); J. H. Hessel (Stanford University); R. W. Holm (Stanford University); S. C. McIntosh, Jr. (Stanford University); K. E. F. Watt (University of California, Davis). This work was supported in part by a grant from the Ford Foundation.

[9] Since the first draft of this article was written, the authors have seen the manuscript of a timely and pertinent forthcoming book, *Resources and Man*, written under the auspices of the National Academy of Sciences and edited by Preston E. Cloud. The book reinforces many of our own conclusions in such areas as agriculture and fisheries and, in addition, treats both short- and long-term prospects in such areas as mineral resources and fossil fuels in great detail.

[10] This conclusion has also been reached within the specific context of aid to underdeveloped countries in a Ph.D. thesis by Douglas Daetz: "Energy Utilization and Aid Effectiveness in Nonmechanized Agriculture: A Computer Simulation of a Socioeconomic System' (University of California, Berkeley, May 1968).

## REFERENCES

Anonymous. 1968a. India aims to remedy fertilizer shortage. *Chem. Eng. News,* **46** (November 25): 29.

————. 1968b. Scientists Studying Nuclear-Powered Agro-Industrial Complexes to Give Food and Jobs to Millions. *New York Times.* March 10, p. 74.

————. 1968c. Food from the atom. *Technol. Rev.,* January, p. 55.

————. 1968d. Norway—The end of the big blubber. *Time,* November 29, p. 98.

————. 1968e. Nuclear fuel cycle. *Nucl. News,* January, p. 30.

Bender, R. J. 1969. Why water desalting will expand. *Power,* **113** (August): 171.

Blanko, R. E., J. O. Blomeke, and J. T. Roberts. 1967. Solving the waste disposal problem. *Nucleonics.* **25:** 58.

Borgstrom, Georg. 1965. *The Hungry Planet.* Collier-Macmillan, New York.

Bump, T. R. 1967. A third generation of breeder reactors. *Sci. Amer.,* May, p. 25.

Christy, F. C., Jr., and A. Scott. 1965. *The Commonwealth in Ocean Fisheries.* Johns Hopkins Press, Baltimore.

Clawson, M., H. L. Landsberg, and L. T. Alexander. 1969. Desalted seawater for agriculture: Is it economic? *Science,* **164:** 1141.

Cloud, P. R. 1968. Realities of mineral distribution. *Texas Quart.,* Summer, p. 103.

Cole, LaMont C. 1968. Can the world be saved? *BioScience,* **18:** 679.

Curtis, R., and E. Hogan. 1969. *Perils of the Peaceful Atom.* Doubleday, New York, p. 135, 150-152.

Ehrlich, P. R. 1968. *The Population Bomb.* Sierra Club/Ballantine, New York.

Ehrlich, P. R., and Anne H. Ehrlich. 1970. *Population, Resources, and Environment.* W. H. Freeman, San Francisco (In press).

Ennis, C. E. 1967. Desalted water as a competitive commodity. *Chem. Eng. Progr.,* **63** (1): 64.

Galstann, L. S., and E. L. Currier. 1967. The Metropolitan Water District desalting project. *Chem. Eng. Progr.,* **63** (1): 64.

Gúeron, J., J. A. Lane, I. R. Maxwell, and J. R. Menke. 1957. *The Economics of Nuclear Power. Progress in Nuclear Energy.* McGraw-Hill Book Co., New York. Series VIII. p. 23.

Hardin, G. 1968. The tragedy of the commons. *Science,* **162:** 1243.

Hubbert, M. W. 1962. Energy resources, A report to the Committee on Natural Resources. National Research Council Report 1000-D, National Academy of Sciences.

International Atomic Energy Agency. 1964. Desalination of water using conventional and nuclear energy. Technical Report 24, Vienna.

Kelly, R. P. 1966. North American water and power alliance. In: *Water Production Using Nuclear Energy,* R. G. Post and R. L. Seale (eds.). University of Arizona Press, Tucson, p. 29.

Lelyveld, D. 1968. Can India survive Calcutta? *New York Times Magazine.* October 13, p. 58.

Mason, E. A. 1957. Economic growth and energy consumption. In: *The Economics of Nuclear Power. Progress in Nuclear Energy.* Series VIII, J. Gúeron et al. (eds.). McGraw-Hill Book Co., New York, p. 56.

McIlhenny, W. F. 1966. Problems and potentials of concentrated brines. In: *Water Production Using Nuclear Energy,* R. G. Post and R. L. Seale (eds.). University of Arizona Press, Tucson, p. 187.

McKenzie, John. 1968. Nutrition and the soft sell. *New Sci.,* **40:** 423.

McNeil, Mary. 1964. Lateritic soils. *Sci. Amer.,* November, p. 99.

Meseck, G. 1961. Importance of fish production and utilization in the food economy. Paper R11.3, presented at FAO Conference on Fish in Nutrition, Rome.

Milliman, J. W. 1966. Economics of water production using nuclear energy. In: *Water Production Using Nuclear Energy.* R. G. Post and R. L. Seale (eds.). University of Arizona Press, Tucson, p. 49.

Mills, R. G. 1967. Some engineering problems of thermonuclear fusion. *Nucl. Fusion,* **7:** 223.

Molloy, J. F., Jr. 1968. The $12-billion financing problem of U. S. airlines. *Astronautics and Aeronautics,* October, p. 76.

Novick, S. 1969. *The Careless Atom.* Hougton Mifflin, Boston.

Oak Ridge National Laboratory. 1968. Nuclear energy centers, industrial and agro-industrial complexes, Summary Report. ORNL-4291, July.

Paddock, William. 1967. Phytopathology and a hungry world. *Ann. Rev. Phytopathol.,* **5:** 375.

Paddock, William, and Paul Paddock. 1964. *Hungry Nations,* Little, Brown & Co., Boston.

————. 1967. *Famine 1975!* Little, Brown & Co., Boston.

Parikh, G., S. Saxena, and M. Maharaja. 1968. Agricultural extension and IADP, a study of Surat. *Econ. Polit. Weekly,* August 24, p. 1307.

Parker, F. L. 1968. Radioactive wastes from fusion reactors. *Science,* **159:** 83. Parker, F. L., and D. J. Rose, *Science,* **159:** 1376.

Parker, H. M. 1966. Environmental factors relating to large water plants. In: *Water Production Using Nuclear Energy,* R. G. Post and R. L. Seale (eds.). University of Arizona Press, Tucson, p. 209.

Population Reference Bureau. 1968. Population Reference Bureau Data Sheet. Pop. Ref. Bureau, Washington, D.C.

PSAC. 1967. *The World Food Problem.* Report of the President's Science Advisory Committee. Vol. 1-3. U.S. Govt. Printing Office, Washington, D.C.

Rose, D. J., and M. Clark, Jr. 1961. *Plasma and Controlled Fusion.* M.I.T. Press, Cambridge, Mass., p. 3.

Schmitt, W. R. 1965. The planetary food potential. *Ann. N.Y. Acad. Sci.,* **118:** 645.

Sporn, Philip. 1963. *Energy for Man.* Macmillan, New York.

————. 1966. *Fresh Water from Saline Waters.* Pergamon Press, New York.

Sukhatme, P. V. 1966. The world's food supplies. *Roy. Stat. Soc. J.,* **129A:** 222.

United Nations. 1968. *United Nations Statistical Yearbook for 1967.* Statistical Office of the U.N., New York.

U.S. Dept. of Commerce. 1966. *Statistical Abstract of the U.S.* U.S. Govt. Printing Office, Washington, D.C.

Wadleigh, C. H. 1968. Wastes in relation to agriculture and industry. USDA Miscellaneous Publication No. 1065. March.

Woodwell, George M. 1967. Toxic substances and ecological cycles. *Sci. Amer.,* March, p. 24.

# Population, Food Supply, and Economic Development

## MAX F. MILLIKAN*

In 1961, at the urging of President John F. Kennedy, the United Nations declared the 1960's to be the "Decade of Development." The General Assembly passed a variety of resolutions in that year with the intention of stimulating economic progress in the underdeveloped countries during the decade. A target was established: that by 1970 the gross national product of each of these countries—the total output of goods and services—would be growing at a rate of 5 per cent per year. To make this possible it was proposed that the developed countries increase their capital contribution to the resources available to the underdeveloped countries. An amount equal to 1 per cent of national income of the developed countries was established as a reasonable target for resource transfers of all kinds to the less-developed nations. This amount was intended to include foreign aid, private capital investments, and surplus food transfers.

Now, as this decade closes, there is a mounting feeling that the progress of the less-developed countries has been inadequate. This sense of inadequacy has two sources. Economists who have been following closely

Population, Food Supply, and Economic Development. Reprinted from *Technology Review*, February, 1970. Published at the Massachusetts Institute of Technology, © 1970 by the Alumni Association of the M.I.T.

* This article is based on a seminar given by the late Professor Millikan to the Department of Nutrition and Food Science at M.I.T. in November, 1969. Following Dr. Millikan's death on December 14, it has been prepared for publication by the Editors of *Technology Review* with the assistance of Donald L. M. Blackmer, Associate Professor of Political Science, who is Acting Director of the Center.

the progress of development itself by the usual economic indicators suggest that development has not been fast enough to improve standards of living in the underdeveloped world. Economists and nutritionists concerned with food and nutrition feel that there is a growing disparity between the expanding population of underdeveloped countries and their efforts to increase their available food supplies.

As we approach the end of the first "Decade of Development," there is a scurry of preparation for a new effort for the 1970's.

The Commission on International Development, headed by Lester Pearson of Canada and appointed by the International Bank for Reconstruction and Development, has now reported on what will be required for the advancement of the underdeveloped world in a "second development decade." Each specialized agency has developed its own plan: the World Food and Agricultural Organization, the International Labor Organization, the U. N. Conference on Trade and Development, and the U. N. Organization for Industrial Development, among others, have all set goals. These reports will be coordinated next summer when the United Nations General Assembly considers a program for the 1970's.

An examination of American aid programs is underway in the United States. President Nixon has appointed the Peterson Commission to review the whole structure and organization of our foreign aid effort and to make recommendations to him and to the Congress by the end of this month.

Why this new concern with an accelerated pace of development in a "second development decade?" Was the first a failure? Is it now necessary to find reasons for its failure and to correct the errors?

The answer to these questions is no. The "Decade of Development" was not a failure; it was an overwhelming success—a success in its own terms. The records of the less-developed countries (we have information, some of it statistical, about most of the non-Communist countries) will probably show that the average rate of growth of their gross national products during the 1960's was slightly more than 5 per cent per year. For the transfer of resources from developed to underdeveloped countries, the target of 1 per cent of national income has very nearly been reached, according to the Development Advisory Commission of the Organization for Economic Cooperation and Development. The O.E.C.D. members—the nations of Western Europe, Japan, and the United States—have averaged about 0.96 per cent of their national incomes. However, at the U.N. Conference on Trade Development in New Delhi a year ago, the target was raised from 1 per cent of national income to 1 per cent of gross national product —some 20 to 25 per cent more than the previous target. We are now nowhere close to that. The United States is only eighth or ninth in the proportion of gross national product devoted to resource transfers, both private and public, to the underdeveloped countries. France, West Germany, Great Britain, Holland, Denmark, and Austria are well ahead of us, despite the fact that we are more than twice as wealthy per capita as any of these countries.

## ECONOMIC GROWTH VERSUS AGRICULTURAL PRODUCTIVITY

In historical terms, the 5 per cent rate of growth achieved by the underdeveloped countries is a remarkable performance. It vastly exceeds anything achieved by the developed countries in the comparable periods of their histories during the nineteenth century; none grew at a rate as high. The average for the United States and Western Europe was 3 or 3½ per cent per year at the end of that century. So this is, in fact, a development record in which to take pride.

And within this average of 5 per cent there are some countries that are really almost successful; some of them seemed, a decade ago, without hope. The common view of South Korea, for example, was bleak indeed. Yet South Korea has grown over the last five years at close to 8 or 9 per cent per year—perfectly extraordinary progress. Taiwan, Iran, Mexico, and Pakistan have also achieved remarkable growth.

If, in fact, we have had this rather extraordinary performance during the 1960's, what explains our unease as we begin the 1970's? Two or three years ago, essentially two problems were recognized as crucially inhibiting a more rapid growth of per capita income in the underdeveloped countries. The first was the unprecedented explosion—no other word is appropriate—in their populations, an explosion which has literally eaten up their substantial increase in output. This is an explosion which has no historical parallel, a rate of population growth much more rapid in the past few decades than ever existed in any of the presently developed countries. The second problem is that, in spite of a very substantial rate of growth in many aspects of these countries' economies—growth in their industries, and transportation and communications networks—there has been a lag in their agricultural productivity. Agriculture has not kept pace with the growing demand for food.

Within the last two or three years, we have had a number of encouraging developments in both population control and agricultural productivity. Now two quite different worries arise. The first is that unless the general growth in per capita income is accelerated beyond the level of the 1960's, it seems unlikely that either advances in population control or expanded prospects for food supply, which now look so promising, can be realized. Though the aggregate growth rate was about

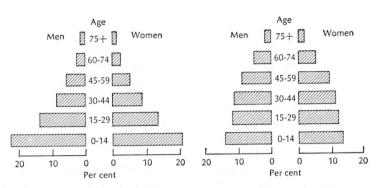

These two graphs show the distribution by age of the populations of the under-developed countries (left) and the developed ones (right). The former shows its greatest bulk in youth; the largest numbers represent children who may not even now grow to productive maturity. The latter shows a more balanced proportion, in which children who are fed and schooled live to put energy back into the economy.

5 per cent, the growth in per capita income was between 2 and 2½ per cent per year in this decade; the population growth rate was about 2½ to 3 per cent, so less than half of the 5 per cent growth was free to increase per capita standards of living. But even if development is accelerated, even if the rate of growth of per capita incomes is increased to the U.N. goal of 4 to 4½ per cent per year, this rate of increase will not by itself confront these countries' crucial nutritional problems.

This is my second worry. Specialists in economic development have tended to assume that rising incomes would naturally improve nutrition. It is now increasingly apparent that quality of diet will not be improved rapidly enough if nutritional problems are left to the normal process of economic development. In other words, development plans must now contain specific nutritional strategies.

## FROM A CENTURY TO A YEAR

Perhaps we should now briefly review some statistics of the population explosion. Every population curve has a sharp corner in it—a change from moderate to very rapid increase. There are a number of ways of drama-

tizing this. One of my favorites is that until roughly the year 1600 the rate of population growth in the world at large was of the same order of magnitude per century as it now is annually.

Acceleration of world population began around the year 1600. By 1900, the growth rate was about 1 per cent per year; between 1900 and 1970, population was multiplied more than 2½ times. The rate of population growth in the world now averages a little more than 2.0 per cent per year. The increase in the underdeveloped world is very close to 3 per cent; in some countries of Latin America, it reaches 3½ per cent. There is added to the population of India each year a Belgium—approximately 12 million people a year.

We can now explain why a 5 per cent growth rate in overall gross national product for underdeveloped countries produces such an unsatisfactory rate of growth and living standards, compared with the relatively satisfactory rate of improvement produced by a 3 per cent growth rate in the United States in the nineteenth century. Because we had only 1 per cent population growth, we realized a 2 per cent per capita income growth. In contrast, of the 5 per cent growth rate in today's underdeveloped countries, nearly 3 per cent is used merely to provide food, housing, and clothing at a bare level of subsistence.

Birth rates have thus far contributed very little to the changing rate of population development. Infant mortality is still high. The large decline in death rates has been the result of a decline in the principal communicable diseases of childhood and adulthood, such as malaria and scarlet fever. Infant mortality, which is very closely related to malnutrition, is still very high. In human terms, this is a great deal of suffering. But in the cold-blooded terms of economic efficiency, this is an enormous amount of waste because a large fraction of the population brought into existence and fed in its very early years never reaches its maturity in intellectual or physical productivity.

Several years ago, the common impression, based on anthropological literature, was that motivation was the basic problem in population control. It is now recognized, however, that there is much greater demand for the limitation of births among all populations than we had believed. However, despite this favorable indication, the new programs now being inaugurated will be slow to reduce the population growth rate even if they are mildly successful. Indeed, our best hope is that by 1980 the population growth rate of the less-developed world will not have significantly increased above its present level. Even this should be regarded as a triumph if it is achieved.

Population control takes time. And during these decades the composition of the populations remaining in the world will be altered; there is already a substantially larger fraction of child-bearing mothers than existed eight or ten years ago. The aggregate birth rate per 1,000 will increase because the number of mothers of child-bearing age in that 1,000 will be significantly higher.

The present view is that the birth rate tends to follow the death rate down after a lag of several generations. The primary motivation for having a large family is to provide some assurance that the parents will have at least a single grown, male son. We may hope, then—if infant mortality is reduced through improved medical care and nutrition—that the motivation for having large families will be correspondingly reduced with a lag of several generations, and that ultimately the population explosion will be controlled. This will probably take 20 or 30 years. A further complication is that we have no satisfactory and uncomplicated methods of contraception which can be widely disseminated without mere medical expertise than we now have.

For several reasons, therefore, the prospects of a significant drop in the population explosion over the next decade are not very good, although the prospects over 30 to 50 years look quite promising. Does that mean desperate problems for the 1970's? I do not believe so, because we have also had a breakthrough in agricultural productivity—the green revolution—which may permit us to stay ahead of the population explosion for at least the next decade.

Until about 1955, agriculture barely kept ahead of population in the underdeveloped world. Its rate of growth was about 3 per cent per year, and population growth was only about 2½ per cent. But that ½ per cent lead was not enough, because it existed amidst gross malnutrition. As people's incomes rise in these underdeveloped countries, they spend a substantial fraction of the increase on more food. There is a useful equation for this relationship. It is: $F = p + \eta y$.

In this expression, "F" represents the annual rate of growth in the demand for food, in per cent per year; it is determined partly by the rate of population growth—"p"—in per cent per year. The other determinant is the increase in the demand for food which results from rising income. If "y" represents the per capita rate of growth in incomes—this is not just cash income, but the value of everything consumed—and we then multiply that by the "income elasticity of demand" for food—the ratio of one per cent by which demand for food rises when income rises by one per cent—we obtain an indication of how food demand is related to both population and income. For example, if the rate of population growth p is 2.5 and if we hope for a growth in per capita income of about 3.5 per cent, the

| | Gross national product (billions of dollars) | Per capita income (dollars) | Population (millions) |
|---|---|---|---|
| Near East (excluding Greece and Turkey) | 23.3 | 263 | 88.5 |
| Latin America (excluding Brazil) | 69.0 | 447 | 154 |
| Far East | 35.7 | 129 | 276 |
| India, Pakistan, Brazil | 82.4 | 120 | 686 |
| Tropical Africa | 22.9 | 107 | 213 |
| North Africa | 7.0 | 225 | 31.3 |
| Rest of South Asia | 3.7 | 100 | 37.0 |
| Greece, Turkey, Spain, Puerto Rico, and miscellaneous | — / 39.9 | — / 534 | — / 78.4 |

Gross national products, levels of populations, and per capita incomes for regions of the developing world. The total gross national product for the areas shown is $284 billion, the total population is 1,564 million, and the average per capita income is $182. (The data was taken in 1965.) The United States at that time had a population of 194 million and a gross national product of over 630 billion.

income elasticity of demand—the percentage increase in food consumption which will result from a 1 per cent increase in incomes of about $100 per year—is about .66, and this means that the growth in food demand under these circumstances is roughly 5 per cent per year, of which about half is to meet population growth and half to meet the growth in food demand from rising income.

In the 1960's, "y" was about 2.5 and therefore the growth in the demand for food was roughly 4 per cent per year. The growth in agricultural productivity was only slightly above 3 per cent per year; the difference was made up by transfers of food from the developed countries.

But finally this lag in agriculture began to hold down overall economic growth. This was dramatized by the crisis in 1965 and 1966 when two bad monsoons led to a severe threat of famine in India. Only massive shipments of surplus food from the West averted disaster. The most important consequence of the bad harvests was not the increased shipments from the West; rather, it was to bring home to offi-

cials in India and throughout the underdeveloped world the importance of planning for agricultural productivity. Just at this time came the green revolution, and the new varieties of wheat and rice won rapid acceptance. Indeed, much less adaptation turned out to be necessary than was presumed; particularly the wheats have done extraordinarily well in Pakistan, India, the Philippines, and elsewhere, and even the rices have been successful. Agricultural production has grown at 6 or 7 per cent per year for the last two or three years, and the prospects for the continued rapid growth in agricultural productivity are now quite favorable.

The green revolution has limits: when it is fully exploited, there will be once again the problem of how to continue to expand agricultural productivity. Thus we may have further difficulties 20 or 30 years hence. But, at least for the next decade, consistent effort on the part of all concerned may mean that the world's food production can stay ahead of the population explosion. Indeed, the green revolution may make possible a slight improvement in the gross caloric undernourishment; perhaps half the rate of growth of food production can be devoted to increasing per capita levels of consumption.

## PROSPERITY AS A CONDITION FOR PRODUCTIVITY

Now the two concerns which I described at the beginning become more evident. If incomes do not grow, there will be no increase in the demand for food. If incomes increase more rapidly than 3 per cent, the demand for food will rise more quickly. As incomes rise and diets become adequate, the income elasticity demand for food falls off. There is a very real prospect that if nonagricultural incomes do not go up by 7 or 8 per cent per year in the less-developed world, the green revolution will be aborted. One of the reasons it has taken hold so quickly is that the lag of food production behind incomes during the

1950's and early 1960's made farming relatively profitable. The two bad Indian monsoons particularly had this effect. Food prices have been high because there has been demand from the nonagricultural population for substantially more food than agriculture has been able to supply. If that demand is not sustained and a surplus occurs, the green revolution can be stopped in its tracks.

A crucial aspect of the new agricultural technology is that it requires purchased input by the farmer. The new rices and wheats do well only with heavy doses of fertilizer and with more water, usually from irrigation, than traditional strains. Farmers will not buy fertilizer and irrigation water if the price drops out of the market for farm products—the situation that existed before the bad monsoons. Farming has changed from a subsistence activity to a commercial one; farmers must be able to sell their products to nonfarmers to have the cash to buy the raw materials needed to grow their next crop. That will only be possible, of course, if the nonagricultural population has more money to buy food.

Nonfarmers in turn cannot buy more food unless their productivity goes up—and the nonfarm productivity can only go up if there is an ample supply of capital from a foreign exchange. This means accelerated foreign aid from the developed countries. And the trend in transfers has not been encouraging in the last few years. The United States program has been sharply cut in each of the last three years; we now devote only .3 per cent of our gross national product to aid, compared to the United Nations target of 1 per cent.

## THE INTERRELATIONS OF NUTRITION AND ECONOMICS

The United Nations and the Pearson Committee have determined that the developing world needs a growth rate of 6 or 7 per cent. This is not an impossibly ambitious target—it means accelerating growth by only 1 or 2 percentage points beyond the average

achieved for the 1960's. What it does mean is a substantial increase in capital transfers from the developed to the underdeveloped world.

My fourth worry now comes into focus. Even if the second development decade begins well, and even if particularly the American aid performance of the last two or three years is reversed and we now add the several billion dollars needed to support a growth rate of 6 or 7 per cent, the question still arises: What will happen to nutrition? Will improved nutrition not naturally follow?

One point must be made to nutritionists: Without high economic growth there is no possibility of improving nutrition in the underdeveloped world. So those whose basic concern is with improved nutrition must also get behind the efforts for generally expanded economic development.

A second point must be made to developers, whose basic concern is economic development, timing, and strategy. Without a specific nutritional strategy, a rising level of income will not by itself alleviate the nutrition problem.

It is quite clear that, at an income level of $75 to $100 a year—this is not cash income but value in market terms of everything consumed—it is impossible to provide enough simple calories. And it certainly is not possible to provide any increase in the quality of the diet. The higher the rate of growth of per capita incomes, the larger the fraction of any increase that can go into improvement of quality. At a very low increase in income the increase goes simply into increasing the bulk of caloric intake. It is only as incomes rise substantially more rapidly that people are enabled to purchase a little bit of milk or a little bit of meat.

There are many subtler connections between economic development and improved nutrition. In underdeveloped countries, which still have largely subsistence economies, there is no commercial access to a farmer's food supply if he grows it on his own land and consumes it all himself. There is no food processing industry and no way to introduce additives into his diet to improve its protein

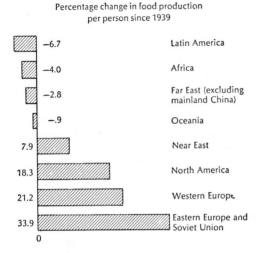

Percentage change in food production
per person since 1939

| | |
|---|---|
| −6.7 | Latin America |
| −4.0 | Africa |
| −2.8 | Far East (excluding mainland China) |
| −.9 | Oceania |
| 7.9 | Near East |
| 18.3 | North America |
| 21.2 | Western Europe |
| 33.9 | Eastern Europe and Soviet Union |

This equilibrium in food per person is not spread evenly across the world, however. Since 1939, some regions have increased their supplies drastically, while others, the underdeveloped ones, have lessened theirs.

content. If a farmer does not buy seed, there is obviously no way to supply him with a higher protein yield.

One of the main accesses proposed to children's nutritional problems is through school lunches. But education rests on development. And if children are not in school they obviously will not eat school lunches. If per capita gross national product does not exceed $75, there are not the resources to support universal primary education.

I thus conclude that improved nutrition is not possible without rising incomes.

But now I want to argue the other side of the case, to explain to economists why they must consider a special nutritional strategy even if incomes are moving up. It is true that increased incomes will mean better nutrition after a time, but this process is slow. For example, at $100 per capita you need all the land available to produce grain for direct human consumption simply for minimal caloric intake. If your nation chooses to obtain

its calories by feeding grain to animals, it will use five to seven times as much grain to produce a calorie of animal protein. This has economic as well as agricultural implications.

To rely on traditionally preferred animal proteins, purchased in the market, means that a significant effect on protein nutrition cannot be obtained unless incomes rise to $700 to $800 per year. At the current 2 per cent per year target rate an eight-fold multiplication of income will take a century. We cannot wait a century to eliminate nutritional deficiencies, particularly in the school-age children. Even if incomes were good, we are aware that, in the United States, which has an average per capita income of $4,000 per year, we have serious nutritional deficiencies in a significant portion of our population.

All indications are that the maldistribution of income in the underdeveloped world will be worse before it is better. The agricultural areas affected by the green revolution may progress quite rapidly, but this affects only 10 to 20 per cent of the rural population. Only a limited fraction of the people for whom the green revolution is appropriate have access to it, for the new grains will grow only with abundant irrigation, with fertilizers, and on certain types of soils, and these are not present in many parts of the underdeveloped world.

So the green revolution will mean an increased disparity in the incomes in rural populations. Concern exists for urban populations as well: the growth of industry is proceeding too slowly to provide employment for the large numbers of people being released from agriculture and flooding into the cities. Unemployment has been rising in the underdeveloped countries, and studies by the International Labor Organization and other agencies estimate that even with industrial growth rates at 7 to 9 per cent per year, the capital requirements in industry are so heavy and the number of new workers per dollar of new capital so small, that employment prospects outside of agriculture for this burgeoning 2½ per cent population growth are not good.

## TOWARD
## A NUTRITIONAL STRATEGY

What does this mean for nutrition? It means that the disparities in income will tend, within averages that are already very low, to be greater rather than smaller in the future than they have been in the past.

This demonstrates to me a case for explicit government programs to provide nutritional supplements, particularly for infants and for mothers, in the entire population. These supplements must be provided outside of normal market channels because, distributed through normal market channels, they will not reach the right people in the right quantities. We desperately need a nutritional strategy in the development plans of the underdeveloped countries. Fortunately this is beginning to be recognized—India's Fourth Five-Year Plan includes a chapter on nutrition. This has not happened before. It is coming to be recognized that more explicit attention needs to be paid to institutional and organizational devices for insuring that the next generation of children is not subjected to impossible handicaps—permanent deficiencies, both mental and physical—because of the failure to deal with the nutrition problem.

# Photosynthesis and Fish Production in the Sea

JOHN H. RYTHER

Numerous attempts have been made to estimate the production in the sea of fish and other organisms of existing or potential food value to man (1-4). These exercises, for the most part, are based on estimates of primary (photosynthetic) organic production rates in the ocean (5) and various assumed trophic-dynamic relationships between the photosynthetic producers and the organisms of interest to man. Included in the latter are the number of steps or links in the food chains and the efficiency of conversion of organic matter from each trophic level or link in the food chain to the next. Different estimates result from different choices in the number of trophic levels and in the efficiencies, as illustrated in Table 1 (2).

Implicit in the above approach is the concept of the ocean as a single ecosystem in which the same food chains involving the same number of links and efficiencies apply throughout. However, the rate of primary production is known to be highly variable, differing by at least two full orders of magnitude from the richest to the most impoverished regions. This in itself would be expected to result in a highly irregular pattern of food production. In addition, the ecological conditions which determine the trophic dynamics of marine food chains also vary widely and

Photosynthesis and Fish Production in the Sea. From *Science*, Vol. 166, October 3, 1969, pp. 72-76. Copyright 1969 by the American Association for the Advancement of Science. Reprinted by permission of the author and the publisher

**TABLE 1**

Estimates of potential yields (per year) at various trophic levels, in metric tons. [After Schaeffer *(2)*]

| | Ecological efficiency factor | | | | | |
| | 10 per cent | | 15 per cent | | 20 per cent | |
| Trophic level | Carbon (tons) | Total weight (tons) | Carbon (tons) | Total weight (tons) | Carbon (tons) | Total weight (tons) |
|---|---|---|---|---|---|---|
| 0. Phytoplankton (net particulate production) | $1.9 \times 10^{10}$ | | $1.9 \times 10^{10}$ | | $1.9 \times 10^{10}$ | |
| 1. Herbivores | $1.9 \times 10^{9}$ | $1.9 \times 10^{10}$ | $2.8 \times 10^{9}$ | $2.8 \times 10^{10}$ | $3.8 \times 10^{9}$ | $3.8 \times 10^{10}$ |
| 2. 1st stage carnivores | $1.9 \times 10^{8}$ | $1.9 \times 10^{9}$ | $4.2 \times 10^{8}$ | $4.2 \times 10^{9}$ | $7.6 \times 10^{8}$ | $7.6 \times 10^{9}$ |
| 3. 2nd stage carnivores | $1.9 \times 10^{7}$ | $1.9 \times 10^{8}$ | $6.4 \times 10^{7}$ | $6.4 \times 10^{8}$ | $15.2 \times 10^{7}$ | $15.2 \times 10^{8}$ |
| 4. 3rd stage carnivores | $1.9 \times 10^{6}$ | $1.9 \times 10^{7}$ | $9.6 \times 10^{6}$ | $9.6 \times 10^{7}$ | $30.4 \times 10^{6}$ | $30.4 \times 10^{7}$ |

in direct relationship to the absolute level of primary organic production. As is shown below, the two sets of variables—primary production and the associated food chain dynamics—may act additively to produce differences in fish production which are far more pronounced and dramatic than the observed variability of the individual causative factors.

## PRIMARY PRODUCTIVITY

Our knowledge of the primary organic productivity of the ocean began with the development of the $C^{14}$-tracer technique for *in situ* measurement of photosynthesis by marine plankton algae *(6)* and the application of the method on the 1950–52 *Galathea* expedition around the world *(5)*. Despite obvious deficiencies in the coverage of the ocean by *Galathea* (the expedition made 194 observations, or an average of about one every 2 million square kilometers, most of which were made in the tropics or semitropics), our concept of the total productivity of the world ocean has changed little in the intervening years.

While there have been no more expeditions comparable to the *Galathea*, there have

been numerous local or regional studies of productivity in many parts of the world. Most of these have been brought together by a group of Soviet scientists to provide up-to-date world coverage consisting of over 7000 productivity observations *(7)*. The result has been modification of the estimate of primary production in the world ocean from 1.2 to $1.5 \times 10^{10}$ tons of carbon fixed per year *(5)* to a new figure, 1.5 to $1.8 \times 10^{10}$ tons.

Attempts have also been made by Steemann Nielsen and Jensen *(5)*, Ryther *(8)*, and Koblentz-Mishke et *al. (7)* to assign specific levels or ranges of productivity to different parts of the ocean. Although the approach was somewhat different in each case, in general the agreement between the three was good and, with appropriate condensation and combination, permit the following conclusions.

1. Annual primary production in the open sea varies, for the most part, between 25 and 75 grams of carbon fixed per square meter and averages about 50 grams of carbon per square meter per year. This is true for roughly 90 per cent of the ocean, an area of $326 \times 10^{6}$ square kilometers.

2. Higher levels of primary production occur in shallow coastal waters, defined here as the area within the 100-fathom (180-meter) depth contour. The mean value for this region

may be considered to be 100 grams of carbon fixed per square meter per year, and the area, according to Menard and Smith (9), is 7.5 per cent of the total world ocean. In addition, certain offshore waters are influenced by divergences, fronts, and other hydrographic features which bring nutrient-rich subsurface water into the euphotic zone. The equatorial divergences are examples of such regions. The productivity of these offshore areas is comparable to that of the coastal zone. Their total area is difficult to assess, but is considered here to be 2.5 per cent of the total ocean. Thus, the coastal zone and the offshore regions of comparably high productivity together represent 10 per cent of the total area of the oceans, or $36 \times 10^6$ square kilometers.

3. In a few restricted areas of the world, particularly along the west coasts of continents at subtropical latitudes where there are prevailing offshore winds and strong eastern boundary currents, surface waters are diverted offshore and are replaced by nutrient-rich deeper water. Such areas of coastal upwelling are biologically the richest parts of the ocean. They exist off Peru, California, northwest and southwest Africa, Somalia, and the Arabian coast, and in other more localized situations. Extensive coastal upwelling also is known to occur in various places around the continent of Antarctica, although its exact location and extent have not been well documented. During periods of active upwelling, primary pro-

duction normally exceeds 1.0 and may exceed 10.0 grams of carbon per square meter per day. Some of the high values which have been reported from these locations are 3.9 grams for the southwest coast of Africa (5), 6.4 for the Arabian Sea (10), and 11.2 off Peru (11). However, the upwelling of subsurface water does not persist throughout the year in many of these places—for example, in the Arabian Sea, where the process is seasonal and related to the monsoon winds. In the Antarctic, high production is limited by solar radiation during half the year. For all these areas of coastal upwelling throughout the year, it is probably safe, if somewhat conservative, to assign an annual value of 300 grams of carbon per square meter. Their total area in the world is again difficult to assess. On the assumption that their total cumulative area is no greater than 10 times the well-documented upwelling area off Peru, this would amount to some $3.6 \times 10^5$ square kilometers, or 0.1 per cent of the world ocean. These conclusions are summa.ized in Table 2.

## FOOD CHAINS

Let us next examine the three provinces of the ocean which have been designated according to their differing levels of primary productivity from the standpoint of other pos-

## TABLE 2

Division of the ocean into provinces according to their level of primary organic production.

| Province | Percentage of ocean | Area (km²) | Mean productivity (grams of carbon/m²/yr) | Total productivity (10⁹ tons of carbon/yr) |
|---|---|---|---|---|
| Open ocean | 90 | $326 \times 10^6$ | 50 | 16.3 |
| Coastal zone* | 9.9 | $36 \times 10^6$ | 100 | 3.6 |
| Upwelling areas | 0.1 | $3.6 \times 10^5$ | 300 | 0.1 |
| Total | | | | 20.0 |

* Includes offshore areas of high productivity.

sible major differences. These will include, in particular, differences which relate to the food chains and to trophic efficiencies involved in the transfer of organic matter from the photosynthetic organisms to fish and invertebrate species large and abundant enough to be of importance to man.

The first factor to be considered in this context is the size of the photosynthetic or producer organisms. It is generally agreed that, as one moves from coastal to offshore oceanic waters, the character of these organisms changes from large "microplankton" (100 microns or more in diameter) to the much smaller "nannoplankton" cells 5 to 25 microns in their largest dimensions *(12, 13)*.

Since the size of an organism is an essential criterion of its potential usefulness to man, we have the following relationship: the larger the plant cells at the beginning of the food chain, the fewer the trophic levels that are required to convert the organic matter to a useful form. The oceanic nannoplankton cannot be effectively filtered from the water by most of the common zooplankton crustacea. For example, the euphausid *Euphausia pacifica*, which may function as a herbivore in the rich subarctic coastal waters of the Pacific, must turn to a carnivorous habit in the offshore waters where the phytoplankton become too small to be captured *(13)*.

Intermediate between the nannoplankton and the carnivorous zooplankton are a group of herbivores, the microzooplankton, whose ecological significance is a subject of considerable current interest *(14, 15)*. Representatives of this group include protozoans such as Radiolaria, Foraminifera, and Tintinnidae, and larval nuplii of micro-crustaceans. These organisms, which may occur in concentrations of tens of thousands per cubic meter, are the primary herbivores of the open sea.

Feeding upon these tiny animals is a great host of carnivorous zooplankton, many of which have long been thought of as herbivores. Only by careful study of the mouthparts and feeding habits were Anraku and Omori *(16)* able to show that many common copepods are facultative if not obligate carnivores. Some of these predatory copepods may be no more than a millimeter or two in length.

Again, it is in the offshore environment that these small carnivorous zooplankton predominate. Grice and Hart *(17)* showed that the percentage of carnivorous species in the zooplankton increased from 16 to 39 per cent in a transect from the coastal waters of the northeastern United States to the Sargasso Sea. Of very considerable importance in this group are the Chaetognatha. In terms of biomass, this group of animals, predominantly carnivorous, represents, on the average, 30 per cent of the weight of copepods in the open sea *(17)*. With such a distribution, it is clear that virtually all the copepods, many of which are themselves carnivores, must be preyed upon by chaetognaths.

The oceanic food chain thus far described involves three to four trophic levels from the photosynthetic nannoplankton to animals no more than 1 to 2 centimeters long. How many additional steps may be required to produce

## TABLE 3

Estimated fish production in the three ocean provinces defined in Table 2.

| Province | Primary production [tons (organic carbon)] | Trophic levels | Efficiency (%) | Fish production [tons (fresh wt.)] |
|---|---|---|---|---|
| Oceanic | $16.3 \times 10^9$ | 5 | 10 | $16 \times 10^5$ |
| Coastal | $3.6 \times 10^9$ | 3 | 15 | $12 \times 10^7$ |
| Upwelling | $0.1 \times 10^9$ | 1½ | 20 | $12 \times 10^7$ |
| Total | | | | $24 \times 10^7$ |

organisms of conceivable use to man is difficult to say, largely because there are so few known oceanic species large enough and (through schooling habits) abundant enough to fit this category. Familiar species such as the tunas, dolphins, and squid are all top carnivores which feed on fishes or invertebrates at least one, and probably two, trophic levels beyond such zooplankton as the chaetognaths. A food chain consisting of five trophic levels between photosynthetic organisms and man would therefore seem reasonable for the oceanic province.

As for the coastal zone, it has already been pointed out that the phytoplankton are quite commonly large enough to be filtered and consumed directly by the common crustacean zooplankton such as copepods and euphausids. However, the presence, in coastal waters, of protozoans and other microzooplankton in larger numbers and of greater biomass than those found in offshore waters (15) attests to the fact that much of the primary production here, too, passes through several steps of a microscopic food chain before reaching the macrozooplankton.

The larger animals of the coastal province (that is, those directly useful to man) are certainly the most diverse with respect to feeding type. Some (mollusks and some fishes) are herbivores. Many others, including most of the pelagic clupeoid fishes, feed on zooplankton. Another large group, the demersal fishes, feed on bottom fauna which may be anywhere from one to several steps removed from the phytoplankton.

If the herbivorous clupeoid fishes are excluded (since these occur predominantly in the upwelling provinces and are therefore considered separately), it is probably safe to assume that the average food organism from coastal waters represents the end of at least a three-step food chain between phytoplankton and man.

It is in the upwelling areas of the world that food chains are the shortest, or—to put it another way—that the organisms are large enough to be directly utilizable by man from trophic levels very near the primary producers.

This, again, is due to the large size of the phytoplankton, but it is due also to the fact that many of these species are colonial in habit, forming large gelatinous masses or long filaments. The eight most abundant species of phytoplankton in the upwelling region off Peru, in the spring of 1966, were *Chaetoceros socialis, C. debilis, C. lorenzianus, Skeletonema costatum, Nitzschia seriata, N. delicatissima, Schroederella delicatula,* and *Asterionella japonica (11, 18)*. The first in this list, *C. socialis,* forms large gelatinous masses. The others all form long filamentous chains. *Thalossiosira subtilis,* another gelatinous colonial form like *Chaetoceros socialis,* occurs commonly off southwest Africa *(19)* and close to shore off the Azores *(20)*. Hart *(21)* makes special mention of the colonial habit of all the most abundant species of phytoplankton in the Antarctic—*Fragiloriopsis antarctica, Encampia balaustrium, Rhizosalenia alata, R. antarctica, R. chunii, Thallosiothrix antarctica,* and *Phaeocystis brucei*.

Many of the above-mentioned species of phytoplankton form colonies several millimeters, and, in some cases, several centimeters in diameter. Such aggregates of plant material can be readily eaten by large fishes without special feeding adaptation. In addition, however, many of the clupeoid fishes (sardines, anchovies, pilchards, menhaden, and so on) that are found most abundantly in upwelling areas and that make up the largest single component of the world's commerical fish landings, do have specially modified gill rakers for removing the larger species of phytoplankton from the water.

There seems little doubt that many of the fishes indigenous to upwelling regions are direct herbivores for at least most of their lives. There is some evidence that juveniles of the Peruvian anchovy *(Engraulis ringens)* may feed on zooplankton, but the adult is predominantly if not exclusively a herbivore *(22)*. Small gobies *(Gobius bibarbatus)* found at mid-water in the coastal waters off southwest Africa had their stomachs filled with a large, chain-forming diatom of the genus *Fragilaria (23)*. There is considerable interest at present in the possible commercial utilization of the large Antarctic krill, *Euphausia superba*, which feeds primarily on the colonial diatom *Fragilariopsis antarctica (24)*.

In some of the upwelling regions of the world, such as the Arabian Sea, the species of fish are not well known, so it is not surprising that knowledge of their feeding habits and food chains is fragmentary. From what is known, however, the evidence would appear to be overwhelming that a one- or two-step food chain between phytoplankton and man is the rule. As a working compromise, let us assign the upwelling province a 1½-step food chain.

## EFFICIENCY

The growth (that is, the net organic production) of an organism is a function of the food assimilated less metabolic losses or respiration. This efficiency of growth or food utilization (the ratio of growth to assimilation) has been found, by a large number of investigators and with a great variety of organisms, to be about 30 per cent in young, actively growing animals. The efficiency decreases as animals approach their full growth, and reaches zero in fully mature or senescent individuals *(25)*. Thus a figure of 30 per cent can be considered a biological potential which may be approached in nature, although the growth efficiency of a population of animals of mixed ages under steady-state conditions must be lower.

Since there must obviously be a "maintenance ration"" which is just sufficient to accommodate an organism's basal metabolic requirement *(26)*, it must also be true that growth efficiency is a function of the absolute rate of assimilation. The effects of this factor will be most pronounced at low feeding rates, near the "maintenance ration," and will tend to become negligible at high feeding rates. Food conversion (that is, growth efficiency) will therefore obviously be related to food availability, or to the concentration of prey organisms when the latter are sparsely distributed.

In addition, the more available the food and the greater the quantity consumed, the greater the amount of "internal work" the animal must perform to digest, assimilate, convert, and store the food. Conversely, the less available the food, the greater the amount of "external work" the animal must perform to hunt, locate, and capture its prey. These concepts are discussed in some detail by Ivlev *(27)* and reviewed by Ricker *(28)*. The two metabolic costs thus work in opposite ways with respect to food availability, tending thereby toward a constant total effect. However, when food availability is low, the added costs of basal metabolism and external work relative to assimilation may have a pronounced effect on growth efficiency.

When one turns from consideration of the individual and its physiological growth efficiency to the "ecological efficiency" of food conversion from one trophic level to the next *(2, 29)*, there are additional losses to be taken into account. Any of the food consumed but not assimilated would be included here, though it is possible that undigested organic matter may be reassimilated by members of the same trophic level *(2)*. Any other nonassimilatory losses, such as losses due to natural death, sedimentation, and emigration, will, if not otherwise accounted for, appear as a loss in trophic efficiency. In addition, when one considers a specific or selected part of a trophic level, such as a population of fish of use to man, the consumption of food by any other hidden member of the same trophic level will appear as a loss in efficiency. For example, the role of such animals as salps, medusae, and ctenophores in marine food chains is not well understood and is seldom even considered. Yet these animals may occur sporadically or periodically in swarms so dense that they dominate the plankton completely. Whether they represent a dead end or side branch in the normal food chain of the sea is not known, but their effect can hardly be negligible when they occur in abundance.

Finally, a further loss which may occur at any trophic level but is, again, of unknown or unpredictable magnitude is that of dissolved organic matter lost through excretion or other physiological processes by plants and animals. This has received particular attention at the level of primary production, some investigators concluding that 50 per cent or more of the photoassimilated carbon may be released by phytoplankton into the water as dissolved compounds (30). There appears to be general agreement that the loss of dissolved organic matter is indirectly proportional to the absolute rate of organic production and is therefore most serious in the oligotrophic regions of the open sea (11, 31).

All of the various factors discussed above will affect the efficiency or apparent efficiency of the transfer of organic matter between trophic levels. Since they cannot, in most cases, be quantitatively estimated individually, their total effect cannot be assessed. It is known only that the maximum potential growth is about 30 per cent and that at least some of the factors which reduce this further are more pronounced in oligotrophic, low-productivity waters than in highly productive situations. Slobodkin (29) concludes that an ecological efficiency of about 10 per cent is possible, and Schaeffer feels that the figure may be as high as 20 per cent. Here, therefore, I assign efficiencies of 10, 15, and 20 per cent, respectively, to the oceanic, the coastal, and the upwelling provinces, though it is quite possible that the actual values are considerably lower.

## CONCLUSIONS AND DISCUSSION

With values assigned to the three marine provinces for primary productivity (Table 2), number of trophic levels, and efficiencies, it is now possible to calculate fish production in the three regions. The results are summarized in Table 3.

These calculations reveal several interesting features. The open sea—90 per cent of the ocean and nearly three-fourths of the earth's surface—is essentially a biological desert. It produces a negligible fraction of the world's fish catch at present and has little or no potential for yielding more in the future.

Upwelling regions, totaling no more than about one-tenth of 1 per cent of the ocean surface (an area roughly the size of California) produce about half the world's fish supply. The other half is produced in coastal waters and the few offshore regions of comparably high fertility.

One of the major uncertainties and possible sources of error in the calculation is the estimation of the areas of high, intermediate, and low productivity. This is particularly true of the upwelling area off the continent of Antarctica, an area which has never been well described or defined.

A figure of 360,000 square kilometers has been used for the total area of upwelling regions in the world (Table 2). If the upwelling regions off California, northwest and southwest Africa, and the Arabian Sea are of roughly the same area as that off the coast of Peru, these semitropical regions would total some 200,000 square kilometers. The remaining 160,000 square kilometers would represent about one-fourth the circumference of Antarctica seaward for a distance of 30 kilometers. This seems a not unreasonable inference. Certainly, the entire ocean south of the Antarctic Convergence is not highly productive, contrary to the estimates of El-Sayed (32). Extensive observations in this region by Saijo and Kawashima (33) yielded primary productivity values of 0.01 to 0.15 gram of carbon per square meter per day—a value no higher than the values used here for the open sea. Presumably, the discrepancy is the result of highly irregular, discontinuous, or "patchy" distribution of biological activity. In other words, the occurrence of extremely high productivity associated with upwelling conditions appears to be confined, in the Antarctic, as elsewhere, to restricted areas close to shore.

An area of 160,000 square kilometers of upwelling conditions with an annual productivity of 300 grams of carbon per square meter would result in the production of about $50 \times 10^6$ tons of "fish," if we follow the ground rules established above in making the estimate. Presumably these "fish" would consist for the most part of the Antarctic krill, which feeds directly upon phytoplankton, as noted above, and which is known to be extremely abundant in Antarctic waters. There have been numerous attempts to estimate the annual production of krill in the Antarctic, from the known number of whales at their peak of abundance and from various assumptions concerning their daily ration of krill. The evidence upon which such estimates are based is so tenuous that they are hardly worth discussing. It is interesting to note, however, that the more conservative of these estimates are rather close to figures derived independently by the method discussed here. For example, Moiseev (34) calculated krill production for 1967 to be $60.5 \times 10^6$ tons, while Kasahara (3) considered a range of 24 to $36 \times 10^6$ tons to be a minimal figure. I consider the figure $50 \times 10^6$ tons to be on the high side, as the estimated area of upwelling is probably generous, the average productivity value of 300 grams of carbon per square meter per year is high for a region where photosynthesis can occur during only half the year, and much of the primary production is probably diverted into smaller crustacean herbivores (35). Clearly, the Antarctic must receive much more intensive study before its productive capacity can be assessed with any accuracy.

In all, I estimate that some 240 million tons (fresh weight) of fish are produced annually in the sea. As this figure is rough and subject to numerous sources of error, it should not be considered significantly different from Schaeffer's (2) figure of 200 million tons.

Production, however, is not equivalent to potential harvest. In the first place, man must share the production with other top-level carnivores. It has been estimated, for example, that guano birds alone eat some 4 million tons of anchovies annually off the coast of Peru, while tunas, squid, sea lions, and other predators probably consume an equivalent amount (22, 36). This is nearly equal to the amount taken by man from this one highly productive fishery. In addition, man must take care to leave a large enough fraction of the annual production of fish to permit utilization of the resource at something close to its maximum sustainable yield, both to protect the fishery and to provide a sound economic basis for the industry.

When these various factors are taken into consideration, it seems unlikely that the potential sustained yield of fish to man is appreciably greater than 100 million tons. The total world fish landings for 1967 were just over 60 million tons (37), and this figure has been increasing at an average rate of about 8 per cent per year for the past 25 years. It is clear that, while the yield can be still further increased, the resource is not vast. At the present rate, the industry can continue to expand for no more than a decade.

Most of the existing fisheries of the world are probably incapable of contributing significantly to this expansion. Many are already overexploited, and most of the rest are utilized at or near their maximum sustainable yield. Evidence of fishing pressure is usually determined directly from fishery statistics, but it is of some interest, in connection with the present discussion, to compare landings with fish production as estimated by the methods developed in this article. I will make this comparison for two quite dissimilar fisheries, that of the continental shelf of the northwest Atlantic and that of the Peruvian coastal region.

According to Edwards (38), the continental shelf between Hudson Canyon and the southern end of the Nova Scotian shelf includes an area of 110,000 square miles ($2.9 \times 10^{11}$ square meters). From the information in Tables 2 and 3, it may be calculated that approximately 1 million tons of fish are produced annually in this region. Commercial landings from the same area were slightly in excess of 1 million tons per year for the 3-year period 1963 to 1965 before going into a decline. The decline has become more serious each year, until it is now proposed to regulate the landings of at least the more valuable species such as cod and haddock, now clearly overexploited.

The coastal upwelling associated with the Peru Coastal Current gives rise to the world's most productive fishery, an annual harvest of some $10^7$ metric tons of anchovies. The maximum sustainable yield is estimated at, or slightly below, this figure (39), and the fishery is carefully regulated. As mentioned above, mortality from other causes (such as predation from guano birds, bonito, squid, and so on) probably accounts for an additional $10^7$ tons. This prodigious fishery is concentrated in an area no larger than about $800 \times 30$ miles (36), or $6 \times 10^{10}$ square meters. By the methods developed in this article, it is estimated that such an upwelling area can be expected to produce $2 \times 10^7$ tons of fish, almost precisely the commercial yield as now regulated plus the amount attributed to natural mortality.

These are but two of the many recognized examples of well-developed commercial fisheries now being utilized at or above their levels of maximum sustainable yield. Any appreciable continued increase in the world's fish landings must clearly come from unexploited species and, for the most part, from undeveloped new fishing areas. Much of the potential expansion must consist of new products from remote regions, such as the Antarctic krill, for which no harvesting technology and no market yet exist.

## REFERENCES AND NOTES

1. H. W. Graham and R. L. Edwards, in *Fish and Nutrition* (Fishing News, London, 1962), pp. 3–8; W. K. Schmitt, *Ann. N.Y. Acad. Sci.* 118, 645 (1965).
2. M. B. Schaeffer, *Trans. Amer. Fish. Soc.* 94, 123 (1965).
3. H. Kasahara, in *Proceedings, 7th International Congress of Nutrition, Hamburg* (Pergamon, New York, 1966), vol. 4, p. 958.
4. W. M. Chapman, "Potential Resources of the Ocean" (Serial Publication 89–21, 89th Congress, first session, 1965) (Government Printing Office, Washington, D.C., 1965), pp. 132–156.
5. E. Steemann Nielsen and E. A. Jensen, *Galathea Report*, F. Bruun et al., Eds. (Allen & Unwin, London, 1957), vol. 1, p. 49.
6. E. Steemann Nielsen, *J. Cons. Cons. Perma. Int. Explor. Mer* 18, 117 (1952).
7. O. I. Koblentz-Mishke, V. V. Volkovinsky, J. G. Kobanova, in *Scientific Exploration of the South Pacific*, W. Wooster, Ed. (National Academy of Sciences, Washington, D.C., in press).
8. J. H. Ryther, in *The Sea*, M. N. Hill, Ed. (Interscience, London, 1963), pp. 347–380.
9. H. W. Menard and S. M. Smith, *J. Geophys. Res.* 71, 4305 (1966).
10. J. H. Ryther and D. W. Menzel, *Deep-Sea Res.* 12, 199 (1965).
11. ———, E. M. Hulburt, C. J. Lorenzen, N. Corwin, "The Production and Utilization of Organic Matter in the Peru Coastal Current" (Texas A & M Univ. Press, College Station, in press).
12. C. D. McAllister, T. R. Parsons, J. D. H. Strickland, *J. Cons. Cons. Perma. Int. Explor. Mer* 25, 240 (1960); G. C. Anderson, *Limnol. Oceanogr.* 10, 477 (1965).
13. T. R. Parsons and R. J. Le Brasseur, in "Symposium Marine Food Chains, Aarhus (1968)."
14. E. Steemann Nielsen, *J. Cons. Cons. Perma. Int. Explor. Mer* 23, 178 (1958).
15. J. R. Beers and G. L. Stewart, *J. Fish. Res. Board Can.* 24, 2053 (1967).
16. M. Anraku and M. Omori, *Limnol. Oceanogr.* 8, 116 (1963).
17. G. D. Grice and H. D. Hart, *Ecol. Monogr.* 32, 287 (1962).
18. M. R. Reeve, in "Symposium Marine Food Chains, Aarhus (1968)."
19. Personal observation: T. J. Hart and R. I. Currie, *Discovery Rep.* 31, 123 (1960).
20. K. R. Gaarder, *Report on the Scientific Results of the "Michael Sars" North Atlantic Deep-Sea Expedition 1910* (Univ. of Bergen, Bergen, Norway).
21. T. J. Hart, *Discovery Rep.* 21, 261 (1942).
22. R. J. E. Sanchez, in *Proceedings of the 18th Annual Session, Gulf and Caribbean Fisheries Institute, University of Miami Institute of Marine Science, 1966*, J. B. Higman, Ed. (Univ. of Miami Press, Coral Gables, Fla., 1966), pp. 84–93.
23. R. T. Barber and R. L. Haedrich, *Deep-Sea Res.* 16, 415 (1952).
24. J. W. S. Marr, *Discovery Rep.* 32, 34 (1962).
25. S. D. Gerking, *Physiol. Zool.* 25, 358 (1952).
26. B. Dawes, *J. Mar. Biol. Ass. U.K.* 17, 102 (1930–31); ibid., p. 877.
27. V. S. Ivlev, *Zool. Zh.* 18, 303 (1939).
28. W. E. Ricker, *Ecology* 16, 373 (1946).
29. L. B. Slobodkin, *Growth and Regulation of Animal Populations* (Holt, Rinehart & Winston, New York, 1961), chap. 12.
30. G. E. Fogg, C. Nalewajko, W. D. Watt, *Proc. Roy. Soc. Ser B Biol. Sci.* 162, 517 (1965).
31. G. E. Fogg and W. D. Watt, *Mem. Inst. Ital. Idrobiol. Dott. Marco de Marshi Pallanza Italy* 18, suppl., 165 (1965).
32. S. Z. El-Sayed, in *Biology of the Antarctic Seas III*, G. Llano and W. Schmitt, Eds. (American Geophysical Union, Washington, D.C., 1968), pp. 15–47.
33. Y. Saijo and T. Kawashima, *J. Oceanogr. Soc. Japan* 19, 190 (1964).
34. P. A. Moiseev, paper presented at the 2nd Symposium on Antarctic Ecology, Cambridge, England, 1968.
35. T. L. Hopkins, unpublished manuscript.
36. W. S. Wooster and J. L. Reid, Jr., in *The Sea*, M. N. Hill, Ed. (Interscience, London, 1963), vol. 2, p. 253.

37. *FAO Yearb. Fish. Statistics* **25** (1967).
38. R. L. Edwards, *Univ. Wash. Publ. Fish.* **4,** 52 (1968).
39. R. J. E. Sanchez, in *Proceedings, 18th Annual Session, Gulf and Caribbean Fisheries Institute, University of Miami Institute of Marine Science* (Univ. of Miami Press, Coral Gables, 1966), p. 84.

40. The work discussed here was supported by the Atomic Energy Commission, contract No. AT(30-1)-3862, Ref. No. NYO-3862-20. This article is contribution No. 2327 from the Woods Hole Oceanographic Institution.

# Non-Fuel Mineral Resources in the Next Century

## T. S. LOVERING

The total volume of commercial mineral deposits is an insignificant fraction of 1 per cent of the earth's crust and each deposit represents some accident of geology in the remote past. It must be exploited where it occurs. Each has it limits, however, and if worked long enough must sooner or later be exhausted. No second crop will materialize; rich mineral deposits are a nation's most valuable but ephemeral possession—its quick assets. Continued extraction of ore leads to increasing costs as the material mined comes from greater and greater depths, but sometimes improved technology make˙ possible continuation or renewal of work in deposits that would otherwise have been shut down because of competition with deposits more favorably situated or where cost per unit of output was appreciably less.

Demand for mineral products comes chiefly from the chemical and manufacturing industries and from agriculture. The constant arrival of large quantities of raw materials is essential to maintaining output and continuing output is vital to a healthy industrial economy. An adequate supply is more easily assured if the mineral deposits are under domestic control and within the national boundaries of the country where they are to be consumed. The greater the dependence on foreign sources the greater the risk of industrial stress caused by foreign institutional action such as price rises due to cartel action, trade barriers set up by governments, or by adverse military action.

Satisfactory substitutes for most raw materials exist if the price of the substitute is not a consideration. Some minerals, however, have unique properties for which there is no satisfactory substitute and many others are essential to successful commercial competition in the world markets. The minerals that are currently most essential to civilization are probably coal, iron, copper, aluminum, petroleum, and the fertilizer minerals. Only a very few industrial countries have adequate internal sources of all these minerals to supply their current industrial needs and none have reserves adequate for the next century using foreseeable technology. Although it is possible in times of distress, when free access to world sources is cut off, to work deposits that otherwise are noncommercial, it must be remem-

Non-Fuel Mineral Resources in the Next Century. From *Texas Quarterly*, Summer 1968, pp. 127–147. Reprinted by permission of the author.

bered that low-grade deposits require much time and capital to develop. Economic chaos can result if foreign sources of supply are denied to a country that has allowed itself to become dependent on them. And dependent all industrial nations are, entirely or in large part, on foreign sources of supply for some or most of the essential metals demanded by their industries. This dependence grows ever greater with the years.

That sources of supply will inevitably shift is evident not only from the hard geological facts but also from a review of historical events. Three thousand years ago the Middle East was the center of the iron mining industry of the ancient world. For several hundred years ancient Greece was the center of lead and silver mining of the western civilized world. For a long time Germany was the leading producer of lead, zinc, and silver in medieval Europe, but Belgium became the chief producer of zinc at the beginning of the industrial era. In the nineteenth century Great Britain was successively the world's foremost producer of lead, of copper, of tin, of iron, of coal, and during that period she was the wealthiest nation in the world; from 1700 to 1850 the United Kingdom mined 50 per cent of the world's lead, from 1820 to 1840 she produced 45 per cent of the world's copper, from 1850 to 1890 she increased her iron production from one-third to one-half of the entire world output. At the turn of the century, Russia was the leading producer of petroleum in the world and during the latter part of the nineteenth century she was the foremost gold producer—until the discovery of the great Transvaal gold deposits in South Africa. Most of the manganese ore mined until after the second World War, came from a comparatively small area in southern Russia. Now large new deposits in Africa, Australia, and Brazil threaten the dominance of the U.S.S.R. and have cut deeply into the manganese market.

Hewett (1929) made a penetrating analysis of the normal history of mineral exploitation in a nation and recognized five stages between discovery and exhaustion. In the forty years since his study, exploitation of mineral resources has strengthened his conclusions that discovery is followed successively by flush production, proliferation of smelters, decline in production, cessation of export metal, growing dependence on imports, and ultimately complete dependence on imported metals.

Between 1905 and 1938 more metal was produced than had been consumed in the entire history of the world prior to 1905; a similar amount of metal was produced and consumed in a far shorter interval after the start of World War II. In the meanwhile the world population has more than doubled so that per capita consumption has not increased appreciably even in industrial countries. The reserves of known and undiscovered ore deposits of commercial grade are finite and diminishing, whereas the demand for metals is growing at an exponential rate; it is clear that exhaustion of deposits of currently commercial grade is inevitable. The cost of mining deposits of lower grade involves increased costs for capital, labor energy, and transportation; decreased costs of energy from the ultimate development of breeder reactors will only cut energy costs a relatively small amount because their major cost is that of invested capital.

It would seem that grave concern may be justified over mineral supplies during the lifetime of those now living. There is, however, an optimism among mineral economists now (1968) that may be shortsighted. Future mineral resources depend on the cost of supplying market places, and this in turn is a function of relative locations, cost per unit of mine output, market price, the market location, and any institutional incentives or restrictions placed on operations. The current but questionable assumptions of the majority of mineral economists as given in The Paley Report, the book *Scarcity and Growth* (Barnett and Chandler, 1963) and *Natural Resources for U.S. Growth* (Landsberg, 1964) may be summarized as follows:

1. Technology for the past fifty years has steadily made increasing amounts of raw ma-

terial available at lower costs per unit and, therefore, will continue to do so into the "foreseeable future";

2. As the grade of a mineral deposit decreases arithmetically the reserves increase geometrically;

3. Non-renewable resources are therefore inexhaustible;

4. Scarcity can always be prevented by a rise in price of the raw materials and

5. Since the cost of raw materials is only a fraction of the final cost, a material rise in price for any raw material will have an insignificant effect on the price of manufactured items and on the general economy;

6. Any industrial nation will have adequate access to deposits throughout the world;

7. There will be only insignificant institutional restraints on access;

8. The United States and other industrial nations must have an "ever-expanding economy"—the GNP (Gross National Product) increasing continuously at an annual rate of about 4 per cent because their economic well-being requires it;

9. The population of western industrial nations will continue to increase at a rate of about 1.5 per cent per year for several generations; and finally,

10. The under-developed nations will achieve a per capita income comparable to that currently enjoyed by the United States within one or two generations.

All these assumptions are debatable; some are based more on rhetoric than reason, some seem a sort of struthionic optimism unrelated to physical factors, some are simply wrong. If accepted as guides to future policy they may lead to a lethal complacency as to natural resources.

The basic assumptions underlying the current optimism concerning the adequacy of mineral resources stems in large part from Lasky's classic paper (Lasky, 1948, 1950) in which he analyzed the relations between grade and reserves of ore in eight copper porphyries of the Southwest. The optimism

generated by the current interpretation of Lasky's work has been greatly increased by Barnett and Morris (1963) whose book *Scarcity and Growth* and summary article "The Myth of Our Vanishing Resources" (Barnett, 1967) formulate clearly, specifically, and persuasively the basic position and the happy philosophy of most mineral economists. They reformulate the Ricardian hypothesis of scarcity as follows (p. 249): "The character of the resource base presents man with a never ending stream of problems;—that man will face a series of particular scarcities as the result of growth, is a foregone conclusion; that these problems will impose general scarcity as shown by increasing costs per unit output is not a legitimate corollary." According to them (p. 230), "technological progress is automatic and self-reproducing in modern economies." They state that "natural resource building blocks are now to a large extent atoms and molecules...units of mass and energy, and the problem thus is one of manipulating the available stores of iron, magnesium, aluminum, carbon, and oxygen atoms—even electrons—so that we obtain those resources required by industry." The exuberant optimism reflected in such a belief leads Barnett and Morris to conclude: "The progress of growth generates antidotes to a general increase in resource scarcity" (p. 290), and to believe also that the sea is a continually augmenting store of resource of all kinds, ready at hand to supply man bountifully for all future time. Barnett and Morris state (p. 249) that principles "that have clear relevance in a Ricardian world where today's depletion curtails tomorrow's production, have little if any relevance in a progressive world." This will be heartening news to all mine owners!

Barnett and Morris looked at the net decrease in unit costs for the mineral industry and certain specific commodities over a period of some seventy-five years and concluded that the improvement in efficiency caused by improved technology had resulted in a continuing net decrease in the cost per unit of mineral extracted; furthermore, that this increased efficiency would continue into the indefinite future. Within the mineral industry, the increased mechanization that accompanied the increased production of coal and oil, resulted in current costs of one-third to one-fourth those of 1920; this Barnett interprets as showing the opposite of increased scarcity or the lessening of economic quality. The curves for lead and zinc, however, show no such change and rather an increase during this period. For copper and for iron, the trend towards lower unit cost flattens greatly between 1940 and 1960 and as shown in their graph for timber, the trend for many years has been the opposite of that which Barnett postulates for minerals. Conservationists, who are unduly belabored by Barnett (1967) might make something of this!

Changing costs in mineral extraction reflect the relative efficiency of operation as opposed to the increasing costs of capital, labor, and energy. The efficiency in operations must approach an irreducible minimum as maximum mechanization is achieved; it would require major innovations not yet in sight to start another marked downward slope in the curve representing price times grade. The present trend of the ratio of copper grade to price (in constant dollars) is not encouraging (Figure 1) but the discovery rate is.

Lasky's analysis of the relation of reserves to tonnage and average grade of ore produced in copper porphyries (Lasky, 1950) resulted in his stating the principle that is now known as the "arithmetic-geometric ratio" (or simply the A/G ratio): The reserves of ore increase geometrically as the average grade mined decreases arithmetically, or as Lasky (1951) expressed it

$$Grade = K_1 - K_2 \log tonnage.$$

The problem of exhaustibility thus need cause no concern according to current (1967–68) economic philosophy because over a long period of time the decreased grade that is now mined, shows that reserves have increased or at least been maintained. The past half century refutes the gloomy forecasts made in 1912 which indicated that the United States would run out of many major resources long before

now. From this unequivocal fact, some very dubious deductions stem.

In referring to his equation and the curve it generates, Lasky (1948) said, "It fits the porphyry coppers . . . and apparently also other deposits of similar type in which small quantities of ore minerals are scattered through great volumes of shattered rock." According to Lasky then, "It may be stated as a general principle that in many mineral deposits in which there is a gradation from relatively rich to relatively lean material, the tonnage increases at a constant geometric rate as the grade decreases." A typical curve for a porphyry copper plots as a straight line on semilogarithmic paper for which the decrements in grade are represented by the arithmetically spaced vertical lines and the increments in tonnage are scaled by logarithmic ordinate lines. The straight line plot represents the cumulative production or tonnage of a porphyry copper for decreasing average grade of the *total tonnage extracted* as ever leaner ore is mined. *This constraint is a very important one*—but has apparently been misunderstood by many economists who use this analysis as a springboard from which to leap into a sea of optimism.

Lasky averaged the characteristics of the eight major porphyry copper deposits in the United States (as of 1950) and notes that for such an average deposit, there would be somewhat more than 600 million tons of ore averaging about 0.6 per cent of copper when it had been *mined out—down to and including* "zero cut-off grade." In this average deposit, the tonnage increases at a rate of about 18 per cent for each unit decrease in grade of 0.1 per cent. Most of the copper is contained in the 175 million tons having a copper content between 0.5 and 0.9 per cent. Lasky's analysis is a major contribution to our concepts of grade and tonnage for the type of deposit that he considers. It should be noted, however, that the curves rigidly defined the situation over a range of grade of about 1.5 per cent, but that even for porphyry coppers they cannot express the relations for higher grades of ore and for the very lean rocks which should be represented by the extensions of the curve to the left and to the right respectively. For his average copper porphyry deposit which contains sixty million tons of ore averaging 2 per cent copper and six hundred million tons of ore averaging 0.6 per cent of copper, Lasky's mathematical expression is "Grade=12.9−1.4 log tonnage"; from this we deduce that Zero grade=12.9−1.4×9.2 and as 9.2=log (1.58×10$^9$) Zero grade is reached at 1.58×10$^9$ tons, *which is impossible*! The clarke (average abundance of an element) of many igneous rocks is 0.004 to 0.010 per cent copper; for Lasky's average porphyry copper deposit in question, an average grade of 0.3 per cent copper corresponds to a tonnage of one billion tons—not an unreasonable figure if the cut-off grade is held close to the average grade mined. Somewhere between a grade of a few tenths of a per cent and a hundredth of a per cent, the tonnage must increase astronomically but there is no geologic reason why the curve should maintain its slope or change smoothly from the one calculated by Lasky's formula into the curve that might express the change in copper content of the various rock units found in the crust of the earth. It is more than likely that the cumulative curve would first flatten and then rise precipitously. At the other end of the curve, consider what happens for ore minerals. The formula shows a "tonnage" of one milligram of ore having a grade of 24.5 per cent copper or one ton (out of sixty million tons averaging 2 per cent copper) having a grade of 12.8 per cent copper. It is obvious that the curve generated by the Lasky formula departs widely from reality between 0.01 per cent and 0.3 per cent on the one side and for any masses of ore containing substantial amounts of the common copper ore minerals.

Most ores are deposited over an appreciable time interval by complex processes. The large mass of mineralized intensely fractured rock that marks deposits of the porphyry copper type does have its limits, and beyond these limits the metal content drops off sharply. Most such bodies show a history of repeated fracturing and mineralization; in some several stages of metallization are present, in others only one stage of metallization but several stages of barren alteration may be represented. Where the fractured rock has been enriched by successive waves of metalizing solutions, each wave is apt to be localized in somewhat restricted masses of refractured rock; these localized blocks of better ore result in a stepwise change in grade for the deposit as a whole, but such a change is not reflected in the product of mining which represents a predetermined mixture. Where a very low grade protore—less than 0.10 Cu—has been enriched by weathering processes, a shallow mass of ore may carry ten times as much as the protore. In such porphyry copper deposits there is an abrupt transition from ore grade to unmineable rock. Any attempt to use an A/G curve for them is obviously absurd. Lowering the grade by decrements of 0.10 per cent would increase the total tonnages of ore by only a small fraction until the grade of the protore was reached, when an enormous increase might take place in reserves of protore, though not necessarily in total tonnage of contained copper.

Even though the porphyry copper type deposits share many characteristics in common, each individual deposit is unique. It is clear that generalizations based on a few biased samples will not apply to the entire population; the extension of these generalizations to deposits of entirely different origin and geologic habitat is not only unwarranted, unscientific, and illogical, it is also downright dangerous in its psychological effects.

In his cautious first statement of the problem, Lasky says that the curve generated by his equation is meaningful for many types of deposits, but he adds the proviso "the geological evidence permitting." It is this reservation that has been neglected. There is absolutely no geological reason for concluding that the so-called arithmetic-geometric ratio holds for ore deposits in general. Most especially is it an error to believe there must be undiscovered low grade deposits of astronomical tonnage to bridge the gap between known commercial ore and the millions of cubic miles of crustal rocks that have measurable trace amounts of the various metals in them. The closer the mineable grade approaches the clarke of an element for major rocks, the more probable is the existence of an exponential ratio of tonnage to grade far below that of commercial ore.

The geologic processes that operate to give us mineable ores include huge tonnages provided by *sedimentation*; this process will cause dilution as well as concentration in detrital deposits and there are, of course, far larger volumes of sediments containing metals in the parts per million range—except for iron, aluminum, and magnesium—than there are that contain ore metals in per cent amounts. In sedimentary rocks, however, the A/G ratio may well hold far down towards the clarke of certain metals. The areas where the greatest concentrations of a mineral occur in sedimentary precipitates, whether by evaporation, inorganic chemical reactions, or biogenic activity, are much more limited in time and space than in precipitation areas of less intense chemical selectivity contaminated both by other precipitates and by detrital components. A special kind of mechanical precipitates would include some magmatic segregations where a desired mineral constituent has concentrated in a liquid magma as an igneous sediment at high temperatures. Many ores of this type show abrupt gradations and others show gradual changes in concentration, especially when followed along the layers that contain the segregation itself. For some segregation deposits the A/G ratio will hold through a tenfold change in grade, but for many segregations, there is an abrupt change from ore deposit to barren rock.

Both for igneous segregations and for precipitates from aqueous solutions in fractured or chemically reactive rocks such as limestone and dolomite, there is no geologic reason to expect geometric increase in tonnage with decrease in grade beyond certain well defined limits which vary not only with type of deposits but with the individual deposit considered. Nearly all these deposits have an outer margin of mineralization controlled by igneous contacts or by fractures or by hostrock where the grade decreases sharply.

Fracture controlled deposits range from those with abrupt transitions between high and low grade ores such as are found in the typical "fissure" veins characteristic of the western United States to the disseminated ores of the porphyry copper type where the A/G ratios have been established for changes in grade of approximately one order of magnitude. Ore deposits the majority of which do not show the A/G ratio would include those of mercury, gold, silver, tungsten, lead, zinc, antimony, beryllium, tantalum, niobium, and the rare earth elements.

Weathering, the precursor of sedimentation, may result in widespread gradational deposits derived from rock protores of huge tonnage; both residual enrichment through leaching, and secondary enrichment through precipitation of elements at depth form important ore bodies having large tonnages. Some of these deposits show abrupt changes in grade from worthless material to valuable ore, as in the upper part of most sulfide deposits; others show a gradual enrichment, as with many lateritic nickel ores.

In many important types of mineral deposits, all available evidence indicates a paucity of the low-grade material essential to the concept of the arithmetic-geometric ratios. For lead-zinc replacement deposits in carbonate rocks, this zone is commonly but a few feet wide, and limestone carrying 20 or 30 ppm may be within arm's reach of a huge ore body having a grade ten thousand times that of the countryrock (Morris and Lovering, 1952). Lowering the grade of a typical large high-grade lead manta ore body from 20 per cent to 10 per cent would not increase the total quantity of reserves greatly and lowering the grade from 10 per cent to 1 per cent would increase the reserves only as barren rock was added to the ore to bring its average down to the proposed low cut-off value.

Many other geologic types of ore deposits scattered over the surface of our planet have characteristics in common. Bonanza epithermal silver and gold ores are characterized by rich ores that commonly bottom at shallow depths and have relatively sharp boundaries with their wallrocks. Most mercury deposits and antimony deposits fall in this epithermal class. For the vast majority of such deposits there is little hope of a geometric increase in tonnage with arithmetic decrease in grade, but we should expect to find an exceptional deposit occasionally somewhere in the world that shows promise of a geometric (but finite) increase in ore reserves with decreasing grade.

Production of several of the metal vitamins essential to the life of industrial giants is concentrated in a few major deposits contained in very small areas of the world, but minor production may come from a large number of small intermittently worked deposits. Mercury belongs in this class. It is worthy of note that the clarke of mercury is 0.000,04 per cent or 400 ppb; this is four orders of magnitude less than in ore, which commonly contains from 0.2 to 0.5 per cent mercury. A similar range exists for other important industrial elements such as tungsten (clarke less than 2 ppm), tantalum, silver, tin, vanadium, molybdenum, and others. Several metals fall in an intermediate class between the iron-aluminum group and the mercury-tungsten group; these would include copper (ore grade approximately 0.4 to 0.8 per cent and having a clarke in basic igneous rocks of 87 ppm, although in some igneous rock it averages several hundred ppm, only an order of magnitude below the present cut-off grade in some porphyry coppers. Cobalt, nickel, and vanadium have similar abundance ratios of clarke to ore grades. Both zinc and lead approach this group but currently the ratio of ore grade to clarke is distinctly higher than in this latter trio.

It has been optimistically said (Brown, Bonner, and Weir, p. 91, 1957) that with the advent of cheap nuclear energy, common rock—granite—would become "ore" and supply unlimited quantities of all the metals needed by industry, but even the breeder reactor is not expected to make energy costs appreciably less than current costs of cheap hydroelectric or geothermal power (2.5 mills per kilowatt hour). Surprisingly enough, many men unfamiliar with the mineral industry believe that the beneficent gods of Technology are about to open the cornucopia of granite and sea, flooding industry with any and all metals desired. Unfortunately cheap energy little reduces the total costs—chiefly made up of capital and labor—required for mining and processing rock. The enormous quantities of unusable waste produced for each unit of metal also are more easily disposed of on a blueprint than in the field.

The difference in physical and chemical form of the compounds containing the metals in common rock would require development of a new and complex technology to extract them, and the unit costs of labor and capital (and even cheap energy!) could be orders of magnitude above those of the present. For at least another century or so metals will come from ores that have metal concentrations well above the clarkes of metals in rocks, with only few exceptions such as that represented by the magnetic black sands concentrated in the U.S.S.R.

Even where the arithmetic-geometric ratio holds, each deposit will approach zero grade at a very finite tonnage. This does not mean that large tonnages of very low grade currently noncommercial copper-bearing rock will not be developed ultimately in the porphyry type copper deposits. Indeed, with a moderate increase in price and substantial decrease in grade, there would seem to be ample copper within the Western Hemisphere to supply the needs of North America for at least another fifty years. Currently the outlook for adequate supplies of molybdenum also invites cautious optimism.

Few if any mining geologists see any reason to expect semi-infinite volumes of copper-bearing rock containing about 0.1 per cent copper; most especially they do not by analogy with porphyry type deposits assume any A/G increase in tonnage for ore bodies of the many other metals that are totally different in their geologic habitat and genesis. In spite of the excellent start on a continuing inventory of United States and world ore reserves made by the Geological Survey under Lasky's guidance and by the U.S. Bureau of Mines in the early fifties, far too little has been done in this field with geologic guidance since, and we desperately need such studies of a wide variety of ore deposits, guided by geologic insight and much field study.

## TECHNOLOGY AND MINERAL RESOURCES

It may be true that in the future technology and science will always provide answers to our problems but it is also true that much time, money, and effort will be required as grade diminishes, mineralogy changes, and entirely different types of deposits are exploited. The widespread belief that technology is continually lowering the unit costs while allowing us to work lower grade deposits is belied by the trends revealed in the copper industry as shown in Figure 1. Here the continuing change in average grade of copper as mined is shown, ranging from a high of 2.12 per cent to the current low of about 0.70 per cent; the tonnage produced yearly shows a general upward trend as would be expected. Assuming that the price of copper represents the summation of costs plus profit and that the costs of capital, labor and energy comprise the total costs, it then follows that the product of grade times price should give us an index representing the contribution of technology in lowering the cost per unit produced. The three-year moving average of this "grade times price" is shown in the same illustration and exhibits the expected sharp down slope from the early 1920s to the end of World War II; during the past twenty years, however, this type curve is nearly horizontal. Improving technology was almost compensating for the ever decreasing grade of ore mined and the increasing costs of capital and labor. Of especial interest is the plot for corrected price representing zero profit; the average price is reduced by the percentage of the total sales represented by net earnings of the major cop-

per companies each year since 1954 to indicate the break-even price at which they might have operated. (Figures taken from annual review of 500 major U.S. corporations in *Fortune* Magazine.)

When this break-even price is used and multiplied by the current average grade of copper mined, the line plots with a perceptible upward trend showing that current technology is not quite keeping pace with the increased costs of extraction; contrary to the Barnett school of thought, *unit costs are not* declining. The major costs of extraction are those of labor and capital, so that a decline in the cost of energy from 3 to 2.5 mills per kilowatt hour will not greatly affect the cost of extraction. To maintain the current dividend rate the major porphyry copper producers will need a continued price increase or will have to devise an entirely different and appreciably more efficient way of extracting copper from the ores. A rough approximation for zero profit is price times grade must equal 0.20. To maintain present production at the average grade of copper mined in the United States and to allow the net earnings comparable to those currently had by the major copper companies, price times grade (in constant dollars 1958–59 base) would have to be 0.24. To maintain present returns on investment, assuming average grade of copper ore mined times the price must be 0.24, an average grade of 0.5 per cent (average grade in 1966 was 0.7 per cent cu.) would require a price in constant dollars (1958–59 base) of forty-eight cents per pound in the United States. For this type of deposit, it seems probable that an increase in price, if guaranteed and maintained, would bring out a corresponding increase in production. This is not true, however, of some other metals. Some elements occur in minor amounts in ores exploited chiefly for some other metal; molybdenum is a valuable by-product of the concentrating processes used for getting copper from porphyry coppers. Tin and tungsten are worthwhile by-products from some molybdenum deposits that have all the characteristics of the copper porphyries except that copper is present in only trace amounts.

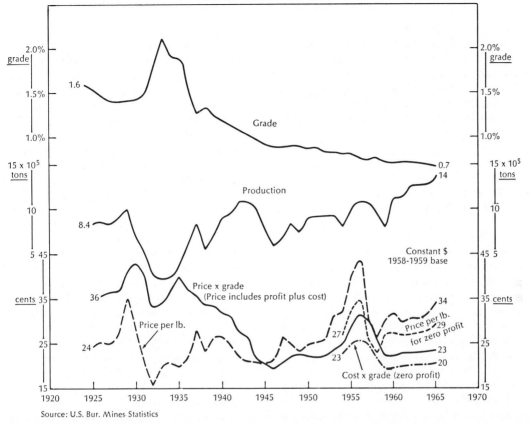

COPPER INDUSTRY 1924–1965

Source: U.S. Bur. Mines Statistics

**Fig. 1.**

Most of the production of silver, gold, and antimony in the United States comes as by-products from the mining of other ores and such deposits can form a limited source of additional by-product metals for a sufficient increase in price of the by-product metal, but at the risk of flooding and depressing the market for the major constituents. When this happens, most such deposits would become uneconomic to operate.

It is often suggested that successful development of the breeder reactor will bring unlimited quantities of cheap (almost free!) power and revolutionize mining and other industries. The cost of nuclear fuel for the breeder reactor will indeed be negligible, but the cost of the large capital investment, of power transmission, of waste disposal, and of operation, combine to bring the price per kilo-

watt hour to essentially that of cheap steam-coal electric generating plants. Breeder reactors will be a wonderful asset to industrial nations not because they provide power at very low cost but because they may provide desperately needed power when fossil fuels are depleted.

Mining costs always increase with depth, and for those deposits which have an A/G ratio that extends down to low grades and huge tonnages, technology will inevitably cease to produce larger tonnages at lower unit costs; the trend that is currently evident in open pit copper mines manifests itself also in other types of deposits. To maintain production would require a gradually rising price for the domestic product, or increased dependence on foreign sources and new discoveries. For types of deposits other than those characterized by an A/G ratio, the increase in price may not be gradual, but instead may accelerate rapidly to where the metal will price itself out of the market except for the most unusual and essential uses. In other words, a real scarcity will develop as measured by the change in price.

If the change in grade with time is gradual as with copper, the change in price (in constant dollars) should also be gradual. The assumption that a similar slow change in price will hold for other mineral industries is not borne out by either geologic theory or current mineral statistics. A 20 per cent increase in the price of copper, if maintained, would certainly stimulate activity in the copper industry and increase the production more than 20 per cent within a year or so; for deposits that characteristically lack the Lasky grade/tonnage relation but instead show an abrupt transition between ore and country rock, no such increase in production will result.

Rise in price may well increase production temporarily, hastening producers toward exhaustion, stimulating marginal and submarginal mines into a flurry of activity, with the result that industrial nations increasingly are vulnerable to the vagaries of outside institutional action. For some commodities, however, a substantial rise in price does not bring about any commensurate production of a new material either at home or abroad, though it may make available temporarily ore from marginal producers and sufficient secondary or hoarded metal (a stockpile may be regarded as a "hoard") to satisfy demand—as witness the supply-price behavior of mercury for the past few decades.

As a pointed illustration of the impropriety of generalizing about all mineral deposits from data on a special kind of deposit the two basic assumptions for copper are considered in relation to mercury: (1) geometric increase in tonnage accompanies an arithmetic decrease in grade; (2) a moderate increase in price brings a large increase in production. Bearing significantly on the A/G ratio as applied to mercury, we have the figures resulting from an intensive exploration effort by the Bureau of Mines and the Geological Survey during World War II. More than 330 examinations of mercury occurrences were made and forty-three deposits were explored. Commercial ore was developed on thirty-eight of them; 370,000 tons of ore averaging 0.8 per cent (16.2 pounds per ton); 1,220,000 tons averaging 0.125 per cent (2.5 pounds per ton), and only 285,000 tons averaging 0.08 per cent or 1.6 pounds per ton. This is equivalent to 2,960 tons of mercury in the 0.8 per cent ore, 1,525 tons of mercury in the 0.12 per cent ore, and only 228 tons of mercury in the 0.008 per cent ore. To sum up the relations, an arithmetic decrease in grade from 0.8 per cent to 0.125 per cent (and actually a sixfold change) resulted in a geometric increase in tonnage of threefold *but the total mercury in the larger tonnage was only one-half* that in the smaller high-grade tonnage. A further decrease of 0.004 per cent in grade resulted in additional tonnage containing only one-tenth as much mercury as that in the high-grade ore.

The U. S. Bureau of Mines Yearbook figures for mercury show the lowest output in twenty-five years for the United States was 5,000 flasks (of seventy-six pounds each) in 1950 when the price was approximately $90 per flask, which was the average price from 1946 to 1950, during which time the output fell steadily from 25,000 to 5,000 flasks. From 1951 to 1953, the price rose rapidly to an average of $200 per flask and in 1954, the United States government guaranteed a minimum price of $225 a flask for a three-year period—a 250 per cent increase in the 1946–50 price! United States production climbed to nearly 12,000 flasks by the end of 1953, about half the 1946 production. Although the price after 1956 fluctuated on both sides of $200 per flask, this is not far from the average that obtained until a few years ago. During this period the production from the United States mercury mines reached a high of 38,000 flasks in 1958 but from then on dropped steadily until it reached a low of 14,000 flasks in 1964. In that year, however, the price of mercury again more than doubled, reaching an all-time high of about $800 per flask in the latter part of 1965, resulting in an average price of over $500 a flask. The substantial increase in price —a sixfold increase in twenty-one years— resulted in another increase in domestic production which reached 22,000 flasks in 1965, somewhat less than was produced in 1947 when the average price of mercury was only $83 per flask. It is worthy of note that at $1,500 per flask the price of mercury would approximate the coinage value of silver at $1.35 per troy ounce.

Mercury resembles silver in many of its occurrences but most silver now produced comes as a by-product of mining complex lead ores. The high-grade silver mines are depleted just as most of the high-grade mercury mines have been depleted. Very little mercury is recovered as a by-product from complex ores so that this source will contribute only an insignificant amount of mercury in the future whereas silver will continue to increase as the production of the complex ores continues to increase. The average consumption of mercury in the United States has increased at a rate of 3 per cent per year for twenty years, equivalent to a doubling in consumption every twenty-three years. But in the same period *the price of mercury has increased more than 500 per cent!* Presumably a price of more than $1,000 per flask might maintain world production of mercury for fifty years or more but the source of this mercury would be increasingly concentrated in a few large deposits such as those of Spain and Italy where cartel action rather than costs per unit output determine market price.

## DISTRIBUTION OF FUTURE DEMAND AND SUPPLY

Hans Landsberg (1964, p. 6) in his scholarly study of the sources of natural resources for the United States during the next forty years, has based his projections on the following assumptions: "Three basic assumptions built in from the start were: continuing gains in technology, improvements in political and social arrangements, and a reasonably free flow of world trade . . . and that there will be neither a large scale war nor a widespread economic depression like that of the early 1930's." There is little evidence in the history of the past half century to justify such an optimistic outlook, but there is some encouragement if one believes, with the writer, that history does *not* repeat itself. Perhaps Landsberg's assumptions will be justified by the next few decades, but only if attention is given to their alternatives, and if policy is devised to prevent the unpleasant consequences of failure to achieve conditions implicit in the assumptions.

Before considering future supplies of the non-fuel minerals, it is necessary to consider potential future demands. The demand for products in a modern world is a function of culture and population, of the relation of the growth rates of GNP and specific populations as well as their particular type of culture (Blackett, 1967). At present cultures all over the world show a marked convergent trend toward a materialistic western way of life which demands an increasing standard of living for the average person; such an increased standard is quickly reflected in the per capita income of the population.

The average income in the United States in 1965 was something over $2,500 per capita. In India the average income then was about $80 per capita, and the average income from some underdeveloped countries was even less. For several years the GNP in the United States has grown at a rate of about 4 per cent per annum while the rate of population growth has been about 1.5 per cent per annum; this results in a per capita income growth rate of approximately 2.5 per cent per year. Projected into the future this would suggest a per capita income increase from $2,500 in 1965 to $5,000 in 1993 and to $10,000 in the year 2021. Meanwhile if the effective fertility rate of 2.5 per cent per year for India were maintained, its population would double every twenty-eight years. The per capita income increase in India, if governed by the present ratio of GNP to population increase, would be far slower; if the GNP were to increase at 4 per cent per annum but the population continued to increase at 2.5 per cent, the actual increase in per capita income would be at the rate of 1.5 per cent per annum. The current per capita income of about $80 would reach $160 in the year 2012 and $320 in the year 2060. Such figures cannot be dismissed as unrealistic unless we also dismiss the basic premise of an "ever expanding economy" at 4 per cent and a population increasing at a constant rate as also unrealistic. Even if population growth slows down substantially in the underdeveloped countries and their GNP is greatly increased, it may be many generations before per capita income can approximate that currently enjoyed by the United States. In the meantime the disparity between incomes will not only be maintained but greatly increased unless a drastic and dramatic change in current trends takes place.

During the early years of industrialization, however, the rate of increase of GNP in backward countries where outside financial assistance is available may be phenomenal. The investment of excess Japanese capital in Korea together with a campaign to control family size has resulted in a steady decline in the birth rate (about 0.1 per cent per year decrease) and an increase in the GNP of approximately 8 per cent per year from 1964-67.

A few demographers (Bogue, 1965) believe that the present population explosion will soon be regarded as an anachronism and that populations will stabilize themselves shortly. This hopeful attitude is not shared by the majority of demographers and is not even considered by economists. The dramatic decline in birth rate in Japan during the fifties following a year of intensive propaganda and appropriate legislation startled the western world. The steady but slow decline in birth rate in the United States since the introduction of modern (1963) contraceptives is also worthy of note. If the industrial and political leaders of a nation become convinced that it is helpful to the national economy and the strength of the nation as a whole to slow down the rate of effective fertility, this can happen within a surprisingly short time.

The demand for goods whether in small amounts per capita for rapidly increasing population or in large amounts per capita for a static population will strain industrial capacity and mineral productivity for the next century. Per capita consumption in the industrial nations first shows exponential growth, usually for a few decades, and then flattens to a merely arithmetic increase usually at a relatively low figure. A nearly static population in underdeveloped countries would certainly result in a tremendous surge in the demand for the nonrenewable resources of the world. For this reason it would seem the current estimates of the United States and world consumption during the rest of the twentieth century as given in Landsberg's study (1964) are too conservative. All available evidence indicates that demand for minerals will increase at an exponential rate for at least fifty or seventy-five years before it begins to level off—as it must do eventually if for no other reason than that the supply is finite.

If events in South Korea and Japan foreshadow those in other Asiatic nations, the demand for minerals and other resources clearly will increase far faster than the rate of 1.5 per cent per year suggested by projection of current fertility rates and an assumed 4 per cent increase in GNP. The world's demand (i.e., production) for industrial metals has been growing at a rate of more than 6 per cent per annum for nearly a decade. It is most unlikely that all underdeveloped nations will want a completely western type culture, but enough of them have already indicated their desire to become industrialized to justify the conclusion that major demands will be made on mineral resources far into the twenty-first century. Industry requires an increasing tonnage and variety of mineral raw materials. Many that are deemed essential to modern industry have understudies that can play their part adequately, but technology has found no satisfactory substitute for some. The locations of mineral raw materials are fixed by geologic accident in the remote past and many potential sources of supply lie far from the centers of consumption.

In considering future mineral resources certain factors stand out. Because all known individual deposits will be exhausted sooner or later if present patterns of use are maintained, future production depends on the continued discovery of new deposits. Currently discovery techniques seem to be developing rapidly and many new deposits have been found by the application of geology, geophysics and geochemistry. Future sources of ore will be of two types; many known noncommercial deposits will become ore through technical innovations, future availability of cheaper transportation, or a rise in price. The second and larger group includes future sources that are now unknown but will be discovered by exploration. These deposits will be chiefly in remote or underdeveloped areas if they crop out at the surface, and will be found more and more by a combination of geology, geophysics and geochemistry. Such deposits are expensive to find and will require well financed companies or government supported groups because of the high cost of exploration and development far from supply centers. A second type of unknown ore bodies includes those that do not come to the surface—blind ore bodies. To search successfully for them is even more expensive than to find exposed ore bodies in remote areas. Much money will be spent in preliminary exploration and reconnaissance for every drill hole that zeros in on a commercial ore body. It might be said that the cost of discovery and the cost of development are proportional to the depth below the surface of the ore body.

The kind and locale of blind ore bodies can be guessed by a study of the metalogenetic provinces of the world and their geology. At present our geologic theories are inadequate to say with confidence where to drill for blind ore bodies and a substantial amount of adequately financed well planned research should be devoted to establishing sound theories of ore genesis.

Since the number of deposits is finite, the lead time necessary for successful search increases as the number of shallow deposits found grows larger. Both time and money must be allocated for an inventory of known resources and for planning programs and program revision.

The amount of metal consumed in one generation at the current rate of increase in consumption approximates all the metal that has been used previously. The entire metal production of the world prior to World War II is about that which has been consumed since the beginning of that unhappy event. Ore deposits have been sought most actively ever since the industrial era began and the major industrial powers have a similar history of mineral exploitation and exhaustion. The Middle East, Greece, Spain, England, Belgium, France, Germany, Sweden, Mexico, Peru, and the United States have all had their day as the world's foremost producer of one or several metals only to become plagued by either exhaustion or continuing decline.

As individual nations use up the cheap supplies in their own countries first, they inevitably become more and more dependent on foreign sources for most of their raw materials. At present all industrial nations except possibly the U.S.S.R. are net importers of most of the metals or the ores used by them. This dependence on foreign sources will almost certainly grow far greater for the United States during the next generation except possibly for molybdenum, magnesium, copper, and the fertilizer minerals potash, sulphur, and phosphate. Increasing dependence on foreign sources inevitably brings increased vulnerability to military, political or economic action. Some of the metals most vital to the economic well-being of industrial nations are in areas of political instability or lie in the Communist countries with which many nations are currently at odds. Most of the known reserves of tungsten and antimony lie in Communist lands, as well as a large part of the world's manganese, nickel, chromium, and platinum. The future and present sources of manganese for Europe and North America are mostly in Africa; of tin, in Southeast Asia; of aluminum ore, in various underdeveloped tropical countries. If the present dichotomy in the world economy persists, the non-

Communist nations must develop a technology that will insure a viable economy which is independent of Communist control of vital resources, or else exploit Communist scarcities in those commodities of which they have an inexplorable surplus. It would seem profitable to further the policy of "co-existence."

Discovery is required that will develop reserves at an exponential rate until a static population is achieved together with a constant per capita demand for metals. The lead time from discovery to production of a major deposit averages three to five years or more and a similar time is usually required for the exploration involved in its discovery. It is apparent then that mineral reserves should be available for a minimum of ten years future production on the basis of present demand and that for those metals which show increasing demand, the reserves must increase even faster.

The resources ready to hand are those first mined, and hence future resources will come from less industrialized countries which, however, will be making maximum efforts to become industrialized. The increased vulnerability of industrial nations in both peace and war suggests that the assumption of equitable access will be affected in the future as it has in the past by institutional restraints and the counter measures which will seem in the best interests of the countries concerned. National attitude, economic advantages, military advantages, and current leaders, will all change with time. Their interplay will require constant vigilance on the part of the industrial nations if they are to maintain a healthy economy. In order to plan for the decades ahead which may be needed to give sufficient lead time for economic and technical adjustments, national and international watchdog groups of experts will be required to warn of impending critical resource situations and to recommend the most desirable remedies. For such groups industrial countries should begin at once to develop continuing national inventories of reserves both at home and abroad. Unfortunately the results of studies guided primarily

by mineral economists have led to a "cornucopian" concept of mineral resources that allows policy makers to ignore potential mineral shortages. We are rapidly approaching a time when indifferences can be disastrous.

The main escape hatch for scarcity is technical advance along a broad front, as noted by Landsberg (p. 240), and this will depend on extensive and effective programs of research and development in science, engineering, economics, and management. The more immediate the promise of practical results the greater the willingness of private industry to finance the necessary research. Much of the required research, however, would be of the more exploratory kind, the results of which cannot be guaranteed, but from which eventually answers of crucial importance will come. Planning and prosecution of such research should be a continuing function of the government of major industrial nations. There is a desperate need for integrated national and international resources policies that harmonize or adjudicate the needs of the many special segments of an economy that utilizes natural resources. We especially need research on blind bodies and the factors that are critical to their implacement, research on the genesis of ore bodies. This should lead to new discovery techniques which must be tested by the drill. Exploration should emphasize metals in short supply or which have diminishing reserves. The over-all policy concerning mineral resources should be in the hands of a continuing group of legislative officers working in close cooperation with a full time watchdog group of experts from business, government and the educational field. With such a group functioning effectively, stresses caused by utilization of exhaustible foreign and domestic ore sources should be minimized; without it recurrent or persistent shortages will occur in the supply of some metals. Periods of needlessly high prices for some mineral products will alternate with prices so low that many potential sources of ore will be lost, and certain it is that many disastrous political errors will be made through lack of appreciation of the future importance of trade between areas of industry and potential mineral raw materials.

At present we are living in an epoch of localized affluence such as has recurred throughout historical time when new treasures of metal or mineral were discovered. In the past mineral deposits have led to invasion, conquest, and wealth, for a comparative few. Now, more happily, the utilization of mineral resources of not only the industrial countries but also of some of the underdeveloped countries has led to affluence for many people rather than a select few, but it is well to realize that mineral deposits are still the "quick assets" of the country that possesses them and that ultimately these resources will be exhausted or will decrease their contribution to a fraction of their flush protection. To insure a more equitable distribution of end results of the exploitation of mineral wealth, is one of the foremost but rarely stated objectives of successful, modern economic systems. During the next century this will not be achieved merely by recycling metal as scrap, nor by processing dozens of cubic kilometers of common rock to supply the metal needs of each major industrial nation. When the time comes for living in a society dependent on scrap for "high grade" and on common rocks for "commercial ore," the "affluent society" will be much overworked to maintain a standard of living equal to that of a century ago. The foreseeable exhaustion of ores of some metals and the continually decreasing grade of most ore deposits now used show that it is no small prudence to provide ample lead time for technology to work out such answers as it can and to allow the economy time to make the necessary adjustments to changing mineral supplies.

## BIBLIOGRAPHY

Barnett, H. J. and Morris, Chandler, 1963. Scarcity and Growth. Johns Hopkins Press, Baltimore, Maryland.
Barnett, H. J., 1967. The Myth of Our Vanishing Resources. Transactions Social Science and Modern Society, June, p. 7–10.
Blackett, P. M. S., 1967. The Ever Widening Gap. Science Feb. Vol. 155, No. 3765, p. 959–964.
Bogue, D. J., 1965. The prospects for world population control. Community and Family Study Center, University of Chicago.
Brown, Harrison; Bonner, James; and Weir, John; 1957. The next hundred years. Viking Press, New York, 193 p.
Bureau of Mines Staff, 1965. Minerals Year Book, Vol. 1, Metals and Minerals. U.S. Government Printing Office, Washington.
———, 1965. Mercury potential of the United States. U.S. Bureau of Mines, I. C. 8252, U.S. Government Printing Office, 376 p.
———, 1956. Mineral Facts and Problems. U.S. Government Printing Office, Washington, D.C., 1042 p.
Landsberg, H. M., 1964. Natural Resources for U.S. Growth. The Johns Hopkins Press, Baltimore, Maryland, 260 p.
Lasky, S. G., 1948. Mineral Resources Appraisal by the U.S. Geological Survey. Colorado School of Mines Quarterly, Golden, Colorado, p. 1–27.
Lasky, S. G., 1950. How Tonnage Grade Relations Help Predict Ore Reserves. Engineering and Mining Journal, Vol. 151, No. 4, p. 81–86.
Lasky, S. G., 1951. Mineral Industry Futures. Engineering and Mining Journal, Vol. 152, No. 8, p. 60–63.
Lasky, S. G., 1955. Mineral Industry Futures Can Be Predicted II. Engineering and Mining Journal, Vol. 155, No. 9.
McMahon, A. D., 1965. Copper, a Material Survey. U.S. Bureau of Mines Information Cir. 8225, U.S. Government Printing Office.
Morris, H. T., and Lovering, T. S., 1952. Supergene and hydrothermal dispersion of heavy metals in wall rocks near ore bodies, Tintic district, Utah: Econ. Geol., v. 47, p. 685–716.
Staffs, Bureau of Mines and U.S. Geological Survey, 1948. Mineral Resources of the United States. Public Affairs Press, Washington, D.C. 212 p.

# *From* Resources and Man:
# A Study and Recommendations

### COMMITTEE ON RESOURCES AND MAN
### (NATIONAL ACADEMY OF SCIENCES–NATIONAL
### RESEARCH COUNCIL)

A prime conclusion of ecology is that species whose populations exceed or approach too closely the carrying capacity of resources in the space occupied undergo reduction. Such reductions are often severe and may lead to extinction because of disease, pestilence, predation, or aggressive competitors. Although it is true that man has repeatedly succeeded in increasing both the space he occupies and its carrying capacity, and that he will continue to do so, it is also clear that both the occupiable space and its carrying capacity have finite limits which he can approach only at great peril.

It is essential, therefore, that we carefully assess and continually reassess these limits, and that we take steps to assure that future generations, as well as people now living, will have the resources necessary for a satisfying life. These resources, moreover, must be so distributed as to exclude catastrophe as a factor in limiting population density. Few species of animals ever really multiply to the absolute limit of their food supply under natural conditions; other controlling factors intervene, often of the sort that humans would call psychic or psychosomatic. Man also must

adapt to his ecosystem—to his physical environment and its biologic components. We cannot long operate as a force apart from it, for we are not. Above all, we must be wary of man's tendency to reduce the variety of components in his ecosystem, for this increases susceptibility to adverse change.

Many people outside the Atlantic community of nations are now threatened with poverty and famine as a result of population increases that locally exceed the carrying capacity of the land. To a greater or lesser degree the same potential danger threatens all people, as Malthus first clearly recognized in 1798. Wishful thinking does not banish the problem. Harrison Brown asked in 1954[1] "Is betterment of the situation really within the realm of possibility? And if betterment is possible, at what level can the greatly increased numbers be supported? Lastly are the earth's resources sufficient to meet the enhanced demand?" The same questions haunt us with increasing intensity—an intensity as yet almost unrelieved by significant decreases in rates of population growth. By average American standards, two thirds of the world's people are still ill-fed, ill-housed, and ill-clothed, including many in North America. What can we in North America do to aid our own underprivileged, to meet the population increases that will yet precede real popula-

From the Introduction to *Resources and Man: A Study and Recommendations* by the Committee on Resources and Man of the Division of Earth Sciences, National Academy of Sciences–National Research Council, with the cooperation of the Division of Biology and Agriculture. W. H. Freeman and Company. Copyright © 1969.

[1] *The Challenge of Man's Future*, Viking Press, New York, p. 61.

tion control, and to help the rest of the world?

The answer is that much can be done, given sufficient effort in resource management. But other dangers arise. The quality of life, which we equate with flexibility of choices and freedom of action, is threatened by the demands of an expanding economy and population. This happens in three principal ways: (1) through the restrictive and harmful effects of pollution; (2) through the increasing frequency and complexity of unconstructive but unavoidable human contacts; and (3) through the necessary increase of regulatory measures—all in consequence of increasing use of and competition for resources, space, recreation, transportation, housing, and even educational facilities.

Thus, in addition to energy, mineral, and food resources, the quantity and quality of the human resource itself are critical components of the equation. [For] man is not only a part of his ecosystem, he is the most powerful influence in it. He is simultaneously its potentially most precious resource and its most serious threat. The gains from technological development must always be balanced in as much detail as possible against its costs. Man's own best interests plead for a more generous attitude toward the rest of nature and for less materialistic measures of well-being and success—especially in the developed countries. Such changes in attitude would make it easier to bring about dynamically balanced relations between the need for materials and the quantity available on the one hand and the quality of life and quantity of consumers on the other.

The growing quantity of people is a key factor whose future dimensions we should like to be able to estimate. Only two things seem certain: there are going to be more people are still ill-fed, ill-housed, and ill-denser aggregates. The number of people to be accommodated by the end of the century, moreover, adds a new dimension to current crises. To accommodate these populations, the developed world will require, by the year 2000, additional urban facilities equivalent to all of those already in existence, and corre-

spondingly more for the underdeveloped world. This calls for an entirely different view of our cities and their resource requirements than if we think only of ameliorating specific crises step by step as they arise. Complete urban renovation, the creation of new and better living clusters throughout the country, and better and more diversified use of suburban and rural space are a big order; but it is an order that is practicable, necessary, and urgent. There is no simple "best solution." A variety of solutions must be tried, and for all of them the resource component (including clean air and water) will be central.

Somehow we must manage by the year 2000 to support a population increase in the United States from the present 200 million people to between 300 million and 340 million, and an increase in world population from the now more than 3.5 billion people to between 6 billion and 7 billion—an increasing proportion of them in cities. Failure to support that population increase would have unacceptable consequences. Population control, essential in the long run, cannot come soon enough to eliminate the challenge. To stabilize populations requires that the birth rate not exceed 14 live births per year per thousand people at the 70-year life expectancy sought as a goal for all. Only Hungary, Japan, and Bulgaria currently have such a low birth rate. This shows that a stabilized population can be achieved, but as Kingsley Davis has emphasized,[2] the inadequate measures that now pass for population control at best eliminate only unwanted births. Birth rates over most of the world cannot be brought to control levels by presently accepted measures. Steps must be taken to realize a zero rate of population increase as the ultimate goal. In the meanwhile, the increasing number of people to be accommodated will severely tax the capacity of the human ecosystem.

Nutrition is the first essential; yet problems of distribution, of local failure to exploit potentialities, and with social customs that dictate what food is acceptable are more im-

[2] *Science*, 1957, vol. 158, p. 730.

mediately urgent than the problem of quantity of food available or producible on a global scale. If present world food production could be evenly rationed, there would be enough to satisfy both energy (calories) and protein requirements for everyone—although with drastic reductions for the now affluent. All-out effort, including the provision of ample fertilizer, and genetic, ecological, and chemical research, could probably quadruple production from the lands and double production from the waters by the end of the century. If such increased production were evenly distributed, it could keep up with population growth expected during the same time and even permit some improvement of diet. But will such all-out effort be started and sustained?

The probable ultimate increase in production of food from the sea on a sustained basis is not likely to be much more than about two and one-half times the present annual production of 60 million metric tons of fish, containing 12 million tons of usable protein. An increase to as much as four times the present production is unlikely. Perhaps the most important thing to bear in mind about aquatic food products, however, is that although they are an excellent source of protein they are a poor source of calories. Only the land can supply calories in adequate quantity for the needs anticipated, an eventual increase of possibly eight times the present land production being foreseen. To attain this, however, will call for maximum increases in productivity of existing lands, cultivation of all potentially arable lands, new crops, the use of more vegetable and less animal protein, continued risky use of ever-new but hopefully degradable biocides, chemical or microbiological synthesis of foods, and other innovations.

Foreseeable increases in food supplies over the long term, therefore, are not likely to exceed about nine times the amount now available. That approaches a limit that seems to place the earth's ultimate carrying capacity at about 30 billion people, *at a level of chronic near-starvation for the great majority* (and

with massive immigration to the now less densely populated lands)! A world population of 30 billion is only slightly more than three doublings from the present one, which is now increasing at a doubling time of about 35 years. At this rate, there could be 30 billion people by about 2075 in the absence of controls beyond those now in effect. Hopeful allowance for such controls suggests that populations *may* level off not far above 10 billion people by about 2050—and that is close to (if not above) the maximum that an *intensively managed* world might hope to support with some degree of comfort and individual choice, as we estimate such immeasurables. If, in fulfillment of their rising expectations, all people are to be more than merely adequately nourished, effort must be made to stabilize populations at a world total much lower than 10 billion. Indeed it is our judgment that a human population less than the present one would offer the best hope for comfortable living for our descendants, long duration for the species, and the preservation of environmental quality.

Man must also look with equal urgency to his nonrenewable resources—to mineral fuels, to metals, to chemicals, and to construction materials. These are the heritage of all mankind. Their overconsumption or waste for the temporary benefit of the few who currently possess the capability to exploit them cannot be tolerated.

The nonfuel mineral resources are very unequally distributed, both as to location and as to grade. No nation is self-sufficient in all of them, even in the short term. The ultimate resources of major industrial metals such as iron and aluminum, to be sure, are very large, for their availability depends mainly on improvements in recovery methods. But true shortages exist or threaten for many substances that are considered essential for current industrial society: mercury, tin, tungsten, and helium for example. Known and now-prospective reserves of these substances will be nearly exhausted by the end of this century or early in the next, and new sources or substitutes to satisfy even these relatively near-term needs will have to be found. It is not true, although it is widely believed, that tonnages of metalliferous rock generally increase geometrically with arithmetic decrease in grade; this is an invalid generalization that encourages a dangerous complacency. Neither is abundant cheap energy a panacea for waning resources. Innovation of many kinds will be needed—in methods of finding ore, in mining, in extraction of metals, in substitution, in transportation, and in conservation and waste disposal. For all reusable materials in short supply, appropriate laws or codes restructuring economic incentives could facilitate conservative recovery, more efficient use, and reuse, thereby appreciably extending now foreseeable commodity lifetimes.

It is not certain whether, in the next century or two, further industrial development based on mineral resources will be foreclosed by limitations of supply. The biggest unknowns are population and rates of consumption. It is self-evident, however, that the exponential increases in demand that have long prevailed cannot be satisfied indefinitely. If population and demand level off at some reasonable plateau, and if resources are used wisely, industrial society can endure for centuries or perhaps millenia. But technological and economic brilliance alone cannot create the essential raw materials whose enhancement in value through beneficiation, fabrication, and exchange constitutes the basic material fabric of such a society.

The mineral and chemical resources of the sea will increasingly supplement those from the land—but only for a few of the many commodities we need. Information on which to base a durable assessment of such resources is not now available, but it can be expected to improve as research and exploration increase. Although ocean waters cover two-thirds of the earth, what little is known about the composition and probable history of the three quarters of the sea bottom that lies beyond the continental rises does not support the popular belief that this region harbors great mineral wealth. Beneath a thin veneer of young sediments, the floor of the

ocean basins appears to consist of young basaltic rocks, only sparsely metalliferous and in constant slow motion toward and beneath the continents. Much more promising are the potentialities of the submerged parts of the continents—of oil from the sediments of the continental shelves, slopes, and rises and of mineral placers near the coast. Seawater is also an important source of some useful elements and salts, but only for a few of those needed.

On the one hand, therefore, mineral and mineral-fuel production from the sea are certainly worth going after and will increasingly help to meet needs and shortages in certain commodities. On the other hand, there is little basis for assuming that many marine mineral and chemical resources are of large usable volume or feasible recoverability or that for many essential substances there are any marine resources at all. The roughly $4 billion 1964 world production of offshore mineral resources shows clearly that profits are to be had from the sea. Whether offshore minerals will provide an adequate supplement to the mineral resources of the lands in the needed variety of products is quite another matter.

Finally, energy resources must be considered. Known or potential energy resources include power from flowing waters, tidal power, geothermal power, solar energy, and mineral fuels. Of these, conventional water power, if fully developed, would be about equal to that currently generated from fossil fuels. Important as they could be, however, especially in presently underdeveloped parts of the southern hemisphere, conventional sources of water power are erratically distributed, and reservoirs silt up. Tidal power and geothermal power are only locally available and neither represents a potential energy supply of more than about 2 per cent of that available from water power. Solar energy, although daily renewable and enormous in amount, offers little promise as a major source of industrial power because of the difficulty of achieving the essential concentration and continuity of energy and because of the large quantities of metals and other materials that would be required for solar energy plants of significant capacity.

Sources of power for the future are to be sought among the mineral fuels, and above all in nuclear energy. It will take only another 50 years or so to use up the great bulk of the world's initial supply of recoverable petroleum liquids and natural gas! Recoverable liquid fuels from tar sands and oil shales, although their estimates are very uncertain, might supplement conventional petroleum fuels sufficiently to extend the total lifetime of the petroleum family of fuels as an important source of industrial energy to as much as a century from now. The remaining effective lifetime for coal, if used as the principal source of energy at expected increased demands, would be no more than two or three centuries (although the normal tapering-off in use of a diminishing resource will assure its continued production for perhaps another 500 years from the present). Moreover, we cannot simultaneously use the fossil fuels for fuels, petrochemicals, synthetic polymers, and bacterial conversion to food without going through them even more rapidly. A major side benefit from converting to nuclear energy as our main energy source, therefore, could be the adoption of measures to conserve the fossil fuels for other useful purposes and for *essential* liquid fuels.

Nuclear power from naturally fissionable uranium-235 and from fissionable isotopes obtained by neutron irradiation of uranium-238 and thorium-232 is potentially orders of magnitude larger than that obtainable from all the fossil fuels combined. The supply of uranium-235 from high-grade ores, however, is severely limited, and the production of nuclear power at a cost competitive with fossil fuels or water power, using the present light-water converter reactors and uranium-235 as the principal energy source can be sustained for only a few decades.

If the potential of nuclear power based on the fission reaction is to be realized, therefore, this can be accomplished only by an early replacement of the present light-water reactors (which can use only about 1 per cent of natural uranium) by fully breeding reactors capable of consuming the entire amount of natural uranium or thorium supplied to them.

Controlled fusion has not yet been achieved and may never be. Should it be, however, the energy obtainable from the deuterium contained in 30 cubic kilometers of seawater would be about equal to that of the earth's initial supply of fossil fuels!

On a long-term basis, an achievement no less essential than a practical nuclear-energy economy itself must be the development of an adequate system of safe disposal of nuclear-fission wastes. Much progress has been made within the last decade by the U.S. Atomic Energy Commission in the processing and safe underground disposal of low-volume, high-level wastes. Less satisfactory progress has been made in the handling of the voluminous low-level wastes and solid trash. In fact, for primarily economic reasons, practices are still prevalent at most Atomic Energy Commission installations with respect to these latter categories of waste that on the present scale of operations are barely tolerable, but which would become intolerable with much increase in the use of nuclear power.

[In summary, the problem may be posed in these terms]: since resources are finite, then, as population increases, the ratio of resources to man must eventually fall to an unacceptable level. This is the crux of the Malthusian dilemma, often evaded but never invalidated. [We have considered] the possibility of a final evasion of this dilemma by population control and the possibility of escape by increasing resources of food, minerals, and energy. The inescapable central conclusion is that both population control and better resource management are mandatory and should be effected with as little delay as possible.

We must add an elaboration, however. Studies of animal populations suggest that environmental factors other than simple limitation of material resources may act in unexpected ways to limit populations before theoretical maxima are reached. To consider whether the earth might support three more doublings of the human population is probably to consider a purely hypothetical situation. It seems more likely that further crowding, the necessary social and governmental restrictions that accompany dense settlement, and certain kinds of boredom resulting from isolation from nature in an immense, uniform, secular society may prove so depressing to the human spirit or so destructive of coherent social organization that no such population size will ever be reached.

Current urban problems are perhaps premonitory of what can come in the absence of more effective attention to the broader problems of resources and man. In attempting to deal with such problems we would do well to consider the basic causes as well as the symptoms. To delay progress toward full self-regulation of population size is to play "Russian roulette" with the future of man.

# PART TWO

# Environmental Roulette

*Mit der Dummheit kämpfen Götter selbst vergebens.*[*]

A member of the Army Corps of Engineers is reputed to have said "if I have to choose between the environment and people, I'll choose people every time." His attitude, shared by a vast number of politicians, businessmen, technologists and laymen, is a monument to the failure of biological education. Evidently, many people never had the opportunity to learn that man, like every other organism, is totally dependent on his environment for survival. His food, his water, his waste disposal, and ultimately his oxygen are provided or renewed by environmental systems for which there is no known substitute.

In the first paper of this section, "Overpopulation and the Potential for Ecocide," we provide an overview of man's assaults on the life support system of Spaceship Earth. The papers which follow provide more detail, occasionally on a more technical level, in specific areas. For example, Reid Bryson in "All Other Factors Being Constant . . ." considers the inadvertent modification of climate by man. In discussing the many competing factors which determine the climate, he makes clear the dilemma of the contemporary meteorologist: we know enough to appreciate the possibilities for man-induced changes, but too little to say for certain which ones will be important in the short term. To speculate about the *consequences* of even such changes as may already be occurring is beyond the intent of Dr. Bryson's paper. We note here, however, that the probable immediate consequence of a major climatic perturbation of *any* sort is a precipitous decline in the productivity of world agriculture.

A factor not yet large enough to be considered in Bryson's analysis is the introduction into the global energy balance of heat released by the activities of man. The possibility that this phenomenon will grow to significant proportions in the next century is examined in Holdren's article, "Global Thermal Pollution." Lest the bit of mathematics there obscure the conclusions, we summarize them here: Heat is the ultimate pollutant—man's energy use will probably be limited not by how much power he can produce but rather by

[*] "Against stupidity even the gods do battle in vain." Schiller, *Jungfrau von Orleans.*

the impact of the associated heat on climate. Simple calculations show that present growth rates in energy consumption would carry us to such a limit in perhaps one hundred years; ill-understood complexities in the meteorological system may mean the actual period of grace will be much less.

Most of the papers in this section deal primarily with man's *alteration* of the environment. Earth scientist Richard Jahns adds a dimension to these concerns by documenting our ingenuous inattention to its geological characteristics—earthquake faults and flood plains, for example. His discussion of how human intervention in the form of mining activities, irrigation, and construction may change the shape of the earth to the further detriment of *Homo sapiens* is also most instructive.

The now well-publicized threat from broadcast poisons is discussed by Stanford biologists Donald Kennedy and John Hessel in "The Biology of Pesticides." The irresponsibility of both the government (especially the United States Department of Agriculture) and the pesticide industry in promoting exceedingly dangerous and ineffective methods of "controlling" agricultural pests may well be the blackest chapter in the history of the destruction of our planet for profit. In reading "The Biology of Pesticides" you should recall the fears expressed in the introductory essay about the consequences of spreading the philosophy of American "agri-business" to the underdeveloped countries. Should we make that blunder, the resultant tragedy may dwarf all others in human experience.

"Low-dose Radiation and Cancer" by Drs. John W. Gofman and Arthur R. Tamplin of the Lawrence Radiation Laboratory is destined to become a landmark in the field of science and public policy. It initiated a storm of controversy when first presented at a technical meeting in November of 1969, and the uproar shows no signs of diminishing today. At issue are not only the quantitative aspects of interpreting available data on biological effects of low doses of radiation; the adequacy of the present system of balancing costs and benefits in the implementation of new technology is itself being called into question. It is too soon to be certain whether Gofman and Tamplin's estimate for the number of deaths to be expected from nationwide exposure to current guidelines is substantially correct. No completely definitive data exists, animal experiments are not entirely relevant, and a large-scale experiment involving the requisite numbers of humans over several decades is out of the question—except insofar as the presumption that present standards represent a "safe" exposure encourages precisely such an experiment, with all of us unwitting guinea pigs. Unfortunately, while Gofman and Tamplin continue to publish additional data in support of their position, the discussion from their critics has proven largely unenlightening. Most of them have chosen to express their indignation over the tone and style of the Gofman/Tamplin position, rather than to offer any substantial refutation of it.

More important, however, are three basic issues which are independent of the radiological data. Indeed, they are fundamental to the wise management of *any* large technology. First, in matters of public health, the burden of proof must lie with those who argue that the technology is safe; more specifically, one must accept for working purposes the most conservative interpretation consistent with whatever data are available. Second, cost-benefit analyses must not be carried out by technical bodies alone. In most cases it is ostensibly the public which is to receive the benefits, and it is inevitably the public which pays the costs. The proper forum for striking a balance is therefore open consideration by responsive elected representatives; the role of scientists and technologists should be to provide such bodies with the most accurate possible *information* concerning risk and costs, and, separately, concerning potential benefits. Vague statements from "experts" that the benefits (unquantified) exceed the costs (unspecified) are operationally useless and socially irresponsible. Third, the promotional and regulatory functions of all government agencies must be separated. The two roles are patently inconsistent, and it is unrealistic to expect vigorous, uncompromising enforcement of standards from the same individuals charged with promoting the technology in question. Thus, for example, one function or the other should be removed from the responsibilities of the Atomic Energy Commission at once. Gofman and Tamplin have performed a great service in calling public attention to these general and unexceptionable propositions. It will be a tragedy if scientists of any persuasion permit the highly charged debate over the radiation standards themselves to obscure the underlying issues.

Taken together, the papers in this section—a tiny sampling from the burgeoning literature on man's growing impact on the environment—suggest the following analogy for our behavior: We are playing a vast game of "Russian roulette", in which the environment can be described as a pistol with uncounted thousands of chambers. No one knows as yet how many of these may be "loaded", but he who persists in pulling the trigger repeatedly is assured of finding out. There are, of course, shortcomings in the environmental roulette analogy. Most importantly, it overlooks a *systematic* (as opposed to hit-or-miss) component in man's impact on the ecosystem: the loss of complexity which, as we argue in the opening selection, must ultimately lead to instability and collapse. In the final paper, ecologist George Woodwell amplifies this argument by using the effects of radiation on plant communities as a case study in the simplification of ecosystems. His clear discussion of the importance of structure and diversity in such systems is most educational. His concluding paragraphs on the direction of present trends indicate that the words "environmental roulette" are really too hopeful— continuation of our present behavior leaves nothing to chance.

# Overpopulation
# and the Potential for Ecocide

PAUL R. EHRLICH AND JOHN P. HOLDREN

## INTRODUCTION

**The Ascendancy of Man.** The most startling terrestrial event in the two billion year history of life on the Earth has been the rise of the species *Homo sapiens* to its present position of global preeminence. A mere ten thousand years ago mankind was but one of many species of large mammals. He numbered perhaps five million individuals, at that time a far smaller population than that of such species as the bison. But even then, man's skill at hunting and his mastery of fire foreshadowed the colossal threat to the planetary ecology he was to become. There is substantial evidence that Pleistocene man in America caused the extinction of 70 per cent of the land mammals of large size, such as mammoths, horses, and camels. In Africa, he wiped out perhaps 30 per cent of the megafauna. Finally, many ecologists attribute the existence of the world's great grasslands to primitive man's use and misuse of fire.

At about 8000 B.C., on the edge of the Fertile Crescent in western Asia, the first groups of men gave up the nomadic life and started to practice agriculture. This change, which marked the inception of a revolution which is still in progress today, was perhaps the most important single happening in the history of the earth. It started a trend toward increased security from hunger for mankind, and initiated an irregular but persistent decline in the death rate in the human population. As the beginning of the systematic modification of the planet for the support of human beings, it provided the springboard for mankind's dramatic leap to dominance.

The agricultural revolution has been going on now for some 10,000 years; until a few hundred years ago it was the major cause of the decline in the death rate. Since population growth is a function of the difference between the birth rate and the death rate, and since the birth rate over these many centuries has remained relatively high, the spectacular rise of the human population during this period can be attributed directly to the agricultural revolution. It, virtually alone, caused the 100 fold increase from some 5 million people in 8000 B.C. to 500 million in 1650 A.D. And thus it fueled the first long pull in man's unconscious quest to determine by experiment the ultimate carrying capacity of this planet.

Since 1650, the agricultural revolution has been joined in the work of shaping civilization by two further revolutions, industrial and biomedical. And while the fruits of these two newcomers have in large measure been unequally enjoyed, their effects in further reducing the death rate have been almost universal. Hence, while quality of life has gone up dramatically in some places, the quantity of life has gone up dramatically everywhere. At this writing the human population, at over 3.5 billion, is more than 700 times its size at the start of the agricultural revolution; an increment equal to that "initial" 5 million human beings is now added every twenty-six days.

**The Price of Growth.** The achievement of these remarkable figures through the interacting effects of the agricultural, industrial, and

Overpopulation and the Potential for Ecocide. Published by the Center for the Study of Democratic Institutions, Santa Barbara, 1970 (in press). Copyright © P. R. Ehrlich and J. P. Holdren. Reprinted by permission of the authors.

biomedical revolutions has entailed not only the profound modification of man's environment, but also its piecemeal disintegration. This is not surprising in view of man's historical and persistent reluctance to consider goals and consequences which transcend the immediate or the local. We have occupied ourselves with constructing the ingredients of the revolutions themselves because these ingredients met immediately perceived needs. But we have failed to develop the social machinery to direct and control our expanding manipulative and technological abilities, because the consequences of not doing so have not been obvious. Indeed, it is our ever growing expertise at building our technology and modifying ourselves and our planet, all in the absence of carefully considered goals, that is at the heart of what is today being called the Biological Revolution.

The consequences of our short sightedness are now being more widely felt, for two reasons. First, improved communications have heightened our awareness of human misery which has always existed, but was once easier to ignore. Second, the sheer weight of our numbers and the unprecedented power of our technology has so overtaxed the buffering capacity of the globe that only the most unperceptive can dispute the rapid deterioration of the environment on every side. Unfortunately, the recognition of the symptoms is even today only rarely accompanied by a grasp of the cause. Thus we are still promised relief by ardent advocates of the same patchwork combination of heedless growth and technological band-aids which has put us where we are today.

It is worth reviewing briefly just where that is. Of the 3.5 billion people packed onto the planet, over half a billion are undernourished (they receive too few calories) and over a billion are malnourished (their diets are deficient in some essential constituent, usually protein). The consequences are especially severe among children—those who escape death by starvation often suffer permanent mental retardation from the lack of high quality protein. And while it would take an overnight increase of perhaps thirty per cent in world food production to feed today's population decently, that population is growing at a rate which will double its size in only thirty-five years. The contention of certain well-fed journalists that the "Green Revolution" will keep food production ahead of population growth over the next few decades is patent nonsense—food production has hardly begun to catch up. Hunger is of course only one aspect of the incredibly low standard of living in the "less developed" countries of the world. At last count, the relatively well-off one third of the world's population accounted for 87½ per cent of the global equivalent of gross national product. The remaining 2.4 billion people had 12½ per cent of the goods and services to divide among them. Despite intensive international efforts to reduce this politically explosive gap between the "haves" and the "have-nots," the disparity is at this moment still increasing.

**The Pursuit of Disaster.**   It is widely held that the "solution" for these difficulties is to develop the rest of the world after the standard of today's industrial nations. Most observers acknowledge, of course, that so complex a process will be too slow to avert entirely the convulsions of famine and social disintegration whose precursors are already being felt. But all too few have questioned the validity of the development concept itself. We are suggesting here that the overdeveloped West, with all the short-sighted exploitation of the environment and pillage of resources which have attended its "progress," makes a miserable model for anyone to follow. Indeed, in view of the grave threats which the abuse of technology has already posed to the environmental systems on which all life depends, one can argue that to batter the rest of the world into "prosperity" with the same technological bludgeons would be ecological suicide.

This is not to belittle the need for improving the quality of life in most of the world, or even the role that technology must play in the attempt. But it must be made clear that even *one* three hundred horsepower automobile per family represents a level of consumption inconsistent with the long term sustenance of even the present population of this planet;

that the elevation of the poor to a nominal degree of affluence must be accompanied by the descent of the rest of us from the excessive affluence we enjoy today; that "quality of life" means breathable air, drinkable water, and the hope of a future for one's children, none of which are measured by GNP; and, finally, that all the technology brought to bear on the considerable problems of mankind must be tempered with an unprecedented concern for the long-term livability of this fragile and finite "Spaceship Earth."

For the lack of such a perspective we are today in a precarious position indeed. The remainder of this article elaborates the threats to our health, sanity, and survival which overpopulation and our attempts to support it have so sorely aggravated. The subject matter is categorized according to the "level of insult" to man and his environment; direct or subtle, continuous or discrete, catastrophic or merely corrosive. Some of the threats, such as persistent pesticides, appear in more than one category. Others are only vaguely understood, and may ultimately prove to be less (or more) serious than we imply. Nor do we claim that this bleak survey is exhaustive—new threats materialize regularly—but those we cite are reason enough to question the ethic of unending growth which spawns or nurtures all of them.

## CONTINUOUS ASSAULTS ON MAN AND HIS PERCEIVED ENVIRONMENT

**Air Pollution.** Virtually every major metropolis in the world has an air pollution problem, and the rate of expansion of urban complexes everywhere is rapidly making the brown pall and smarting eyes ubiquitous symbols of "progress." Unfortunately, there is more to air pollution than darkened skies and minor discomfort. Human death rates, particularly among the very young, very old, and those with respiratory ailments, are correlated with heavy smog concentrations. The few dramatic disasters associated with smog to date (such as the estimated 4000 fatalities in London in the 1952 episode) are nevertheless overshadowed by the potential long-term health hazard to vastly greater numbers of people.

The amounts of material involved are staggering and the physiological consequences extensive. In the United States alone, automobiles spew 66 million tons of carbon monoxide, 12 million tons of hydrocarbons, 7 million tons of sulfur and nitrogen oxides, and 1 million tons of miscellaneous particulate matter into the atmosphere every year. Steel and paper mills, refineries, chemical plants, power stations, heating, and trash burning add more of the same, to a grand total of 140 million tons of filth and assorted poisons annually. Symptoms of acute carbon monoxide poisoning—headache, nausea, decrease of coordination—are not uncommon in freeway traffic jams, and cases of chronic carbon monoxide poisoning have been reported. Sulfur dioxide reacts with airborne droplets to form sulfuric acid and is suspected in increasing rates of acute and chronic asthma, bronchitis, and emphysema. Nitrogen oxides react to form photomechanical smog, and, in higher concentrations, cause constriction of the bronchi and tissue damage in the lungs. Various hydrocarbons and some kinds of particulate matter are known or suspected carcinogens; a number of studies have demonstrated a strong correlation between incidence of lung cancer and geographical distribution of air pollutants.

Animals other than humans are of course also adversely affected by air pollution, as are plants. High levels of pollution can be expected to have immediate effects on plant and animal productivity and even survival. Lower levels do systematic damage which may be longer in showing up, but is eventually devastating. A current example is the demise of some 100,000 acres of pines in the mountains overlooking Los Angeles, due to the unfortunate location of the trees at the elevation of that city's infamous inversion layer.

Our limited knowledge of the details of air pollution permits little hope for early relief. The meteorology of air pollutants is in its infancy, and only a few of the chemical reactions which these substances undergo in the atmosphere are well understood. It has been said that 70 per cent of the particulate contaminants in urban air have not even been *identified*. The biological effects of these unknown substances are open to speculation. As their concentrations increase, we will certainly find out. It is also worth noting that first-generation automotive smog-control devices, while they reduce carbon monoxide and hydrocarbon emissions, actually *increase* those of the nitrogen oxides. Panaceas are not easily found. Electric cars, for example, would simply shift part of the pollution burden to the locations where power is generated. Some pollutants, such as asbestos particles from brake linings and miscellaneous polymers from tires grinding against pavement, are independent of the source of motive power.

**Water Pollution.** Civilized man is by now well aware of the more obvious symptoms of water pollution: scum-covered rivers, stinking bays, and shorelines littered with bloated fish. The cause of much of it is equally clear: the indiscriminate dumping of raw sewage and industrial sludge into the nearest body of water has exceeded the absorptive capacity of the environment. Because the symptoms of this overflow are so compelling, it seems likely that we will finally attempt to do something about it. But continued population growth makes it improbable that we will find the funds to do more than skim off the chunks.

Unfortunately, the most serious water pollution threats are those which cannot be seen, smelled, or picked up by the handful. The organic content in many domestic water supplies which have been treated to some degree is apparently still high enough to protect viruses from the effects of chlorine. Hence tap water is a suspected transmission route for the alarming rise of infectious hepatitis in the United States today. Moreover, the vast array of chemicals which industry spews into the environment in many cases defies filtration. These chemicals now pervade not only rivers, lakes, and even oceans but also vast reservoirs of ground water. As with air pollutants, their possible toxic effects have in most cases not even been adequately catalogued. Many, of course, are *known* to be fatal to fish, the main-

stay of high-quality protein supplies in much of the world.

Several particularly insidious forms of water pollution result from the extensive use of fertilizers in modern agriculture. These nutrients are carried by irrigation and rainfall runoff into rivers and lakes, which they effectively overfertilize. The result is the rapid growth of certain kinds of algae, which periodically reach incredible abundance in "blooms," then die. The decay of the great masses of algae depletes the supply of oxygen dissolved in the water, leading to massive fish kills. A second and only recently discovered consequence of heavy fertilization is the accumulation of nitrates in local supplies of ground water. Unfortunately, the digestive tracts of farm animals and human infants often contain bacteria which convert the harmless nitrates to highly toxic nitrites. The result is a blood disease, methemoglobinemia, characterized by labored breathing and possible suffocation. Cases have been reported in California and in the Midwest. In view of such problems, the projected ten-fold increase of inorganic fertilizer consumption in the U.S. in the next thirty years poses a frightening threat.

**Pesticides.** The harmful effects of persistent pesticides, principally the chlorinated hydrocarbons such as DDT, have only recently attracted public attention. Most of the consequences of their widespread use are quite subtle and slow to be detected; accordingly, these aspects will be discussed in the next section. Two effects which could now be called obvious, however, are the frequent failure of pesticides to achieve one of their stated objectives, namely increased productivity, and the related problem of eradication of useful, non-target species. The difficulty is that the population most resistant to the pesticide is often that of the target pest and the most susceptible populations are those of the pest's natural enemies. One reason for this is that the population of the pest is larger than those of the creatures which feed upon it, and the probability of a resistant strain developing increases with population size. As a result, broadcast use of non-selective pesticides tends to kill more useful organisms than pests (the farmer is then encouraged to apply larger doses to cope with the population explosion of, say, weevils, whose natural enemies have been eradicated). Available evidence indicates that although use of persistent pesticides has increased many times over in the last twenty years, the *fraction* of food crops lost to pests in the fields has remained relatively constant at about ten per cent.

It is now well established that certain birds and fishes are already being poisoned as a result of chlorinated hydrocarbons being concentrated as they pass up the biological food chains. Some species of birds, particularly fish-eating hawks, eagles, and sea birds (which eat four or more steps up from the base of food chains), may be threatened with complete extinction. Part of the difficulty is that the pesticides interfere with the birds' calcium metabolism in such a way that the eggshells are too thin and are thus easily crushed. Coho salmon, which also feed high on the food chain, have been passing pesticide residues into their eggs. In 1968, almost 700,000 young Lake Michigan salmon died as they absorbed the last drop of DDT-rich oil from their yolk sacs. And DDT concentrations are now rising ominously in such important food fishes as tuna, mackerel, and hake. The more subtle effects of biological concentration of pesticides will be mentioned later; the birds and fish are cited here because the problem is already quite visible. As will become clear, there is good reason to believe that the birds and fish are only the *first* victims.

**Soil Erosion.** Soil is not just a collection of crushed rock arranged to keep plants from blowing down in the wind. It is a complicated collection of organisms—bacteria, fungi, protozoa, worms, and insects, to name a few— all of which participate in the retention, conversion and processing of the nutrients used by plants. The biological community of fertile topsoil is "produced", as it were, at the rate of about one inch every three hundred to one thousand years. The dispersal of the same amount by wind or water, aided by the short-

sighted logging, grazing, and cultivation practices of man, may take as little as a day or even an hour. The process of erosion is of course not deterred by the use of fertilizer, nor can the addition of these few inorganic chemicals be expected to compensate for long for the loss of the topsoil itself.

At a time when population growth demands ever increasing areas of productive land, the record of our essentially permanent losses to erosion is most discouraging. The fraction of the Earth's land surface classified as desert and wasteland has increased from less than ten to over twenty-five per cent in the last century. The Sahara, in part a man-made desert, is advancing at several miles per year over a broad front. The Great Thar desert of India, also partly man-made, is advancing at 5 miles per decade around its entire perimeter—its area has increased by 60,000 square miles in 90 years. And it is worth noting that in India, one of the hungriest countries on earth, over half the existing farmland is inadequately protected against erosion today.

Secondary to the immediate loss of agricultural productivity, but still very costly, is the damage done by the soil once it has been ripped from the land. The burden of silt carried by many of the world's rivers fills irrigation and hydroelectric reservoirs on a time scale of decades for significant loss and a century or so for total destruction. Thus are defeated some of the very measures intended to compensate for the original erosion losses elsewhere. A final casualty of the silt load in rivers are the gravel beds needed by anadromous food fishes, principally salmon, to spawn. The beds not already made inaccessible or unusable by dams are being continuously converted to pebble-bearing muck, carrying yet another species further down the road to extinction.

**Thermal Pollution.** The combination of growing population and increasing per capita use of energy has led to a phenomenal growth in the power requirements of civilization— world energy consumption is doubling every 17 years or less, more than twice as fast as population. Herein lies yet another threat to both local and global environments. For according to the laws of thermodynamics, waste heat is the inevitable companion of usable energy—not only is heat a by-product of power generation processes, but even the useful power itself is ultimately degraded to heat. The former effect manifests itself as the heat which goes up the stack in a coal-fired electric power station, and in the heat transferred to water used for cooling in both fossil- and nuclear-fueled plants; the latter effect is seen in the heat from cities, which in some instances already perceptibly alters the climate in surrounding areas. The problem of disposing of the heat at the consumption end of civilization's energy flow will ultimately be a global one; it is discussed in the section on "subtle assaults" on the environment.

The problem of handling the relatively concentrated heat at the sites where power is generated is upon us today, and is worsening rapidly. It has been aggravated by the fact that nuclear generating plants are thermally less efficient than their fossil-fueled counterparts; that is, they produce more waste heat per kilowatt of electricity. Moreover, nuclear plants become more economical with increasing size, so the trend has been toward larger and larger installations. This increases still further the amount of heat which must be handled at one site.

The numbers involved virtually dictate the use of water, as opposed to air, as the primary coolant, and the amount of water required (1 to 2 cubic feet per second for every megawatt of installed capacity) makes borrowing from a lake, river, or ocean almost a necessity. The water is returned to its source from 12 to 25 degrees Fahrenheit hotter than it started, and herein lies the threat—immediate and potentially catastrophic damage to aquatic animals and plants. Installations on the open coastline will be least harmful because of the enormous volume of cold water available to dilute the heated discharge—but even here local effects on kelp and other inshore biological communities can be anticipated. Outfalls on estuaries, bays, and inland lakes, where dilution is much less effective, will cause

drastic changes in marine ecology. By far the worst prospects, however, are those for the world's river systems. It is estimated that by 1985 fully one quarter of the total annual runoff by the United States will be cooling power plants. Since much of the total actually occurs during a relatively short flood season, the fraction will be closer to half for most of the year. This will mean the virtual extinction of much of the flora and fauna which inhabit our rivers today, including a number of valuable food species. It should be noted that part of the threat which warm water poses to aquatic life is its reduced content of dissolved oxygen. Since other pollutants already discussed consume water-borne oxygen, we can expect destructive reinforcement of these effects to hasten the demise of freshwater life.

The few alternatives to the use of ocean, lake, or river water for cooling plants are expensive and hence unpopular with utilities. Open-cycle cooling towers are costly to build and require the purchase of water which is consumed by evaporation. Closed-cycle towers, which use the same water over and over, cost even more to build, and cooling ponds require the acquisition of two acres of increasingly expensive land per megawatt of plant capacity. All of these alternatives spare marine life by pumping the heat into the atmosphere. The consequences are then climatological; some which have already been experienced in Europe and heavy ground fogs and frosts (associated with the water vapor from open-cycle towers).

Utility companies argue, as do polluters of every stripe, that mankind must choose between their indispensable product and some "minor" aspect of an evidently very dispensable environment. They seem unable to grasp that the real choices are not of the form, "energy—take it or leave it," but rather of the nature, "energy—increase the supply hastily (at the expense of the habitat) or moderate the demand (at the expense of population growth and 300 horsepower cars)."

**Noise.** The spectacle of headlong mechanization and urbanization of growing populations has been accompanied by a veritable cacophony of ever louder and more discordant sounds. Today the problem is most clearly recognized by people unfortunate enough to live in airport landing and takeoff patterns, and those whose teenagers have suffered permanent hearing impairment at rock concerts. And while "noise pollution" is undoubtedly more amenable to solutions employing technology and determination than are most pollution problems, these ingredients are not being applied to the task in the requisite amounts today. Sound levels are customarily measured in decibels—a logarithmic scale on which a tenfold increase in the intensity of the noise adds ten decibels. Thus a 100-fold increase in loudness adds 20 decibels, a 1000-fold increase adds 30. On this scale, the threshold of hearing is zero decibels, a typical conversation is 60, heavy traffic or a jet passing overhead is 100, and a jet taking off or a machine gun at close range is 120. Sleep interference can occur as low as 50–55 decibels, and there is growing evidence that noise in the 90 decibel range causes irreversible changes in the autonomic nervous system. There are also indications that noise is a factor in such stress-related conditions as peptic ulcer and essential hypertension. And while the data are still spotty, we can rest assured that the "experiment," with most of mankind serving as guinea pigs, will go on.

Representative of our cavalier attitude toward noise as a concomitant of "progress" is the recent Presidential go-ahead for the supersonic transport. It is now asserted that the SST, whose usefulness and cost-benefit ratio are debatable even without considering the inevitable sonic boom, will be permitted to fly supersonically only over water. The resulting limitation of boom effects (although not takeoff and landing noise) to fisherman, island dwellers, and oceanic travellers is another demonstration of our remarkable ability to endure the acute discomfort of someone else. The world perspective which must be acquired if a livable environment is to be preserved is obviously not yet at hand.

## ONE-SHOT ASSAULTS

**Thermonuclear War.** Most of us are aware of the possibility that thermonuclear war will cause more destruction in an hour than man's prolonged insults to the environment could manage in decades. Nevertheless, since some strategic planners continue to argue that such a war is "survivable" and hence a viable policy alternative, it is worth reviewing some pertinent facts. The strategists seem to base their arguments on calculations of the number of millions of people who might survive blast and short-term radiation effects in various postulated attacks. Unfortunately, their projections overlook or underestimate ecological and sociological effects which, in the aftermath of a nuclear war, could easily result in the complete demise of civilized man.

Consider the effects of a rather limited exchange among the United States, Russia, China, and various European powers. The flow of food and technological aid from the developed to the underdeveloped nations would cease instantaneously. In the absence of the wheat, seeds, fertilizers, and mechanical equipment previously supplied by the now-devastated countries, much of the unscathed but also undeveloped world would promptly be pitched into massive famines. Blast effects and huge fires burning in the warring nations would fill the atmosphere with debris. The resulting reduction of sunlight for at least a year thereafter would significantly lower the mean surface temperature of the earth, compounding famines by reducing agricultural production still further.

The direct effects of the blasts and fires themselves have possibly been badly underestimated. Germany's experiences with firestorms several square miles in area during World War II presage such catastrophes in much greater dimensions in the event of a nuclear conflict. Individual firestorms, generating extreme temperatures, might then incinerate hundreds or thousands of square miles apiece in forest or metropolitan areas. Not only would vegetation be removed, but vast areas of soil might be sterilized. Rains washing away the unprotected topsoil would then insure the permanent loss of productivity of much of the hemisphere's agricultural land, and the silt and radioactive debris deposited in the fragile offshore waters would wreak havoc on ocean fisheries.

In short, in the face of widespread famine, soaring disease and mutation rates from radio-active fallout, raging epidemics in the absence of much of the world's medical technology, and generally harsher environmental conditions than man has ever faced before, it is problematical whether the survivors of even "limited" thermonuclear war will survive for very long. It is not our intention here to delve into the correlation between population pressures and the probability that such a conflict will occur; it suffices to point out that few students of the psychology and economics of war dispute the connection.

**Epidemics: Natural and Man-Made.** The present world population is not only large, crowded, and malnourished beyond precedent, it is also the most mobile the world has ever seen. People, potential carriers of disease of every description, move routinely and in substantial numbers from continent to continent in matters of hours. Thus the potential for world-wide epidemic has never been greater, notwithstanding the popular belief that modern medicine has made such a catastrophe impossible.

Consider, in this connection, the difficulty experienced in the United States in coping with the relatively mild Asian flu epidemic of 1968. It proved impossible to manufacture and distribute enough vaccine in time to protect most of the population. That relatively few deaths were associated with the epidemic was not due to modern public health measures; this particular virus happened to be non-fatal for victims in otherwise good health. Our knowledge of viruses, while incomplete, is sufficient to indicate that the spontaneous development of highly lethal strains is possible— in other words, we may not be so lucky the next time.

Another area in which we might not remain lucky is the transfer of lethal viruses from animal populations to man. Recently a new virus, the Marburgvirus, was transmitted from green monkeys to workers in a German laboratory. Among 32 people contracting this highly contagious disease, there were 7 deaths. Only the appearance of the disease in a medically sophisticated environment permitted its containment and minimized the number of deaths. If the virus had escaped into the population at large (the monkeys had been in the London Airport on their way to Marburg) a billion deaths might possibly have occurred.

We have already witnessed the vulnerability of our highly mechanized society to such comparatively minor disruptions as power outages and snow storms. One can perhaps imagine, then, the almost total societal breakdown which could result from a serious epidemic. Millions of vital jobs would go unattended, while still healthy individuals fled the cities to avoid infection. Such consequences of the disease itself would seriously impede the use of any ameliorative measures which happened to be available.

In many parts of the world, health conditions with the potential for initiating such a disaster are worsening. Rats thriving on stored grain in India have revived the spectre of bubonic plague there. The serious parasitic disease, bilharzia, is spreading across Egypt through new irrigation canals connected with the Aswan Dam project. And wholesale use of chemotherapy and antibiotics has resulted in the development of resistant strains of bacteria and other parasites. The same conditions of crowding, malnourishment, and mobility which make mankind so vulnerable to epidemic also magnify the potential consequences of chemical and biological warfare. CBW is, unfortunately, the poor man's atomic bomb—a few dollars and one or two trained microbiologists can put any country in the business of developing its own biological doomsday weapons. The possibilities are abundant: drug-resistant strains of known diseases, new ways to transmit old foes (such as rabies), altogether new viruses, and chemical or biological attacks on food supplies, to name a few. One can hope that the world's arsenals of such material will never be used. But even if they are not, the abundant potential for accidents remains (it has already been demonstrated in this country at Skull Valley, Utah, where the victims happened to be sheep). Surely there are more pleasant, if less comprehensive, solutions to overpopulation.

**Man-Made Earthquakes.** Man has already demonstrated the ability to trigger inadvertently the release of vast amounts of destructive energy stored in the stress field of the earth. His most long-standing activity of this sort is the construction of large dams, whose enormous reservoirs result in substantial loading of the earth's crust. When Lake Mead was first filled during the period from 1935 to 1939, thousands of seismic events were recorded in that previously inactive area. The largest earthquake involved had a magnitude of 5 on the Richter scale. Other dams in relatively inactive regions have caused numerous earthquakes with magnitudes greater than 6— sufficient to do substantial damage to urban areas. A quake registering 6.4, associated with the filling of the Kogna dam in India, was responsible for 200 fatalities in 1967.

Underground nuclear explosions provide another potential means for achieving similar results. The fact that the recent Amchitka test did not induce a major quake proves nothing but the good fortune of everyone involved. It must be emphasized that stresses associated with either reservoirs or nuclear explosions may act as *triggers* and not as the principal source of energy for an earthquake (although a nuclear explosion itself can have an equivalent magnitude of 6 or 7). There is therefore no reason to expect that a much larger quake than any associated with these causes to date will not eventually result. The consequences of the associated earth movement and possible tidal waves will of course be directly proportional to the number of people crammed onto the world at the time.

## SUBTLE ASSAULTS: CHIPPING AWAY AT THE "INVISIBLE ENVIRONMENT"

**Persistent Pesticides and Other Chemicals.** Instances of the poisoning of important food

fishes and birds of prey by chlorinated hydrocarbon pesticides were given in the previous section. Probably much more dangerous are long-term effects which cannot yet be measured in numbers of corpses; damning evidence that it will come to that is accumulating steadily. The alarming distribution of DDT and its relatives is accounted for by their mobility, by the long time period over which these compounds remain intact before being degraded by natural processes, and by their solubility in fat. The first property means that the compounds move easily from the places where they are deposited. They vaporize into the atmosphere, cling to moving dust particles, and move along with ground water, etc. The second property—a half-life of a decade or more—means that the substances remain active during and after their dispersal by wind and water over the entire face of the earth. The third property promotes the movement of these compounds from the nonliving environment into living systems, all of which have fatty components. This leads to their accumulation at increasing concentrations as they move up the biological food chains—from plant to herbivore to carnivore to secondary carnivore, and so on. The mass of organisms at each trophic (feeding) level is constrained by the laws of thermodynamics to be less than the mass on the next lower level. In terms of a simple example, this means that it may take 100 pounds of grass to make ten pounds of steer, which in turn may be used to make a pound of man (here, the third trophic level). But while only 10 per cent of the grass itself ends up as steer, a much higher percentage of the DDT *on* the grass does, because it tends to dissolve in the first fat it encounters, and little DDT is lost as energy and materials pass from trophic level to trophic level. In food chains with many trophic levels, such as many aquatic ones, such fat-soluble pesticides may be concentrated to thousands of times their initial environmental levels. Even at low trophic levels, filter feeding organisms such as oysters may build up astonishingly high concentrations.

These mechanisms explain why pesticide levels in lake-dwelling plankton were found in a representative instance to be 250 times the concentration of application (to control gnats). The concentrations in frogs, sunfish, and fish-eating birds inhabiting the same lake were, respectively, 2000, 12,000, and 80,000 times that of the application. Equally ominous, the intake of DDT by infants around the globe is now about twice the maximum recommended by the World Health Organization. In adult humans, DDT is often found at concentrations of 12 parts per million (ppm) in fat. In mother's milk, concentrations of .2 ppm are not unusual; for comparison, we note that the permissible levels in cow's milk is set by the FDA at .05 ppm.

The producers of persistent pesticides argue that these levels are harmless and cite two poorly designed studies of adults exposed to heavy doses of DDT over several years. The fact that none of the subjects displayed symptoms of acute poisoning during the observation period is not particularly reassuring; by the same criteria, cigarette smoking and fallout would also be judged perfectly safe. Against this shaky evidence are arrayed innumerable ominous studies of the toxic effects of DDT and other pesticides on various animals: DDT in large doses increases incidence of cancer in mice (similar evidence on cyclamates recently resulted in an FDA ban); DDT interferes with the reproductive physiology of rats, which resembles that of humans; various chlorinated hydrocarbons can cause abnormal changes in animal brain wave patterns, and trout exposed to 20 ppm DDT lose the ability to learn to avoid electric shock.

Evidence of long-term pernicious effects on human beings is just beginning to come in, some twenty years after the introduction of DDT (how long did it take to get the goods on cigarettes?). Perhaps the most significant recent study correlated high fat concentrations of DDT and its breakdown products with human deaths from softening of the brain, cerebral hemorrhage, hypertension, cirrhosis of the liver, and various cancers. These results are only preliminary, but they are ominous. Finally, it should be noted that we have no experience with the effects of DDT over a typical human lifespan—the first people to

have been exposed to DDT from conception are now only in their early twenties.

Nevertheless, the persistent pesticides pose a far greater threat than the rather direct one to man's health—they have the potential to undermine the food production of both land and sea. As regards the sea, DDT at a few parts per billion concentration has been shown to inhibit photosynthesis in phytoplankton, the tiny green plants which are at the bottom of the ocean food pyramid. Again the results are preliminary but frightening. If photosynthesis in the ocean as a whole were affected, the total amount of food available to man from that source would diminish correspondingly. Far more likely than the _end_ of photosynthesis in phytoplankton is a rise to dominance of some particular form which is _least_ susceptible to the low concentrations of DDT (less than 1 part per billion) in most seawater today. This could lead to huge "blooms" of one species or another, with serious consequences throughout the oceanic food chains. Or it could lead to a change in the size of the dominant phytoplankton species—an occurrence which could dramatically decrease fisheries' yields. In this entire area, mankind is operating largely from a position of ignorance; scientific knowledge has barely scratched the complexities of the life and chemistry of the sea. But such facts as are available suggest that the potential for man-induced disaster is there.

We are on equally uncertain ground in regard to the effects of pesticides on topsoil. As was pointed out in an earlier section, soil is a complicated biological community in itself. Its continued fertility is dependent, among other things, on the unhindered operation of natural cycles involving nitrogen, carbon, and phosphorous. All these cycles depend in part on living organisms—bacteria, fungi, and others—whose defenses against the long-lived pesticides now accumulating in soils everywhere is a matter of conjecture. The nitrogen cycle is particularly vulnerable, being in several essential steps _completely_ dependent on certain bacteria. It has been said, perhaps only slightly overstating the case, that the extermination of any of several of these crucial populations would mean the end of life on earth.

Nor are pesticides the only slow-acting poisons with which we are lacing the environment. Some, like lead, are not merely persistent, they do not degrade at all. Symptoms of chronic lead poisoning in humans include miscarriage, weakness, and lesions in various parts of the circulatory, digestive, and nervous systems (it doesn't miss much). Such descriptions are particularly discouraging in view of the fact that the atmospheric lead level from all sources (including gasoline additives, smelting, lead piping, and lead-bearing paints, ceramics, and glassware) increased some 400 per cent between 1750 and 1940 and another 300 per cent between 1940 and 1967. There is considerable disagreement about what level of lead can be tolerated by humans without substantial ill effects. But since lead is a *cumulative* cellular poison, it seems unwise to wait until everyone is displaying symptoms before attempting to reduce its concentration in the environment.

We remain uncertain of all the consequences of lead in ecological systems, although its effects on people should give even the biologically uninitiated a clue. Nevertheless, as a result of man's activities some 100,000 tons of lead particles fall into the oceans every year, and the lead concentration in the Pacific is up by a factor of 10 since the first gasoline additives were introduced 45 years ago. It should be noted in this connection that lead, like pesticides, concentrates heavily along food chains.

Many other industrial metals form toxic compounds—nickel is one, and it too has been added to gasoline. Altogether, it is estimated that man is putting about half a million different pollutants into the ocean, and about three thousand into the air. The associated risks, already monumental, will increase as proliferating populations demand—and dispose of —more of everything.

**Radiation.** Radioactive substances are those which undergo spontaneous changes in nuclear structure accompanied by the emission of energetic particles and, usually, penetrating electromagnetic waves. The latter, called gamma rays, are identical to x-rays of equal energy in every respect except origin. The particles (principally helium nuclei and electrons), the gamma rays, and x-rays are all lumped under the term "radiation." The debilitating or lethal effects of acute doses of radiation—such as those associated with nuclear warfare or with serious accidents in the handling of nuclear reactors and isotopes— have been well publicized, and we will not discuss them here.

The dangers of prolonged, low-level exposures to radiation are more insidious and have some similarity to those of pesticides: the absence of immediate and obvious symptoms does not imply that the exposure is harmless; radioactive substances remain dangerous for extended lengths of time; and many are concentrated in biological systems. The differences of degree, however, are very important ones. For example, the half-lives of two particularly dangerous fission products, strontium 90 and cesium 137 are about 30 years, and because of the potency of these substances a nominal initial amount of either remains hazardous for centuries. Indeed, if lethality is given its customary definition as destructive effect per unit of energy released in tissue, radiation is 100,000,000 times as deadly as cyanide.

Radiation from cosmic rays and from radioactive material in the earth's crust has always been with us. It amounts to an average of from .08 to .15 rad per person per year. (The rad is the customary unit of absorbed ionizing radiation, and amounts to 100 ergs of energy per gram of absorber.) There is a great temptation to regard this so-called background level of radiation as a yardstick for safety, in particular, to regard any man-made increment of radiation as safe if, averaged over the exposed population, it is smaller than or comparable to the natural background. There are three flaws in this approach. First, available evidence indicates that *no* amount of ionizing radiation, not even the relatively low background, is completely safe—some mutations are always induced, and if the exposed population is large enough and the data complete enough a statistical increase in deformities, stillbirths, and cancers will always appear. (In the case of natural background radiation, there is no unexposed "control" group for comparison; however, it is reasonable to suppose that a historical burden of mutations, albeit small, has been associated with the background.) The second flaw arises because, with respect to genetic effects, at least, radiation doses are cumulative—a given man-induced dose must be considered in combination with all other sources of exposure, natural and artificial, past, present, and future. The third flaw stems from the frequent assumption that the dose can be determined essentially by dividing the total radioactivity involved (measured in nuclear disintegrations per second) by the area of the part of the planet exposed. The biological concentration of many radioactive substances makes nonsense of this assumption.

There will be some environmental and human cost associated with *any* increase in radiation dose, just as such costs accrue from the consumption of gasoline, the use of pesticides and fertilizers, and so on. The pertinent question in every case is: at what point do the incremental penalties outweigh the incremental gain? The peculiar problem with radiation is that the penalties are so far removed in time from the activity and its benefits. By the time the price is clear, the damage is done.

Standards for "permissible" radiation exposure vary somewhat among the various national and international agencies which promulgate them. Nor can the standards be easily summarized, for they specify not only a variety of absorbed doses depending on occupation, length of exposure, and organs exposed, but also fix maximum environmental concentrations for a vast assortment of isotopes of varying biological effectiveness. Two numbers which are representative are the International Commission for Radiation Protection's recommendations of no more than 5 rads accumulated total in the first 30 years of life (.17 rad/yr. average) for the general population, and 5 rads/yr. for workers in x-ray and nuclear technology (both these figures refer to radiation *in addition to* the natural background). Unfortunately, many of the

guidelines in use today were last substantially revised in the fifties; prominent scientists affiliated with nuclear programs in the United States have recently suggested that, in view of recent knowledge, some of these levels may be ten times too high. It is true that, *on average*, exposures have not yet approached the guideline levels, but there is reason to believe they will. And individual and local overdoses have occasionally occurred.

At the moment, by far the bulk of man-made radiation exposure is attributable to medical and dental x-ray equipment—over ninety per cent—and the vast majority of radiation induced deaths are caused by these sources. A single pelvic x-ray examination to determine the position of a fetus delivers 1.3 rads to the mother and 2.7 to the unborn child, appreciably increasing the probability that the child will eventually contract leukemia. X-ray leakage from color television sets is becoming a non-negligible source of exposure for many Americans, and even a radioactive wrist watch may cause an exposure of up to .6 rad/year (mostly to relatively insensitive parts of the body).

Potentially the most serious radiation threat related to population growth is the proliferation of nuclear reactors for the generation of electric power. The highly concentrated radioactive wastes produced by these reactors have been the subject of much study and concern. Although there is cause for uneasiness in the present disposition of these wastes (which remain dangerous for hundreds of years and more) in underground tanks and, at more moderate concentrations, in concrete-lined barrels at the bottom of the sea, the AEC's proposal to store them in the future in abandoned salt mines seems sound. Far more bothersome are the comparatively small amounts of radioactive isotopes which are released to air and water at virtually every step of the nuclear power production process—from mining and processing the fuel, to running the reactor, to transporting and reprocessing the spent fuel elements. Because of the low concentrations of the substances involved, their control and removal is technically difficult and correspondingly expensive. And because price is the name of the game in power production, there is a temptation to encourage standards based more on what is economically feasible than on what is biologically acceptable.

Today's standards on the emission of radioactive pollutants at the various steps in power production are often applied on a one-installation-at-a-time philosophy: if the anticipated levels of radiation from a single facility do not pose a clear hazard to health, such levels are judged safe. As we have pointed out above, such an approach is inconsistent with much of our knowledge about radioactive substances and radiation—particularly the concentration of some of the isotopes in biological systems and the existence of additive destructive effects from radiation of all origins. The consequences of this philosophy are not yet pronounced because the number of facilities is still small (although local violations of even today's overgenerous standards have occasionally occurred). But if nuclear power plants undergo the hundred-fold or greater proliferation predicted for them, and if the present concept of "safe" is not revised, the consequences may be totally unacceptable. If the concept *is* revised, the cost of meeting the more realistic standards will slow the proliferation.

As with pesticides, the threat of radiation overdoses may be even more severe for the environmental life-support systems than for the physical health of man. The effects of radioactive isotopes on many of the organisms which concentrate them are incompletely known. The long-term consequences of further irradiating the microorganisms which provide the fertility of the soil and sea are largely matters of speculation. Because of the additivity and longevity of radiation damage, once we go too far there will be no turning back the clock.

**The Alteration of Climate.** Numerous inspired publicity agents for science have long made glowing statements about control of the weather—the individual occurrences of rain and snow, sunshine and clouds, tornadoes and hurricanes, which taken together comprise the climate. Nevertheless, an inspection of the batting average of weather forecasters suggests that our ability to predict, much less control, the weather is still in its infancy. It is therefore both remarkable and disconcerting to discover that the activities of man are unintentionally altering climate and weather not only locally (as in ground fogs from cooling towers and inversion changes over cities) but also globally.

The global situation is of course of greater significance, and while it is still only poorly understood, a semblance of an explanation can be given. The surface temperature of the earth is determined by a heat balance, a simplified version of which is as follows: incident energy from the sun, largely in the visible part of the electromagnetic spectrum, warms the surface of the earth and drives the winds, ocean currents, water cycle, photosynthesis, and so on. These processes in themselves lead to the dissipation of heat, which, together with that absorbed directly by the earth from the sun, is reradiated outward in the infrared part of the spectrum. Substantial interference by man with any part of this process can result in changing the average surface temperature and atmospheric circulation pattern.

Such interference currently takes several forms. One is the steady increase of the carbon dioxide content of the atmosphere, believed to be due primarily to increasing combustion of hydrocarbon fuels. Carbon dioxide is essentially transparent to incoming visible light, so it doesn't change the input to the heat balance; but being opaque to part of the outbound infrared energy, it does reduce the amount of heat which can escape. This effect, if it were the only one operating, would result in a warming trend. (Glass has similar properties which account for the warmth of a greenhouse —and for the name "greenhouse effect" applied to the $CO_2$ phenomenon.)

It seems, however, that a competing effect has dominated the situation since 1940. This is the reduced transparency of the atmosphere to incoming light as a result of urban air pollution (smoke, aerosols), agricultural air pollution (dust), and volcanic ash. This screening phenomenon is said to be responsible for the present world cooling trend—a total of about .2°C in the world mean surface temperature over the past quarter century. This number seems small until it is realized that a decrease of only 4°C would probably be sufficient to start another ice age. Moreover, other effects besides simple screening by air pollution threaten to move us in the same direction. In particular, a mere one per cent increase in low cloud cover would decrease the surface temperature by .8°C. We may be in the process of providing just such a cloud increase, and more, by adding man-made condensation nuclei to the atmosphere in the form of jet exhausts and other suitable pollutants. A final push in the cooling direction comes from man-made changes in the direct reflectivity of the earth's surface (albedo) through urbanization, deforestation, and the enlargement of deserts.

The effects of a new ice age on agriculture and the supportability of large human populations scarcely need elaboration here. Even more dramatic results are possible, however; for instance, a sudden outward slumping in the Antarctic ice cap, induced by added weight, could generate a tidal wave of proportions unprecedented in recorded history.

If man survives the comparatively short-term threat of making the planet too cold, there is every indication he is quite capable of making it too warm not long thereafter. For the remaining major means of interference with the global heat balance is the release of energy from fossil and nuclear fuels. As pointed out previously, all this energy is ultimately degraded to heat. What are today scattered local effects of its disposition will in time, with the continued growth of population and energy consumption, give way to global warming. The present rate of increase in energy use, if continued, will bring us in about a century to the point where our heat input could have drastic global consequences. Again, the exact form such consequences might take is unknown; the melting of the icecaps with a concomitant 150 foot increase in sea level might be one of them.

**Ecosystem Destabilization.** A common thread runs through the discussions in this section on "subtle" assaults on the environment—that thread is the utter inadequacy of

man's knowledge in the face of the problems he confronts. For many of the most serious difficulties involve the effects of substances or phenomena we do not understand very well (pesticides, radiation, air pollution) on systems we do not understand very well either (soil microorganisms, ocean food chains, climate). What is becoming clear is that man's activities are modifying the planet so extensively that the natural stability of the ecosystems we inherited is imperiled. The crime we are committing is the destruction of the life support systems of our planetary spaceship, the death of our environment, in short—ecocide.

The ecosystem concept means no less than the totality of the biological community, the physical environment in which these organisms exist, and the intricate web of relationships which interconnects the whole. It is the very complexity of the interrelationships which imparts stability to the ecosystem—the existence of many alternative links in a food chain insures the success of the enterprise even if the population of a species or two declines or explodes; the presence of many alternative paths in a mineral cycle serves the same function. A complex forest or jungle community may persist for centuries (in the absence of interference by man); by contrast, a simple cornfield is subject to instant ruin if not vigilantly protected.

Mankind, even since before the agricultural revolution, has been a simplifier of the ecosystem. He has decimated species, and, both literally and figuratively, replaced the forests with cornfields. Today, with his pesticides, radiation, and miscellaneous pollution, he threatens to remove altogether links whose functions he does not even understand. He is by the entire process inevitably pushing the world toward instability.

In this analysis, we have considered threats to various components of the ecosystem as if those components were separate entities. They are not, of course, and neither are the threats. A discouraging concept in this regard is that of synergistic interaction, in which the effect of two causes operating together is greater than the sum of their effects if they operated separately. Some examples of synergisms which are known are enhanced toxicity of benzyprene and sulfur dioxide when the two are present together, and the interaction of asbestos particles with smoking and other air pollutants in accelerating lung disease. Possible synergisms between pesticides and air pollution or pesticides and radiation are fertile areas for speculation.

## SUMMARY AND CONCLUSION

The direct threats to health which result from man's activities in support of his ever-growing population are many. But the threats which the same activities pose to the systems on which *all* life depends are still more numerous—and less well understood. It is a safe assumption that as population continues to grow, and as technology is pressed harder and harder to devise means to cope with more and more people, more frequent and more serious mis-

takes will be made. Even the mistakes already with us are aggravated simply because they are made on behalf of so many people, and because so many people are here to be affected.

It is remarkable that nature's systems—plant communities, mineral cycles, food chains—become more stable with increasing complexity, while man's systems—cities, power grids, instruments of defense and war—appear to grow less stable as their complexity increases. It should worry us more than it does that we are pushing *both* in the wrong direction.

Simple arithmetic makes it plain that indefinite population growth in the finite space allotted to us is impossible. In this article we have posed the cost-benefit question several times in regard to different activities; we pose it once more with respect to the concept of the previous sentence: What is gained and what is lost in the pursuit of the impossible? We have enumerated here the possible costs—they include the destruction of all life on this planet. Where is the gain that justifies this risk?

# "All Other Factors Being Constant..." A Reconciliation of Several Theories of Climatic Change

REID A. BRYSON

"Something is wrong with the weather" is the title of a recent article in *U.S. News and World Report*, and an article in *Saturday Re-*

view *asks*, "Is man changing the climate of the earth?"[1] The layman, and the nonspecialist on reading these articles and the many others in the newspapers will probably be convinced that the climate *is* changing, for the accumu-

"All Other Factors Being Constant...," A Reconciliation of Several Theories of Climatic Change. From *Weatherwise*, Vol. 21, No. 2, April 1968, pp. 56–62. Reprinted by permission of the author and the publisher

[1] *U.S. News and World Report*, July 10, 1967, p. 38; *Saturday Review*, April 1, 1967, p. 52.

lating evidence is considerable. He will probably be confused also, for the reasons given for the change are as varied as the authors. One author will blame the change on sunspots, another on the consumption of fossil fuels producing an increase in the carbon dioxide content of the atmosphere. Still another author will suggest air pollution as a significant cause, and another maintains that a complicated feedback of energy between sea and air is sufficient to produce irregular climatic fluctuations. On the other hand, the man next door *knows* that it is due to all those atom bombs, or the cloud seeders, or automobiles, etc.

Who is right? Which of these answers is the correct one? These are questions that I am frequently asked by my colleagues and friends. These questions can only be answered by saying that none are and all are! All are at least partly right, because each of the factors does contribute to climatic change in larger or smaller measure, contributing to rising or falling world temperatures. All are at least partly wrong in failing to emphasize that there is more than one factor.

There is really no good reason why this confusion should exist, for the various factors fit into a quite well-known basic relationship. The principle is that the heat supplied to the earth's surface by the sun and from the interior of the earth must be disposed of or the surface will get hotter and hotter. This heat income is balanced by infrared radiation from the earth to space.

Neglecting the very small flow of heat from the earth's interior, this basic relationship may be expressed by a simple equation

$$ScA = KeT^4 \text{ (4c)}$$

or in words:

"The intensity of the sunlight arriving at the earth (*S*), times the cross-sectional area of the earth (*c*), times the fraction of that radiation which is absorbed (*A*) is equal to a constant *(K)*, times the "effective emissivity" of the earth (*e*), times the average temperature of the earth raised to the fourth power $(T^4)$, this outward heat radiation flowing from the entire surface of the earth (*4c*)." In still plainer English this says that the sunlight is absorbed on the cross-section "target area" of the earth, but lost by heat radiation over the whole surface. This heat radiation is proportional to the fourth power of the temperature and to an "effective emissivity" of the earth (i.e., how good the earth is as a radiator). With this simple equation the various theories of climatic change may be related.

Numbers may be put into this simple equation to test it. The intensity of the solar beam reaching the earth is about 2 calories per square centimeter per minute. The fraction of the radiation absorbed by the earth, which must then be re-radiated away, is 60 to 65%. The amount of energy which must be lost by each square centimeter of the earth's surface, on the average, must then be 0.30 to 0.325 calories per minute.* This is about what the artificial satellite measurements show,—a fact which gives us some confidence in the equation! Fig. 1. If the earth were a perfect radiator, however, this value for the outward radiation would require a mean world temperature of 22 to 26 degrees celsius below freezing, or −7 to −15 degs. F. Fortunately, near the ground the temperature averages something on the order of 60° F. Most of the solar heat is absorbed at or near the surface, because the air is nearly transparent to the wavelengths of solar radiation. The earth emits infrared radiation, to which the air is quite opaque, mostly due to water (clouds), water vapor, and carbon dioxide in it. Some of the solar heat absorbed at the surface heats the air by conduction, and then the atmosphere itself must radiate some of the heat away, but about half of this atmospheric radiation is back downward. Even that which is radiated upward is partly absorbed by higher layers of air unless one goes high enough for most of the water vapor, clouds, and carbon dioxide to be left behind. At this level the temperature is well below freezing. In essence, the equation says that the atmosphere acts as though it were

---

* One-fourth of 2 times 0.60 or 2 times 0.65, because the area of the earth is four times the cross-sectional area. The income is on the cross-section, but the loss is over the whole surface.

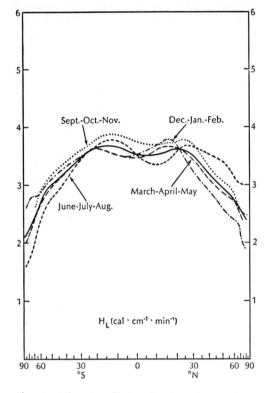

**Fig. 1.** Infrared radiation leaving the earth, as measured from meteorological satellites, averaged along latitudes. Abscissa is latitude compressed to allow for the smaller area of the earth at higher latitudes, and the ordinate is langleys/minute. The average value agrees quite well with the known values of the solar constant and earth albedo. (From Vonder Haar, 1967.)

radiating perfectly from some upper level where the temperature is minus 22 to minus 26 degrees celsius.

In order to get the heat from the surface up to where it is finally lost by radiation there must be a temperature difference. In effect this temperature difference is on the order of 40 to 50 degrees celsius, the surface where we live averaging that much warmer. Vive l'atmosphere! This is the so-called "greenhouse effect," which is simulated in the simple equation by throwing in an "effective emissivity."

At this point we must digress momentarily to consider what the average temperature of

the earth is. For the purposes of the present discussion it is the temperature averaged over the whole earth and whole year, measured near the surface of the earth. All other factors being constant, the effect of increasing sun intensity is to raise the average temperature of the earth. It is this effect that is being single out by those meteorologists who maintain the fluctuating solar output, perhaps related to sunspots, is responsible for the ups and downs of the climate over the past few centuries. Hurd Willett of M.I.T. represents this group. A one per cent increase in the solar intensity would raise the average temperature of the earth about 0.8° C. or 1.4° F.

All other factors being constant, the effect of changing the fraction of the sunlight absorbed by the earth is to change the average temperature of the earth. The absorptivity* of the earth depends on such things as the amount of snow and ice on the ground, the amount of cloud, the dustiness of the atmosphere, and the nature of the ground cover. Any change which makes the earth a brighter planet, that is, which results in more of the sunlight being reflected, lowers the mean temperature of the earth. Increased cloudiness, snow cover, or dustiness of the atmosphere makes the earth a brighter planet. In fact, the "dark" side of the moon at new moon is less dark when there is much cloud on the sunlit side of the earth or much dust in the air—it is illuminated by sunlight "reflected" by the clouds and dust—and becomes faintly visible.

An increase of one per cent in the normal reflectivity or "albedo" of the earth from perhaps 37% to 38% would lower the mean temperature of the earth about 1.7° C. or 3.1° F.

Proponents of variation in cloudiness, volcanic dust, and man-made dust as factors causing climatic change emphasize this factor. I am one of these.

All other factors being constant, an increase of the "effective emissivity" of the earth for infrared radiation will result in a cooler earth. This is the rather complicated factor

* Meteorologists normally measure the reflectivity, the fraction reflected, rather than the fraction absorbed or absorptivity. The reflectivity is called the *albedo*.

discussed in a previous paragraph which involves the mechanism by which the solar heat absorbed at the surface of the earth works its way up to the levels in the atmosphere from which it is finally lost to interstellar space. Part of this "greenhouse effect" is due to the carbon dioxide, clouds, moisture, dust, and ozone in the atmosphere. Those scientists who say that the rising world temperature observed between 1880 and 1940 was due to the observed increase of carbon dioxide in the atmosphere during that time are emphasizing a change of one part of the "effective emissivity."

A one per cent increase in the "effective emissivity" from say 55% to 56% would lower the mean world temperature by about 1.2° C. or 2.2° F. A one per cent change in carbon dioxide would give a much smaller change.

So far the story is simple and straightforward. Change one of the three factors—solar intensity, reflectivity, and "effective emissivity"—and the mean temperature of the earth changes. However true this may be, most of us are concerned with local temperature, not the annual average for the whole world. In general, the local climatic change is not the same as the average, but differs from it by an amount dictated by the circulation patterns of the atmosphere. These patterns do not change in a simple way as the solar intensity, absorptivity, and "emissivity" change.

We do know that one of the most important relations is that which exists between the *differential* heating of the atmosphere and the circulation pattern. It is not the average temperature of the earth which counts so much as the equator to pole contrast of temperature which determines the circulation pattern of the atmosphere, and thus the local climate change. This is why summer circulation patterns are not like those of winter. Just how the pattern changes is quite complicated, but it is sufficient at this point to say that a change in temperature contrast from equator to poles will generally change the pattern of circulation to a *different* pattern.

In general, changes in sunshine intensity, absorptivity, and "emissivity" will change both the average annual temperature of the earth *and* the circulation pattern because the equator to pole contrast is changed. Changing radiation or circulation patterns may also change the distribution of sea temperatures which in turn further modifies the climate. This gets to be so complicated that for purposes of this discussion we will stick to considerations of the mean annual temperature of the earth.

Now the really sticky question is, "Which of these factors is the more important?" Framed in a different way the question is whether the observed variations of sunshine, absorptivity, and "emissivity" give equal effects. According to J. Murray Mitchell, Jr., the increase in world mean annual temperature from the 1880's to the 1940's was about 0.7° F. From the figures given above one can see that this could be due to an increase in the intensity of the solar radiation reaching the earth of about half a per cent, a decrease of reflectivity of about a quarter of a per cent, or a decrease of "effective emissivity" of about a third of a per cent. None of these factors can be measured with this precision!

This leaves us in the unfortunate position of not being able to resolve the question of relative importance at present. In theory it should be possible to measure the sunlight intensity as it reaches the earth, the reflectivity of the earth, and earth's back-radiation to space from artificial satellites. It is likely that these measurements will soon be made with sufficient accuracy. To establish, however, whether the variations with time are enough to explain climatic fluctuations will probably require decades of observations, which doesn't help us answer the question now.

Still, we might be able to throw some light on some of the questions which have been raised concerning climatic change if we consider whether the observed changes go in the right direction. Let us assume that the number of sunspots varies with the solar heat output. If a small increase in solar heat output means a large increase in sunspots, then perhaps observed increase in sunspots since about 1900 might indicate the presence of a small but unmeasurable increase in solar intensity.

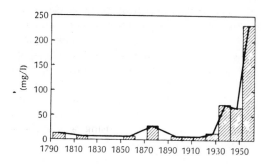

**Fig. 2.** Dust fall trapped in the firn of the glaciers of the high Caucasus according to F. Davitaya. He believes that the rapid increase in recent decades is due to human activity.

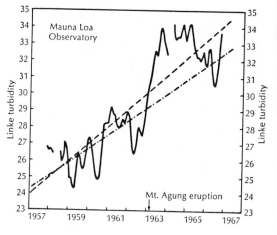

**Fig. 3.** Trend of Linke Turbidity coefficient at Mauna Loa Observatory, Hawaii, with mean annual variation removed. The dotted line represents the line of least-squares best fit to all the data, and the dash-dot line is for the data with the three years following the Mt. Agung eruption omitted. (Compiled by Mr. James Peterson.)

An increase of carbon dioxide in the atmosphere increases the "greenhouse effect" and thus decreases the "effective emissivity." Since carbon dioxide provides only a small part of the "greenhouse effect" an easily measurable change in carbon dioxide content of the atmosphere would be necessary to change the "emissivity" by the required amount. The carbon dioxide content of the atmosphere has increased by about 11 per cent since 1870.

Except for seasonal changes, the reflectivity of the seas and land seems to be quite constant, the largest variations being due to cloud and dust in the atmosphere itself. Whether the cloud cover varies from decade to decade is simply not known—the observational system is inadequate. There is better information on dust in the atmosphere, though it is less than needed. Fortunately, dust gets well mixed in the atmosphere so that measurements at a point are often more representative than those of clouds. Robert A. McCormick and John H. Ludwig, of ESSA, have shown that the turbidity of the air (roughly the "dustiness") increased 57% over Washington, D.C., in about 60 years, and 88% over Davos, Switzerland, in about 30 years.[2] They concluded that while perhaps two-thirds of the Washington increase was local, there was a significant increase in worldwide "dustiness." My own studies suggest a turbidity increase of 30% per decade over the Mauna

Loa Observatory in Hawaii, far from sources of pollution. A turbidity change of 3–4%, averaged over the world, appears to be adequate to change the world mean temperature by 0.7° F. Certainly the observed fluctuations in turbidity are large enough to explain the climatic change. The question is whether it is in the right direction.

J. Murray Mitchell, Jr. has published a diagram which makes it possible to at least see whether the proposed causes of climatic change work in the right direction.[3] Fig. 4. He showed that from the 1880's to the 1940's the mean temperature of the world rose by 0.7° F. as mentioned above. His diagram also shows the increase of sunspots during that time and the increase of carbon dioxide in the atmosphere over the same time. These changes are in the right direction to produce the observed change of world temperature. However, Mitchell's diagram shows that after 1940 the world began to cool off, and by 1960 had cooled about 30% of the previous rise—yet

[2] *Science*, **156**–3780 (9 June 1967), 1358–59.

[3] *Annals N.Y. Academy of Science*, **95** (1961), 248.

the sunspots and carbon dioxide continued to increase. This diverging trend has continued into the 1960's and hints strongly that something other than sunspots and carbon dioxide is more important.

Mitchell suggested in 1961 that this other factor might be dust from volcanic eruptions, such as Mt. Spurr in Alaska in 1953 and Mt. Bezymyannaya, Kamchatka, in 1956, but concluded that the volcanic activity was insufficient to explain the recent cooling. There have been other dusty eruptions since, such as Agung on Bali, which produced easily measurable increases in atmospheric turbidity. I believe that the increasing turbidity of the air due to these volcanic eruptions *plus human activity*, which Mitchell ignored, is now overshadowing the increase of carbon dioxide and sunspots and is now causing a worldwide cooling.

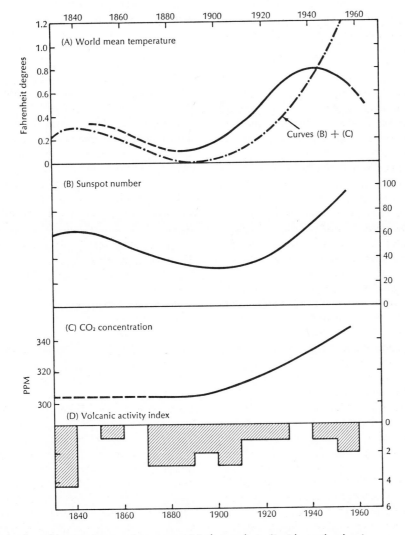

**Fig. 4.** Trends of world mean temperature, sunspot index, carbon dioxide, and volcanic activity. (After Mitchell, 1961.) The curve for temperature has been extended to include data available since Mitchell constructed the diagram.

All other factors being constant, an increase of solar output, which may be indicated by increased sunspot activity, will produce increased world temperature—but recent cooling of the earth while the sunspots increased suggests that other factors were operative.

All other factors being constant, an increase of atmospheric carbon dioxide, by decreasing the ease with which radiant energy leaves the earth's surface, should cause world temperatures to rise—but they have been falling while the carbon dioxide continued to rise. Some other factor must be more important and varying.

All other factors being constant, an increase of atmospheric turbidity ("dustiness") will make the earth cooler by scattering away more incoming sunlight. A decrease of dust should make the earth warmer. Mitchell's diagram shows that volcanic activity, as a source of atmospheric dust, varied in the right direction to produce warming from the 1880's to the 1940's followed by cooling. The continued rapid cooling of the earth since World War II is also in accord with the increased global air pollution associated with industrialization, mechanization, urbanization, and an exploding population, added to a renewal of volcanic activity.

Though changes in solar intensity, earth reflectivity, and "effective emissivity" may each produce climatic change alone, it appears that there is a complex interplay of factors, some dominating at one time, others dominating at other times I believe that increasing global air pollution, through its effect on the reflectivity of the earth, is currently dominant and is responsible for the temperature decline of the past decade or two.

It has been suggested that the increase of carbon dioxide over the past century is due to human activity also—the burning of fossil fuels since the Industrial Revolution. If this were the case then the carbon dioxide increase and the air pollution increase might balance each other in terms of effect on climatic change in the future. However, radiocarbon assays by Hans Suess, of the Scripps Institution of Oceanography, have shown that most of the carbon dioxide increase is not from the burning of fossil fuels, but must come from the modern plant materials, such as the slow oxidation of peat bogs or the slash-and-burn clearing of farm fields would produce.[4] Edward Deevey, Jr., of Yale, believes that peat bogs and soil humus are the source.[5] Perhaps, then, the increased carbon dioxide is the effect of increased temperature rather than its cause.

The atmospheric balances and complexities rival those of politics!

[4] *Tellus.* **9** (Feb., 1957), 18–27.
[5] *Scientific American.* **199**–4 (Oct. 1958), 114–122.

# Global Thermal Pollution

JOHN P. HOLDREN

## INTRODUCTION

Mention of the term "thermal pollution" most commonly calls to mind the local consequences of waste heat from the generation of electrical power. While the warming of rivers, bays, and estuaries by this means is indeed a matter for concern, it is but one aspect of a more fundamental problem. Specifically, *all* human activities—from metabolism to plowing a field to driving (and stopping) an automobile —result in the dissipation of energy as heat. In the case of a power plant, the heat delivered to the environment ultimately includes not just the waste heat at the site but all the useful output as well: the electricity itself is transformed to heat in passing through wires, toasters, air conditioners, lightbulbs, and more complicated paths too numerous to mention. It is to be emphasized that mankind is stuck with this situation; no technological gadgetry or scientific breakthrough will circumvent it. The ultimate degradation to heat of all the energy we use is a consequence of the second law of thermodynamics, to which no exception has ever been observed and none is anticipated.[1]

Little attention has been called to the disposition as heat of man's energy budget because, historically, it has been of no significance. The amount involved on a global scale

[1] The reader who does not wish to tackle a thermodynamics book will find a brief but instructive introduction to the laws of thermodynamics in this context in *Population, Resources, Environment,* Paul R. Ehrlich and Anne H. Ehrlich, W. H. Freeman and Co. (San Francisco, 1970), p. 54.

was and is dwarfed by the major components of the earth's natural energy balance (as discussed below and in the preceding paper by Prof. Bryson). But this may no longer be true a century from now: the unprecedented growth rate of the human population, coupled with an even more rapid increase in per capita consumption of energy, could lead to significant global warming by then if the rates persist. Of course, there is some reason to believe that other factors will put a catastrophic end to the growth of population and energy consumption much sooner, as we discuss elsewhere in this book. And one might argue that there is little utility in worrying about threats a century off in any case.

It is nevertheless instructive to examine the situation now, for a variety of reasons. First, enormously increased use of energy is nearly every technologist's prescription for prosperity in an overpopulated world—energy to wrest raw materials from common rock, to distill fresh water from the oceans, to reconcentrate and reuse dispersed materials now regarded as pollutants. Assuming for a moment that the economic, logistic, and more immediate ecological obstacles confronting such measures can be overcome, it seems only fair to ask what problems may plague the energy-intensive world to which today's decisions commit our descendants. Second, there are still individuals whose childlike faith in science permits no concession to the finite ability of this planet to support people. While other problems of sociological or biological origin threaten to demonstrate the absurdity of this position well before global warming does, the more readily quantifiable ones (e.g., famine) are solvable "in theory,"[2] and those not so easily quantified (e.g., plague, stresses arising from crowding, ecosystem destabilization) are not credible to congenital optimists. Since universal acknowledgment of an ultimate limit on human population and activities should make population control more palatable in some quarters (if we must stop eventually, why not do so while some hope for a decent future remains?), the quantifiable and inevitable restrictions of thermodynamics deserve attention. Finally, the speed with which mankind is approaching so fundamental a global disruption is a sobering lesson in the power of short doubling times.

## THE BASIC ENERGY BALANCE

In simplified terms, the mean temperature of the earth is established by an energy balance between what comes in and what goes out. The principal components of the balance are represented in the equation

$$-\pi R_E^2 S + M = \pi R_E^2 SA + H\pi R_E^2 \varepsilon\sigma T^4 \quad (1)$$

$$\underbrace{\qquad\qquad}_{\text{input}} \quad \underbrace{\qquad\qquad\qquad}_{\text{output}}$$

where the symbols are defined as follows:

$S$ is the *solar constant,* defined as the energy arriving from the sun at the earth per unit of time, per unit of area perpendicular to the flux. $R_E$ is the mean radius of the earth, so $\pi R_E^2$ is the cross-sectional area, and the first term in Equation (1) is therefore the solar energy incident on the earth.

$M$ represents miscellaneous inputs of energy to the earth's surface, including tidal (gravitational) energy from the moon and sun, energy released in chemical and nuclear reactions in the earth's crust, thermal energy from the earth's interior, and energy released by certain activities of man (as discussed in detail below).

$A$ is the *albedo,* or the fraction of incident solar energy directly reflected by the earth (including atmosphere and clouds). Thus the first output term in Equation (1) is just $A$ times the solar input.

$\varepsilon$ is the "effective emissivity" of the earth. The term in Equation (1) in which it appears represents heat radiated away from the earth into space, which, according to the Stefan-Boltzmann law, is given for an ideal radiator ("blackbody") by the fourth power of the temperature times a proportionality constant ($\sigma$), times the area radiating. Since the entire surface of the earth participates, the multiplier is $4\pi R_E^2$. The quantity $\varepsilon$ corrects for the fact that the earth is not a perfect blackbody radiating at the mean surface temperature. In fact, the effective "radiator" for the earth is in the upper atmosphere, and the corresponding temperature is $-24°C$ rather than the $15°C$ mean surface temperature.[3] For present purposes and over a small range of temperature, the vast complexity of the actual global meteorological system is concealed in the use of an "effective emissivity" with the space- and time-averaged surface temperature.

Activities carried on by man and subsumed under the quantity $M$ in Equation (1) are combustion, fission, and fusion. As noted above, the second law of thermodynamics insures that all the energy released in these processes will ultimately be dissipated as heat. Energy which man obtains from the sun in the form of hydroelectric power or direct harnessing of the sun's rays must also be dissipated as heat, but this same transformation would take place without man's intervention as an intermediary, and it is already included in the energy balance. (There may be *local* effects from man's use of hydroelectric and solar power, since man may dissipate the energy in a different place than nature would have done—for example, concentrated in metropolitan areas.) Combustion of fossil fuels does not fall in the same category with hydroelectric and solar power, even though the original energy source was the sun, because man is burning these fuels far faster than

---

[2] But see the first paper in Part One, "Population and Panaceas: A Technological Perspective."

[3] See the discussion in the foregoing paper by Prof. Bryson.

present solar energy is being stored in the same forms.

Finally, it should be noted that energy in transit between the solar input on the left of Equation (1) and the long-wavelength (heat) output on the right serves many purposes and takes on many forms. It drives the winds and ocean currents and the hydrological cycle, and part of it is stored, through photosynthesis, in plants and the rest of the biological food web. The energy emerges from these intermediate categories as heat through the processes of condensation, friction, and metabolism.

## QUANTITATIVE EVALUATION AND MAN'S CONTRIBUTION

The accepted values of the parameters introduced in the basic energy balance equation are

$$S = 0.135 \text{ watts/cm}^2$$
$$A = 0.37$$
$$R_E = 6.37 \times 10^8 \text{ cm}$$
$$\sigma = 5.67 \times 10^{-12} \text{ watts/cm}^2 - {}^\circ K^4$$
$$\varepsilon = .55$$
$$M \approx 27 \times 10^{12} \text{ watts, of which } M_m \approx$$

$5 \times 10^{12}$ watts is man's contribution at the present time.[4]

Use of the figures for $S$ and $R_E$ gives $17.2 \times 10^{16}$ watts for the solar input, which is 6400 times $M$ and 34000 times man's contribution. Obviously, both $M$ and, of course, man's contribution to it are insignificant compared to the solar input in determining global temperature today. Solving Equation (1) for the temperature, we find

$$T = \left[ \frac{(1-A)\pi R_E^2 S + M}{4\pi R_E^2 \varepsilon \sigma} \right]^{1/4} \quad (2)$$

and using the numbers given above yields

$$T = 388 \text{ }^\circ K = 15^\circ C = 59^\circ F$$

[4] $M_m$ was estimated at $4 \times 10^{12}$ watts in 1966 by M. I. Budyko, *Modern Problems of Climatology* (Hydromet. Publishing House, Leningrad).

(as it must, since $\varepsilon$ was defined to give this result!).

We now consider what the future may hold as man increases his contribution to the energy balance. Many meteorologists feel that if man's activities were to add as much as one per cent to the heat naturally radiated by the earth-atmosphere system, serious consequences could occur. Since there is far more complexity in the earth's climatological system than is represented in Equation (2)—or in any set of equations we can yet write down—no one can say exactly what those consequences might be. But it is instructive to determine how fast we may reach the one per cent level of "intervention," and what increase in mean surface temperature would result if Equation (2) were exactly right. The heat now radiated by the earth and atmosphere is $(1 - A) \times$ (solar input), or

$$R \equiv (1 - A) \, 4\pi R_E^2 S = 10.8 \times 10^{16} \text{ watts}$$

which is 21,200 times man's present contribution. Hence man's contribution will reach one per cent of $R$ when it is 212 times larger than today's; this amounts to fewer than 8 doublings ($2^8 = 256$). Worldwide, man's energy production is increasing at between 4 and 5 per cent per year, corresponding to doubling times of 17 and 14 years, respectively. Working out the numbers shows that persistence of this trend would lead to $M_m/R = .01$ in 107 years at the faster rate and 134 years at the slower one.

The corresponding temperature increase is obtained by taking the logarithm of Equation (2) and differentiating. For small changes, that is, for

$$T_2 - T_1 \equiv \Delta T \ll T_1 = 288^\circ K$$

we find

$$\Delta T/T_1 = 0.25 \, M_m/R.$$

Thus, when $M_m/R$ equals .01, we get

$$\Delta T = .025 \, T_1 = .72^\circ K \quad \text{or} \quad 1.3^\circ F.$$

If this number appears innocuous, recall that an increase of only a few degrees could melt the icecaps. Moreover, any such "mean" temperature change will inevitably entail major changes in circulation patterns, especially because the human energy dissipation will be unevenly distributed.

Some observers suggest that a more refined analysis should compare man's energy input with the so-called *radiation balance* at the earth's surface, rather than with the total heat flow to space. (Recall that the energy balance represented by Equation (1) holds for the earth-atmosphere *system*. The actual surface of the planet is not in radiative equilibrium since it absorbs more radiation that it emits. The difference between the radiant energy absorbed and that radiated from the earth's surface is called—somewhat confusingly—the radiation balance. This energy leaves the surface principally by conduction and in connection with the evaporation of water. If one per cent of the *radiation balance* should prove to be the threshold for serious consequences of man's heat input, ninety one years at a five per cent rate of growth in energy use will get us there (the radiation balance is equal to about half of *R*). If one per cent of the radiation balance *over land areas only* is the threshold, sixty seven years will suffice.

These numbers make it clear, as suggested at the outset, that global thermal pollution is hardly our most immediate environmental threat. It could prove to be the most inexorable, however, if we are fortunate enough to evade all the rest. Certainly, long continuation of present trends has the potential for making us uncomfortably warm (if one degree does not trigger disaster, wait for a few more doubling times!).

Of course, our real uncertainty as to the exact time scale and early consequences of the problem must be emphasized. There is, for example, nothing magic in the figure of one per cent used in much of the foregoing discussion—it is simply a round number for a level at which serious effects seem plausible. Time may prove this number too low or too high. Certainly, one cannot be sure from so simple and conservative a model as Equation (2) that energy consumption at, say, half a per cent of *R* will be innocuous globally (yet two prominent and usually more cautious technologists recently made precisely that assertion[5]). There is at least more hope in this situation than in most that the analysis will improve before mankind succeeds in carrying out the experiment.

[5] A. M. Weinberg and R. P. Hammond, *American Scientist*, July–August, 1970, p. 412.

# The Biology of Pesticides

## DONALD KENNEDY AND JOHN HESSEL

On March 18, 1969, Dr. Robert Riseborough of the University of California's Institute of Marine Resources led three colleagues on a short expedition to the Channel Islands

The Biology of Pesticides. From *Cry California,* Vol. 4, No. 3, Summer, 1969, pp. 2–10. Published by California Tomorrow, San Francisco. Reprinted by permission of the authors and the publisher.

off Santa Barbara. The islands they visited were the object of national biological concern at the time: colonies of sea lions and seals, as well as various oceanic birds, were threatened by a huge oil slick accidentally released as a result of offshore drilling operations. Riseborough and his group undoubtedly saw enough oil damage to last them a good while;

but on Anacapa Island, they made an entirely different and even more disturbing discovery. The brown pelican rookery there had about 300 nests that had obviously been constructed this year; but of these, only 12 contained intact eggs. The rest held, or were surrounded with, broken eggs. All of their shells were spongy in texture, and in many places the shell material had flaked away, exposing the membrane below. It was evident that the structural weakness of the shells had led to a massive reproductive disaster.

When a home gardener selects a particular pesticide—or when he chooses *not* to use one—he makes an ecological decision. That decision does not apply to his own land; it is not in the nature of ecological systems to be subdivided by backyards. Instead, that decision, along with thousands made by other such individuals and, of course, the far more momentous ones made by those in agriculture and government, influences the future of the planet-wide web of life to which we all belong. There is a direct and inexorable environmental calculus linking these decisions with the tragedy of the Anacapa pelicans, and with a global tragedy which becomes more pressing each day. It is the purpose of this article to explain why that it so.

## KINDS OF PESTICIDES

We have at our disposal a remarkable arsenal for use against the pests—mostly insects—that threaten our gardens. From the shelves of any garden center, one can select from a highly varied array of preparations that run the chemical gamut from new, synthetic chlorinated hydrocarbons like DDT and chlordane to old-fashioned, natural products like pyrethrum. We may apply them to plants as sprays or dusts, set them out as bait, or put them into the soil as "systemic" poisons to be absorbed by the plant's roots and carried to the leaves, stems and flowers, or buy them combined with fertilizer or herbicides.

Insecticides are of three general types—inorganic, botanical or synthetic organic. Such highly toxic inorganics as the arsenic and fluorine compounds are now seldom used because they are extremely poisonous to man and his pets and they are distressingly persistent in soils. Substances derived from plants (for example, the pyrethrins from chrysanthemums and rotenone from derris) have been widely used in the past, and because of their very low mammalian toxicity are still considered especially desirable for use in "home and garden" sprays and dusts.

Since 1945, synthetic organic insecticides have largely replaced the botanicals and inorganics. Three general types, the chlorinated hydrocarbons, the organophosphates and the carbamates, are available and widely used both in commercial agriculture and in the home garden. The usual shelf assortment contains various chlorinated hydrocarbons—DDT, chlordane, lindane, methoxychlor, heptachlor, toxaphene, dieldrin and aldrin; such organophosphates as malathion, diazinon, meta-systox, and nalad; several carbamates (Carbaryl [Sevin] and vapam, for example); and a few botanicals (nicotine sulphate, pyrethrum, rotenone).

Often several insecticides are packaged together: Ortho Isotox spray, for example, consists of carbaryl, meta-systox, and kelthane—a carbamate, an organophosphate, and a chlorinated hydrocarbon. Insecticides are now also combined with fertilizers as a "two-for-the-price-of-one" bargain for the home gardener. Ortho's Western Crab Grass Control+fertilizer +insecticide combination goes one step further: it allows the lawn-grower to control crabgrass with an herbicide, fertilize his lawn, and apply chlordane to such lawn pests as might be present—all in one application.

Recently it was discovered that 14 years after application, 40 per cent or more of the original amounts of aldrin, endrine, dieldrin, chlordane, toxaphene and DDT were still present in the soil of the original test plots. Although these figures probably represent upper limits for the longevity of chlorinated hydrocarbons, not even the most ardent advocate of these compounds denies that they are extremely persistent. Chlorinated hydrocarbons are today found in virtually all living organisms, and in all places on the earth. Arctic seals, for example, have significant amounts in their fat deposits—so do the Eskimos who eat them. The air we breathe has detectable quantities of chlorinated hydrocarbons—and the total now includes the polychlorobiphenyls, a group of DDT-like compounds released in certain industrial processes.

To ecologists, the quality of persistence is the most important factor differentiating types of pesticides. An organophosphate compound and a chlorinated hydrocarbon, for example, may be equally poisonous to their insect targets when *first* applied. However, the organophosphate compound, although it may severely disrupt the local plant and animal community, will disappear from the environment within a few weeks through biological degradation or weathering. By contrast, fully half of the chlorinated hydrocarbon may still be present ten years after the application. Put in another way, insecticides like malathion or the botanicals are acute poisons, with a relatively immediate action and local effects; the ecologist calls them "soft" insecticides. The "hard" insecticides, because of their persistence, produce long-term as well as immediate effects upon the ecological system, and have influences far from the site of original application.

These terms, of course, refer only to the longevity of the pesticide in the environment, and not to their immediate toxicity. Many of the most persistent chlorinated hydrocarbons are not initially poisonous to man and other vertebrates as the organophosphates. This is not surprising; the first organophosphates were developed in Nazi Germany in the 1930's, in the course of research on antipersonnel nerve gases. The now famous sheep kill near Dugway, Utah, in 1968 was the result of an accident in which an organophosphate nerve gas "escaped" from a test center several miles away.

The immediate actions of pesticides are complex, multiple, and not well understood. Some affect the chemistry of energy production in cells; others influence transmission in the nervous system. They have been selected by considering only their effectiveness in control of the target organism, and although toxicity to man was considered as a negative factor, DDT and its derivatives are accumulating in the fat deposits of people, especially *users* of pesticides, and there is increasing doubt that this is a medically insignificant problem.

## RESISTANCE

Those of us who remember the introduction of DDT aerosol sprays recall their devastating effect on mosquitoes and flies in the household. But within a few years, these formulations lost their effectiveness. This very localized phenomenon paralleled a worldwide one in which DDT control of, for example, malarial mosquitoes became ineffectual in the years following World War II. The development of resistance is actually a predictable response of any insect population we try to control with insecticides. In turn, it has encouraged the chemical companies to escalate the rate of development and introduction of new compounds—simply to substitute for old ones to which the insects have become resistant.

What is the basis of the resistance phenomenon? In essence, it is an example of extreme selection. Suppose that rare individuals in an insect population are able to detoxify or immobilize the pesticide used. In the large and extensive populations characteristic of insects, the probability is high that a few such individuals will occur. Since insects have large numbers of offspring and short generation time, the increase in relative abundance of such a rare variety will be very rapid in the presence of the pesticide.

Moreover, plant-eating insects have contended with chemical warfare for hundreds of million of years before man entered the struggle. It is no accident that such insecticides as pyrethrum and rotenone are produced by plants; they are representative of a variety of compounds evolved by the plants to discourge insect attacks. (In many instances, these substances have been eliminated from cultivated varieties of plants, either purposefully because they are poisonous, bitter, or distasteful to humans, or simply by accident; this, of course, makes man's food crops especially attractive to insects.) Plant-feeding insects have, in their turn, developed mechanisms for coping with a variety of plant poisons, and this versatile set of countermeasures is often applicable to man's current assault with synthetic poisons.

## ECOSYSTEMS

The case of the Anacapa Island pelicans is a dramatic—but entirely typical—instance of the ecological ties that bind the life of this planet into a single system. It is now clear beyond doubt that the reproductive catastrophe of these birds, as well as those affecting the bald eagle, the peregrine falcon, Bermuda petrels, and other species, is a direct consequence of the spread of hard pesticides. Equally inescapable is the conclusion that things will get much, much worse.

What has happened? Like any compound added to the physical environment, a pesticide molecule enters a kind of global chemical economy; if it is long-lived, like the chlorinated hydrocarbons, it may take up semipermanent membership. It moves through the system along various pathways. Much of the DDT sprayed onto foliage or put on the ground washes away and eventually ends up in the soil or in water. Some is absorbed by biological systems—only a small part, ironically, by the tissues of the pests that were its original targets. Some also volatilizes: DDT is now found in air and in rainwater, through which it returns to the land and, ultimately, the sea. All of the world's oceans now contain measurable quantities of DDT and its derivatives; the concentration of these compounds is, furthermore, increasing steadily due to runoff from the land.

What happens when such long-lived compounds attain a widespread distribution in natural waters and are then taken up by living organisms? Their fate is determined by a set of ecological relationships among the organisms inhabiting the environment. These relationships, put in simplest form, involve who eats whom: ecologists often describe the ecosystem as a pyramid. In a small, freshwater pond, for example, various floating, single-celled algae provide the basis for all subsequent commerce. Since they fix the sun's energy in the form of stored chemical reserves through the process of photosynthesis, they are called *primary producers*. Their total mass is greatest, and they form the base of the pyramid. The algae are eaten by small herbivorous crustaceans, which in turn are fed upon by primary carnivores—small fish, for example. These, in their turn, are preyed upon by such secondary carnivores as black bass. The imaginative reader can complete the chain by adding layers of carnivores (example: kingfisher, peregrine falcon). Such straightforward *food chains* are the exception in most complex ecosystems; instead, there is an elaborate network of alternate relationships that is much more aptly described as a *food web*. The total mass of organisms continues to get progressively smaller as one progress toward the highest carnivores in the system. The shape of the pyramid is an inevitable result of the Second Law of Thermodynamics: energy is lost at each step, and the inefficiency of the conversion makes each level a small percentage of the next lower one.

One of the first warnings that the ecosystem is actually a highly efficient machine for the concentration of hard pesticides came from what we might now call the Clear Lake Experiment—though it was hardly conceived as an experiment at the time. Clear Lake is a large, attractively situated body of water in northern California; its shores are dotted with summer homes and small resorts. An annoying plague of gnats in the late 1940's and 1950's led to a decision to treat the lake with DDD, a less toxic relative of DDT. Applications were made in 1949, 1954 and 1957. Within three years of each treatment, the gnats—the intended victims—had reappeared in dismaying numbers. Not so fortunate were the 1,000 pairs of western grebes that formerly bred at the lake; by 1960 *no* young were being produced, though adults continued to visit the lake. Major die-offs occurred during three of the years, and examination of fatty tissues revealed DDD concentrations of 1,600 parts per million in the birds. In passing through several layers of the Clear Lake food chain to the grebes, the compound had become concentrated by a factor of 80,000 over its occurrence in the lake.

The Clear Lake Experiment, one might suppose, could be written off as a once-in-a-lifetime error in judgment. We must have learned something from it; no one would propose such a method of pest control in a lake again. Perhaps not; but it appears that we are trying the Clear Lake Experiment on a much larger, albeit slower scale—with the ocean. Here the pesticide concentrations, which are derived from runoff or at atmospheric fallout, are much lower. But they are ubiquitous; even the Antarctic Ocean has DDT in it. The food chains of the oceans are among the most complex known, and the concentrating power of an ecological system is proportional to the number of steps that make it up. At each one, an organism must harvest large numbers of prey, because metabolism—like other processes in which energy is transformed from one kind into another—is inefficient. Only about ten per cent of the tissue at any one level in the ecosystem is converted into tissue at the next. The rest is lost in the form of heat during the various chemical reactions that comprise metabolism. The pesticide, since it resists these chemical attacks, remains—and is thereby concentrated tenfold. Thus, in a Long Island estuary investigated by biologists at the State University of New York and at Brookhaven National Laboratory, planktonic organisms had 0.04 parts per million (ppm) of DDT and its relatives, small fish that fed directly on them had 0.23 ppm, larger predaceous fish about 2 ppm, and ospreys 13.8 ppm.

Such concentration processes are not restricted to special situations; they have become global effects and now threaten not only the California brown pelican but a number of other bird species as well. Many are birds of prey that feed near coastlines. Peregrine falcons and bald eagles both show high amounts of chlorinated hydrocarbons in their tissues, and both are showing reductions in breeding success. In each case, a perplexing thinness of eggshells, such as that found among the Anacapa Island pelicans, appears to be the direct cause of reproductive failure. Apparently, DDT and related compounds have an indirect effect upon the hormones that control deposition of the shell by the female bird. Though the details of the biochemistry involved are not yet clear, the correlation between the defective shells and the presence of pesticide residues in the birds is too persuasive to ignore.

Still another feature of ecological systems is of special significance for pesticide effects. The organisms that comprise an ecosystem can be defined, in part, by a set of job descriptions; indeed, an ecologist's job in specifying an ecosystem bears many resemblances to the task of an anthropologist in defining the organization of a new culture. Each organism has a "niche," which is approximated by his status in the food chain (primary carnivore, for example) and defined much more specifically by *how* he makes his living. A particular species of aphid, for example, is an herbivore; its niche is further specified by the fact that it feeds by piercing plant cells with a long beak and sucking out the juices, and that it restricts its attention to the tender shoots of roses and their relatives. Collectives of organisms that all have generally similar ways of feeding—sometimes called "guilds"—may share susceptibility to the same kinds of pesticides. Beyond this sort of specificity, however, few pesticides are really selective. Since most of them are general metabolic or nervous poisons, they will affect most insect species, and usually other animals as well.

In different parts of the world, ecosystems differ radically in their richness and complexity. Typically, tropical ecosystems contain very large numbers of species compared to temperate ones: this means that the interrelationships within them form highly complex networks. (It is also true that aquatic food chains are generally longer than terrestrial ones; this is why the ecological concentration of pesticides is more impressive in aquatic situations.) Complexity, in turn, confers stability and balance; tropical animal populations, for example, do not show the violent, boom-and-bust cycles frequently exhibited by such arctic rodents as the lemming. Even the simplest natural ecosystems, however, are complex by comparison with the artificial ones created by man in his agricultural practices. It is partially because they are "monocultures" that crop acreages are so precarious and require so much protection. In dealing with his own simplified ecosystems, man thus finds that it is easy to blunder, and that the consequences of blunders are unexpected and harsh.

An interesting—and tragic—illustration of this situation is provided by the use of Azodrin, a new organophosphate insecticide marketed by Shell Chemical Company for use against cotton pests. In the huge cotton acreages of the San Joaquin Valley in California, farmers have been persuaded to subscribe to regular early-season spraying programs in order to rid their crops of lygus bugs. Ironically, this particular pest—though it can produce impressive-looking infestations—has been shown experimentally *not* to decrease cotton yields. On sprayed fields, however, the bollworm (a later-appearing, *bona fide* pest) often shows unusually high population densities. The spray may kill natural predators of the bollworm; or quite possibly, by killing other, benign insects it opens up new areas for bollworm occupation. For whichever reason, its effect is not the predicted one. The response of Shell's agricultural "advisers" to this result, however, *is* perfectly predictable: "Increase the dosage and spray again."

The user of pesticides frequently encounters a perplexing problem. An initially successful spraying program is followed by seasons in which the pest returns, with even *higher* abundance than before. In many cases, this results from the destruction of insects that prey upon the pest. The unintentional slaughter of the predators releases the pest population from natural control, so that once it develops resistance to the pesticide an unchecked growth, often of spectacular proportions, is possible. Predatory insects are much less able to develop chemical resistance than the plant-feeding species upon which they feed. In part, this is because—being at a higher level in the ecosystem—they have populations that are numerically smaller, and they therefore show a lowered probability of having members with the "rare" genes that confer resistance. In addition, predatory insects, since they do not feed on plants, lack the evolutionary history of dealing with "natural" insecticides that has proved so beneficial to pest species in waging their war with man's agriculture.

## MAN IN THE ECOSYSTEM

The foregoing example illustrates as clearly as anything could the dual role of man in the global ecosystem. He is, obviously, very much a member of it; he is also, by virtue of being so overwhelmingly the dominant species, its custodian. In the closed system we all inhabit, bad decisions are likely to have pervasive and long-lasting effects. At the moment, we are spending our ecological capital at a record rate. The advances in agricultural methods made in recent years may be economically efficient; but they are at the same time ecologically inefficient, trading short-term caloric gains for long-term productivity impairment. One factor forcing us toward such a policy is the pressure of population growth. The specter of starvation is singularly unattractive, and the promoters of agricultural chemicals frequently employ the argument that their use is essential for increased food production to meet growing needs. Ultimately, population control is essential for sound environmental policy.

How can agricultural practices be made less ecologically disastrous? One very real prospect is to alter the ones that are neither economically *nor* ecologically efficient. Of the insecticides put on the land, the majority are not even needed for their advertised purpose. The application of Azodrin to the California cotton crop is an example; so are spraying practices that depend entirely upon a schedule, rather than upon the appearance of insect pests. So, too, are many of the formulations in which the insecticide is included along with some needed component, like fertilizer—riding, as it were, piggyback. Each of these practices doses the environment with huge amounts of unneeded pesticide, whose presence is thus more a tribute to salesmanship than to agricultural need.

Broadcast application methods themselves are a large part of the problem. Only a tiny fraction of the pesticide molecules that load our environment actually reach their intended target; that load could be substantially reduced by the passage of laws banning "scheduled" spraying of hard pesticides as well as all applications by airplane and helicopter. Unfortunately, the agricultural chemicals industry, which has deliberately encouraged such methods in order to increase the sales of their products, has been a formidable defender of its own economic self-interest. The corporations prominently involved—Shell Oil, Standard Oil of California and the like—are among the giants of American industry, and they wield enormous political influence.

A further step in reducing the pesticide level must involve a change in the "level of expectation" of the American consumer. The home gardener demands that every leaf on his rose bush be perfect; the government requires purity of processed foods, to the extent that an entire pack can be condemned if a few insect parts are discovered in it. Some requirements are ecologically unrealistic, and the unreasonable standards we have imposed accounts for a substantial portion of the pesticide load with which we currently stress ourselves and our environment. In actual fact, the chemicals we add to our produce while it is still growing often merely substitute potentially harmful pesticide impurities for harmless insect impurities.

The curtailment of such habits will reduce the problem. It will not be adequate, as long as the hard pesticides continue to be used. Will new technology give us some help? There are a few sources of hope. Biological control methods, such as introducing natural predators, are effective in certain rather special circumstances. The genetic management of cultivated plants so as to produce "natural" resistance has worked in some cases, and is being tried in others. There may be a new generation of soft pesticides based upon very much more specific physiological interventions: for example, several species of coniferous trees and ferns produce compounds that mimic insect hormones crucial for the control of development. Though the possible ecological consequences of their use have not yet been thoroughly investigated, there is promise in the idea that compounds of this sort would have less widespread environmental consequences than the general poisons we now use.

One billion pounds of DDT or its toxic derivatives are now in circulation in our environment. Even if we stopped all use of DDT and its relatives *tomorrow*, one-half billion pounds would still be sharing the environment with us in 1979—and half that much in 1989. Ecological concentration will continue during that period, so that in fact the situation will deteriorate even without new additions. There is something especially disturbing about watching the development of an inevitable disaster—it is like seeing a horror movie for the second time. That is why it seems so incredible to many biologists that we continue to spread onto the earth a *dangerous chemical that will not go away.*

Political decisions come slowly in the United States—though encouragingly, most Western European nations and the Soviet Union have now banned the manufacture and use of DDT. An ultimate international agreement would be an effective device, and a model is readily available. The nuclear test-ban treaty was, in part, motivated by deep concerns about the biological effects of long-lived, dangerous molecules—in that case, radioactive ones. A very similar threat is present now, and a similar mechanism may be needed to alleviate it.

Many gardeners have concluded that they would rather live with some insects than poison their gardens. Others have made only limited use of non-persistent compounds for special purposes. Such decisions have, in the past, been made largely by conservation-minded people who are exercising ecological responsibility.

Now, however, there are potentially more urgent reasons for avoiding pesticide use, and they are medical. Two recently published reports hold serious implications for human health. The first reports that Carbaryl, along with such herbicides as 2,4-D and 2,4,5-T, is capable of causing birth defects and reducing litter size in laboratory animals. This HEW report is careful to point out that the failure of many of the other pesticides tested to show such teratogenic effects may have been due to the small number of litters tested and do not constitute a clean bill of health for the "negative" compounds. Therefore, it certainly seems advisable for pregnant women to avoid contact with all pesticides.

The second report concerns the finding of elevated amount of DDT and its derivatives in autopsy material from persons previously suffering from liver diseases, various cancers, and brain diseases. The quantity of DDT contained in these individuals could be correlated with their own use of it in garden sprays. While as yet the correlation is only strongly suggestive, it surely spells a danger more immediate —though perhaps not more ultimately tragic— than the ecological threat.

# Geologic Jeopardy

### RICHARD H. JAHNS

Not long ago, man was often inclined to reflect with unqualified satisfaction upon his growing record of accomplishment in competing with nature. But as he has continued to reshape the terrain, to modify much of its drainage, to extract useful materials from the subsurface, and to control various elements of his environment on larger and larger scales, it has become less and less clear that so pleasant a view is justified by the record. Today man is being more widely recognized as the kind of schizoid competitor he really is—imaginative, ingenious, resourceful, and remarkably coura-

Geologic Jeopardy. From *Texas Quarterly*, Vol. XI, No. 2, Summer, 1968, pp. 69–83. Reprinted by permission of the author and the publisher.

geous, but with distressing capacities for vastly increasing his own numbers, for enveloping himself with wastes of many kinds, and for making serious mistakes in dealing with his natural surroundings.

As human population has burgeoned and clustered during recent decades, unpleasant confrontations with geologic reality have become more frequent and more challenging. Among the so-called geologic hazards, or risks, those most commonly encountered are related to floods, earthquakes, and various kinds of unstable ground, and as such they are normal and widespread manifestations of natural processes operating upon and within the earth's crust. From time to time some of the risks are translated into disasters, either unavoidably or through the active cooperation of man; the nature, location, and even the magnitude of such disasters often can be predicted well in advance of their occurrence, but the advance dating of these occurrences is another matter. Intervals between successive natural catastrophes of the same kind ordinarily are so great that studies of the geologic and historic records rarely lead to forecasts sharply enough focused to be useful without supplementary information of other kinds.

A brief sampling of well-documented geologic risks and disasters from the state of California may provide some notion of the diversity of problems that have been recognized. By no means does California have a corner on such problems, but its great variety of geologic materials and features, combined with major concentrations of population, establishes it as an excellent testing ground for the basic wisdom of its occupants. And in few other places are large numbers of residents confronted by such stimulating assemblages of natural hazards as those in the Los Angeles and San Francisco regions, where contrasts in topography, climate, and geology are especially prominent.

California's climate is rather pleasant over much of the state for much of the time, yet it is distinguished by episodes and periodic trends whose results are something less than benign. Years of excessive precipitation, swollen streams, and flooded valley floors are no strangers to the record, which for a period of more than two centuries indicates some remarkable variations from the climatic norm. At several localities where long-term average rainfall is about fifteen inches per year, for example, the known range between annual extremes is thirty inches or more. Usually wet years have occurred both singly and in clusters, but they have tended strongly toward concentration in recurring sequences of years separated by sequences during which precipitation has been prevailingly deficient.

Combinations of weather records and tree-ring data have shown that during the past six centuries the median length of dry periods

in much of the state has been approximately fifteen years, and the median length of wet periods approximately twelve years. Most of the cycles have included one or more exceptional years; for instance, a long period of near-average to markedly dry years was interrupted by an extraordinary "wet spell" during the winter of 1861–62 when, according to numerous colorful accounts by contemporary residents and travellers, half the state seemed to be under water for months!

Relatively quiet inundation is not a prime characteristic of the most damaging floods, which generally result from individual great storms or series of storms. Rainfall during some of these storms has been extremely intense, with one spectacular record of 1.02 inches in one minute and several records of more than an inch per hour averaged over 24-hour periods. Such contributions of moisture form torrents that rush down steep mountain slopes and canyons, picking up heavy charges of debris en route, and thence debouch onto adjacent lowland areas where the ground already is saturated or even flooded. Where towns and cities are spread across sloping alluvial fans at the base of mountain fronts, as in the San Gabriel Valley northeast of Los Angeles and the Peninsula area south of San Francisco, damage and destruction by uncontrolled runoff result mainly from accelerated erosion, battering by boulders and other debris, and widespread deposition of coarse-grained detritus. In flatter areas the greatest damage results from inundation and the unwanted delivery of mud and trash.

Until recent decades the measure of loss has increased for successive great floods, chiefly because of increased settlement in the lowland areas. Thus the floods of 1883–84 and 1916 affected crops but few homes in the La Cañada and San Fernando Valleys of southern California, whereas residential damage in these areas was enormous during the New Year's Day Flood of 1934 and the great March Flood of 1938. During the intervening years extensive development of communities across the natural patterns of alluvial-fan drainage had involved modification and even the filling of many channels without adequate provision for future runoff; any implied assumption that excessive volumes of surface water nevermore would put in an appearance was proved tragically incorrect.

Problems of uncontrolled runoff are complicated in many lowland areas by a steadily expanding blanket of pavement, buildings, and other impervious works of man. And as settlement in major cities has reached near-saturation in terms of available flat and gently sloping ground, the adjacent hills and mountains have been invaded by heavy earthmoving equipment for the establishing of additional building sites. Ridges and slopes have been notched and benched, too often with little regard for the nature of the materials removed or newly exposed, and numerous canyon bottoms have been filled to provide more space for homes and other structures. The inevitable result has been less infiltration and more runoff during periods of heavy rainfall. The faces of many new cuts and masses of fill in the hillside areas have been deeply gullied, readily yielding impressive volumes of solid material to the rapidly moving surface waters.

Thus debris flows, generally restricted to the interior desert regions, have become increasingly frequent visitors in the more populous coastal parts of the state. Consisting typically of solid fragments with lesser amounts of water, they range from slurries of mud to coarse fluosolids that contain huge boulders. Most appear as tongue-like masses that are much heavier and move more slowly than ordinary flood runoff, and their effects can be devastating as they clog drainage facilities, fill streets, homes, yards, and swimming pools, and even carry away automobiles, buildings, and other heavy objects. They can be expected whenever large quantities of detachable solid matter are exposed to extremely intense rainfall on relatively steep slopes, and their size and coarseness are governed principally by the amounts and nature of available debris. Thus the bouldery slurries that moved across the La Cañada Valley on January 1, 1934, can be attributed mainly to cloudburst rainfall on adjacent precipitous mountainsides from which a protective cover of vegetation had been burned away by a major forest fire during the previous fall season.

Fortunately, the problem of recurring floods has long been recognized in California, and during recent decades its complex shape has become increasingly understood through vigorous study by several state, county, and local agencies. If it is only practical to acknowledge that cities will remain where they are, and that they will expand in certain predictable directions regardless of flood hazard, then the approach to more peaceful coexistence with this element of nature must lie in more effective flood control. Already in service toward this end are numerous installations that include water regulating and conserving dams in major canyons, debris dams and basins near mountain fronts, flood-control basins and water-spreading grounds in valley areas, and a host of improvements along both natural and man-made channels of valley drainage.

Despite the considerable progress to date, geologists and engineers are painfully aware that many additional facilities are urgently needed, that it is all but impossible to keep pace with requirements for the protection of many rapidly growing communities, and that it is not economic to design any facility for the greatest flood that reasonably can be expected in the future. And finally comes the sobering thought that the tremendous growth in population and hillside development since World War II has corresponded to one of California's rainfall-deficient periods; the coming decade, in contrast, is likely to represent an opposite swing in the cyclic pattern known to have characterized past centuries of precipitation.

## FAULT MOVEMENTS AND GROUND SHAKING

From California's subsurface come those recurring violent actions known as earthquakes, several of which have dealt rather harshly with man and his works during the period of historic record. These shocks have originated along faults, or breaks in the earth's crust that represent repeated slippage over very long spans of time. Thousands of faults are known within the state, and many of them can be classed as large in terms of their total displacements. Many of them also are geologically active in the sense of having moved within the past 10,000 years, and more than a few have been active in historic time.

The release of energy in the form of a large earthquake can be assumed to begin with sudden fault movement initiated at some depth in the earth's crust, and to continue as this slippage is rapidly propagated in all directions along the fault. Under appropriate conditions, the displacement may reach the earth's surface and appear as horizontal, vertical, or oblique offsets along the trace of the fault. Such surface faulting also may accompany a relatively small earthquake if the focus, or point of original rupture, is sufficiently shallow.

During the San Francisco earthquake of 1906, predominantly horizontal surface displacement occurred along perhaps as much as 270 miles of the San Andreas fault, California's widely known master break. Maximum observed offset of reference features such as roads and fences was nearly twenty feet. Displacements of similar magnitude may well have occurred farther south along the same fault during the great Fort Tejon earthquake of 1857. Among earthquakes originating in California and nearby parts of Nevada during the past century, at least twenty are known to have been attended by measurable surface faulting. The largest offsets observed in relatively recent years were nineteen feet (horizontal) with the Imperial Valley earthquake of 1940, and twelve feet (horizontal component) and fourteen feet (vertical component) with the Fairview Peak, Nevada, earthquake of 1954.

Although surface rupture is neither common nor widespread over periods of human generations, there is obvious risk in erecting homes or other structures athwart the most recent traces of past movements along active faults. Yet this is precisely what has been done, especially along the San Andreas fault south-ward from San Francisco and along the San Andreas and San Jacinto faults in the San Bernardino area of southern California. Moreover, this kind of "gamble-in-residence" is being taken more and more often, and in areas where the positions of active faults are well known; it is particularly distressing to note the number of schools represented among installations that some day might serve as reference features for large-scale shear. The gamble might seem safe enough in terms of the odds against losing, but any loss in this ill-advised game could be a major disaster. Fortunately, the nature of such risk is being increasingly noted and appraised for aqueducts, dams, and other special engineering works, if not for housing developments.

A more immediate threat to some installations that extend across fault traces is the slow creep, or progressive slippage in the apparent absence of earthquakes, that is being recognized as currently characteristic of several major breaks in California. These include the Hayward fault on the east side of San Francisco Bay, the Calaveras fault in the vicinity of Hollister, and parts of the San Andreas fault for a distance of about two hundred miles southeastward from San Francisco. Tunnels, railroad tracks, roads, fences, culverts, and buildings are being deformed and displaced where they straddle the narrow strands of creep, with cumulative offsets generally measured in inches over periods of years or decades. At the Almaden-Cienega winery southeast of Hollister, horizontal slippage along the San Andreas fault averages more than half an inch per year; the main building, which evidently lies astride the active fault trace, has been aptly described as experiencng "obvious structural distress."

Returning now to large earthquakes, it should be emphasized that by far their most widespread effects upon man are results of severe ground shaking that accompanies the sudden rupturing along faults. For a given amount of energy released, the severity of shaking can vary greatly from one locality to another according to the interplay of many factors. Perhaps most important among these is the nature of the rocks or other foundation materials at the site in question, as demonstrated by marked variations in the distribution of damage from individual historic shocks. In general, shaking is least intense in hard, firm rocks like granite and gneiss, and most intense where the energy is coupled into relatively soft and loose materials like alluvial silts, sands, and gravels, swamp and lake deposits, and hydraulic fill. The oft-used analogy of a block of jello on a vibrating platter is grossly simplified but nonetheless reasonable, and assuredly a structure that in effect is built upon the jello must be designed to accommodate greater dynamic stresses if it is to survive the shaking as effectively as a comparable structure built upon the platter.

This focuses principally upon California's metropolitan areas, large parts of which are underlain by relatively soft and poorly consolidated materials, and it further points up the need for prudent design of buildings to be erected on reclaimed marsh land or filled portions of lakes and bays. Much of value has been learned during recent decades in the important field of earthquake-resistant design for structures, and a great deal of this knowledge has been wisely applied in actual construction. Unhappily, however, it rarely is possible to offer more than broad generalizations concerning the nature of ground motion to be expected beneath these structures during future earthquakes. Relations between the release of energy at its source and the attendant ground response at a given surface locality are incompletely understood, and pertinent empirical data are still sketchy at best; thus the engineer with capability for earthquake-resistant design cannot be readily supplied with precise design criteria.

A considerable sum of recorded observations indicates that strong shaking during past California earthquakes has found expression in many different ways. In addition to its widely known effects upon man-made features, it has led to cracking, fissuring, warping, lurching, and local elevation or depression of the ground, to triggering of slumps, landslides, avalanches, and debris flows, to shifting of surface drainage and groundwater circulation, and to broad-scale sloshing of lakes and other water bodies. Various combinations of these and other abrupt changes in the normal scene doubtless will accompany future earthquakes that are certain to occur; indeed, the notion that the state is now "overdue" for another great earthquake is not without some foundation.

## UNSTABLE GROUND

All but a very few California residents have been spared the kinds of violent ground settlement and collapse that have plagued several mining districts and limestone sinkhole areas elsewhere in the United States, yet they have had numerous disagreeable experiences with unstable ground. For example, prolonged extraction of water, oil, and gas from the subsurface has prompted gradual surface subsidence in many valley and basin areas, the changes in level ranging from fractions of an inch to tens of feet. Irrigation in some arid parts of the state also has caused differential subsidence through marked compaction of susceptible near-surface materials, in places on a spectacular scale. Though rarely so sudden or so localized as to endanger human life, such kinds of ground behavior impose serious problems in the maintenance and repair of roads, canals, levees, wells, buildings, and other engineering works, especially in the more populous areas.

Hitting closer to home are the small-scale ups and downs of residential and commercial buildings founded upon so-called expansive soils. These widespread surficial materials, which generally are rich in clay minerals, expand and contract in response to changes in their moisture content, and the attendant effects on thousands of buildings with inappropriately designed foundations have ranged from minor cracks and the nuisance of doors and windows that do not function properly to severe structural damage.

Lateral stability is an added factor of importance on slopes underlain by expansive soils, weathered bedrock, or other relatively soft and weak materials that tend to migrate slowly downhill in response to gravity. Aprons, tongues, and thin but extensive mantles of "creep debris," derived from such source materials at points higher on the slopes, are responsible for the attractively smooth appearance of many California hills. Some of these accumulations have become essentially static, and others continue to move at rates that are insignificant relative to the useful life of a typical building. All, however, are capable of renewed or markedly quickened movements, as countless home owners have sorrowfully discovered over periods as short as a few hours or as long as several years.

Damaging and destructive travel of surficial debris that at best was in an earlier state of tentative equilibrium has been triggered by single or variously combined actions of man, of nature, or of both in operational concert. Typical among these unwise or unavoidable actions have been earthquakes, heavy rains, excavation of downslope supporting materials, and the loading of slopes with structures or masses of fill. More than a few purchasers of new homes in several of the state's hillside areas have made a particularly unpalatable discovery—the imposed weight of a single home can be more than enough to send the immediately underlying materials on their way.

By far the most spectacular expressions of slope failure in California are landslides that involve large masses of bedrock. Although specific conditions vary from one occurrence to another, all these slides reflect an unfavorable relationship between geometry of slope and effective strength of the underlying ground. On this score, the most troublesome rocks in relatively populous areas are fine-grained sedimentary types, generally of late Mesozoic or Tertiary age, in which slippage readily occurs along surfaces of stratification. Rocks of this kind crop out extensively in the region between San Francisco and San Diego, where fifty million people may reside within another generation or so. Rocks of many additional kinds also can be liable to

sliding if they are soft or are weakened by the presence of numerous structural discontinuities such* as bedding and foliation surfaces, fractures, and faults.

Geologic evidence indicates that landslide movements have occurred, either in single or repeated episodes, at thousands of localities within the state. Some of the known slides have been inactive for as long as several hundred thousand years. A great many more are considerably younger, and scores of them have been in motion during the present century. Late Pleistocene times, dating back from about 10,000 years ago, were specially characterized by vigorous and widespread landsliding in California, and many of the topographic benches that mark sites of such ancient ground failure are occupied today by residential structures ranging from shacks to mansions. It is fortunate indeed that relatively few of these landslides have been reactivated during the past few millennia, but if great moistness of California's climate during parts of the Pleistocene epoch was a principal cause of the ground slippage, those people who currently reside upon the old slide masses should have a more than casual interest in the amounts of water entering their respective properties in the future.

The hand of man, ironically enough, is commonly responsible for improving the predictability of major ground failure, whether or not landsliding has occurred in the past at the locality in question. Thus, ill-considered modification of the terrain for homesites in an urban area can prompt a confident forecast of serious landsliding to occur within weeks or months, and certainly before the mortgages are paid on the to-be-affected homes. Repeatedly emphasized by past disasters over a wide range of scales is the basic lesson that many natural hillsides are in a state of gross equilibrium, but only by the tiniest of margins. And so—a small cut near the toe of an old slide mass can trigger renewed movement that destroys property on hills near Santa Cruz or Malibu Beach, cutting from below and introduction of water from above can contribute to large-scale failure on steep slopes in the Berkeley Hills or the Pacific Palisades area, and various combinations of cutting, loading, water saturation, and perhaps other factors may be responsible for damaging slippage in San Diego, San Jose, Ventura, or San Francisco. A dismal host of additional examples could be cited.

The landslide syndrome is not always fully understood, especially for those occurrences in which the presence of extraordinary amounts of subsurface water cannot be readily accounted for. Yet it is quite improper to conclude, as many citizens and even a few geologists have suggested, that the study of potential ground failure is all art and no science, and that "little or nothing really can be done." Indeed, soundness of the contrary view already has been demonstrated by the City of Los Angeles and several of the state's most populous counties.

Through the Grading Ordinance of 1952, the first regulatory measure of its kind, Los Angeles set forth specific requirements for the development of hillside areas within the city; input of geologic data and interpretations was included among these requirements for certain kinds of terrain. During the first fifteen years since adoption of this pioneering ordinance, more than fifty thousand hillside sites were graded according to its provisions. Within that same period of time, approximately thirty-five homes were totally destroyed through landsliding, but more than half of these either were built prior to 1952 or were built at sites graded prior to 1952. According to a special investigating committee of the American Institute of Professional Geologists, review of the record indicates that "Without question, efforts made by the City of Los Angeles to protect its citizens from geologically-related disasters have yielded highly worthwhile results. Their total benefits cannot be fully assessed, however, as the basic aim has been preventive and as there is no satisfactory means for determining how many occurrences of ground failure have been forestalled in the face of the rapidly increasing development of hillside terrain during recent years. The number of these averted disasters probably is very large."

It seems obvious that man cannot take for granted the ground he occupies, and that responsibility for troubles stemming from a careless attitude cannot be easily fixed upon someone else, legally or otherwise. Nor can a defeatest attitude survive under the growing pressure of population increase, with corollary expansion of settlement into areas where questions of ground stability must be faced and answered. Here some real progress already has been made, especially in the San Francisco and Los Angeles regions, as more geologists, engineers, land developers, and public officials appear to be asking themselves:

> Will posterity participate
> In chaos we create,
> Or will our heirs commemorate
> Mistakes we didn't make?

Granting man's limitations in controlling certain important elements of his geologic environment, in California and elsewhere, at least he is learning that when he imposes improperly upon nature, nature is likely to respond by imposing more seriously upon him. He has been modifying his approach by seeking better to understand natural processes and more effectively to apply this understanding in the primary struggle, which really lies more with himself than with nature. Nature now can be identified less as the antagonist than as the arena in which ever-increasing numbers of people are competing with one another for food, for air and water, for energy, and for space—there is no other readily available arena, hence this one needs a bit more respect and care.

Toward environmental understanding and improvement, geological scientists and engineers are vigorously investigating many kinds of so-called natural hazards. Active and potentially active faults are now being precisely mapped over large areas, and their respective styles of behavior during the geologic past are being deciphered via a remarkable variety of approaches. New data on creep along faults, the accumulating strain in ground adjacent to faults, and the behavior of the ground during recent earthquakes are revealing some instructive and unexpected relationships. Engineering seismology has fully emerged as a highly significant field of study, with major efforts now being devoted to determining the response of bedrock terranes and surficial deposits to earthquake shaking, the behavior of buildings and other structures during earthquakes, and the most satisfactory types of seismic design for many kinds of structures.

Prediction of earthquakes no longer seems to be an objective for some future century; indeed, at least one important break-through in this area can be expected within the coming decade. Soon perhaps we shall have warning of a few minutes to as much as an hour in advance of strong shocks along two or three of this country's most prominent active faults, a contribution of incalculable value to people if not to their property. In the meantime, increasing coordination of empirical and basic data and of observation, experiment, and theoretical analysis can be expected further to improve our dealings with floods, landslides, ground subsidence, and other kinds of natural hazards. May we look forward to the days when all kinds of ground failure can be forestalled or reduced in impact, when existing landslides can be made safe for useful development, when our buildings and utilities can survive the severest earthquake, and when sound programs for disaster insurance can be predicted upon knowledge not yet available.

The human side of these dealings is even more complex than the problems posed by nature. The general public and numerous stewards at all levels of government have been rapidly awakening to the existence and scope of geologic jeopardy in its numerous forms, with reactions ranging from apathy to panic but tending properly to consolidate into deep concern. The growing record of damage and death, especially in some thickly populated areas, has become so compelling that direct responses are now extending beyond temporary reactions to individual disasters. Homeowners and public officials, scientists and engineers, universities and utilities, conservation groups and industrial organizations, government agencies and legislatures, and increasingly large numbers of individual citizens are discovering that they have a common stake in learning how better to live with their physical environment, regardless of their other interests. As more and more of them come to recognize the game we all have been playing in nature's arena for so many centuries, more and more of them will want to know what the score is. Geoscientists and engineers must be continuingly ready with the answer, however constrained or unpalatable it might be at any given place or time.

## FOR A START ON FURTHER READING

Allen, C. R., Housner, G. W., and others, 1967, Earthquake and geologic hazards in California, Report of Geologic Hazards Advisory Committees, Resources Agency of California.

Bailey, E. H. (editor), 1966, Geology of Northern California: California Division of Mines and Geology, Bulletin 190.

Iacopi, Robert, 1964, Earthquake country, Lane Magazine and Book Company, Menlo Park, California.

Jahns, R. H. (editor), 1954, Geology of Southern California: California Division of Mines and Geology, Bulletin 170.

Lung, Richard, and Proctor, Richard (editors), 1966, Engineering geology in Southern California, Association of Engineering Geologists, Los Angeles Section, Special Publication, Glendale, California.

Richter, C. F., 1958, Elementary seismology, W. H. Freeman and Company, San Francisco, California.

# Low Dose Radiation
# and Cancer

JOHN W. GOFMAN AND ARTHUR R. TAMPLIN

**Summary.** Contrary to a widespread notion that only leukemia plus certain rare cancers are radiation-induced in man, the evidence now points strongly to the induction of all forms of human cancer plus leukemia by ionizing radiation.

These data amply justify the following three general laws of radiation-induction of cancer in man.

**Law I.** "All forms of cancer, in all probability, can be increased by ionizing radiation, and the *correct* way to describe the phenomenon is either in terms of the dose required to double the spontaneous incidence rate of each cancer or, alternatively, as the increase in incidence rate of such cancers per Rad of exposure."

**Law II.** "All forms of cancer show closely similar doubling doses and closely similar increases in incidence rate per Rad."

**Law III.** "Youthful subjects require less radiation to increase the incidence rate by a specified fraction than do adults."

The currently allowable radiation dose (Federal Radiation Council Guidelines) of 0.17 Rads per year to the population-at-large from peaceful development of atomic energy would, *if* everyone received this dose, lead to a minimum estimate of 16,000 additional cancer plus leukemia cases annually in the USA. The only hope for a lower risk is either (a) existence of a threshold or (b) protection by protraction over time of the radiation damage.

Since neither protraction nor threshold can be counted on, the only reasonable procedure is to revise the Federal Radiation Council guidelines downward by at least a factor of 10, to a dose of less than 0.017 Rads per year for the allowable population exposure to ionizing radiation.

The most crucial pressing problem facing everyone concerned with any and all burgeoning atomic energy activities is to secure the earliest possible revision *downward,* by at *least a factor of tenfold,* of the allowable radiation dosage to the population from peaceful atomic energy activities. The Federal Radiation Council allowable dose of whole body ionizing radiation is 0.17 Rads per year. Evidence is presented here that leads us to recommend that this be reduced *now* to 0.017 Rads or even less. And we shall also estimate the disastrous consequences to the health of the public if this recommendation receives less than immediate, serious attention.

## THE FEDERAL RADIATION
## COUNCIL GUIDELINES

There has been ample reason for skepticism concerning the FRC guides for many years.[1] In essence, this is the case because a

Low Dose Radiation and Cancer. From *IEEE Transactions on Nuclear Science*, Vol. NS-17, No. 1, February 1970, pp. 1–9. Reprinted by permission of the authors and the publisher.

valid scientific justification for the allowable dose of 0.17 Rads of total body exposure to ionizing radiation has never been presented. The general, vague statement is usually repeated that the risk to the population so exposed is *believed* to be small compared with the benefits to be derived from the orderly development of atomic energy for peaceful purposes.

Dr. Brian MacMahon, Professor of Epidemiology at Harvard, writing as recently as early 1969, stated,

"While a great deal more is known now than was known 20 years ago, it must be admitted that we still do not have most of the data that would be required for an informed judgment on the maximum limits of exposure advisable for individuals or populations."[2]

This is vastly different from the bland reassurances of the Federal Radiation Council Guidelines. We find ourselves in general agreement with Professor MacMahon, except that we go further and feel the already-documented evidence amply justifies a drastic revision *downwards*—and now.[3, 4]

There is an even more hazardous situation associated with the vagueness of the justification for FRC Guidelines. This hazard has become apparent to us through extensive contact with people in radiation surveillance work in the atomic energy industry, and in atomic energy laboratories. Widely prevalent is the notion that the existing standards have a wide margin of safety built in. Many such individuals refuse to believe that any responsible body would even set a guideline dosage into the Federal Statutes without a wide margin of safety.

How is it possible that our current Federal Radiation Council Guidelines may have falsely lulled us into complacency? Let us trace the evidence, and restrict our considerations to two major effects of radiation upon humans; namely, cancer and leukemia—in this generation—that is, effects upon those humans actually receiving the radiation. *Any conclusion* we draw concerning the hazard of the current radiation guidelines can only be amplified and buttressed by consideration of the additional burden of human misery associated with genet-

ic defects, fetal deaths, and neo-natal deaths.[3] The case against perpetuation of the existing FRC Guidelines is overwhelmingly strong just on the basis of the cancer-leukemia risk, without even considering the potentially much larger problem of effects upon future generations.

## HOW DID
## THE COMPLACENCY ARISE?

First of all, there once existed a very great paucity of data concerning the dose versus effect relationship between radiation and cancer or leukemia induction in man. Steadily, however, during these past 20 years, parts of the story have come to light from a combination of several extremely important sources:

(a) Study of survivors of Hiroshima-Nagasaki by the Atomic Bomb Casualty Commission.

(b) Study of patients *treated* with radiation for non-malignant diseases earlier in life and then developing cancer or leukemia.

(c) Study of children who commonly received irradiation to the neck area in one unfortunate era of American Medicine.

(d) Study of the occurrence of lung cancer in uranium miners in the USA.

(e) Study of cancer and leukemia in children whose mothers had received irradiation (diagnostic) during pregnancy.

As the early results started to come forth from the Atomic Bomb Casualty Commission, it was noted that *leukemia* might be appearing more frequently in those persons irradiated in Hiroshima and Nagasaki. Attention became centered upon leukemia as a sort of "special" response to ionizing radiation and not much thought was given to other forms of cancer. From the ABCC studies[5] and from wholly independent observations,[2] it is now clear, and we believe no one disputes the estimate that, at least for total doses of 100 Rads or more, the leukemia risk may be expressed as follows: 1 to 2 cases of leukemia per $10^6$ exposed persons, where each of them has received 1

Rad of total body exposure. This does not require 1 Rad per year; rather, we are talking about the above rate of disease occurrence with a total integrated exposure of 1 Rad. Furthermore, this incidence of 1 to 2 cases per $10^6$ people per year persists for many years, once the latency period* is over, ultimately declining somewhat, at least for chronic leukemia.[5]

An incidence rate of 1 or 2 cases per million people per year *sounds* like a small number, especially when this number is viewed in isolation. Indeed, many have hastened to add that spontaneously, without any man-made radiation, leukemia occurs with a frequency of 60 cases per million per year, which makes it a relatively rare disease. So, 1 or 2 cases per year sounds small by itself, and sounds even smaller viewed against a spontaneous rate of 60 per million persons per year. And, as a result, with the *early* atomic bomb survivor data *only* showing leukemia, a widespread complacency set in concerning long-term effects of ionizing radiation, a complacency extending to high circles.

For two very major reasons, this error in thinking has *turned out to be a mistake of the first order of magnitude*.

1. Leukemia happens to show a shorter latency period than most other forms of cancer. Therefore, the reason it appeared *early* to be the *only* malignancy in the Hiroshima-Nagasaki survivors was simply that not enough time had elapsed for other cancers to become manifest.

2. The *proper* way to look at the incidence rate of 1–2 per $10^6$ persons per year from radiation and the 60 per $10^6$ persons per year spontaneously is *not* in isolation from each other, *but in relation* to each other. Thus, viewed in this light, 1 Rad of ionizing radiation *increases* the leukemia incidence between 1.6 and 3.3%. Or, we can state that the doubling dose for leukemia (namely, that amount of radiation which will double the spontaneous

*It is a known fact, from many observations, that leukemia or cancer is *not* an immediate response to radiation. There is a period of years (different for different forms of cancer) *before* the clinical disease is manifest. This period is called the latency period.

rate) is between 30 and 60 Rads. (Doubling a spontaneous rate of 60 cases per million each year means producing an additional 60 cases per million per year.)

## WHAT ABOUT
## OTHER FORMS OF CANCER?

It now becomes an issue of paramount importance to know whether other forms of cancer behave similarly in response to ionizing radiation. *Are* other forms of cancer describable by a fractional increase in occurrence rate per Rad, and if so, how do the fractions compare with those for leukemia? We need no longer speculate about such matters because *hard, incontrovertible data* are available for human cancers induced by radiation. These data represent *facts, not opinions*. Estimates are available for several forms of cancer from worldwide data, US data, and from the studies by the Atomic Bomb Casualty Commission of survivors of Hiroshima and Nagasaki. Let us consider a variety of forms of human cancers.

**(a) Thyroid Cancer.** The Japanese data, primarily based upon adults, show an approximate doubling dose of 100 Rads for development of thyroid cancer, or approximately a 1% increase in incidence rate of thyroid cancer in the population per Rad of exposure of the population.[5]

We can arrive at the risk for younger people in the USA from two items of data. (a) Pochin gives the figure of 1 case of thyroid cancer per $10^6$ persons per Rad.[6] (b) Carroll et al reported that the spontaneous incidence rate for thyroid cancer is ~5–10 cases per $10^6$ persons per year in the age range of 10–20 years.[7]

Combining these two items of information, it is estimated that between 5 and 10 Rads is the doubling dose for thyroid cancer in young people in the US. This means a 10 to 20% increase in risk of thyroid cancer in the youthful population per year per Rad of exposure. Thus, considering the youthful group (USA) and the adults (Japan), the range is between 1% and 20% increase in thyroid cancer per year per Rad of exposure.

**(b) Lung Cancer.** Estimates are available from several sources for radiation-induction of lung cancer. The ABCC studies in Japan indicate an approximate doubling of lung cancer incidence rate for 100 Rads of exposure, or a 1% increase in risk of lung cancer in the population for an exposure of 1 Rad.[5] The experiences of the uranium miners in the USA are complicated by two factors: (a) the dosimetry is poorly known, and (b) many of the workers are still in the latency period.[8] What estimates have been made for the uranium miners suggest the doubling dose for lung cancer to be between 250 and 500 Rads. If the correction for latency is estimated as twofold, the final estimate would be 125–250 Rads as the doubling dose.[8]

Miller has questioned the Japanese data because of non-specificity of the histology of the cancer cells.[9] On the other hand, the similarity of the ratio of lung cancer to leukemia in the Japanese as compared to the British patients studied by Court-Brown and Doll suggests the Japanese data to be quite reasonable.[10] As a compromise estimate, we shall average the Japanese and USA data to obtain 175 Rads as the estimate for the doubling dose for lung cancer, or a 0.6% increase in the annual incidence rate of lung cancer in the population per Rad of exposure.

**(c) Breast Cancer.** Breast cancer has been found to be radiation-induced in the Japanese studies.[5] The estimated doubling dose is approximately 100 Rads for breast cancer, or, again, a 1% increase in incidence rate per year of breast cancer in the population per Rad of exposure.

**(d) Other Forms of Cancer.** From some important studies on humans receiving therapeutic radiation for the arthritis-like disorder known as rheumatoid spondylitis, Court-Brown and Doll[10] have studied the subsequent occurrence of many forms of cancer in organs heavily exposed, *incidental* to irradiation of the primary disease in the spine. We don't know that all the heavily exposed regions received equivalent doses, but it appears reasonable to estimate that the *various* heavily exposed regions were within a factor of 2 on either side

of the median value for the group. If we use Court-Brown and Doll's value for bronchiogenic cancer of the lung as a reference value, (and for this form of cancer we have used 175 Rads above as an estimated doubling dose), we can then estimate the doubling dose for radiation for several additional cancers. Uncertainty of precise dose comparisons makes these numbers uncertain by a factor of two or thereabouts either on the low or high side. We shall, therefore, not only show the estimated doubling doses for all these additional cancers, but also a range to take this dose uncertainty into consideration. Table 1 shows the results for these additional cancers.

Now we are in a position to summarize the radiation-induced cancers for all sites, utilizing *all* the data available. The summary is presented in Table 2. For such an array of widely divergent organ systems, *already including* hard data for nearly all the forms of human cancers, it is amazing indeed that there is such a small range for the estimated doubling dose. Correspondingly, there is a very small range in the estimated increase in incidence rate per Rad for these widely differing organ sites in which cancers arise.

The only number that is different, and *that one* indicates an *even higher* susceptibility to radiation-induction of cancer, is for thyroid cancer induction in youthful persons (under 20 years of age). As we shall see below, this is *not* at all surprising or inconsistent, for the data presented below suggest a very high sensitivity of embryos-in-utero to irradiation, causing subsequent leukemia and cancer during early childhood.

Furthermore, in some of these studies, aside from leukemia, the persons at risk were most probably still in the latency period when studied, so that full expression of the disease has not yet been reached. This would mean that an *even smaller* radiation dose is required to double the incidence rate, or expressed otherwise, the percent increase in incidence rate per Rad of exposure is even higher than that tabulated above. We know, from extensive other data, that bone cancer and skin cancer have definitely been produced by radiation. With further observation and study, the

**TABLE 1**

| Site of Cancer | Doubling Dose (Rads) | | Increase in Incidence Rate per Rad | |
|---|---|---|---|---|
| | Mean | Range | Mean | Range |
| Pharnyx | 40 Rads | (20–80) | 2.5% | (1.2–5.0) |
| Stomach | 230 Rads | (115–460) | 0.4% | (0.2–0.8) |
| Pancreas | 125 Rads | (60–250) | 0.8% | (0.4–1.6) |
| Bone* | 40 Rads | (20–80) | 2.5% | (1.2–5.0) |
| Lymphatic plus other hematopoeitic organs | 70 Rads | (35–140) | 1.4% | (0.7–2.8) |
| Carcinomatosis of miscellaneous origin | 60 Rads | (30–120) | 1.7% | (0.9–3.4) |

(* Bone may possibly have received higher irradiation dose than other sites. If this were true, the estimated doubling dose is too low for bone.)

**TABLE 2**

Best estimates of doubling dose of radiation for human cancers and the increase in incidence rate per Rad of exposure.

| Organ Site | Doubling Dose | % Increase in Incidence Rate per Rad |
|---|---|---|
| Leukemia | 30–60 Rads | 1.6 – 3.3% |
| Thyroid Cancer | | |
| (adults) | 100 Rads | 1% |
| (young persons) | (5–10 Rads) | (10–20%) |
| Lung Cancer | ∼ 175 Rads | 0.6% |
| Breast Cancer | ∼ 100 Rads | 1% |
| Stomach Cancer | ∼ 230 Rads | 0.4% |
| Pancreas Cancer | ∼ 125 Rads | 0.8% |
| Bone Cancer | ∼ 40 Rads | 2.5% |
| Lymphatic plus other hematopoeitic organs | ∼ 70 Rads | 1.4% |
| Carcinomatosis of miscellaneous origin | ∼ 60 Rads | 1.7% |

ABCC data will provide firm estimates of the doubling dose for the induction of cancer by radiation at the *few* remaining other major organ sites. At present the *only* malignant disease reputedly *not* induced by radiation is chronic lymphatic leukemia. And even this may be in doubt since malignant lymphoma, a highly related cancerous disorder, is radiation-induced, both from the data of Court-Brown and Doll[10] and from Japanese data.[11]

## IN-UTERO RADIATION AND SUBSEQUENT DEVELOPMENT OF CHILDHOOD LEUKEMIA AND CANCER

Stewart and co-workers originally[12] and MacMahon[13, 14] and Stewart and Kneale[15] re-

cently have presented evidence that implicates in-utero radiation of embryos (carried out for *diagnostic* purposes in the mother) with the development of subsequent leukemia plus other cancers in the first ten years of life of the child. The general estimate of the amount of radiation delivered in such diagnostic procedures is 2 to 3 Rads to the developing fetus. From the Stewart and Kneale data, we have, for the following forms of cancer, the estimates of the increase in numbers of cancers for several organ sites:

| Type of Cancer | Radiation Induced Increase | | |
|---|---|---|---|
| Leukemia | 50% over spontaneous incidence | | |
| Lymphosarcoma | 50% | " | " |
| Cerebral Tumors | 50% | " | " |
| Neuroblastoma | 50% | " | " |
| Wilms' Tumor | 60% | " | " |
| Other cancers | 50% | " | " |

From the MacMahon data, we have the following highly similar estimates:

| | | | | |
|---|---|---|---|---|
| Leukemia | 50% | " | " | " |
| Central Nervous System Tumors | 60% | " | " | " |
| Other cancers | 40% | " | " | " |

If we now take the central values from both the MacMahon evidence and the Stewart-Kneale evidence, we have as a best estimate, 50% increase in incidence rate for all forms of cancer plus leukemia, associated with diagnostic irradiation of the infant in-utero, and the numbers are closely similar for US practise and British practise. So, for 2–3 Rads to the infant in-utero, a 50% increase in incidence rate of various cancers leads to an estimate of 4 to 6 Rads as the doubling dose for childhood leukemia plus cancer due to diagnostic irradiation in-utero. Let us underestimate the risk, and use the higher number, 6 Rads, as the doubling dose for in-utero induction of subsequent leukemia plus other childhood cancers. This means a 17% increase in the incidence rate of such leukemia plus cancers per Rad of in-utero exposure of the infant.

It is not at all surprising that infants in-utero should appear *most* sensitive to irradiation, children *next* in sensitivity, and adults *third* (but *by no means* low). This is precisely the order in which these groups stand in terms of the fraction of their cells undergoing cell division at any time—and much evidence suggests these are the cells most susceptible to cancer induction.[16]

## GENERAL LAWS OF CANCER INDUCTION BY RADIATION

In view of the widely diverse forms of human cancers plus leukemia showing such striking similarity in their risk of radiation induction, it does not appear at all rash to propose some fundamental laws of cancer induction by radiation in humans.

**Law I** "All forms of cancer, in all probability, can be increased by ionizing radiation, and the *correct* way to describe the phenomenon is either in terms of the dose required to double the spontaneous incidence rate of each cancer or, alternatively, as the increase in incidence rate of such cancers per Rad of exposure."

**Law II** "All forms of cancer show closely similar doubling doses and closely similar increases in incidence rate per Rad."

**Law III** "Youthful subjects require less radiation to increase the incidence rate by a specified fraction than do adults."

Based upon these laws and the extensive data already in hand and described above, the following assignments appear reasonable for all forms of cancer.

| | |
|---|---|
| For Adults | ~100 Rads as the doubling dose. ~1% increase in incidence rate per year per Rad of exposure. |
| For Youthful Subjects (< 20 years of age) | Between 5 and 100 Rads as the doubling dose. Between 1 and 20% increase in incidence rate per year per Rad of exposure. |
| For Infants in-Utero | ~6 Rads as the doubling dose. ~17% increase in incidence rate per year per Rad of exposure. |

For the radiation of infants in-utero, Stewart and Kneale[15] clearly stated the outlines of these general laws. For adults, Court-Brown and Doll[10] clearly stated the outlines of these general laws.

With all the additional data available plus the data of Stewart and Kneale, MacMahon, and Court-Brown and Doll, we consider the enunciation of these general fundamental laws as having a better experimental base than many laws of physics, chemistry, or biology had when first proposed. Furthermore, we would estimate that the absolute numbers, if anything, probably underestimate the risk. For purposes of setting radiation tolerance guidelines, one might even be advised to use lower doubling doses than those estimated above.

## THE IMPLICATION OF
## THESE LAWS FOR THE POPULATION
## EXPOSURE ASSOCIATED
## WITH ATOMS-FOR-PEACE PROGRAMS

The *statutory allowable dose* to the population-at-large in the USA is 0.17 Rads per year from peaceful uses of atomic energy in all forms. If everyone in the population were to receive 0.17 Rads per year from birth to age 30 years, the integrated exposure (above background) would be 5 Rads per person. If the risk for all forms of cancer plus leukemia is an increase of 1% in incidence rate per Rad, we have 5 × 1 = 5% increase in incidence rate for all forms of cancer plus leukemia per year.

For a population of 2 × 10$^8$ persons in the USA ½ can roughly be estimated to be over 30 years of age. In this group, irradiated from birth, the latency period might, on the average, be expected to be over by ~35 years of age.

The *spontaneous* cancer incidence is ~280/10$^5$ persons per year.

5% × 280 = 14.0. Therefore, 14 additional cancer cases per 10$^5$ persons per year due to irradiation.

Thus, *14,000 additional cancer cases per year* in the USA, considering *only* those over 30 years of age.

If we estimate that latency plus lower accumulated dosage provides a smaller number of additional cases in the under 30-year age group, it would by no means be an overestimate to add 2,000 additional cases for the under 30-year age group. (Especially is this true when we see the data above concerning the greater sensitivity of this group to radiation-induced cancer.)

There should be added some contribution of additional cases each year to take into account the fact that 0.13 Rads will have been received by each infant in-utero (0.17 Rads/year × 40/52 years). It is hard to know whether this in-utero radiation carries an increased cancer risk for the whole lifetime or not. The additional contribution for the in-utero radiation (at a period when the effectiveness per

Rad is very high) could be between a few hundred and several thousand additional cancer cases per year. We shall not attempt to guess the additional contribution due to in-utero irradiation.

Therefore, 14,000 + 2,000 = *16,000 additional cancer plus leukemia cases* per year in the USA if everyone received the Federal Radiation Council statutory allowable doses of radiation. This would, for the several reasons outlined, appear to be a *minimum* value. 16,000 cases is equivalent to the mortality rate from one recent high year of the Vietnam war! It would appear that this is rather a high price to consider as being compatible with the benefits to be derived from the orderly development of atomic energy.

And we must add to these estimates the comment that we have used only the *hard data* in hand based upon cancer and leukemia induced in humans by radiation. We have said *nothing* of the additional possible burden of loss of life and misery from genetic disorders in future generations, fetal deaths, and neonatal deaths.[3] Furthermore, we have not used the vast array of experimental animal data which indicate that not only does cancer mortality increase from irradiation, but that many, if not all, causes of death increase—and in about the same proportion as does cancer mortality.

## WHAT MUST BE DONE?

In the *absence of any direct evidence* in man that factors will operate to reduce these estimated cases of cancer plus leukemia, it would appear that the only sensible thing to do right now is to reduce *drastically* the Federal Radiation Council dose allowable to the population-at-large—by at *least* a factor of 10. The new figure should be below 0.017 Rads for peaceful uses of atomic energy. We are well aware that this suggestion recommends that man-made radiation exposure be limited to a *small* fraction (0.1 or less) of natural background sources.

## ARE THERE
## ANY COUNTER-ARGUMENTS?

A *number* of counter-arguments may be raised against this proposal by some advocates of the peaceful uses of the atom. Before demonstrating to you the lack of validity of every one of these arguments in turn, we must emphasize that this is *not* a proposal against peaceful uses of the atom. Rather, it is a proposal for the use of common sense discretion in atomic energy development, weighted always in favor of the health and welfare of the people of the USA.

**Argument 1.** "Atomic energy projects thus far have *not* delivered 0.17 Rads to everyone in the population."

That is perfectly true! But the nuclear power industry is only now getting going, and 0.17 Rads per year *is* on the Federal Statute Books as allowable. Additionally, Plowshare proposals and industrial uses of radiation sources will surely add some increment to the population dosage.

**Argument 2.** "We *don't plan* to deliver the allowable 0.17 Rads per year to everyone in the population-at-large from peaceful uses of atomic energy."

We should certainly hope not! But, if it be true that such doses are unnecessary in the peaceful development of atomic energy, and if it be true that we can develop atomic energy for electric power and other uses with a much lower delivery of radiation to humans, that is indeed excellent news. Surely there can be no objection to immediate codification of this welcome news into *law* so that no one can possibly be confused by a *high* allowable standard and the concomitant promise that we will stay *well below* that figure.

We have alluded previously to our experience indicating that misinformation concerning potential hazard is widespread, with numerous responsible people in atomic energy development laboring under the impression

that the *current* standards have a wide margin of safety built in. Just recently an eminent authority in nuclear safety, Professor Merrill Eisenbud, expressed his *opinion* that, "The standards contain enormous built-in conservatism" and "that 50–100 millirads per year (1/3 to 1/2 FRC Guideline values) will produce no harm."[17] We would indeed be relieved of our concern if Professor Eisenbud would replace his *opinion* with some hard *evidence* to refute the facts presented here today.

Industry *urgently* needs a real standard that can be expected to hold up over time, since a *later* revision downward can lead to excruciatingly costly retrofits in a developed industrial application of nuclear energy. It is *far* better to lower the guidelines for radiation exposure now and do our engineering accordingly. We believe engineering talent can direct its effort to essentially absolute containment of radioactivity *at every step* in any useful atomic energy development.

If we are fortunate enough later to find that some unknown effect operates to protect against the hazards we have demonstrated here, it will be easy enough to raise the guidelines for radiation exposure *then*. In this way we can avoid irreversible injury to our environment and to a whole generation of humans *while* we find out the true facts.

**Argument 3.** "We live in '*a sea of radioactivity*' and man has for time immemorial been exposed to ionizing radiation. Why worry about adding a little?"

This argument presumes that natural radiation does no harm! As we can demonstrate readily by elementary arithmetic, natural radiation, in all likelihood, does just about as much harm as we would expect from all the evidence we have laid before you.

Let us apply our factor of a 1% increase in cancer incidence rate per Rad. A reasonable value for average radiation due to natural causes is approximately 0.1 Rad per year. At 30 years of age, the average man has received $30 \times 0.1 = 3.0$ Rads of radiation from natural sources. (It is higher in some locations, and we shall consider that in a few moments.)

Now 3 × 1 = 3, *so we expect a 3% increase* in the spontaneous cancer rate due to natural radiation. We doubt very, very much that many persons informed in this field would be prepared to argue that 3% of "spontaneous" cancer plus leukemia is *not* due to natural radiation. So, this argument concerning the sea of radioactivity falls of its own weight.

**Argument 4.** "But possibly there is a 'threshold' dose of radiation below which no harm accrues to man. Aren't you, therefore, unduly pessimistic about our standards?"

There are two crucial answers to this question.

1. Before the work of Stewart, Kneale, and MacMahon, all the data concerning cancer plus leukemia induction in man was for total doses of 100 Rads or more. But their data for irradiation of infants in-utero are for *2 or 3 Rads*. And, even more importantly, their data indicate that each Rad may be even 10 times *more effective* in inducing cancer at these *extremely low total doses* than is each Rad at the high doses. So the threshold concept has suffered some rather severe reverses!

2. We and others are doing experiments on human cells actively to determine the effect per Rad at various *total* doses to see if threshold type effects *ever* exist for man. But to use a *hope* that such thresholds may exist in setting guidelines for the exposure of our population *now* would seem like absolute folly.

**Argument 5.** "But isn't it true that delivering radiation slowly over a period of years, as would be the case for peaceful applications of atomic energy, may be less harmful with respect to cancer induction than the same dose delivered rapidly?"

It is perfectly true that, for *some* biological effects, the ability of the body to repair damage from previous radiation makes the effect of slow, protracted radiation less than for the same dose delivered rapidly. *No* evidence exists for such an effect on cancer or leukemia induction by radiation in man. Furthermore, the uranium miners received *their* irradiation slowly over a period of years, and it appears that any protection this provides, if there *is any,* is not enough to appreciably alter any of our major conclusions.

Further, it may take 10 or 20 years to ascertain whether such protraction of radiation lessens cancer induction in man. This only militates in *favor* of reducing the allowable dosage standards rather than against reducing them. Why, during such an interval of 10–20 years, should we take the high risk, *at the expense of the people of the USA,* of producing extensive irreversible injury?

**Argument 6.** "But isn't it true that some children have received large dosages of radiation to their thyroid glands from radio-iodine from fallout, as in St. George, Utah, and have failed to show a high incidence of thyroid cancer?"

Let us look very closely at this issue. Tamplin has presented evidence, never refuted, that high levels of radio-iodine were indeed deposited in the St. George area during the Nevada tests *above ground* during 1952–55.[18] If children in that area consumed 1 liter of milk each day from cows grazing upon contaminated pastureland, he calculated that the radio-iodine dosage to their thyroid glands would have been approximately 120 Rads. Now, there are several points to consider:

(a) There are some 2,000 children in St. George, Utah.

(b) When these children were examined, years after the possible exposure, some of the children in St. George were those who had moved there *since* the exposure, so the true number who might have been exposed is less than 2,000.

(c) Some of the children probably didn't drink 1 liter of milk per day.

(d) Some of the cows were *not* grazing on contaminated pastureland. They were eating uncontaminated stored feed.

But, for the sake of argument, let us *assume* all 2,000 children *were* in St. George, and *did* drink 1 liter per day of radio-iodine-contaminated milk, and *did* receive 120 Rads to their thyroid glands. How much cancer should have been expected?

Again, by simple arithmetic, we can use the mid-figure for increased incidence of thyroid cancer in children per Rad as 15% of the spontaneous rate. If the spontaneous rate is ~ 10 cases per million per year, our expectation would be, for St. George:

$$\left(\frac{2,000}{10^6}\right)\left(\frac{15}{100}\right)(10)(120)=0.36 \text{ cases per year.}$$

Thus, every three years, 1 case of thyroid cancer would be *expected*. With this expectation, one could go 6 or 10 years and not see that one case. Further, the points mentioned above in (b) through (d) would have reduced even this small expectation! So, the data from St. George, Utah don't prove at all that radio-iodine exposure doesn't produce cancer in children. The St. George Studies just prove if an inadequate study is done, an inadequate result is obtained.

**Argument 7.** "But isn't it true that living in Denver at high altitudes exposes people to more cosmic radiation and that as a result, their annual "natural" radiation dose is 1.5 to 2.0 times what it is at sea level?"

The answer is, "Yes."

"Then why don't they have a higher cancer incidence than people at sea-level?"

This particular argument is brought out and burnished brightly at regular intervals.

The answer is that the excessive radiation due to cosmic rays probably produced precisely as much extra cancer in Denver as our calculations would indicate. Let us make those extremely simple calculations.

First, to compare Denver with a sea-level region, we would have to know that the medical reporting of disease categories were just as good both in Denver and the sea-level community.

Second, we would want to be sure that the people at risk in Denver had lived there all their lives, and the people at sea-level had lived *there* all their lives.

Third, we would want to be sure that all other factors, aside from radiation, were identical in Denver and the sea-level community.

We don't know all these points, but let us suppose we were satisfied on all three. Let us say, to exaggerate the case, that Denver residents get 0.2 Rads per year versus 0.1 Rads per year at sea-level. In 30 years, the average Denver resident would accumulate 6 Rads; the average sea-level resident would accumulate 3 Rads.

Using our increase in cancer incidence rate of 1% per Rad, we would estimate,

for Denver, a 6% increase in the cancer incidence rate;

for Sea-Level, a 3% increase in the cancer incidence rate.

So, if we set all other "spontaneous" causes of cancer at 100%, we would say, Denver residents should experience 100 + 6 = 106; Sea-Level residents should experience 100 + 3 = 103.

*No expert in the field of Vital Statistics* would be prepared to contest that Denver residents might be experiencing a 3% increase in cancer incidence rate due to cosmic radiation compared with otherwise equivalent people at sea-level.

**Argument 8.** "But aren't medical x-rays also capable of producing cancer along the lines of your argument?"

Absolutely! There is no justification whatever for *non-essential* x-rays in the course of medical practise. Every physician should acquaint himself with the facts described above and he should be convinced that the risk to his patient is greater by *not* having a particular x-ray taken than by having it taken. There is ample evidence of a concerted campaign within the medical profession to reduce the radiation exposure through diagnostic x-rays.

**Argument 9.** "Why do you criticize the guidelines for radiation exposure from the development of nuclear energy for electricity generation and say nothing of the hazard to the public from fossil-fuel electricity generating plants?"

Our answer is that we don't condone homicide with knives any more than homicide with guns.

We are in the field of atomic energy and we believe our knowledge enables us to speak to the issue of atomic energy. Therefore, we are presenting the evidence upon which a reasonable set of guidelines for radiation exposure from the peaceful atom can be based. We are *not* against nuclear generation of electricity. We have great confidence that our engineers have the talent to design reactors, reprocessing plants for spent nuclear fuel, transport systems, and waste storage facilities in such a manner that any release of radioactivity that might conceivably expose humans be kept so low as to preclude harm.

If fossil-fuel plants are causing diseases in our population, this issue should be evaluated as soon as possible, and the fossil-fuel generating plants should be redesigned to remove effluents that are producing harm.

The general argument that making either nuclear plants or fossil-fuel plants safe will increase the cost of electricity does not impress us. Probably a dollar per month added to electricity cost per family would allow super-clean plants either of fossil-fuel or atomic variety. We submit it is much better to pay a little more for electricity than to die prematurely of cancer or leukemia.

**Argument 10.** "Experts have estimated that the dosage levels we are discussing in the existing Federal Radiation Council Guidelines might only shorten the average life-span of humans some weeks or months. Isn't this worthwhile compared to the benefits?"

Absolutely not! First, even the *average* life-shortening may be greater than estimated. Let us assume, however, that the experts are right. The real answer is that this argument is totally immoral. Let us *assume* it is true that the average life expectancy is reduced only by several weeks. But how, we must ask, does this average reduction come about? It arises because many of the victims of premature cancer (those 16,000+ cases per year we re-referred to previously) lose 10, 20, 30, 40, or 50 years of their potential life-span. While 16,000 cases is a large number, when it is diluted into the couple of hundred million people in the country, the resulting *average* reduction of life-span due to radiation-induced cancer comes out only several weeks. This monstrous hoax should stop recurring.

**Closing Remarks** Unfortunately, there is a recent tendency to create an apparent "adversary" position between so-called "environmentalists" and "those in favor of technical progress." This, we believe, is dangerous nonsense. We feel certain that the Atomic Energy Commission, the scientific and engineering community, and the electrical power industry are as concerned as we are to keep the environment safe for human habitation and to bring society the earliest possible benefits of the peaceful atom. And because we are certain of this, we urge all of these groups to join us in seeking an early revision downward by at least a factor of ten in the Federal Radiation Council Guidelines for allowable exposure to the population-at-large.

**REFERENCES**

1. Gofman, J. W. "The Hazards to Man from Radioactivity" in *Proceedings of the 3rd Plow-share Symposium,* "Engineering with Nuclear Explosives," April 21–23, 1964, Davis, California, TID-7695. (Reprinted in "Scientist and Citizen," 5–10, Aug. 1964.)
2. MacMahon, B. "Epidemiologic Aspects of Cancer," "Ca-a Cancer Journal for Clinicians," **19,** 1, 27–35, 1969.
3. Tamplin, A. R. "Fetal and Infant Mortality and the Environment," *Bulletin of the Atomic Scientist* **25,** No. 10, December, 1969.
4. Gofman, J. W., and Tamplin, A. R. "Low Dose Radiation and Cancer," see Summary—this paper.
5. Maki, H., Ishimaru, T., Kate, H., Wakabayashi, T. "Carcinogenesis in Atomic Bomb Survivors."

*Technical Report 24–68*, Atomic Bomb Casualty Commission, November 14, 1968.

6. Pochin, E. E. "Somatic Risks—Thyroid Carcinoma" (The Evaluation of Risks from Radiation), *International Commission on Radiation Protection, Publication 8*, p. 9, Pergamon Press, Oxford, 1966.

7. Carroll, R. E., Haddon, W., Jr., Handy, V. H., and Weeben, E. E., Sr. "Thyroid Cancer: Cohort Analysis of Increasing Incidence in New York State, 1941–1962," *J. Natl. Cancer Inst.*, **33**, 277–283, 1964.

8. *Hearings of the Joint Committee on Atomic Energy*, "Radiation Exposure of Uranium Miners," Part 2, p. 1047, 90th Congress, 1967.

9. Miller, Robert W. "Delayed Radiation Effects in Atomic Bomb Survivors," *Science*, **166**, 569–574, 1969.

10. Court-Brown, W. M., and Doll, R. "Mortality from Cancer and Other Causes After Radiotherapy for Ankylosing Spondylitis," *Brit. Med. J.*, **2**, 1327–1332, 1965.

11. Anderson, R. E., and Ishida, K. "Malignant Lymphoma in Survivors of the Atomic Bomb in Hiroshima," *Ann. Intern. Med.* **61**, 853–862, 1964.

12. Stewart, A., Webb, J., and Hewitt, D. "A Survey of Childhood Malignancies," *Brit. Med. J.*, **1**, 1495–1508, 1958.

13. MacMahon, B. "Pre-Natal X-Ray Exposure and Childhood Cancer," *J. Natl. Cancer Inst.*, **28**, 1173–1191, 1962.

14. MacMahon, B., and Hutchinson, H. *Rev. Acta Un. Int. Cancer* **20**, 1172, 1964.

15. Stewart, A., and Kneale, G. W. "Changes in the Cancer Risk Associated with Obstetric Radiography," *Lancet*, **1**, 104–107, 1968.

16. Gofman, J., Minkler, J., and Tandy, R. "A Specific Common Chromosomal Pathway for the Origin of Human Malignancy," UCRL–50356, November 20, 1967.

17. Eisenbud, M. "Standards of Radiation Protection and Their Implications to the Public Health" plus discussion comments in "Symposium on Nuclear Power and the Public," Minneapolis, Minnesota, October 10–11, 1969.

18. Tamplin, A. R., and Fisher, H. L. "Estimation of Dosage to Thyroids of Children in the U.S. from Nuclear Tests Conducted in Nevada during 1952 through 1955," UCRL–14707, May 10, 1966.

19. Ng, Yook C., Burton, C. Ann, Thompson, Stanley E., Tandy, Robert K., Kretner, Helen K., and Pratt, Michael W. "Predictions of the Maximum Dosage to Man from the Fallout of Nuclear Devices, IV. Handbook for Estimating the Maximum Internal Dose from Radionuclides Released to the Biosphere," UCRL–50163 Part IV, May 14, 1968.

## ACKNOWLEDGMENT

This work was performed (in part) under the auspices of the U.S. Atomic Energy Commission.

# Effects of Pollution on the Structure and Physiology of Ecosystems

G. M. WOODWELL

The accumulation of various toxic substances in the biosphere is leading to complex changes in the structure and function of nat-

Effects of Pollution on the Structure and Physiology of Ecosystems. From *Science*, Vol. 168, April 24, 1970, pp. 429–433. Copyright 1970 by the American Association for the Advancement of Science. Reprinted by permission of the author and the publisher.

ural ecosystems. Although the changes are complex, they follow in aggregate patterns that are similar in many different ecosystems and are therefore broadly predictable. The patterns involve many changes but include especially simplification of the structure of both plant and animal communities, shifts in the ratio of gross production to total respiration, and loss of part or all of the inventory of nutrients. Despite the frequency with which various pollutants are causing such changes and the significance of the changes for all living systems (1), only a few studies show details of the pattern of change clearly. These are studies of the effects of ionizing radiation, of persistent pesticides, and of eutrophication. The effects of radiation will be used here to show the pattern of changes in terrestrial plant communities and to show similarities with the effects of fire, oxides of sulfur, and herbicides. Effects of such pollutants as pesticides on the animal community are less conspicuous but quite parallel, which shows that the ecological effects of pollution correspond very closely to the general "strategy of ecosystem development" outlined by Odum (1) and that they can be anticipated in considerable detail.

The problems caused by pollution are of interest from two viewpoints. Practical people —toxicologists, engineers, health physicists, public health officials, intensive users of the environment—consider pollution primarily as a direct hazard to man. Others, no less concerned for human welfare but with less pressing public responsibilities, recognize that toxicity to humans is but one aspect of the pollution problem, the other being a threat to the maintenance of a biosphere suitable for life as we know it. The first viewpoint leads to emphasis on human food chains; the second leads to emphasis on human welfare insofar as it depends on the integrity of the diverse ecosystems of the earth, the living systems that appear to have built and now maintain the biosphere.

The food-chain problem is by far the simpler; it is amenable at least in part to the pragmatic, narrowly compartmentalized solutions that industrialized societies are good at. The best example of the toxicological approach is in control of mutagens, particularly the radionuclides. These present a specific, direct hazard to man. They are much more important to man than to other organisms. A slightly enhanced rate of mutation is a serious danger to man, who has developed through medical science elaborate ways of preserving a high fraction of the genetic defects in the popula-

tion; it is trivial to the rest of the biota, in which genetic defects may be eliminated through selection. This is an important fact about pollution hazards—toxic substances that are principally mutagenic are usually of far greater direct hazard to man than to the rest of the earth's biota and must be considered first from the standpoint of their movement to man through food webs or other mechanisms and to a much lesser extent from that of their effects on the ecosystem through which they move. We have erred, as shown below, in assuming that all toxic substances should be treated this way.

Pollutants that affect other components of the earth's biota as well as man present a far greater problem. Their effects are chronic and may be cumulative in contrast to the effects of short-lived disturbances that are repaired by succession. We ask what effects such pollutants have on the structure of natural ecosystems and on biological diversity and what these changes mean to physiology, especially to mineral cycling and the long-term potential for sustaining life.

Although experience with pollution of various types is extensive and growing rapidly, only a limited number of detailed case history studies provide convincing control data that deal with the structure of ecosystems. One of the clearest and most detailed series of experiments in recent years has been focused on the ecological effects of radiation. These studies are especially useful because they allow cause and effect to be related quantitatively at the ecosystem level, which is difficult to do in nature. The question arises, however, whether the results from studies of ionizing radiation, a factor that is not usually considered to have played an important role in recent evolution, have any general application. The answer, somewhat surprisingly to many biologists, seems to be that they do. The ecological effects of radiation follow patterns that are known from other types of disturbances. The studies of radiation, because of their specificity, provide useful clues for examination of effects of other types of pollution for which evidence is much more fragmentary.

The effects of chronic irradiation of a late successional oak-pine forest have been studied at Brookhaven National Laboratory in New York. After 6 months' exposure to chronic irradiation from a $^{137}$Cs source, five well-defined zones of modification of vegetation had been established. They have become more pronounced through 7 years of chronic irradiation. The zones were:

1. A central devastated zone, where exposures were >200 R/day and no higher plants survived, although certain mosses and lichens survived up to exposures >1000 R/day.
2. A sedge zone, where *Carex pensylvanica* (2) survived and ultimately formed a continuous cover (>150 R/day).
3. A shrub zone in which two species of *Vaccinium* and one of *Gaylussacia* survived, with *Quercus ilicifolia* toward the outer limit of the circle where exposures were lowest (>40 R/day).
4. An oak zone, the pine having been eliminated (>16 R/day).
5. Oak-pine forest, where exposures were <2 R/day, and there was no obvious change in the number of species, although small changes in rates of growth were measurable at exposures as low as 1 R/day.

The effect was a systematic dissection of the forest, strata being removed layer by layer. Trees were eliminated at low exposures, then the taller shrubs *(Gaylussacia baccata)*, then the lower shrubs *(Vaccinium* species), then the herbs, and finally the lichens and mosses. Within these groups, it was evident that under irradiation an upright form of growth was a disadvantage. The trees did vary—the pines *(Pinus rigida)* for instance were far more sensitive than the oaks without having a conspicuous tendency toward more upright growth, but all the trees were substantially more sensitive than the shrubs (3). Within the shrub zone, tall forms were more sensitive; even within the

lichen populations, foliose and fruticose lichens proved more sensitive than crustose lichens (4).

The changes caused by chronic irradiation of herb communities in old fields show the same pattern—upright species are at a disadvantage. In one old field at Brookhaven, the frequency of low-growing plants increased along the gradient of increasing radiation intensity to 100 per cent at >1000 R/day (5). Comparison of the sensitivity of the herb field with that of the forest, by whatever criterion, clearly shows the field to be more resistant than the forest. The exposure reducing diversity to 50 per cent in the first year was ~ 1000 R/day for the field and 160 R/day for the forest, a greater than fivefold difference in sensitivity (3).

The changes in these ecosystems under chronic irradiation are best summarized as changes in structure, although diversity, primary production, total respiration, and nutrient inventory are also involved. The changes are similar to the familiar ones along natural gradients of increasingly severe conditions, such as exposure on mountains, salt spray, and water availability. Along all these gradients the conspicuous change is a reduction of structure from forest toward communities dominated by certain shrubs, then, under more severe conditions, by certain herbs, and finally by low-growing plants, frequently moses and lichens. Succession, insofar as it has played any role at all in the irradiated ecosystems, has simply reinforced this pattern, adding a very few hardy species and allowing expansion of the populations of more resistant indigenous species. The reasons for radiation's causing this pattern are still not clear (3, 6), but the pattern is a common one, not peculiar to ionizing radiation, despite the novelty of radiation exposures as high as these.

Its commonness is illustrated by the response to fire, one of the oldest and most important disruptions of nature. The oak-pine forests such as those on Long Island have, throughout their extensive range in eastern North America, been subject in recent times to repeated burning. The changes in physiognomy of the vegetation follow the above pattern very closely—the forest is replaced by communities of shrubs, especially bear oak (*Quercus ilicifolia*), *Gaylussacia*, and *Vaccinium* species. This change is equivalent to that caused by chronic exposure to 40 R/day or more. Buell and Cantlon (7), working on similar vegetation in New Jersey, showed that a further increase in the frequency of fires resulted in a differential reduction in taller shrubs first, and a substantial increase in the abundance of *Carex pensylvanica,* the same sedge now dominating the sedge zone of the irradiated forest. The parallel is detailed; radiation and repeated fires both reduce the structure of the forest in similar ways, favoring low-growing hardy species.

The similarity of response appears to extend to other vegetations as well. G. L. Miller, working with F. McCormick at the Savannah River Laboratory, has shown recently that the most radiation-resistant and fire-resistant species of 20-year-old fields are annuals and perennials characteristic of disturbed places (8). An interesting sidelight of his study was the observation that the grass stage of long leaf pine (*Pinus palustris*), long considered a specific adaptation to the fires that maintain the southeastern savannahs, appears more resistant to radiation damage than the mature trees. At a total acute exposure of 2.1 kR (3 R/day), 85 per cent of the grass-stage populations survived but only 55 per cent of larger trees survived. Seasonal variation in sensitivity to radiation damage has been abundantly demonstrated (9), and it would not be surprising to find that this variation is related to the ecology of the species. Again it appears that the response to radiation is not unique.

The species surviving high radiation-exposure rates in the Brookhaven experiments are the ones commonly found in disturbed places, such as roadsides, gravel banks, and areas with nutrient-deficient or unstable soil. In the forest they include *Comptonia peregrina* (the sweet fern), a decumbent spiny *Rubus*, and the lichens, especially *Cladonia cristatella.*

In the old field one of the most conspicuously resistant species was *Digitaria sanguinalis* (crabgrass) among several other weedy species. Clearly these species are generalists in the sense that they survive a wide range of conditions, including exposure to high intensities of ionizing radiation—hardly a common experience in nature but apparently one that elicits a common response.

With this background one might predict that a similar pattern of devastation would result from such pollutants as oxides of sulfur released from smelting. The evidence is fragmentary, but Gorham and Gordon (10) found around the smelters in Sudbury, Ontario, a striking reduction in the number of species of higher plants along a gradient of 62 kilometers (39 miles). In different samples the number of species ranged from 19 to 31 at the more distant sites and dropped abruptly at 6.4 kilometers. At 1.6 kilometers, one of two randomly placed plots (20 by 2 meters) included only one species. They classified the damage in five categories, from "Not obvious" through "Moderate" to "Very severe." The tree canopy had been reduced or eliminated within 4.8 to 6.4 kilometers of the smelter, with only occasional sprouts of trees, seedlings, and successional herbs and shrubs remaining; this damage is equivalent to that produced by exposure to 40 R/day. The most resistant trees were, almost predictably to a botanist, red maple (*Acer rubrum*) and red oak (*Quercus rubra*). Other species surviving in the zones of "Severe" and "Very severe" damage included *Sambucus pubens, Polygonum cilinode, Comptonia peregrina,* and *Epilobium angustifolium* (fire weed). The most sensitive plants appeared to be *Pinus strobus* and *Vaccinium myrtilloides.* The pine was reported no closer than 25.6 kilometers (16 miles), where it was chlorotic.

This example confirms the pattern of the change—first a reduction of diversity of the forest by elimination of positive species: then elimination of the tree canopy and survival of resistant shrubs and herbs widely recognized as "seral" or successional species or "generalists."

The effects of herbicides, despite their hoped for specificity, fall into the same pattern, and it is no surprise that the extremely diverse forest canopies of Viet Nam when sprayed repeatedly with herbicides are replaced over large areas by dense stands of species of bamboo (11).

The mechanisms involved in producing this series of patterns in terrestrial ecosystems are not entirely clear. One mechanism that is almost certainly important is simply the ratio of gross production to respiration in different strata of the community. The size of trees has been shown to approach a limit set by the amount of surface area of stems and branches in proportion to the amount of leaf area (12). The apparent reason is that, as a tree expands in size, the fraction of its total surface devoted to bark, which makes a major contribution to the respiration, expands more rapidly than does the photosynthetic area. Any chronic disturbance has a high probability of damaging the capacity for photosynthesis without reducing appreciably the total amount of respiration; therefore, large plants are more vulnerable than species requiring less total respiration. Thus chronic disturbances of widely different types favor plants that are small in stature, and any disturbance that tends to increase the amount of respiration in proportion to photosynthesis will aggravate this shift.

The shift in the structure of terrestrial plant communities toward shrubs, herbs, or mosses and lichens, involves changes in addition to those of structure and diversity. Simplification of the plant community involves also a reduction of the total standing crop of organic matter and a corresponding reduction in the total inventory of nutrient elements held within the system, a change that may have important long-term implications for the potential of the site to support life. The extent of such losses has been demonstrated recently by Bormann and his colleagues in the Hubbard Brook Forest in New Hampshire (13), where all of the trees in a watershed were cut, the cut material was left to decay, and the losses of

nutrients were monitored in the runoff. Total nitrogen losses in the first year were equivalent to twice the amount cycled in the system during a normal year. With the rise of nitrate ion in the runoff, concentrations of calcium, magnesium, sodium, and potassium ions rose severalfold, which caused eutrophication and even pollution of the streams fed by this watershed. The soil had little capacity to retain the nutrients that were locked in the biota once the higher plants had been killed. The total losses are not yet known, but early evidence indicates that they will be a high fraction of the nutrient inventory, which will cause a large reduction in the potential of the site for supporting living systems as complex as that destroyed—until nutrients accumulate again. Sources are limited: the principal source is erosion of primary minerals.

When the extent of the loss of nutrients that accompanies a reduction in the structure of a plant community is recognized, it is not surprising to find depauperate vegetation in places subject to chronic disturbances. Extensive sections of central Long Island, for example, support a depauperate oak-pine forest in which the bear oak, Quercus ilicifolia, is the principal woody species. The cation content of an extremely dense stand of this common community, which has a biomass equivalent to that of the more diverse late successional forest that was burned much less recently and less intensively, would be about 60 percent that of the richer stand, despite the equivalence of standing crop. This means that the species, especially the bear oak, contain, and presumably require, lower concentrations of cations. This is an especially good example because the bear oak community is a long-lasting one in the fire succession and marks the transition from a high shrub community to forest. It has analogies elsewhere, such as the heath balds of the Great Smoky Mountains and certain bamboo thickets in Southeast Asia.

The potential of a site for supporting life depends heavily on the pool of nutrients available through breakdown of primary minerals and through recycling in the living portion of the ecosystem. Reduction of the structure of the system drains these pools in whole or in part; it puts leaks in the system. Any chronic pollution that affects the structure of ecosystems, especially the plant community, starts leaks and reduces the potential of the site for recovery. Reduction of the structure of forests in Southeast Asia by herbicides has dumped the nutrient pools of these large statured and extremely diverse forests. The nutrients are carried to the streams, which turn green with the algae that the nutrients support. Tschirley *(11)*, reporting his study of the effects of herbicides in Viet Nam, recorded "surprise" and "pleasure" that fishing had improved in treated areas. If the herbicides are not toxic to fish, there should be little surprise at improved catches of certain kinds of fish in heavily enriched water adjacent to herbicide-treated forests. The bamboo thickets that replace the forests also reflect the drastically lowered potential of these sites to support living systems. The time it takes to reestablish a forest with the original diversity depends on the availability of nutrients, and is probably very long in most lateritic soils.

In generalizing about pollution. I have concentrated on some of the grossest changes in the plant communities of terrestrial ecosystems. The emphasis on plants is appropriate because plants dominate terrestrial ecosystems. But not all pollutants affect plants directly; some have their principal effects on heterotrophs. What changes in the structure of animal communities are caused by such broadly toxic materials as most pesticides?

The general pattern of loss of structure is quite similar, although the structure of the animal communities is more difficult to chart. The transfer of energy appears to be one good criterion of structure. Various studies suggest that 10 to 20 per cent of the energy entering the plant community is transfered directly to the animal community through herbivores *(14)*. Much of that energy, perhaps 50 per cent or more, is used in respiration to support the herbivore population; some is transferred to

the detritus food chain directly, and some, probably not more than 20 per cent, is transferred to predators of the herbivores. In an evolutionarily and successionally mature community, this transfer of 10 to 20 per cent per trophic level may occur two or three times to support carnivores, some highly specialized, such as certain eagles, hawks, and herons, others less specialized, such as gulls, ravens, rats, and people.

Changes in the plant community, such as its size, rate of energy fixation, and species, will affect the structure of the animal community as well. Introduction of a toxin specific for animals, such as a pesticide that is a generalized nerve toxin, will also topple the pyramid. Although the persistent pesticides are fat soluble and tend to accumulate in carnivores and reduce populations at the tops of food chains, they affect every trophic level, reducing reproductive capacity, almost certainly altering behavioral patterns, and disrupting the competitive relationships between species. Under these circumstances the highly specialized species, the obligate carnivores high in the trophic structure, are at a disadvantage because the food chain concentrates the toxin and, what is even more important, because the entire structure beneath them becomes unstable. Again the generalists or broadniched species are favored, the gulls, rats, ravens, pigeons and, in a very narrow short-term sense, man. Thus, the pesticides favor the herbivores, the very organisms they were invented to control.

Biological evolution has divided the resources of any site among a large variety of users—species—which, taken together, confer on that site the properties of a closely integrated system capable of conserving a diversity of life. The system has structure; its populations exist with certain definable, quantitative relationships to one another; it fixes energy and releases it at a measurable rate; and it contains an inventory of nutrients that is accumulated and recirculated, not lost. The system is far from static; it is subject, on a time scale very long compared with a human life-span, to a continuing augmentive change through evolution; on a shorter time scale, it is subject to succession toward a more stable state after any disturbance. The successional patterns are themselves a product of the evolution of life, providing for systematic recovery from any acute disturbance. Without a detailed discussion of the theory of ecology, one can say that biological evolution, following a pattern approximating that outlined above, has built the earth's ecosystems, and that these systems have been the dominant influence on the earth throughout the span of human existence. The structure of these systems is now being changed all over the world. We know enough about the structure and function of these systems to predict the broad outline of the effects of pollution on both land and water. We know that as far as our interests in the next decades are concerned, pollution operates on the time scale of succession, not of evolution, and we cannot look to evolution to cure this set of problems. The loss of structure involves a shift away from complex arrangements of specialized species toward the generalists; away from forest, toward hardy shrubs and herbs; away from those phytoplankton of the open ocean that Wurster *(15)* proved so very sensitive to DDT, toward those algae of the sewage plants that are unaffected by almost everything including DDT and most fish; away from diversity in birds, plants, and fish toward monotony; away from tight nutrient cycles toward very loose ones with terrestrial systems becoming depleted, and with aquatic systems becoming overloaded; away from stability toward instability especially with regard to sizes of populations of small, rapidly reproducing organisms such as insects and rodents that compete with man; away from a world that runs itself through a self-augmentive, slowly moving evolution, to one that requires constant tinkering to patch it up, a tinkering that is malignant in that each act of repair generates a need for further repairs to avert problems generated at compound interest.

This is the pattern, predictable in broad outline, aggravated by almost any pollutant. Once we recognize the pattern, we can begin to see the meaning of some of the changes occurring now in the earth's biota. We can see the demise of carnivorous birds and predict the demise of important fisheries. We can tell why, around industrial cities, hills that were once forested now are not; why each single species is important; and how the increase in the temperature of natural water bodies used to cool new reactors will, by augmenting respiration over photosynthesis, ultimately degrade the system and contribute to degradation of other interconnected ecosystems nearby. We can begin to speculate on where continued, exponential progress in this direction will lead: probably not to extinction yet—but to a general degradation of the quality of life.

The solution? Fewer people, unpopular but increasing restrictions on technology (making it more and more expensive), and a concerted effort to tighten up human ecosystems to reduce their interactions with the rest of the earth on whose stability we all depend. This does not require foregoing nuclear energy; it requires that if we must dump heat, it should be dumped into civilization to enhance a respiration rate in a sewage plant or an agricultural ecosystem, not dumped outside of civilization to affect that fraction of the earth's biota that sustains the earth as we know it. The question of what fraction that might be remains as one of the great issues, still scarcely considered by the scientific community.

## REFERENCES AND NOTES

1. E. P. Odum, *Science* **164**, 262 (1969).
2. Plant nomenclature follows that of M. L. Fernald in *Gray's Manual of Botany* (American Book, New York, ed. 8, 1950).
3. G. M. Woodwell, *Science* **156**, 461 (1967); _____ and A. L. Rebuck, *Ecol. Monogr.* **37**, 53 (1967).
4. G. M. Woodwell and T. P. Gannutz, *Amer. J. Bot.* **54**, 1210 (1967).
5. _____ and J. K. Oosting, *Radiat. Bot.* **5**, 205 (1965).
6. _____ and R. H. Whittaker, *Quart. Rev. Biol.* **43**, 42 (1968).
7. M. F. Buell and J. E. Cantlon, *Ecology* **34**, 520 (1953).
8. G. L. Miller, thesis, Univ. of North Carolina (1968).
9. A. H. Sparrow, L. A. Schairer, R. C. Sparrow, W. F. Campbell, *Radiat. Bot.* **3**, 169 (1963); F. G. Taylor,

Jr., *ibid.* **6**, 307 (1965).

10. E. Gorham and A. G. Gordon, *Can. J. Bot.* **38**, 307 (1960); *ibid.*, p. 477; *ibid.* **41**, 371 (1963).
11. F. H. Tschirley, *Science* **163**, 779 (1969).
12. R. H. Whittaker and G. M. Woodwell, *Amer. J. Bot.* **54**, 931 (1967).
13. F. H. Bormann, G. E. Likens, D. W. Fisher, R. S. Pierce, *Science* **159**, 882 (1968).
14. These relationships have been summarized in detail by J. Phillipson [*Ecological Energetics* (St. Martin's Press, New York, 1966)]. See also L. B. Slobodkin, *Growth and Regulation of Animal Populations* (Holt, Rinehart and Winston, New York, 1961) and J. H. Ryther, *Science* **166**, 72 (1969).
15. C. F. Wurster, *Science* **159**, 1474 (1968).
16. Research carried out at Brookhaven National Laboratory under the auspices of the U. S. Atomic Energy Commission. Paper delivered at 11th International Botanical Congress, Seattle, Wash., on 26 August 1969 in the symposium "Ecological and Evolutionary Implications of Environmental Pollution."

# Threatened Species, Technological Circuses, and Other Scandals

*At last when his wits were gone beyond repair, he came to conceive the strangest idea that ever occurred to any madman in the world.**

In the face of what has been called an unprecedented concern with environmental problems, the twin juggernauts of unfettered technology and the lust for short-term profit rumble on. If we are to have some chance of coping even with the problems enumerated in the foregoing two sections—to say nothing of our crippling addiction to racism and exploitation—we must come to grips with and ultimately root out such enterprises as are considered in this section: those committed to the senseless extermination of species; those promoting the impoverishment of the environment for the benefit of the privileged; those diverting vast amounts of money and talent to "interesting" technological experiments of virtually no social utility; and those devoted to imposing our will on other peoples without regard for the consequences for them or their environment.

Roger Payne's study, "Among Wild Whales," conveys a sense of the mystery and complexity of these creatures, while marvelling at the puny economic incentive and amazing lack of foresight which drive man to hound them toward extinction. In the catalog of some hundreds of vanishing species, the whales stand out as a particularly compelling example of the self-sustaining momentum built up by a destructive enterprise. Perhaps nowhere else in the field of "resource management" have the predictions of competent biologists (as to diminished yield with increased harvesting pressure) come so quickly and accurately to pass. Yet in the face of this demonstrated understanding of the situation and the patently disastrous consequences of persisting in

* Cervantes, *Don Quixote.*

present practices, the whaling industry persists indeed. It is as if, in Dr. Payne's words, the industry is "bent on its own annihilation."

The similar and awesome momentum of the water-project syndrome, as revealed in Gene Marine's dissection of California's water hucksters, is perhaps easier to explain. For here it is not obvious to the perpetrators (as it should be to the whalers) that their actions will be self-defeating. Indeed, the land developers of the Los Angeles basin (and adjacent deserts) and the corporate landowners of the western San Joaquin Valley have every reason to expect the California water project to bring in handsome profits for decades. The only possible solution here and in all similar situations is a massive public outcry, followed by the prompt ejection of the water lobby's politicians from public office. The case for such action need not be made only on the potential for serious ecological harm associated with large water projects (salination of fertile river deltas *and* the newly irrigated land, aggravation of pollution problems in bays and estuaries once flushed by the diverted rivers, and so forth). Rather, the fundamental bankruptcy of the *philosophy* of large-scale water diversion is sufficient reason to oppose such schemes. They epitomize the development mentality in its two most dangerous aspects: the sacredness of the concept of "demand," and the illusion that the support of human beings is the highest use for *any* piece of land, no matter how deficient it may be in the requisites for life. Thus the developers—and the oilmen, and the power pushers—gleefully accept as "given" the wildest and most unsustainable growth projections for population and per capita consumption. Indeed they labor to bring such disasters to pass with massive advertising campaigns (often, as in the case of the utilities, at public expense). They then assume the role of dutiful public servants in striving to meet the "demand" they have in part created. Finally, in their hot pursuit of the development dollar they justify one environmental disaster to perpetuate another—the rape of resource-rich regions to create tomorrow's urban sprawl wherever it least belongs.

America's supersonic transport program, the principal characteristics and utter disutility of which are  discussed in Holdren's essay, adds a new dimension to the term, "technological circus." The purported social benefits are so far-fetched as to tax credulity, the economic "necessity" of marketing such an aircraft has been thoroughly discredited, and the only significant scientific information which will accrue from the program is the experimental determination of whether the noise or other, more speculative SST-induced environmental disasters will be the worse. It is unfortunate, however, that so much of the public and congressional controversy over this aircraft has focussed on its impact on the environment; for even in the absence of the inevitable boom and unbearable takeoff and landing noise, the program would remain a ridiculous waste of funds and talent. For this, the engineers who support the program cannot be blamed, nor can the good citizens of the state of Washington. Professionals who love their work will forever be campaigning for public support to extend the "state-of-the-art," and everyone cherishes a program to fatten the local economy. The real leverage point in matters of this kind is a functioning legislative body which represents the interests of the *total* citizenry, in practice as well as in name. Such a body is empowered and obliged to select rationally among the sea of demands upon the nation's resources. Its patent failure to do so today, as continued government support of the SST so graphically illustrates, tells us where reform must begin.

The next selection, James Ramsey's "Wonderland Revisited," angrily yet eloquently conveys a sensation known to many who have sought to grasp man's predicament and his present response to it—the sensation that the collective consciousness is addled, the value system gone quite beserk. After a survey of representative idiocies, he focuses on the proposed dismantling and marketing of the Alaskan wilderness as a possible last chance for sanity to prevail. The same mad momentum of institutions and technologies which forms a common thread through the subjects of this chapter now threatens Alaska, where the usual development/conservation dilemma is compounded by the conjunction of exceptional mineral wealth and unusually fragile ecosystems. Man's demonstrated propensity for bungling permits us little confidence under such circumstances, but Ramsey may well be correct when he suggests that Alaska is a crucial test—"a pivotal area in a pivotal time." We still have the opportunity to demonstrate a rational set of priorities and a decision-making process capable of averting disaster rather than merely lamenting it; if that opportunity is wasted, it will signify not just the loss of a battle, but the loss of hope.

The final essay in this section "The Destruction of Indochina" examines one aspect of America's rape of that southeast Asian nation. The full hypocrisy of our official concern with "environment" is here revealed: in a move unprecedented in history, chemical weapons and massive quantities of conventional explosives are being used to destroy the countryside itself, rendering it unfit for agriculture for decades or perhaps centuries. All this is accomplished in the name of denying resources to the "enemy," which translates, as it always has in the history of warfare, to starving women, children, and old folk. The article which describes these atrocities, compiled by a group of Stanford University biologists with the cooperation of scholars at many other institutions, has already been decried by "responsible" members of the scientific community as "political." We include it here not only because of its special relevance to the subject matter of this section (although "scandal" is too weak a word), but also because we deeply believe that science and technology need a great deal more of this brand of "politics," and a great deal less complicity in inhuman and irreversible destruction.

# Among Wild Whales

### ROGER PAYNE

When we talk about the ocean, we are usually only talking about its uppermost, thinnest film—a small fraction of its total volume. We think of a place with ceaseless motion, bright light, sparkling waves and brilliant sunshine. But beneath the turmoil and the light of the first 600 feet lies a different ocean, a profoundly peaceful place of constant darkness and nearly uniform temperature where there are no waves—only slow, drifting currents. The creatures that occupy this largest of the earth's habitats are fed either by sorties to the surface or by waiting for food to sift down to them. This vertical traffic in food can, of course, go both ways and many surface-dwelling animals obtain their food by diving for it.

Sperm whales are probably the deepest diving of all mammals—going down at least 3,000 feet, and perhaps 4 times that far. On long dives from the surface, whales must find whatever they are after without help from their eyes, even though they may have left the surface in broad daylight. It is also well known that they feed routinely on large squid which are found at depths well below any light penetration. Also, sperm whales produce loud, sharp clicks—the sort of sounds useful for sonar (sound navigation and ranging, the type of echolocation employed by porpoises and bats). All of this lends support to the probability that hearing is the non-visual sense most used by whales.

## LARGEST BRAIN

Sperm whales have the largest brain that has ever existed on earth. The combination of a large brain with an elaborate and closely knit social structure is usually found in animals of high intelligence. As well as having large brains, sperm whales are highly social, breeding in large harem herds customarily led by a single bull.

The females in such herds are accompanied by their young of all ages, from infants to adolescents. Because these nurseries are found in equatorial waters, noted for their calmness, it ought to be possible to follow a herd of sperm whales for a long time—perhaps even long enough for the herd to get used to a boat. This is what I want to do: to be among wild whales for prolonged periods and to study them.

If I succeed, there will be many things worth looking for. For example, among the various sounds that have been recorded from whales are some very low tones. Such sounds are reflected well only by large objects such as the most prominent features of the ocean floor—undersea mountains, abyssal plains, wide canyons, the edges of a continental shelf, etc. If one repeatedly noted that a herd of whales changed its heading after a bout of low frequency sound productions, the observation would suggest that echolocation of undersea landmarks was being used for navigation. If, in the process of studying how whales navigate, we also learned their regular migration routes, then we would put our efforts to preserve whales on a much surer basis.

Among Wild Whales. From *The New York Zoological Society Newsletter*, November 1968, pp. 1–6. Reprinted by permission of the author and the publisher.

## THE "TALKING BARNACLE"

The crucial step upon which my plans depend is to develop a reliable way of keeping up with a herd of whales—even in fogs and at night. The Electronics Department at Rockefeller University and the Woods Hole Oceanographic Institution have developed for this project several compact beacons which transmit radio signals whenever the whale surfaces and sound pulses at all times. These ingenious devices also telemeter back the depth at which the whale is swimming. By attaching such a "talking barnacle" to a whale, I hope to follow it under almost any conditions.

We have tested this equipment in mock chases from various boats. But attaching it to the glistening hide of a frightened whale from the bow of a small and tossing boat is quite different.

In order to do this, I went to Bermuda last May. As a sort of practice warm-up for my future among the sperm whale herds, I tried my hand at attaching beacons to the humpback whales found in Bermuda waters in the spring. Humpback whales reach about 45 feet vs. 50 for an average sperm whale. They differ from sperm whales in that they have baleen plates through which they filter water to find small prey, whereas sperm whales have large teeth and eat big animals like giant squid. Other than this, humpbacks seemed at the time to be a good alternative to sperm whales since they are easily accessible from a shore-based boat and swim at about the same rate as sperm whales.

## UNEXPECTED FACTOR

A humpback would also be more vulnerable to attachment than a sperm whale since it returns to the surface more often for air. In one sense humpbacks are a radical departure from all other whales in that they have thin, flexible flippers that are roughly ⅓ as long as their bodies (by contrast, sperm whales have only small, tab-like flippers). I mention this because even though these large flippers seemed inconsequential to the outcome of my tests when plans were being laid, they proved to be the crucial factor in the end.

After many near misses and fruitless tries, I finally succeeded in attaching beacons to two humpbacks on two different days, and in actually following one of them acoustically for a few minutes. What happened next, in both cases, was unexpected. Each whale, using one of its long supple flippers, simply wiped the beacon off its side! (A sperm whale couldn't do this unless the beacon was close to the flipper.) Because those were our last approachable whales of the season, there was no further opportunity of attaching a beacon out of reach of the flippers, and thus the humpbacks won the first round.

Somehow it all seems to be just as it should be since the whales won in such an unexpected way and since I had quite failed to credit them with enough agility. Besides— one of the chief characteristics of any research project is that one invariably has his eye on the wrong ball!

While I was following humpback whales off Bermuda I became interested in the fantastic sounds they produce. (I once heard, through the bottom of a small row boat, one calling for about 15 minutes.) In the vicinity of Bermuda, humpbacks seem to spend most of their time over a pair of offshore banks (the only ones), lying southwest of the island. Nothing is known of what attracts them to the area, but a good guess from their behavior is that they may be using Bermuda and its adjacent undersea mountain peaks (the offshore banks) as a convenient rendezvous for pairing and mating and as a good place to feed. In what may be courtship, I've seen them leap clear of the water on dozens of occasions and have watched pairs lolling at the surface, with their flippers slapping the water or swaying from side to side like palms bending in the wind.

I have a few tapes of humpback whale sounds recorded off Bermuda by Frank Watlington of Columbia University's Lamont

## MODERN WHALING

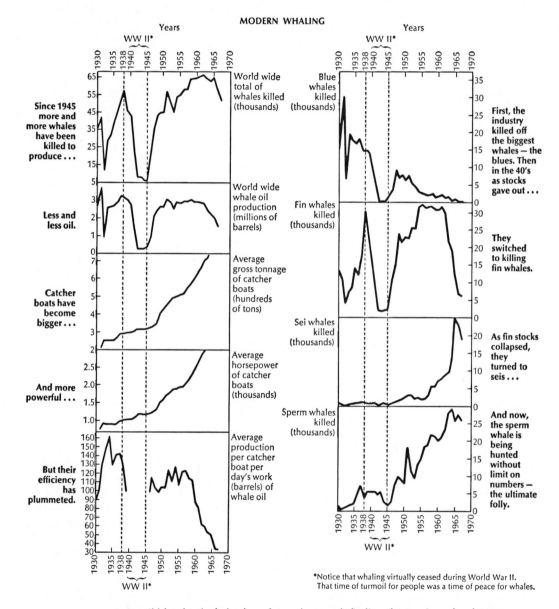

**Since 1945 more and more whales have been killed to produce ...**

*World wide total of whales killed (thousands)*

**Less and less oil.**

*World wide whale oil production (millions of barrels)*

**Catcher boats have become bigger ...**

*Average gross tonnage of catcher boats (hundreds of tons)*

**And more powerful ...**

*Average horsepower of catcher boats (thousands)*

**But their efficiency has plummeted.**

*Average production per catcher boat per day's work (barrels) of whale oil*

*Blue whales killed (thousands)*

**First, the industry killed off the biggest whales — the blues. Then in the 40's as stocks gave out ...**

*Fin whales killed (thousands)*

**They switched to killing fin whales.**

*Sei whales killed (thousands)*

**As fin stocks collapsed, they turned to seis ...**

*Sperm whales killed (thousands)*

**And now, the sperm whale is being hunted without limit on numbers — the ultimate folly.**

*Notice that whaling virtually ceased during World War II. That time of turmoil for people was a time of peace for whales.

As wild herds of whales have been destroyed, finding the survivors has become more difficult and required more effort. As larger whales are killed off, smaller species are exploited to keep the industry alive. However, since there have never been species limits, large whales are always taken wherever and whenever encountered. Thus small whales are used to subsidize the extermination of large ones.

Geophysical Observatory. They are truly extraordinary—they sound like no other earthly thing. The whale produces low sounds containing all the tones that can be heard by people as well as tones that are ultrasonic and infrasonic. Some very preliminary analysis of two of these tapes has led Scott McVay of Princeton University and me to the very tentative and intriguing conclusion that humpback whales may be singing! It's just that they sing a long song, somewhat analogous to the songs of birds (both in style and in function) but lasting minutes rather than seconds.

## 25,911 SPERM WHALES KILLED IN 1967

As fascinating as my preliminary explorations of whales have been to me, there is another compelling aspect of wild whales which interests me: Will there be any whales alive a few years from now?

It is generally assumed that the passing of the great age of sailing ships was accompanied by the disappearance of whaling. Both were abandoned because they could not compete. Sailing ships lost because a steamboat could never be becalmed, and whaling died out because kerosene gave cheaper light than spermaceti candles. Whaling would appear to be in the hands of historians—a forgotten, quaint, and somewhat barbaric art practiced in a distant past. But the real tragedy of this assumption is that it is entirely wrong. Worse— it is a lethal misconception because it may well cost the world its whales. The truth is that the 20th century, and not the 19th, is the great age of whaling, and that right now is when the greatest slaughter ever made is going on.

For example, 100 years ago an average three-year whaling voyage brought back the oil of 37 whales. This is an average of only one whale killed per month. Today a typical catcher boat averages one whale per day; some, routinely, three or four whales per day. There were, as might be expected, more voy-

ages that were worse than better, but even the best three-year cruise ever made in the 1860s returned only 85 whales. In 1967, 25,911 sperm whales were killed. The total killed of all species in 1967 was 52,046, plus 20,000 porpoises slaughtered by Japan.

## THE TECHNOLOGY OF SLAUGHTER

Compare the condition of whaling at the ends of the first and second thirds of the century—i.e. in 1933 and 1966. In 1933, 28,907 whales were killed, resulting in 2,606,201 barrels of oil. In 1966, 57,891 whales produced 1,546,904 barrels of oil—i.e. in 1966 twice as many whales (with almost weird exactness) produced just over ½ as much oil. We can only conclude that each year the whalers must catch smaller and smaller whales in larger and larger numbers. This trend exists despite the fact that there has been an explosive technological improvement in whaling procedures. The most modern technology is now routinely employed by whalers—indeed it is required to keep whaling alive. For example, in all areas where there is pelagic whaling, ship-based helicopters are used for spotting whales. The catcher boats are then radio-guided to the whale from the helicopter. A sonar on the catcher boat can be trained on the whale once it is close by, in order that the boat can maneuver to intercept the whale as it surfaces for air.

Harpoons are, of course, not hand-thrown but fired from a cannon on the bow of the boat. Once fast to the whale the line is handled and cared for, not as in the 19th century by hands and hatfulls of water to keep it from burning as it smoked around a wooden loggerhead, but by a steam-driven winch with a 750-ton ship to back it up. The line, too, has been scaled up from ¾" natural fiber to 1¼" nylon with a breaking strength of 18 tons (even so it is occasionally broken by a particularly frantic whale). To keep the battle short the head of the harpoon is fitted with an exploding grenade which is usually effective in killing a whale after about five seconds (a fight lasting five hours and requiring nine harpoons is on record, however). Once dead, the corpse is inflated with compressed air to keep it from sinking and a floating radio beacon is anchored to it. The signal from this beacon will guide a tow boat to the dead whale, thus freeing the catcher boat immediately for further hunting.

The tow boat drags the body to the factory ship, again using radios and radar if need be. The dead whale is winched up on deck through an inclined slipway in the stern. It is then butchered and melted down, ground up, and stored in tanks.

It is not surprising that the whaling industry's "improvement" in techniques has all but destroyed the resource it has tooled up to exploit. For no animal population can withstand such a technological onslaught. Indeed, it remains to be seen whether even man can withstand his own technology.

## KRILL

The most extraordinary thing about the whaling industry is that it seems to be bent on its own annihilation. It is in such trouble that it may even switch to harvesting krill.

Krill, a shrimp which abounds in the Antarctic ocean, is the principle food of baleen whales. As whales become scarcer, the whaling industry is considering the harvesting of krill for its protein and oil. There are rumors that some krill catchers would exterminate whales to protect krill for man!

This absurd suggestion ignores the fact that sustained harvesting of whales is by far the most efficient way to harvest krill.

Here are the figures: just before World War II, when herds of whales flourished, catcher boats (average weight 260 tons) caught 1.66 whales per hunting day. These whales yielded 26.6 tons of oil and about 49 tons of protein. Krill is 6% oil and 20% protein. If krill fisherman can extract about 80%

(highly efficient) they will still have to catch and process between 300 an 550 tons of krill per day to equal the whales—an impossibility with a 260-ton boat!

To date, the Russians' best krill catch rates (achieved only in the densest swarms and from very large ships) has been "6 tons per half-hour of trawling"—not even half fast enough to keep pace with the whales.

Certainly krill harvesting will someday help feed men—but why consider whales as competitors, when they collect the abundance of krill more efficiently than we can hope to? That is like wiping out beef cattle in order to have the pleasure of eating grass-protein-concentrate.

Unbridled exploitation seems to have been the pattern taken by whaling throughout the 20th century. It is unlikely that whaling will ever stop in any region before it has brought stocks below a density at which whaling still pays. With the present highly efficient means for finding and killing whales, it is likely that this density will fall below the level at which (1) males can still find females; (2) enough traditional herd structure can be retained to raise the young; and (3) enough genetic variability exists for species to survive various regional and natural catastrophies (e.g. famines, diseases, etc.). What is obviously needed is some international control of all oceans. And this control must have some teeth to it.

In protecting whales and controlling their slaughterers, the world would be deprived of no unique food or product. In fact, it is surprising to find what whales are used for. Whales produce two types of oil. That which comes from sperm whales is inedible; that from baleen whales is edible and is used primarily for oleomargarine. The oil collected from all whales during a season is really a raw material. It can be appropriately changed by chemistry to become anything from oleomargarine to lipstick or from shoe polish to transmission oil. There is no hope that one could limit the usages of this oil, since there are innumerable companies that can use it.

## NEITHER UNIQUE
## NOR ESSENTIAL

But it is essential to note that there is nothing taken from whales that has any unique property which cannot be duplicated by some alternative natural or synthetic substitute. In fact, the industry is not really even an important minor contributor to the world's economy. It produces even less oil than exotic sources—1/4 as much oil as rape seeds, 1/7 as much as palm nuts, and 1/7 as much as sunflower seeds. To get some idea of how large the industry actually is, one can calculate that the entire gross receipts for oil collected in the Antarctic in 1967 was about $9,000,000, less money than New York City spent on snow removal during the same period, or less than 1/16 of its garbage removal bill.

## RALLYING POINT

Within the present structure there is really no hope of any change coming in time. With-out a change in tactics the horizon is uniformly black; storms are in all quarters. To get out of this plight we need to be doing a lot of things that are not being done. In fact, they are not being done anywhere by anybody.

We need to create ways for coordinating international concern—to provide a rallying point for Whale Power. This might be a new organization or a fund within an existing one, such as in the New York Zoological Society. Any tightly organized nucleus with clearly stated aims can become a seed crystal to organize about itself a solid body of united concern. And any group is worth launching if it provides realistic hope for international cooperation among private citizens.

Do people throughout the world care whether whales vanish? We think so; but is such a belief real or imagined? Step one seems to be to poll people to find out whether there is a consensus that something should be done to protect whales. If there is total consensus, we will drive ahead hard—otherwise the effort is perhaps better spent on something else.

# The California Water Plan:
# The Most Expensive Faucet in the World

GENE MARINE

One of the most striking things about the ecology bandwagon is that it is becoming badly overpopulated with politicians who a year ago wouldn't have known a food chain from a string of supermarkets. Ecology is, these people assure us, a "safe" issue, best

The California Water Plan: The Most Expensive Faucet in the World. From *Ramparts,* May 1970, pp. 36–41. Reprinted by permission of the publisher.

discussed in tones of restrained alarm and good also for distracting the gullible young from the war in Vietnam.

This just goes to show how little politicians understand the implications of what they've gotten themselves involved in. By its own inevitable logic, an ecological conscience must lead to revolutionary conclusions. And these conclusions will surely be hastened by the politicians' own acts. Selling off a whole area's precious water supply to satisfy certain highrollers who are big in the para-politics of state power is a good example.

Water is neither as clean nor as free as it seems. And when combined with financial power, it becomes a highly volatile substance which does odd things—like flow through the hands of the people into the pockets of a few. In California, water is power. Water is wealth. These are just the most obvious lessons to be learned from the celebrated California Water Plan, which is also a carefully drawn blueprint for ecological disaster.

To understand this disaster, you first have to understand the nature of the ownership of California's major industry—agriculture. When you talk about California agriculture, you're not talking about farmers—at least not the individual, tilling his few hundred acres, normally conjured up by that term. There are those farmers in California—in numbers, a lot of them—and they do dominate a few specialty crops. But real agricultural wealth, which *is* the wealth of the state, lies in the hands of those "farmers" who own most of the land. In California, agriculture is synonymous with corporate empire: 79 per cent of the land is owned by seven per cent of the "farmers."

As agriculture—or agribusiness, if you want to insist on that accurate but repellent word—is the wealth of California, so is it the power. The power structures of New York, Illinois and Pennsylvania are complex. California's is simple—simpler, in fact, than Mississippi's and almost as simple as Honduras'. The people who own the land (not really people, of course: corporations) own the state.

California's aerospace industry, which seems to the casual observer to be extremely important in her economy and therefore in her politics, had prime contracts during the 1968–69 fiscal year (mostly from the Department of Defense and NASA) totaling around $7.5 billion. But by the time California's 200 commercial crops are harvested, transported, processed and packed, their market value is about $16 billion—and almost all that work is done inside the state.

Furthermore, if you search the list of contributors to any major candidate in the state and then run down the occupation of the people whose names you uncover, you'll find only small (and then probably personal) participation by aerospace people. You'll find the "farmers," though, every time—the "farmers" and the oilmen, who are often the same people and who in any case get along together very well. Add in the public utilities and the banks which are intricately tied in with the agricultural giants, and you have the power lineup. And it is these agricultural giants and their allies who, in an effort to control California's water (that precious commodity key to farm wealth) have brought the state to the brink of ecological disaster.

As a glance at any California map will show (a relief map makes it even easier), the Sacramento River, flowing from the north, and the San Joaquin River, flowing from the south, come together to form San Francisco Bay and ultimately to reach the ocean (actually, they don't any more, but that's later in the story). Where they come together is called, in California, "the Delta." The two valleys are thus not separated, and together are called simply the Central Valley.

The Sacramento Valley has, and has always had, enough water to handle agriculture on all its available land and more; but vast acres of the San Joaquin Valley were naturally damned to aridity. The availability of water diminishes sharply as you move south past the Delta. In the 1930's, however, the federal government undertook the gigantic Central Valley Project (CVP) to move "surplus" water from the north into the San Joaquin Valley—and precipitated a fight that lasted for decades and whose implications may be felt for centuries.

The CVP was built under the Reclamation Act of 1902, as subsequently amended. The 1862 Homestead Act provided settlers with a quarter section of land—160 acres—and the Reclamation Act provided for irrigation projects which would deliver to each supposedly small farmer enough water for 160 acres. But because of a number of unanticipated circumstances—vast swindles under the Swamp and Overflow Land Act; huge tracts given away by the federal government for railroads to encourage expansion; and a tangled mess of claims to old Mexican land grants—more than half of California's arable land passed into the hands of huge landowners before small farmers had a chance at it. During the Depression, even as CVP construction of dams and canals for the transfer of water was under way, bank foreclosures added other small holdings to the large tracts.

The Central Valley Project, however, will still deliver to any single landowner only enough water for 160 acres (320 acres if the landowner is married—a dubious but generous concession by the Bureau of Reclamation). If you own, say, 100,000 acres, you can get water to irrigate the entire amount *only* if you agree to sell off all the acreage over 160 within ten years.

Now, the mightier landowners, all-powerful within California's borders, tried for more than a decade to break the federal government's determination to stick to the 160-acre limitation regarding water rights. Unsuccessful, they did succeed at least in keeping CVP out of the west side of the San Joaquin Valley. These lands still sit aridly awaiting the water that to their owners is gold, and awaiting the day when that water will come without pesky federal regulation.

In 1959, when the California Water Plan was placed by legislative decision on the 1960 ballot, these were a few of the west side landowners:

| | |
|---|---|
| Standard Oil Co. of Calif. | 218,000 acres |
| Other oil companies, combined | |
| | 264,000 acres |
| Kern County Land Co. | 348,000 acres |
| Southern Pacific Railroad | 200,000 acres |
| Tejon Ranch Company | 348,000 acres |
| Boston Ranch Company | 37,000 acres* |

And 1,323,000 other acres were in the hands of people who each owned more than 1000 acres. There is oil on some of this land, but it is not as valuable as the crops which, if water were available, could be grown there.

One institution which doesn't appear on the above list but which is indispensable to it is the Bank of America, by deposits the world's largest commercial bank (and itself a large landowner in agricultural California as a whole). The bank finances more than half of all California agriculture. Its former president, Rudolph Peterson, said late in 1968 that the Bank of America was "the world's largest agricultural lender with lines of credit for agricultural production running at about a billion dollars a year." The total commitment of the bank to agriculture is probably more than $3 billion. Rival banks, notably Wells Fargo, have large fingers in the pie, as do other "farmers" like Safeway Stores, Inc., the DiGiorgio Corporation and newcomers like Purex, Dow Chemical and United Fruit. Already for decades the absolute masters of California, these giants were still searching in the late '40's and early '50's, as they are today, for more and greater sources of agricultural wealth. Blocked by the Bureau of Reclamation's 160-acre limitation from any hope of federal subsidy for irrigation of their lands, they first tried unsuccessfully to get the state to finance the entire CVP itself without the federal government, and to give them the water without the 160-acre restriction. But Washington refused to cooperate, and the Big Guys had to look for other tills to tap.

The Central Valley Project's principal features were built by the early '50's and no one was in danger of dying of thirst or going out of business. A rational state power structure might have decided that a point of balance had been reached; that they were getting moderately rich in an effortless sort of way and it was time to sit back and consolidate gains. But rationality has never been the strong suit of power structures. And what was good for California was not good—or at least not good enough—for business. The major discontent came from the southern part of the state.

Southern California hustlers—especially the Los Angeles variety—are a special breed. They have, among other things, perfected the arts of luring people (wealthy people, preferably, although those with retirement savings are also nice) into their part of the state and selling them things (especially real estate). Somebody builds a new apartment house; he gives tenants a month's free rent for moving in; and as soon as it's built and full, he sells it to a little old lady from Iowa. Until this particular con was stopped recently, some couples boasted that they hadn't paid a month's rent in Los Angeles for three years. What you don't do is tell prospective immigrants that Los Angeles sits partly on a thinly covered desert basis, in the shadow of achingly eroded hills that could (and often do) slide down at any minute, bringing their precarious burden of houses with them. You advertise the new suburbs and don't talk about the fact that if there were any reason to live in those locations there probably wouldn't be *new* suburbs there at this late date. Above all, you don't tell them that Los Angeles outran its meager natural water supply more than a half century ago; that the water since stolen from Northern California's Owens Valley and conned from the Colorado (after all these years, Arizona finally won the lawsuit that said California was taking more than its share) is enough today— but won't be if people keep coming in at the rate of 1000 a day. You don't tell them anything. You keep pushing the plastic dream and pitching for more industry and more workers, and you look around for more water to con somebody out of.

That's Southern California today, and that was Southern California in the '40's and in the '50's. Northern Californians, the hustlers noted, had plenty of water. Look at the Feather River—3600 square miles of watershed, an annual average runoff of 4.5 million acre-feet (enough, for instance, to irrigate all the cotton in the state). But they would never give it to the hustlers down south. Northern Californians were wise to the con.

So the Southern California hustlers chafed, while the Big Guys—most of them northerners —waited with their arid, unproductive land while reaping millions from the land they had in production. But time was on their side.

By 1948 it was clear to the Big Guys that their plan to get the state to take over the Central Valley Project and then drop the 160-acre irrigation limitation had been blocked. And so, in hotel bars and the spacious rooms of private clubs, the lords of the Valley talked with their counterparts in Southern California. They decided that together they could pull it off—with taxpayers' money, of course. You take some of the water, we'll take some. You have a majority of the voters down there and they can be conned into supporting the plan. All we have to do is invent an imminent water shortage and then dash in with a scheme for their salvation.

Then the Big Guys turned to something they've always been good at: word games.

There came into being, in 1950 or so, a group called the California Central Valley Flood Control Association (first word game). That group subsidized what looked like a routine flood control investigation by State Water Engineer A. D. Edmonston. His report, however, instead of being a routine report of a routine investigation, was something quite different. Its title (second word game) was *Report on Feasibility of Feather River Project and Sacramento-San Joaquin Delta Diversion Projects Proposed as Features of the California Water Plan.*

The California Water Plan had not yet come into being. But people were talking about a California Water Plan, in some circles anyway, and Edmonston and the people behind him wanted to be sure that their projects were in it.

The Feather River part was a fast shuffle. The important part of the plan, as far as its sponsors were concerned, was in the sneaky end of the title: *Sacramento-San Joaquin Delta Diversion Projects.* Water would be taken out of the Delta and sent south to irrigate the Big Guys' valuable lands, thus cutting the costs on the ones already being irrigated and bringing new lands into production.

The Feather River Project was a dam near the city of Oroville built to regulate the flow of that untamed river into an even and manageable year-round supply. The *reason* for the dam—useful as it proved to be, later, for flood control—had nothing to do with protection for the citizens of Yuba City and Marysville. The dam was constructed because without it the Federal Bureau of Reclamation might stick its nose into the Delta Diversion Project and say that the water being diverted was Central Valley Project water with its 160-acre limitation.

But the Feather River feeds into the Sacramento *below* the CVP projects in the north. By regulating its flow, the project planners could claim that the water being taken from the Delta is the controlled flow of the Feather (i.e., a *state* project) and that no limitations on its use could apply.

What's that you say? Water is water? Not in California.

Problem: At the Delta, the fresh water from the Central Valley meets the salt water of San Francisco Bay; the meeting place moves back and forth, sometimes well out toward the Bay, sometimes dangerously deep into the agricultural areas of the Delta itself. A part of CVP is the Delta Cross-Channel Canal, designed to take fresh Sacramento River water across the Delta without allowing it to mix with the Bay's salt water. But this water has the limitation on it.

Solution: Build another canal (the Peripheral Canal) around the Delta to the east. A pumping plant would lift the water and a new canal would take it down the west side of the San Joaquin Valley, virtually creating money as it flows.

It sounds simple. In principle, it is; but in practice it is something else. When Edmonston talked about moving water, he didn't fool around. The proposed Feather River Project (third word game: call the whole thing by that name) was by far the largest movement of water ever suggested. It has since engendered greater proposals (I have heard one for using Yukon River water in Mexico) but at the time it was, to use a once-familiar California word, colossal. The word about Edmonston's report got around, and pretty soon much of California, without quite understanding why,

was talking about "the Feather River Project." No doubt the Big Guys, long master-users of publicity, had something to do with turning on the public to the exciting project, and seeing to it that the public saw it as an exciting project. Engineers loved it. Men in the street were impressed by it.

Northern Californians hated it.

The next four years brought a few engineering changes in the project, but the time was mostly spent in politics. Regularly the project was brought up in the legislature. Regularly northern senators or assemblymen would offer amendments. Regularly the amendments would lose. Regularly the project would lose. What the northerners were trying to amend into the bill was, believe it or not, a homegrown, California copy of the 160-acre limitation on federal projects. It seemed as though a stalemate had been reached, which was hardly a satisfactory end to the struggle as far as the waterlords of the Valley were concerned.

When liberal "Pat" Brown ran for governor in 1958, backers urged him to endorse a 160-acre limitation for the Water Plan, but he refused; he *did* say he wouldn't stand for any "unjust enrichment" of big landowners. It was supposed to be the sort of liberal compromise which satisfies all parties. It satisfied practically nobody.

It was finally left to newly elected United States Senator Clair Engle to find a way around the 160-acre limitation: a two-price system. The waterlords would have to pay a little more for any water in excess of that necessary for the first 160 acres. But not too much more. Not enough to get in the way of the really massive profits that they would soon realize. And of course, they could have as much water as the size of their holdings made necessary. It was enough to swing a couple of votes in the deadlocked legislature.

The bare minimum cost of the Feather River Project would be, according to the most optimistic estimates of its optimistic partisans, about $2.5 billion. That was something like California's annual budget at the time, and nobody thought the California voters would pass a bond issue for two and a half billion dollars. So they trimmed it down to a figure which they thought the voters might buy, though it was still the largest state bond issue in the history of the United States: $1.75 billion. That's what went on the 1960 ballot as Proposition 1.

Opponents hooted. How, they wanted to know, can you build a $2.5 billion project for $1.75 billion? You can't. Quietly, the engineers cropped the project down to a smaller size, to be ready should the bond issue pass. As they were doing so, opponents of the project had no trouble finding economists to punch holes in the estimates. Inflation, they pointed out, would run the costs up too high. There would be problems selling the bonds. The $1.75 billion project, which was really a $2.5 billion project, would actually wind up costing closer to $4 billion.

They were right on all counts.

Labor (except for steelworkers, operating engineers and teamsters) opposed the bond issue. So did the Grange (historically, in California, the organization representing the "real" farmers). So did two independent consulting firms hired by the state to appraise the financing. So did 50 professors of economics from the state's leading universities. So even did two RAND Corporation scientists who published a paper on Southern California's water supply.

If San Diego had voted two-to-one for the project, it would have lost. San Diego, however, voted *four*-to-one for the project. Out of 5,842,712 voters, the difference was only 173,944 votes—but it was enough for passage. No Northern California county except the one in which Oroville Dam was to be built voted "yes."

The California Water Plan, then, is under way. (Final note on word games: For clarity we have used "Feather River Project" to describe what is properly that project *plus* the Delta diversion project. Today, however, that combination—the total of the project approved by the voters in 1960—has come to be called "The California Water Plan.") It has been under way for almost ten years. Oroville Dam exists, ugly but effective; you can drive

up to an "overlook," view a display replete with superlatives that will tell you far more than you want to know about the dam and its construction, and look down on the dam itself. They had to move a whole railroad to build it. In the meantime, three other things have happened. Some Californians have learned a little more about the plan; some Californians have learned a little more about the costs; and some Californians have learned a little more about what I can only call— overworked word though it has suddenly become—ecology.

The current "official" estimate for the "final" cost of the California Water Plan is $2.75 billion. Whoever makes current "official" cost estimates knows perfectly well that this is hogwash—$4 billion is still closer to the truth. But if that admission were made, too many Californians might get mad. They want Californians to stay happy until this June, when they will be asked to vote "yes" on another ballot measure. It seems that California has this bunch of California Water Plan bonds from the 1960 issue, bonds they hung onto as long as possible—and now nobody will buy them. The state constitution says that you can't pay more than five per cent interest on state bonds (California has one of those constitutions that tell you everything except what color socks the governor may wear), and at five per cent, nobody will buy the damned things.

They have a fast $800 million worth of bonds still to be unloaded, and they figure that if they pay seven per cent, maybe somebody will buy them. If, I should say, Californians pay seven per cent. And whom will they pay? Mainly the Bank of America and its friends, who are the biggest moneylenders in the state, just as they are the biggest underwriters of the Big Guy "farmers."*

So the costs of the California Water Project continue to escalate. Thanks to an ingenious free enterprise system, the people of California have the rare opportunity to pay for the privilege of watering the vast lands of

---

* [Eds. Note: California voters passed the measure to increase the interest on water bonds to seven per cent.]

the rich so that they can grow bigger cash crops and get even richer. But these costs are just the quantitative ones, merely the tip of the iceberg. To appreciate fully the bill which the people of California are going to pay for the honor of living in a society graced by institutions like the Bank of America, let us see what the California Water Plan will *really* do, if the voters let them finish it up this coming election.

First of all, it will—if it is extended to its planned limits, which are far beyond the currently authorized $3 billion or $4 billion project—destroy every natural river in California. There will be none without a dam, none without a man-made lake, none with natural fish and bird and invertebrate life. We don't know what all this will do to the ocean off Northern California; no one has ever asked. We don't know what it will do to the people whose living comes out of that ocean, or in a less important way to those who love to eat what others make their living catching.

Nor do we know what it will do to the climate of some lovely places, like the resort area of the Russian River, or to the Napa Valley, the heart of California's vineyards.

We know that canals and tunnels and dams and whatnot will be all over the place (the master plan calls for 370 more dams). It is already almost impossible to drive through, or to fly over, the Central Valley of California without seeing a canal, a pipeline or a gigantic row of metal towers carrying power lines. They are ugly. Agricultural land, artificial though the rows and crops may be, still somehow looks natural; it makes sense. A concrete canal does not look like a river.

We have talked about the enrichment of the few at the expense of the many. Along with this goes the continuing pollution of our information channels. Californians will be told again this spring that Proposition 7 is necessary so that Los Angeles can have its water (or, rather, they—the Southern Californians with the votes—will be told this). They will be told that again and again. The scare tactics will be dragged out as new appropriations, new authorizations are necessary. Our leaders, as

much puppets on strings as any much-bemedalled Central American dictator, will lie to us. All right, they lie to us all the time; but I still don't like making it easy for them.

It is not only that the real purpose of the whole *megillah* has nothing to do with Los Angeles at all. Los Angeles might know that and still want their end of the culvert. It is that, in fact, Los Angeles does not need the water. The only sense in which Los Angeles (or San Diego, or Orange County or Riverside) can be said to *need* the water is in relation to projected figures of advertising-induced, immigrant population growth. When you provide services for this sort of a hustle, you make a decision: you have decided to support such growth; you have decided that you *want* it.

Thus, in Water Plan-opponent Alvin Duskin's phrase, Northern Californian water will go to Los Angeles in order to make more Los Angeles.

In the meantime, the Sacramento River keeps flowing, despite the existing CVP and the reduction of its flow by dam-building. At present, its fresh water outflow into the Delta is 18 million acre-feet a year. When the California Water Plan is finished, it will be two million acre-feet a year. So what?

So there is irrigation in the Sacramento Valley too, and the water dumps back into the river. It brings with it pesticide residues and minerals from the land; and in addition, the rivers in California, like those in New Jersey or Indiana, get a little industrial pollution. At the moment, in the Sacramento, all those things are diluted by 18 million acre-feet of water. Cut the flow to two million acre-feet, and you get a heavy gravy of pollutants.

In the Delta—one of the most beautiful and delicately balanced ecological systems this side of the Everglades, even as fouled up as it already is—this will make one hell of a lot of difference. If even one species of microscopic, brackish-water life disappears where the fresh water meets the salt water in the Delta, the ramifications, as I'm sure you know by now, can whiplash back through whole life chains, destroying dozens of species.

The land in the Delta—rich agricultural

land—is in some places actually below the water level, and protected by levees. This is because of subsidence; if you fly over some of the islands in the Delta, you can see that they're saucer-shaped. The water underlies, as well as surrounds, the land—but it keeps it rich. Change that water and you can kill that land.

The pollutants in the water, of course, can't stop at the Delta, whatever their effect there. They would flow on out into San Francisco Bay. San Francisco Bay is an ecological mess, but there *are* all kinds of things still alive in it. We can kill the Bay if we want to; the California Water Plan may very well do so.

Okay. So much for the water that *isn't* transferred. What about the water that is?

You know that the Tigris-Euphrates Valley, now a desert, used to be a fruitful irrigated plain. There are areas like that in Pakistan, too, and elsewhere in the world. What happens is that the irrigation water first of all deposits various kinds of salts, thus making the soil more saline (or alkaline). At the same time, the irrigation process leaches some necessary minerals out of the soil, lowering its productivity.

There are ways of slowing up this process (they're very good at it in the Imperial Valley, at the southern end of California, which is a natural desert made to bloom just like in the poems), but in the long run you can't win. With present technology, at least, irrigation means, eventually, desert.

The trend is already clearly noticeable in the Central Valley, and particularly in the San Joaquin Valley, though of course destruction is not imminent. The San Joaquin River, as it used to flow before CVP made it virtually flow upstream, came into the Delta pretty heavily laden with these leached minerals, and it has left a lot of salts behind it. The only difference now is that it starts at the other end, and is then brought back to the Delta through an artificial channel. There was a move not long ago to use the channel for irrigation and to turn the actual San Joaquin River into a pipe. Modern man.

Now clearly, when this Sacramento River water is removed, by whatever means, across the Delta and into the San Joaquin Valley, it does not even have the advantage of being pure water to begin with. It's been used in the north. So it goes on being used, for irrigation, getting dirtier as it goes, not only with leached minerals but with pesticide residues and with anything else you can think of except maybe buffalo chips. But some of it is supposed to go to Los Angeles. Obviously, this now-filthy water can't be put back into the aqueduct and sent through the mountains to our southern neighbors. No, indeed: they get what *hasn't* been taken out for irrigation. What has been taken out is dumped into the San Joaquin drain and taken back to the Delta.

Or it was going to be, until we started to learn a little ecology. Now the Delta people and the Bay people have started to yell so loudly about this poisoned water—water which by the time it reaches the Delta may actually be "strong" enough to poison the land—that the planners have another idea, if you want to call it that.

They're going to divert it into Kesterson Reservoir, which I cannot locate precisely for you because it doesn't exist yet. The poisoned water, according to the current plan, will sit in Kesterson Reservoir until somebody figures out a way to clean it up or get rid of it.

Really. That's the "plan."

To love California is, alas, not necessarily to know it. There are millions of us who wander with delight among her mountains (did you know that Sequoia National Forest was originally created in order to drive out a succeeding socialist commune?), seek with joy her gentle valleys, enjoy her trees, her rolling hills, her awesome battle against the ocean—and who have no idea that she is a feudal state, held in thrall by a tiny few.

We need not kill ourselves through frenzied, irrational, needless growth; we need not labor to build stupid, destructive projects. But to achieve balance, we need first—of all things, in this most modern of states—a "land reform" which will make tortured, expensive and destructive schemes like the California Water Plan impossible.

# The SST:
# Who Needs It?

*It may soon be possible to fly from Watts to Harlem in two hours and to disrupt the lives of everyone in between.\**

Discussions of the U.S. supersonic transport program customarily focus on the aircraft's irremediable sonic boom, its unacceptable takeoff and landing noise, and the other, more speculative, environmental costs of operating a fleet of them. These arguments all mitigate against the expenditure of public funds on such an enterprise, and they will be included for completeness here, but there is no case for the SST even without them. The use of society's limited monies to subsidize the well-off minority of its members who fly at all is itself a dubious proposition; if we really want to do so, there are alternative means to bring greater benefits to the air traveller at less cost; and the contention that the SST program will benefit the U.S. as a whole economically has been descredited by the most distinguished bodies to examine the issue.

As a diversion of society's resources, the SST has in one sense received more attention than it deserves: the 700 million dollars of government money in the project so far is less than a fortieth the sum applied to the destruction of Vietnam last year alone. Were the latter fiasco not available for comparison, however, this figure and the 5 billion dollars the taxpayers stand to lose eventually on the SST would be more appalling. Moreover, as an

The SST: Who Needs It? Copyright © 1971 by J. P. Holdren.

\* William F. Baxter, *Stanford Law Review*, Nov. 1968, p. 1.

example of the mad momentum of technology, to the absurd extreme of the public financing an environmental insult of virtually no demonstrated social utility, the SST program is unexcelled.

The specifications of the American SST call for an aircraft carrying 298 passengers at a cruising speed of 1800 mph, and costing an estimated 52 million dollars each. The first flight of a prototype is not expected until 1972. Both the Soviet Union and a British-French combine have prototypes of smaller and slower SST's in the air today. Both are expected to carry about 125 passengers at 1400 mph, and will cost something like 20 million dollars each. The "head start" now held by the Soviets, the British and the French in getting an SST into commercial operation is offered by the U.S. administration as a compelling reason for us to press ahead with our own program. The argument runs as follows: In the absence of a U.S. SST, our airlines will be forced by the competition with foreign carriers and with each other to purchase large numbers of Anglo-French or (much less probably) Soviet aircraft, worsening the balance-of-payments problem. This argument assumes, of course, that the SST will be a profit-making item for which there will be large airline demand; as will be discussed below, there is no reason to believe this will be true. To the detached observer, in fact, the U.S. must present an amusing spectacle—hastening to join the French, English and Russians in a headlong rush down the road to an economic and environmental debacle.

Let us accept for a moment the premise that improving the lot of the air traveller is a worthy object for government funds. What will the SST do for him? As a start, passage on an SST will be more cramped, less smooth, more expensive, and in all probability less safe than the same ride on the Boeing 747 or air bus with which the SST must compete. It will be more cramped because supersonic aerodynamics requires a long, *slender* fuselage for efficiency in an aircraft of this type, and economics requires that there be lots of seats crammed into it. The flight will be less smooth because a long, flexible fuselage interacts particularly violently with gusts and turbulence in the air through which it passes, and because small bumps at 600 mph become jackhammer jolts at three times the speed. (Concerned aeronautical engineers assure us that the ride can in principle be smoothed somewhat with the use of sophisticated "feedback" techniques; these are expensive, however, and neither Boeing nor the government seems inclined to up the price of an already scandalously expensive technological experiment.) As it stands, the cost per seat mile will be perhaps 40 per cent higher than on the Boeing 747. The speed of the SST, permitting more total flights, cannot compensate entirely for its higher purchase price and huge fuel consumption. The airlines may, of course, elect to artificially hike subsonic fares while depressing fares on the SST, forcing *all* air travelers to subsidize the industry's economic white elephant.

The matter of safety is more speculative, but there is every reason to suspect that the SST will not be as safe as today's jets. It will carry more fuel (and store a greater fraction of it in the fuselage) than any other commercial aircraft, thus increasing the hazard from fire. Existing problems with metal fatigue are far more ominous for an SST: the structure is subjected to greater stresses at supersonic speeds, these are aggravated by surface temperatures approaching 500°F, and we have relatively little experience with the fatigue behavior of

the titanium-alloy components which the SST requires. The SST under cruise conditions will be less maneuverable than a subsonic jet, three times as fast to close the gap in potential collision situations, and far more vulnerable to loss of cabin pressure. Technology of all sorts must be stretched to build an SST—controls, lubricants, engines, sealants, brakes. In these regards, there is no backlog of military experience comparable to that which benefitted subsonic transport development. The U.S. has only one operational military aircraft capable of 1800 mph, the Lockheed SR-71, and it is much smaller than the proposed SST. The trouble-plagued and now retired XB-70, of which only two were built, provided some data on large supersonic aircraft but hardly a reassuring basis for a civilian program. The safety record of the Air Force's B-58 Hustler, capable of 1400 mph sprints but not sustained cruise there, is abysmal.

What then, will the cramped, jolted, and perhaps slightly nervous SST passenger get for his premium fare? The answer is a thirty to forty per cent reduction in travel time, if that is measured (realistically) from home to hotel, rather than runway to runway. (Note that part of the SST's speed advantage on longer flights, such as San Francisco-Tokyo, is lost because the SST must refuel in Hawaii while the Boeing 747 goes nonstop.) Whether reducing travel time further is a worthwhile goal is itself debatable. Even today's subsonic jets cause considerable disruption in the "biological clocks" of travelers crossing many time zones. A number of corporations and even governments forbid their representatives to transact business for 48 hours after transoceanic flights, on the grounds that poor judgment may be part of the disorientation accompanying too rapid change of locale.

The SST does not seem destined for great passenger demand, then, even in a speed-worshipping society such as our own. For the speed, itself a mixed blessing, hardly warrants the host of discomforts and threats likely to accompany it. But if such planes are not popular with passengers, they will certainly not be popular with airlines, and the balance-of-payments argument goes out the window. The airlines are presumably not ecstatic about financing yet another generation of still more expensive aircraft in any case. They had just begun to enjoy some long-awaited profits from the Boeing 707/Douglas DC-8 generation of jets when the smaller jets and jumbos came along to plunge them deep into debt again. The SST, following so close on the jumbos' heels, could easily be the financial death blow for any number of airlines, yet they feel locked into this destructive course by competition and, now, government pressure.[1]

The government's position on the SST is so absurd as to be inexplicable. It's "loan" to Boeing and the engine manufacturers will not be repaid until at least 300 SST's are sold, and it will take 500 sales for the manufacturers to come up with the agreed upon interest. If, against staggering odds, any substantial passenger demand for the SST actually materializes, it is implausible that the airlines could finance this number of 60 million dollar aircraft. It is *impossible* that such a market could exist without flying the SST supersonically over populated areas, and one can only conclude that the government intends to permit this despite its pathetically transparent hedges to the contrary.

So many competent groups have discredited the economic "arguments" in favor of the SST that there is no need to do more than quote a few of them here. The President's own Ad Hoc Review Committee on the SST[2] concluded, on the balance of payments:

If the U.S. overall balance of payments is considered, there is substantial reason for delay in proceeding to the next stage of the SST project.

The Committee argued that, if the plane did happen to sell, the increase in American tourist expenditures abroad would more than cancel the effect of SST purchases by foreign airlines. On the alleged benefits to the U.S.

employment situation, the Committee reported:

Very few unskilled workers will be required ... such employment should not be considered as a justification for proceeding with the program but only as a dividend from it.

Others have pointed out that it is easy to "create" jobs—war does so, as do vandals, arsonists, and hijackers. The more difficult matter, in which the SST fails so miserably, is to create jobs in a way which benefits society.

In a report released August 19, 1970, the joint House-Senate Subcommittee on Economy in Government stated that "No further support of the SST development program is justified at this time," continuing that "it is entirely possible that the government will recover none of (its) investment." Still other critical reports by competent authorities exist, but have been suppressed by the administration. And a group of America's foremost economists, including J. K. Galbraith, Paul Samuelson, Milton Friedman, and Walter Heller, recently concluded that the SST program is utterly without economic merit.[3]

If the government feels it must pour money into commercial aviation, there are ample genuine needs to fill. The air traffic control system is overloaded and its radar antiquated. Collision avoidance systems for all commercial, military, and private aircraft should be developed, short-take-off-and-landing (STOL) aircraft to service population concentrations are needed, and desperately needed rapid transit systems would reduce travel time for air passengers as well as everybody else.

As the foregoing arguments have indicated, there would be no valid case for proceeding with the SST program even if it were free of environmental liabilities. It is not. The now well-publicized sonic boom is an inevitable consequence of supersonic flight through the atmosphere. It is to be emphasized that the boom is created *continuously* (rather than only when the plane passes through the

[1] See, e.g., "For the SST, a Case of Oversell?," Wall Street Journal, Sept. 9, 1970.
[2] Released Oct. 31, 1969 after having been withheld since its completion in March of that year.

[3] *Science*, **169**, 1292 (25 Sept. 1970).

"sound barrier"), and that a supersonically cruising SST will therefore lay down a carpet or swath of booms—some fifty miles wide—for the entire length of its flight path. There is abundant evidence that the boom at "standard" intensities will be intolerable to a considerable fraction of the exposed population, and that damage to property will also result. I refer to "standard" intensities because it also happens that sonic booms can be magnified by atmospheric conditions, by maneuvers of the SST itself, and by the coincidence of the shock waves from more than one such aircraft. It has been shown that a two-fold magnification can be expected to occur about 0.1 per cent of the time, which corresponds to an area of 125 square miles from the 125,000 square miles "boomed" on *every* coast-to-coast flight. (As noted above, the government's assertion that supersonic flights will not be permitted over land is not to be taken seriously.)

Additionally, the sideline noise of the SST on takeoff and landing will be unbearable—some 40 times more intense at 1500 feet than the proposed FAA standard for subsonic jets (which is itself at a level which most people find intolerable). Finally, the responsible bodies which have considered the matter have most recently been unwilling to place any bets on whether a fleet of SST's will substantially alter climates. The introduction of vast quantities of water vapor (a combustion product) into the stratosphere might increase cloud cover, and even if it did not would certainly increase stratospheric humidity. Both phenomena could affect the global energy balance and circulation patterns. Nor is the effect of the SST's combustion products on the stratospheric ozone concentration well understood.

While it seems unlikely that any significant reduction in the amount of ozone present would result, the potential consequences should dictate caution: ozone is our principal protection against ultraviolet radiation from the sun; ultraviolet radiation can be deadly to exposed animals, including man.

The SST, then, is a technological circus *par excellence*. The air traveller doesn't need it, the airlines don't need it, and society certainly does not. If the government claims to need it, one can only ask, whom does the government purport to represent? Indeed, the only *frank* argument which has been advanced for building the SST is that it would challenge the ingenuity of our engineers—we must build it because it can be done. We could perhaps permit out technologists such amusements if there were not real and crying needs for their talents, and if the circuses were not to be pursued with vast amounts of public funds. That this swindle is being justified with specious economic arguments and sanctified with empty words like "prestige" and "leadership," and that it will subject a helpless populace to insufferable sounds and further environmental gambles turns the merely bizarre into the absolutely incredible.

The ultimate responsibility for this debacle must of course rest with government. Engineers do not control the allocation of funds, and if they often advocate projects of less than optimum social utility, society must trust its elected representatives to choose more wisely. Continued governmental support of the SST program, a monument to misplaced priorities, suggests that our trust has been abused.

# Wonderland Revisited

JAMES RAMSEY

> "Would you tell me, please, which way I ought to go from here?" asked Alice.
> "That depends a good deal on where you want to get to," said the Cat.
> "I don't much care where—" said Alice.
> "Then it doesn't matter which way you go," said the Cat.
>
> —from Alice's Adventures in Wonderland

Move over Alice, you've got a couple of hundred million Americans for company. We don't know where we are going or where we want to get to either. Like the guests at the Mad Tea-Party, we eat and move around the table to the next place-setting, leaving the dirty dishes behind, never once facing-up to the question of what happens when we complete the circle. Our national priorities are caricatures without substance, more illusory than the Cheshire Cat. We plan ahead with the same appreciation of the future as that enjoyed by the Mad Hatter. It is always six o'clock.

Consider these scenes from the theater of the absurd:

—At its National Reactor Test Station in Idaho, the Atomic Energy Commission is burying radioactive waste that will be deadly to any living thing exposed to it for the next 1500 years. The burial ground is in the same general vicinity where three rivers flow out of the mountains and disappear into the desert floor.

—This year, the U.S. Army decided it was overstocked with biological warfare weapons and as an economy measure proposed to

dump a quantity of them into the Atlantic Ocean. While Army spokesmen argued the merits of this macabre plan, an entire train-load of the stuff was parked directly off the end of the main Denver airport runway.

In the rush to make it we have created a wonderland of rhetoric, rationalization and double-think that not even Lewis Carroll could have imagined.

—During the Redwood National Park controversy the logging interests complained bitterly that the establishment of a tiny parcel of land as a park would interfere with their sustained yield program. At the same time, they were going ahead with plans to log the last commercial old-growth redwoods on earth within the decade, knowing full well that the growing period is too long, the supply too short for a sustained yield program.

—The dam builders were stopped from flooding the Grand Canyon by an aroused public, and in response proposed to plug Hell's Canyon, the deepest gorge on the North American continent.

—As a deadly twilight descends over our cities, highway departments across the land mid-wife the birth of new freeways, which spawn more automobiles, which demand more freeways . . .

Wonderland Revisited. From Sierra Club Bulletin, Vol. 54, No. 10 October–November 1969, pp. 10–13. Reprinted by permission of the author and the publisher.

—And the President of the United States, faced with the greatest domestic crisis his or any other administration has ever had to deal with, talks of national pride and pushes the development of a monstrous supersonic passenger jet that is neither needed nor wanted by his constituency.

These bizarre actions and hundreds more like them are accompanied by a chorus of Orwellian Newspeak aimed at convincing all of us of the ultimate truth—the stink of a pulp mill is actually the perfume of progress. Humpty Dumpty couldn't have put it better.

The latest symptom of this growing national malaise is taking place now in the mad scramble to explore and exploit the oil reserves of the Alaskan Arctic. The discovery of oil at Prudhoe Bay has been well publicized, as has the near-billion-dollar sale of leases by the State of Alaska in September. Under this barrage of good tidings the plea for ecological sanity is but a squeak. The race to nowhere is on. The long distance runners of this American Dream set piece are the oilmen, the rugged sourdoughs of the late twentieth century. Armed with a bank of computers, a fleet of Lear jets, engineering degrees and a 27.5 per cent oil depletion allowance, a gift from a grateful government, they bravely face the perils of the Arctic. Theirs is a mission of Urgency and Importance. They speak darkly of troubles in the mideast, of the need for a new domestic oil supply, diminishing national reserves, a viable economy, and the spectre of war.

They do not speak to the question of why we should pump billions of barrels of future air pollutants from an area that will almost certainly be irreparably scarred in the process; an area that if left untouched would be a far more valuable national resource in future years than all the oil beneath its surface. But not now, and oilmen have not been programmed to think beyond now.

Wonderland permits no such heresy. The rhetoric says Alaskan wilderness is infinite and therefore indestructible. The rhetoric says there is no connection between the extractors of a resource and its ultimate use, and anyone

suggesting otherwise is demented and very possibly un-American. But rhetoric and reality do not agree. Given the pressures of population and the present state of our technological juggernaut, a relatively pristine Alaska should last at most about twenty years. Coincidentally, this is also about the length of time that urban air will still be breathable, unless something is done, and done quickly.

But the oilmen will not plug up their Alaska wells and go home. Their logic of exploitation has never progressed beyond the level of reasoning expressed by Mallory when asked why he wanted to climb Mt. Everest. "Because it is there" is a fitting reason for climbing a mountain, but shortsighted in the extreme as a basis for establishing a huge industrial operation on the last wild, untouched frontier of this continent, a frontier as fragile as it is beautiful.

It may seem inaccurate to describe the Arctic tundra as fragile with all the powerful environmental forces at work there. But it is precisely these forces—the eternal cold, the long winter nights, the howling blizzards, and the permanently frozen subsoil—that make the Arctic ecologically and esthetically fragile. The complex food chains of the temperate zones are reduced to the bare minimum in the Arctic; often an entire food web consists of only a few species of plants, plant eaters, meat eaters and scavengers. An iron law of nature is that variety means survival, and the Arctic is short on this kind of variety.

Left to themselves, the ecosystems of the Arctic tundra function perfectly, and have done so for millions of years. But they do not have the capacity to withstand any but the most careful incursions of man, particularly mechanized man. The passage of a single, tracked vehicle over thawed tundra may leave a scar that will last for decades, or forever. No one really knows what effect heavy concentrations of humans and their machines will have on the migratory habits of Arctic wildlife such as the caribou, or on already endangered species that live there. In fact, the single most critical issue of the whole Arctic exploitation question is the fact that so little is known about Arctic ecology at this time that it is impossible to assess potential damage.

Given this incontrovertible fact, and in the absence of demonstrable proof that there is any urgent national need for Arctic oil in the immediate future, isn't it reasonable to conclude that the extraction of oil, if it is done at all, should proceed only after careful and extensive ecological studies are made? No, it is not; not in Wonderland. *("But I don't want to go among mad people," Alice remarked. "Oh, you can't help that," said the Cat: "We're all mad here. I'm mad. You're mad.")*

The oil companies, the State of Alaska, and the Federal Government in the person of the Secretary of Interior, are all hell-bent to begin pumping oil out of the ground as soon as possible. They give lip service to the need for ecological studies, but if present plans are consummated, all but cursory investigations will be after the fact, not before.

The oilmen are full of brobdingnagian schemes to transport the oil out of the road-less Arctic to the prime markets in the lower forty-eight. They are predictably products of the engineering mentality so prevalent in the extraction industries where biological considerations are always placed at the bottom of the priority list. One plan calls for a fleet of super tankers equipped with special ice-breaker bows which would transport the oil directly from Prudhoe Bay to the major east coast markets. A "successful" test was conducted this summer with the super-tanker Manhattan reaching the Arctic area, but only after being unstuck from the ice on several occasions by Canadian ice-breakers. No tests were made, of course, on what would happen to Arctic marine life, including polar bears and seals, if one of these oil-bloated ships should duplicate the Torrey Canyon disaster.

Another proposed method of transporting oil to the states is an environmental horror that would put a huge pipeline across the state—an 800-mile long scar from Prudhoe Bay to the port of Valdez. Financed by a consortium of oil companies—Humble, Atlantic-Richfield and British Petroleum—the four-foot diameter pipeline would carry 1 million bar-

rels per day and require a massive construction project involving roads, pumping stations and the pipeline itself cutting directly across the Arctic slope and through the incomparably beautiful Brooks Range. In spite of some serious doubt about the pipeline's technical and economic feasibility the oilmen are already unloading sections of pipe at Valdez.

The oilmen have asked Secretary of Interior Hickel to unfreeze right-of-way areas on Federally owned land presently held up pending settlement of Native Land Claims. The Secretary has displayed a remarkable eagerness to comply with their request. His department has performed one of the miracles of our time by preparing a list of stipulations governing the construction and operation of the pipeline based on ecological information that isn't even known yet. The stipulations and a request for approval to unfreeze the right-of-way were sent to the Senate and House Interior Committees on October 1.

As quoted in the *Oil Daily*, the Secretary embellished his request with a statement that reached new heights in jabberwockian splendor. "The stipulations," he said, "will insure that the wildlife and ecology of the Arctic, along with the culture and opportunities of Alaska's native citizens, will be enhanced." What, on the little that remains of God's green earth, does he mean by that? Federally funded Medicare for Caribou? How can an 800-mile-long mechanical monstrosity "enhance" the ecology of the Arctic? And as for improving the culture and opportunities of Alaska's native citizens, if the Secretary means by *their* standards, not ours, it will be the first time in this nation's history that any of its aboriginal inhabitants have been introduced to such a novel concept.

The Secretary also noted that the stipulations "are designed to meet *all* of the environmental and ecological goals set forth by the department, based on research by its own scientists, independent authorities and public hearings held in Alaska." Nonsense! If the pipeline is allowed at this time it will be installed on a trial and error basis, pure and simple. Most of the studies on just the mechanical phases of pipeline operation in the Arctic—investigations into the effect of the pipeline on permafrost and vice-versa, for example—have not been completed. Hardly any biological studies have been started. Throughout the stipulations the emphasis is placed on remedial action *after* the pipeline ruptures or malfunctions, not on how to prevent it from happening in the first place.

The pipeline fiasco would be ludicrous if it were not the precursor of what is to follow in Alaska. If indeed, Alaska is allowed to be exploited with the mindless planning and narrow economic justifications that have characterized so-called progress in America, the last chance to bring some sanity to our choice of national priorities will have been lost. Alaska is a pivotal area, in a pivotal time. The battles that will be fought in Alaska will not be just to save a chunk of land or a specie of wildlife

—they will be to decide what things are really important for human beings to continue living on this planet. If these decisions are left to those who have made them in the past, it will not be just another ecological battle lost; it will be, in the real meaning of the term, inhuman.

*"First, the Dodo marked out a race-course, in a sort of a circle, and then all the party were placed along the course, here and there. There was no 'one, two, three and away,' but they began running when they liked, and left off when they liked, so that it was not easy to know when the race was over. However, when they had been running a half-hour or so, the Dodo suddenly called out 'the race is over' and they all crowded around it, panting and asking, 'But who has won?'"*

# The Destruction of Indochina:
# A Legacy of Our Presence

### STANFORD BIOLOGY STUDY GROUP

## FOREWORD

At Stanford, as at other American universities, the spring of 1970 was a time of redirected effort. For many students and faculty members, the redirection meant stopping "business as usual" and undertaking political activity on behalf of ending the war in Indochina. In the Department of Biological Sciences, a group of students, fellows and

The Destruction of Indochina: A Legacy of Our Presence. Reprinted with the permission of the Stanford Biology Study Group, Stanford, California.

faculty members were able to relate their own scientific training to the political issues that concerned them so deeply. This pamphlet on the ecological effects of the Indochina War is the result.

It has come out of the labors of a number of Stanford biologists of diverse backgrounds, working as a loosely organized commitee. The group included Howard Edenberg, a graduate student in molecular biophysics; Patrice Morrow and Bruce Bartholomew, graduate students studying physiological ecology of plants; Lawrence Gilbert and Edward Merrell, graduate students in population biology and ecology; Peter Cohen, post-doctoral fellow in molecular genetics; Matthews Bradley, graduate student in developmental biology; and Patricia Caldarola and Paul Grobstein, graduate students in neurophysiology. Professor Colin Pittendrigh and I helped, also. The process of creation was at once gratifying and disturbing. We learned from one another about new things: the ecologists, three of whom have had field experience in the tropics, taught the others about the special qualities of tropical soils and ecosystems; the molecular and cellular biologists in turn looked more critically at the biochemistry of herbicides and the interpretation of the results of bio-assays.

Even in an academic setting where shared intellectual experiences are supposed to happen all the time, this one was unusual. It would have been unambiguously pleasant—were it not for the subject matter. No one can conclude, after looking carefully at the impact of our military strategy in southeast Asia, that we are fighting a war against an army. Instead, we are waging a war against a people and the land they live on. The enormity of our attack upon the Vietnamese environment has, for me, changed entirely the logic with which one evaluates the morality and even the efficacy of our operation there. After reading this report, I hope you will agree that the central question is now a simple one, "How can we claim to be acting on behalf of people when our action itself is prohibiting a future for them?"

Donald Kennedy,
*professor and chairman
of the Department of Biological Sciences,
Stanford University*

The Stanford Biology Study Group is an ad hoc organization of members of the Department of Biological Sciences at Stanford University. Its views do not necessarily represent those of Stanford University as an institution, and the use of titles is for purposes of identification only.

The war in Southeast Asia has gone on for more than 30 years, and during this period, the people of that area have been subjected to intense deprivation and suffering. In the last decade the United States, in its advisory and fighting roles, has not only greatly increased the immediate suffering, it has added a new and terrible dimension to warfare: as a result of strategy used deliberately to destroy the forest cover and enemy food crops and of other programs as well, we are producing devastating, long-term ecological damage. Long

after first-hand memories of the war's horrors have faded, a crippled land will remain the legacy of our presence. This report attempts to evaluate the extent and the seriousness of this destruction.

In making this evaluation, it must be recognized that ignorance of tropical ecosystems is even greater than that of temperate-zone systems. However, ignorance must not be used as a license to plunder. In fact, lack of knowledge is rather a reason for *caution* with policies that affect the environment and human life. We do know enough to state unequivocally that the actions reported here will have serious long-term consequences and that significant damage has already occurred.

United States forces are engaged in two specific programs of environmental destruction. One is the defoliation program, nicknamed Operation Ranch Hand, in which chemical substances that remove leaves (defoliants) are sprayed onto plants from the air. Trees are often killed in the process, and in this case the chemicals act as herbicides. The other program employs aerially sprayed herbicides to destroy croplands in order to deny food to soldiers and civilians in areas controlled by the National Liberation Front (NLF). These and other acts of war of the U.S. military are justified in terms of saving the lives of American and South Vietnamese troops who are fighting for the sake of the people of South Vietnam. However, in view of the permanence of the environmental damage being produced by U.S. military operations in Southeast Asia, it is impossible to identify the benefit to the people living there or to their descendants.

## DEFOLIATION AND CROP DESTRUCTION

Over five million acres, 12 per cent of South Vietnam, have been sprayed with defoliating chemicals.[1] If used in low concentrations, these "defoliants" may indeed merely defoliate some plants. But because the application rate in Vietnam averages 13 times that recommended by the U.S. Department of Agriculture for domestic uses such as weed killing,[2] the chemicals act as herbicides.

The three major herbicides used in South Vietnam are known by the names Orange, White, and Blue. Agent Orange, until recently the most widely used in Vietnam, is a mixture of 2,4-D (n-butyl-2,4-dichlorophenoxyacetate) and 2,4,5-T (n-butyl-2,3,4-trichlorophenoxy-acetate); it is directed mainly against hard-wood trees and other broad-leaved plants. Mangrove forest, an important plant association found along riverbanks, can be severely damaged; one application of Orange usually kills most of the trees. Areas of this kind sprayed as early as 1961 still have shown no significant recovery.[3]

Agent White is primarily used near populated areas because its low volatility makes it less likely to drift off the target. White is, however, soluble in water and as a result it is washed into adjacent croplands and forests by the heavy tropical rains. Picloram, a major component of White, has been called "the most active herbicide yet discovered."[4] It is also the most persistent and has been likened to DDT because it does not break down into biologically inactive substances.[3] Tropical test areas in Puerto Rico which were sprayed with White have remained essentially bare of leaves for more than two years.[4] Of the Picloram applied to a California test area, 80 to 96 per cent was found in the soil 15 months later.[3] Thus the destruction caused by this herbicide will remain long after we have left Southeast Asia. The government has not licensed Picloram for use in the cultivation of a single American crop, apparently because its herbicidal activity varies with climate and soil so unpredictably that no reasonable margin of safety can be guaranteed.[4] Nevertheless, White with Picloram has been used for years in Vietnam.

Agent Blue is more toxic to grasses than to broad-leaved plants and is used mainly to destroy rice crops.[5] Cacodylic acid, a major component of Blue, is 54 per cent arsenic.[3] Because arsenic poisoning of humans can occur by gradual accumulation of small doses until lethal levels are reached, the use of Blue

> Philip Noel-Baker, 1959 winner of the Nobel Peace Prize, recalled a conversation with Henri Bonnet at the Geneva Conference of 1925. Bonnet said "Oh, yes; the form of words they've got is good. It prohibits every kind of chemical or bacterial weapon that anyone could possibly devise. And it has to. Perhaps someday a criminal lunatic might invent some devilish thing that would destroy animals and crops." Noel-Baker added that "in 1925 everyone at the Conference agreed with Henri Bonnet." (See Appendix I.)
>
> Quoted in the *New York Times*, December 9, 1969.

may pose a long-term danger.

Defoliation often affects non-target areas. For example, the U.S. Defense Department claims it has not deliberately defoliated rubber plantations,[2] yet herbicides have severely injured the rubber industry. This and other effects of the war have caused a 25 per cent decrease in the per-acre yield of rubber in Vietnam between 1960 and 1967, while in nearby Malaysia the per-acre yield increased 33 per cent.[2] The total yield of rubber in Vietnam has dropped by over 45 per cent and many small plantations have been forced to close.[2] Cambodian plantations and farms have also been defoliated, some by deliberate overflights of U.S. spraying aircraft (initially denied by the Defense Department but later admitted by the Department of State).[3] About one-third of all rubber trees in production in Cambodia were damaged by defoliation in April and May of 1969, and between May and November of 1969, rubber production in these areas fell by 35 to 40 per cent.[6] An international group of scientists studying the spraying damage estimated losses at $12.2 million.[6]

The U.S. Army admits to having sprayed over 500,000 acres of South Vietnamese crops through 1969.[3] This represents seven per cent of the total acreage under intensive cultivation. However, a 1967 report of the Agronomy section of the Japan Science Council claimed that "... anti-crop attacks have ruined 3,800,-000 acres of arable land in South Vietnam...."[7] Because of official U.S. secrecy, the true figures are not known.

The U.S. policies of direct crop destruction, forced relocation of peasant farmers to refugee camps, bombing and burning of farmland, destruction of food caches, and large Vietnamese military draft all contribute to the severely reduced agricultural production. In 1959, South Vietnam—the "Rice Bowl" of Asia—exported 246,000 tons of rice. In 1968, 850,000 tons had to be imported, over 90 per cent of it from the U.S.[8] Other food crops have suffered as severely.[3, 9, 10] The pineapple crop was reduced by 40 per cent between 1963 and 1968, a period which coincides with the early years of intensive spray operations.[8] Sugar cane, manioc, tomato, beans, papaya, coconut, sweet potato, figs, cassava, and mango are all sensitive to the herbicides and the various yields have decreased from ten to 40 per cent.[9] Overall agricultural production has decreased by about 30 per cent.[8, 9] The crop spraying has continued since 1968 and agricultural production is still low, although reliable figures are not available.

In addition to decreased agricultural production at present, we can reasonably expect, as discussed below, long-term damage to crop and forest land due to the presence of dangerous herbicide residues in the soil; destruction of soil microorganisms necessary for fertility; death or migration of animals responsible for pollination and seed transport; overgrowth of bamboo and other pest species; and greatly increased soil destruction by laterization.

## STARVATION AS A WEAPON OF WAR

The U.S. Army justifies agricultural and ecological destruction in Vietnam for three major tactical reasons: to deny food to civilians and soldiers in "Viet Cong-held areas"

under the "resource denial" program; to prevent ambushes along heavily forested roads and waterways; and to aid in visual reconnaissance of NLF base camps and supply routes by eliminating the forest canopy which hides them.

The rationale behind the "resource denial" program is that the resulting starvation will sufficiently demoralize the NLF troops so that they will surrender. However, previous wars have shown that when food is in short supply, fighting troops are the first to be fed; what is left is then rationed to civilians. Among these, the most severely affected are children, the elderly, and pregnant and lactating women. During the siege of Leningrad, for example, soldiers received 800 grams or more of bread per day while civilians starved on 200 grams per day.[11] The NLF remains an effective fighting force, but the incidence of civilian starvation and starvation-related diseases is rising in the central highlands of Vietnam where extensive crop destruction has occurred.[12] This policy of deliberate starvation contravenes, in the view of many, the Nuremberg Principles which the United States helped establish and has formally accepted (see Appendix II).

The "resource denial" program also wages war against unborn Vietnamese. As a result of two years of malnutrition and starvation experienced by the Biafran people, four out of every ten children born were deformed—with small brain size as well as severe muscular and skeletal malformation.[13] The South Vietnamese public health ministry refuses to provide any statistics on normal and abnormal births,[17] so evidence indicating the extent of birth defects in Vietnamese children is not available. We do, however, know that malnutrition is widespread in the countryside and in refugee camps, so the potential for such abnormalities certainly exists.[12, 14]

## BIRTH DEFECTS

The teratogenic (fetus-deforming) effects of certain chemicals became a matter of public concern when Thalidomide was found to cause birth defects. Until 1965, 2,4,5-T (comprising 50 per cent of Agent Orange) had never been tested for teratogenicity. Forty million pounds of this chemical have been sprayed in Vietnam,[5] without knowledge of its possible effects on man or animals. The widespread use of any chemical, without detailed knowledge of. possible effects, poses grave dangers. In the case of 2,4,5-T the danger is now coming to light.

In late 1967, after two years of greatly accelerated herbicide application, Saigon newspapers began carrying front-page stories of a novel and increasingly common birth defect described as "egg-bundle-like fetus."[20] Some newspapers reported a rise in the incidence of deformed babies in areas that had been sprayed, and questioned whether the defoliation might be causing this. These papers were closed by the Thieu government.[17]

News leaks in October, 1969, forced the National Institutes of Health (NIH) to release reports demonstrating that 2,4,5-T was shown in 1965–1966 to be an exceptionally powerful teratogen. During the time the report was inexplicably suppressed by our government, millions of pounds of 2,4,5-T were used in Vietnam—and, incidentally, in the United States as well.

Producers of 2,4,5-T claimed the teratogenicity shown in these tests was due to a contaminant called "dioxin" (2,3,7,8-tetrachlorodibenzo-p-dioxin), which is found in commercial preparations of 2,4,5-T. Later studies have shown that both extremely pure 2,4,5-T *and* dioxin cause birth defects in the three species of experimental animals tested.[18, 19] In hamsters, for example, commercial 2,4,5-T at dosages of 100 mg/kg (milligrams per kilogram of body weight) killed 80 per cent of the fetuses and deformed many of the survivors.[18] In rats, only 24 mg/kg deformed about 30 per cent of the fetuses (seven-fold increase in deformations).[18, 19]

A Vietnamese woman might ingest 2,4,5-T in dosages shown to be teratogenic. Despite the absence of any actual data, one can make the following calculations based on reasonable assumptions. In an area that had been sprayed with Orange at the usual rate (27 pounds per acre), and with a one-inch rainfall after the spraying, the concentration of 2,4,5-T in the water would be 50 mg/liter.[20] Drinking about two liters of water a day (an average amount) would give a dosage of 3 mg/kg of 2,4,5-T each day. If the spraying plane is forced (in emergency) to rapidly empty its tanks, the dose could increase about eight-fold to 25 mg/kg. Less rainfall would also increase the dose, as would exposure to the contaminated crops or direct contact with the spray.

The contaminant, dioxin, is extremely dangerous by itself. It is highly toxic (0.0005-0.001 mg/kg killed 50 per cent of the male guinea pigs tested) and is a cumulative poison.[19] It also causes birth defects; 0.009 mg/kg given to pregnant hamsters killed 82 per cent of the fetuses and left 82 per cent of the survivors deformed.[19] Since dioxin is formed when substances such as 2,4-D and 2,4,5-T are heated,[18, 19] the combustion of timber or other material exposed to these defoliants may liberate high concentrations of dioxin into the air.[19] Some military men have said that the practice of using wood from defoliated areas for charcoal is a benefit to the Vietnamese. But with the possible formation of dioxin by burning, and the fact that cooking fires are predominantly tended by women, the dangers posed are obvious. Still another danger of dioxin's widespread distribution is that it may, as DDT does, concentrate in food chains.

## BOMBING

Our B-52 bombing of Vietnam has changed rice paddies and forest into a lunar landscape. Each 500- to 750-pound bomb creates a crater as large as 45 feet across and 30 feet deep,[2] rendering this land useless for crops. We have dropped far more bombs in Vietnam than were dropped by the Allied forces in World War II.[21] In 1967–1968 alone,

> Tigers . . . seem to have benefited from the war. In the past 24 years, they have learned to associate the sound of gunfire with the presence of dead and wounded human beings in the vicinity. As a result, tigers rapidly move toward gunfire and apparently consume large numbers of battle casualties.
>
> From *"Ecological Effects of the War in Vietnam,"* by Gordon H. Orians and E. W. Pfeiffer, *Science,* May, 1970.

more than 3,500,000 such bombs were dropped in Vietnam.[2] Were these craters placed end to end, they would form a ditch 30,000 miles long—a distance greater than the circumference of the earth. The area they occupy is nearly 100,000 acres. Nor will the craters disappear with time; the jungles of New Guinea are still pock-marked from bombs dropped more than 25 years ago. Though it is theoretically possible to fill these craters, the job would involve moving more than 2.5 billion cubic yards of earth; clearly a monumental task.

Besides killing and maiming, the bombing forces many people to leave target areas or to live underground. A pediatrician recently returned from Vietnam said that as a consequence of the bombing, "People live underground day and night . . . children are suffering from a number of disorders new to Vietnam. One is rickets, from living without sunlight."[29]

## FIRE AND SHRAPNEL

Fires, some deliberately set and others touched off by artillery and bombing, are a major cause of forest destruction in Vietnam. More than 40 per cent of the pine plantations and an undetermined amount of hardwood forest have been recently destroyed.[2]

Shrapnel is imbedded in trees, both during fighting and when the forests are strafed and bombed immediately before defoliation (to suppress possible sniper fire). Already, sawmills lose from one to three hours each day repairing saw blades damaged by shrapnel in the logs.[2] The economically important lumber industry will be affected by shrapnel-laden logs until these forests are regrown.

## SOCIAL DESTRUCTION

Although this report is primarily concerned with ecological damage in Southeast Asia and the effect of this damage on the people living there, we feel that it is important to point out that other effects of the American presence will also result in permanent damage to this part of the world. The policies of the U.S. military are destroying the Vietnamese culture and social organization. The military is transforming a basically rural agrarian society into an urban nightmare which is economically dependent on the continued presence of the U.S. America and its allies have forcibly transported people from hamlets into refugee camps located in and near cities, and have driven many more off their ancestral lands by bombing and defoliation.[28] Conditions in these camps are often miserable.[28] In the past ten years Saigon has grown from a city of 250,000[2] to become one of the world's largest. It now has 3,000,000[2] people and is the world's most densely populated city with an average density of 148 persons per acre (Tokyo has 63 per acre).[23] The extremely rapid influx into the cities and surrounding camps has created massive problems in housing, feeding and providing medical care for the refugees. This "urbanization" has been caused in part by the inevitable destruction of war, but more by our policy of moving people off the land and into urban areas where they can be effectively under the control of the military.[28]

## THE LONG-TERM ECOLOGICAL EFFECTS

Tropical forests and soils are very different from those in the temperate zone. Thus to understand the long-term effects of the war in Southeast Asia it is necessary to describe certain characteristics of tropical forests and soils.

One such feature is the intricate interdependence of the plants and animals. For instance, the trees of tropical forests depend entirely upon insects, birds, and bats (rather than wind) for pollination. Birds, bats, and ground-dwelling mammals are responsible for dispersing seeds from the parent plants to new clearings. These complex plant-animal relations have reached their greatest intricacy in tropical forests because of the mild and predictable climate. Animals can be active the year around because many flowering and fruiting trees provide food continuously. Massive defolition means an end to this reliable food supply and death for those animals that are most important to the survival of the forest plants.

A second important characteristic of humid tropical forests is that most of the plant nutrients, including nitrates, phosphates, calcium, potassium, magnesium, sulphur and other elements required in smaller amounts, are tied up in the vegetation. Nutrients not contained in the vegetation itself are continuously washed from the soil by heavy rainfall. Under normal conditions, the nutrients released by decaying vegetation are rapidly recaptured and transferred to the roots of the living plants by certain fungi. But large-scale defoliation disrupts this efficient process, and the vital nutrients are quickly lost into streams. Fishing in these streams may temporarily improve because of increased aquatic plant growth due to the higher nutrient levels, but this effect is short term and is gained at the expense of soil fertility. As a direct result of lower fertility and the lack of seeds of the natural colonizing plants, pest species, such as giant bamboo, take over and spread. Once established, bamboo forms an impenetrable thicket which prevents normal forest regeneration and makes future use of the land for agriculture nearly impossible. This bamboo is very resistant to defoliants, and because it reproduces vegetatively from tough underground stems, it cannot be eliminated by burning or cutting once it is established.

From 30 to 50 per cent of Vienamese soils[3, 22] are of a type which have the potential to turn into a brick-like substance known as laterite if they are deprived of the organic covering which protects them from exposure to severe weathering. The potential for laterization is greatest in areas which were already disturbed before herbicide application. Cropland, as well as bombed and bulldozed areas along roadways, fall into this category. The permanence of laterite is well illustrated by the Khmer ruins around Angkor Wat in Cambodia where many of the temples were constructed primarily of this rock nearly ten centuries ago. Obviously, laterized land is useless for agriculture.

Along lowland rivers and waterways in the tropics, rich forests grade into pure stands of mangrove trees. These plants extend stilt-roots into shallow, brackish water; the silt they trap plays an important role in delta formation. They also provide a special habitat for key stages in the life cycles of economically important fish and shellfish. The intensive defoliation program along waterways in Vietnam has killed mile upon mile of this living border. There will undoubtedly be a drastic and long-lasting effect upon river fishing and upon the natural process of delta formation along Vietnamese rivers.

---

*Ralph Dresser, the head of "Ranch Hand," reports that the motto of the Aerial Spray Flight of the 309th Aerial Commando Squadron is "Only We Can Prevent Forests."*

*S. M. Hersh, Chemical and Biological Warfare, 1968.*

The destruction of crop and forest land fertility by herbicides, the alteration of forest composition, and the formation of laterite soil will all result in long-term damage to the agriculture and ecology of Vietnam.

## CONCLUSIONS

This war has two time scales. There is the immediacy of bombs and battles and of instant destruction and death, and there is the prolonged suffering and hardship which will face all survivors for generations. When the fighting has finally ended, the suffering and hardship will have only begun, for our actions in Vietnam have severely upset the environment and greatly reduced the ability of the land to support its people. The defoliation of vast areas of forest and agricultural land by poisonous and teratogenic herbicides, the saturation bombing and extensive burning, the deliberate destruction of crops with resulting starvation, malnutrition, and disease—these we have introduced to Southeast Asia and to the list of available techniques for waging war.

American troops were sent to Southeast Asia, we are told, to protect the interests of the Vietnamese people. The destruction of the Vietnamese and their environment is unfortunate, we are told, but necessary to protect the lives of American troops in wartime. Thus entwined by circular reasoning, our government claims to aid a country and its people by destroying both, and claims to protect freedom while concealing from the American public the facts about our military actions in Southeast Asia. These facts are no secret to the Asians, who experience the truth daily.

All of the military actions described in this report are continuing, and there is no reason to believe they will cease during the time that any gradual withdrawal or "Vietnamization" is attempted. Nor, under the present policy, is there any reason to doubt that during and after withdrawal we will continue to supply the Saigon regime with the tools necessary to pursue the war according to the precedents we have established. The devastation we have already caused is a monstrous legacy for those we call our friends. The environment, the social organization, the very future of Vietnam have been so severely mortgaged by action supposedly on her behalf that an American policy of immediate and permanent cessation of warfare is clearly the most effective aid we can now give.

## APPENDIX I.
## GENEVA PROTOCOL OF 1925

The 1925 Geneva Protocol banned the use in war of all "asphyxiating, poisonous or other gases, and all analogous liquids, materials or devices" and of "bacteriological methods of warfare."[10] To date, 84 states, including almost all of the major industrial powers, have ratified or acceded to the Protocol.[3]

The United States, however, has not ratified it.

There was general agreement at the time the Protocol was drawn that the document prohibited any and all forms of chemical or biological warfare.[24] This interpretation was reaffirmed by the Political Committee of the General Assembly of the United Nations on December 10, 1969; the vote, in specific opposition to United States use of herbicides and tear gases in Vietnam, was 58 yes, 3 no (United States, Australia and Portugal).[25]

The World Health Organization has also condemned the use of herbicides and tear gases in warfare.[3]

## APPENDIX II.
## NUREMBERG PRINCIPLES

The Charter of the International Military Tribunal at Nuremberg (1945) affirmed that war crimes and crimes against humanity are crimes under international law.[26] The Charter defined "murder, extermination, enslavement, deportation and other inhumane acts committed against any civilian population" as "crimes against humanity," and "wanton destruction of cities, towns or villages, or devastation not justified by military necessity" as war crimes.[26] These principles and definitions were stated in an executive agreement concluded by the United States, the USSR, France and Great Britain on August 8, 1945. These same principles and definitions were reaffirmed by the United Nations General Assembly;[27] they are considered binding international law.

The United States and allied forces carry out the destruction of villages and crops, extensive bombing and defoliation, and relocation of people from the countryside to "strategic hamlets" in an attempt to deprive the NLF of potential support.[28] These actions—"wanton destruction," "devastation," and "deportation"—seem clearly to fall within the definition of crimes against humanity and war crimes.

## REFERENCES

1. U.S. Department of Defense Data (MACV); see also reference 15.
2. Orians, G. H. and E. W. Pfeiffer. 1970. Ecological Effects of the War in Vietnam. *Science* 168:544-554.
3. Whiteside, T. 1970. Defoliation. Ballantine Books Inc. New York. 168 pp.
4. Harvey, G. R. and J. D. Mann. 1969. Picloram in Vietnam. *Scientist and Citizen* 10:166-171.
5. Army, U.S. Dept. of. 1969. Employment of Riot Control Agents, Flame, Smoke, Anti-plant Agents, and Personnel Detectors in Counterguerrilla Operations. U.S. Army Trng. Circ. TC 3-16. 85 pp.; portions reprinted in reference 3.
6. Westing, et. al. Report on Herbicide Damage by the United States in Southeastern Cambodia; reprinted in reference 3, pp. 117–132.
7. Hersh, S. M. 1968. Chemical and Biological Warfare. Bobbs-Merrill, New York. 354 pp.
8. The Far East and Oceanic Agr. Situation. 1968. U.S.D.A. Econ. Research Serv. ERS—Foreign 223. 30 pp.
9. Agricultural Statistics Yearbook. 1967. Agr. Econ. Stat. Serv. Republic of Vietnam. 183 pp. p. 29.
10. Rose, S. (ed.). 1968. CBW: Chemical and Biological Warfare. George C. Harrap and Co., Ltd. London. 209 pp.
11. Salisbury, H. 1969. The 900 Days. Harper and Row. New York. 635 pp. p. 377.
12. Mayer, J. 1967. Starvation as a Weapon in Vietnam. *Scientist and Citizen* 9:116–121.
13. Okonkwo, P. O. 1969. Starvation: Weapon of War. *Science* 165:753.
14. Martin, E. 1970. Personal communication.
15. Gruchow, N. 1970. Curbs on 2,4,5-T Use Imposed. *Science* 168:453.
16. Nelson, B. 1969. Herbicides: Order on 2,4,5-T Issued at Unusually High Level. *Science* 166:977-979.
17. Blumenthal, Ralph. *New York Times*, March 15, 1970.
18. *Nature*. 1970. Another Herbicide on the Blacklist. 226:301-311.
19. Epstein, Dr. Samuel S. Testimony before Subcommittee on Energy, Natural Resources and the Environment, of the Senate Committee on Commerce, week of April 15, 1970.
20. Galston, Arthur W. Testimony before Subcommittee on National Security Policy and Scientific Developments, of the Committee on Foreign Affairs, House of Representatives, December 1969; reprinted in reference 3 pp. 107–116.
21. Mitgang, H. *New York Times*, March 2, 1970.
22. Tschirley, F. H. 1969. Defoliation in Vietnam. *Science* 163:779-786.
23. Vietnam Guardian. March 22, 1969.
24. Noel-Baker, Philip. *New York Times*, December 9, 1969.
25. *Los Angeles Times*, December 11, 1969; *New York Times*, December 11, 1969.
26. Woetzel, Robert. The Nuremberg Trials in International Law. 1962. Frederick A. Praeger Inc., N.Y. (the charter is printed in full on pp. 273–281).
27. Resolution No. 95 (1), December 11, 1946 (see ref. 26).
28. Chomsky, Noam. *New York Review of Books*, January 1, 1970.
29. Lewis, Anthony. *New York Times*, March 15, 1970.

# PART FOUR

# Psycho-Social Complications

*The last sound to issue from a human gullet will be three cheers from the last optimist.\**

The word "ecology" all too often conjures up visions of tropical jungles, unspoiled seashores, or hawks swooping down on rabbits. In reality, as the science which deals with the interrelationships of organisms with each other and with their physical environments, ecology is much more than landscapes and food chains. Man is an organism, and a man's environment includes all things living and non-living that influence his life. Therefore, ecology legitimately includes large areas of the behavioral sciences: psychology, sociology, anthropology, economics, and so forth. The ecology of the Chicago ghetto is as legitimate a concern of the ecologist as that of Lake Michigan, which supplies the ghetto with water. The dynamics and genetics of populations of cockroaches and rats must be studied along with those of butterflies and pelicans. Man, in all his conditions, is ineluctably a part of our planetary ecosystem, and no aspect of his existence can be slighted if we are to survive the ecological crisis.

There has been a growing feeling among poor people and minority groups that ecology is, as Robert Chrisman put it, "a racist shuck." They feel that a white racist society has jumped on the ecological bandwagon as an excuse to avoid dealing with the problems of blacks, Chicanos, American Indians, and poverty-stricken whites. Unhappily there is some truth to the accusation, as is evident from the behavior of the executive branch of the Federal Government. Commissions have been formed, reports released, and minor administrative reshuffling ballyhooed. But the public statements of the President, and his pitifully inadequate proposals for coping with a few surface symptoms such as sewage problems, make it abundantly clear he does not comprehend the scope of the problem (beyond its undisputed potential political mileage). Nor does it seem likely that he would be prepared to take the necessary steps even if the light did dawn, for they would be both unpopular

\* H. L. Mencken.

and expensive (of course, so is his war, so perhaps we judge him too harshly). Certainly, he feeds the suspicions of the disadvantaged when he speaks of "environment" while dealing cozily with powerful bigots, maintaining an economic system which has been accurately described as "socialism for the rich and capitalism for the poor," and prosecuting that irrational war in Indo-China.

While the issues of population and environment may have served at times as a "racist shuck," it would only compound the disaster to ignore the problems for the sins of some of the advocates. In *Population Control and Genocide,* the Ehrlichs put these matters in perspective by refuting the misconception that the severest population problems are those of the underdeveloped countries and the poor everywhere. It is true, of course, that overpopulation is a crippling economic disease to every underdeveloped country so afflicted; but it is equally true that overpopulation in the overdeveloped countries is a crippling *ecological* disease for the world. Within a given developed country, moreover, the poor bear more than their share of the costs of the population/environment crunch, while the middle class provides most of the impetus for it.

One can summarize the situation as follows: population control is the sine qua non of survival (contrary to both Marxist and Catholic dogma). From the point of view of the life-support systems of the planet, the affluent populations must be controlled first; but the most immediate and spectacular benefits to populations practicing control would be seen in the underdeveloped countries. The latter is true because, in these nations, some 45 per cent of the people are in the non-productive 0–15 age class. This is the class which would shrink first if population control were achieved, immediately decreasing the non-productive fractions of the population and freeing resources for development.

On a different tack, biologists Hugh Iltis and Orie Loucks and anthropologist Peter Andrews raise some penetrating questions about the kind of environment for which man is evolutionarily suited—questions which should long ago have been a major concern of mankind. In "Criteria for an Optimum Human Environment" they make it clear that we cannot seek the solution to our problems through technology alone, a point which is reemphasized by Garrett Hardin in his superb "Tragedy of the Commons." This paper deserves very careful study. Note in particular the suggestion that there is, in essence, selection against cooperators in voluntary population control programs. Hardin's recommendation of "mutual coercion, mutually agreed upon" has opened the door to much debate, and may well open the door to survival.

A final psycho-social factor central to the population/environment crisis deserves mention here, although considerations of space and the reader's patience mitigated against including a separate paper to illustrate it. We refer to the public's tendency to swallow optimistic pronouncements about the future, from whatever source. Many journalists have mirrored and reinforced this naivety for decades, and—most often armed with myopic analyses by narrowly trained "experts"—they continue to do so today. For example, no one has advanced the cause of complacency more industriously than the editors of *Time Magazine,* who in 1948 (Nov. 8) could write:

> The Neo-Malthusians want to warn man of danger: but their alarm is so loud that it may have the effect of deafening the world to its opportunities. To the real agricultural scientists, close to the soil and its sciences, such pessimism sounds silly or worse. Every main article of the Neo-Malthusian creed, they say, is either false or distorted or unprovable. They are sure that the modern world has both the soil and the knowledge to feed, and feed well, twice as many people as are living today.

The same article ranted on about the ease with which the 2.25 billion people expected to be alive in 1960 could be well fed. (The number was surely a misprint—the population had already exceeded this figure in 1940. And when 1960 rolled around, of course, only one third of the world's 3 billion people enjoyed a decent diet.) Undaunted by the track record of their experts on agriculture, the same magazine reported in 1970 (July 13) that the world has the agricultural potential to feed 157 billion people! We make so much of these otherwise laughable statements—and the many like them—because of the tragedy they reflect: The gullibility of journalists and their public on these matters, their unwillingness to examine "good news" critically, is continuing to hobble efforts to head off disaster.

# Population Control and Genocide

## PAUL R. AND ANNE H. EHRLICH

Many Americans believe that the growth of the U.S. population is mainly due to excessive reproduction among the poor. In fact, more than two-thirds of the babies born each year belong to the wealthy and the middle class. The average American still does not realize that any couple with more than two children is contributing to the population explosion.

Because of their impact on the environment, population growth among the affluent in the U.S. and their counterparts in Europe, the Soviet Union, and Japan is the most serious in the world, even though it is not the most rapid. These people are the main consumers of our planet's non-renewable resources and polluters of its environment; their activities threaten to destroy the Earth's life-support systems. In terms of degradation of the environment, the birth of each American child is 50 times the disaster for the world as the birth of a child in India. In terms of the consumption of non-renewable resources, an American baby is some 300 times as dangerous to our future well-being as an Indonesian baby.

## U.S. POOR PEOPLE

Similarly, poor people in the U.S. have far less power to loot and pollute than does the average American. Therefore, they have much less impact upon the environment, despite their slightly higher birthrates. In general their higher birthrates are a greater liability to themselves than to the public. Statistically, large families tend to be poor; moreover they are more likely to remain poor. Smaller families have been shown to have a greater chance of escaping poverty.

The public, including non-white minorities themselves, tends to equate "poor" with Blacks, Chicanos, and American Indians, because higher proportions of these groups are in low-income groups. Nevertheless, the majority of the poor are white, and the majority of non-white people are not poor. For instance, only about 30 per cent of black families were classified as poor in 1967.

In view of the tendency of affluent Americans to blame U.S. population growth on the poor, it is unfortunate that the Nixon administration has chosen to label the government's new policy of extending family planning services to the poor as "population control." First of all, this served to reinforce the erroneous beliefs of much of the public about the source of American population growth. More importantly, it aroused considerable resentment among minorities, especially among black leaders, who often see such policies as a form of genocide aimed at Blacks.

This point of view is not entirely unjustified, thanks to the attitudes of some population control advocates, who seem mainly interested in controlling other people's populations, and thanks to some abuses in existing birth control programs for the poor.

## MINORITIES

Since minorities have had little to do with generating our environmental deterioration, the most obvious symptoms of overpopulation in the U.S., their leaders can hardly be blamed for a lack of enthusiasm for birth control programs. Nevertheless, it is interesting that minorities are disproportionately victims of environmental deterioration. Poor Blacks are confined to the cores of cities where air pollution is heaviest and urban decay and overcrowding are worst. Black Americans, for unknown reasons, have significantly higher average levels of DDT in their tissues than are found in the general population. Chicanos may be spared the evils of modern urban life, but they suffer directly from polluting agricultural practices, especially the misuse of pesticides.

Reproductive rates in the U.S., as elsewhere, are strongly correlated with such factors as income and educational levels. This is true for Black and other minorities as well as whites. Affluent black couples, for instance, have on the average slightly fewer children than do comparable white couples. When black Americans are given the same economic, educational, and social opportunities as white Americans have, black birthrates will almost certainly be indistinguishable from white.

## SUBSIDIZED ABORTIONS

Contraception and subsidized abortions should be available to all Americans, white, black, or brown, married, or unmarried. No one should be subjected to compulsory pregnancy. Government support of these programs through national health and welfare services is necessary and long overdue. But these programs are not, and should not be considered, population control programs. Rather, they are a logical extension of family planning, which has been part of the American social scene for more than two generations. Population control, on the other hand, is the conscious control of population size and rate of growth by a society. This requires the determination of an optimum population size for the society, and the institution of measures designed to move the society toward that goal.

Since the effects of population growth among affluent white Americans are the most serious, it might be hoped that any governmental population control program will be designed first to reduce the birth rates of that group. American minorities can hardly be expected to look with favor on any programs to control their birth rates imposed by a white government that has barely begun to give them their constitutionally guaranteed rights. When they have those rights, their reproductive responsibilities to society will be the same as those of any other group. Meanwhile, it is up to the rest of us to start exercising our own responsibilities.

# Criteria for an Optimum Human Environment

## HUGH H. ILTIS, ORIE L. LOUCKS, AND PETER ANDREWS

Almost every current issue of the major science journals contains evidence of an overwhelming interest in one urgent question: Shall a single species of animal, man, be permitted to dominate the earth so that life, as we know it, is threatened? The uniformity of the theme is significant but if there is consensus, it is only as to the need for concern. Each discipline looks differently at the problem of what to do about man's imminent potential to modify the earth through environmental control. Proposals to study ways of directing present trends in population, space and resource relationships toward an "optimum" for man are so diverse as to bewilder both scientists and the national granting agencies.

## ARROGANCE TOWARD NATURE

It is no thirst for argument that compels us to add a further view. Rather it is the sad

recognition of major deficiencies in policies guiding support of research on the restoration of the quality of our environment. Many of us find the present situation so desperate that even short-term treatments of the symptoms look attractive. We rapidly lose sight of man's recent origins, probably on the high African plains, and the natural environment that shaped him. Part of the scientific community also accepts what Lynn White has called our Judeo-Christian arrogance toward nature, and is gambling that our superior technology will deliver the necessary food, clean water and fresh air. But are these the only necessities? Few research proposals effectively ask whether man has other than these basic needs, or whether there is a limit to the artificiality of the environment that he can tolerate.

In addition, we wish to examine which disciplines have the responsibility to initiate and carry out the research needed to reveal the limits of man's tolerance to environmental modification and control. We are especially concerned that there is, on the one hand, an unfortunate conviction that social criteria for environmental quality can have no innate biological basis—that they are only conventions. Yet, on the other hand, there is increasing evidence suggesting that mental health and the emotional stability of populations may be profoundly influenced by frustrating aspects of an urban, biologically artificial environment.

There have been numerous proposals for large-scale inter-disciplinary studies of our environment and of the future of man, but such studies must have sufficient breadth to treat conflicting views and to seek to reconcile them. We know of no proposal that would combine the research capabilities of a group studying environmental design with those of a group examining the psychological and mental health responses of man to natural landscapes. The annual mass migration of city man into natural landscapes which provide diversity is a matter of concern to the social scientist, whose research will only be fully satisfactory when joined with studies that quantify the landscape quality, the psychology of individual human response, and the evolutionary basis of man's possible genetic adaptations to nature. The following summary of recent work may provide a basis for scientists in all areas to seek and support even greater breadth of our studies of present and future environments for man.

## "WEB OF LIFE"

Two major theses are sufficiently well established to provide the positive foundation of our argument. First, we believe the interdependency of organisms, popularly known as the "web of life," is essential to maintaining life and a natural environment as we know it. The suffocation of aquatic life in water systems, and the spread of pollutants in the air and on the land, make it clear that the "web of life" for many major ecosystems is seriously threatened. The abrupt extinction of otherwise incidental organisms, or their depletion to the point of no return, threatens permanently to impair our fresh water systems

and coastlines, as well as the vegetation of urban regions.

Second, man's recent evolution is now well enough understood for it to play a major part in elucidating the total relation of man to his natural environment. The major selection stresses operating on man's physical evolution have also had some meaning for the development of social structures. These must be considered together with the immense potential of learned adaptations over the entire geologic period of this physical evolution. Unfortunately, scientists, like most of us moderns, are city dwellers dependent on social conventions, and so have become progressively more and more isolated from the landscape where man developed, and where the benchmarks pointing to man's survival may now be found. They, of all men, must recognize that drastic environmental manipulations by modern man must be examined as part of a continuing evolutionary sequence.

The immediacy of problems relating to environmental control is so startling that the threat of a frightening and unwanted future is another point of departure for our views. At the present rate of advance in technology and agriculture, with an unabated expansion of population, it will be only a few years until all of life, even in the atmosphere and the oceans, will be under the conscious dictates of man. While this general result must be accepted by all of us as inevitable, the methods leading to its control offer some flexibility. It is among these that we must weigh and reweigh the cost-benefit ratios, not only for the next 25 or 50 years, but for the next 25,000 years or more. The increasing scope of the threat to man's existence within this controlled environment demands radically new criteria for judging "benefits to man" and "optimum environments."

It would be perverse not to acknowledge the immense debt of modern man to technological development. In mastering his environment, man has been permitted a cultural explosion and attendant intricate civilization made possible by the very inventiveness of modern agriculture, an inventiveness which must not falter if the world is to feed even its present population. Agricultural technology of the nineteenth and twentieth centuries, from Liebig and the gasoline engine to hybrid corn, weed killers and pesticides, has broken an exploitative barrier leading to greatly increased production and prosperity in favored regions of the world. But this very success has imposed upon man an even greater responsibility for managing all of his physical and biotic environment to his best and sustained advantage.

The view also has been expressed recently that the "balance of nature," upset by massive use of non-disintegrating detergents and pesticides, will be restored by "new engineering." Such a view is necessarily based on the assumption that it is only an engineering problem to provide "an environment [for man] relatively free from unwanted man-produced stress." But when the engineering is successful, the very success dissipates our abilities to see the human being as part of a complex biological balance. The more successful technology and agriculture become, the more difficult it is to ask pertinent questions and to expect sensible answers on the long-range stability of the system we build.

## THE RIGHT QUESTIONS?

Inspired by recent success, some chemical and agricultural authorities still hold firmly that we can feed the world by using suitable means to increase productivity, and there is a conviction that we can and must bend all of nature to our human will. But if open space were known to be as important to man as is food, would we not find ways to assure both? Who among us has such confidence in modern science and technology that he is satisfied we know enough, or that we are even asking the right questions, to ensure our survival beyond the current technological assault upon our environment. The optimism of post-World War II days that man can solve his problems— the faith in science that we of Western culture

learn almost as infants—appears more and more unfounded.

To answer "what does man now need?" we must ask "where has he come from?" and "what evidence is there of continuing genetic ties to surroundings similar to those of his past?"

Theodosius Dobzhansky and others have stressed that man is indeed unique, but we cannot overlook the fact that the uniqueness does not separate him from animals. Man is the product of over a hundred million years of evolution among mammals, over 45 million years among primates, and over 15 million years among apes. While his morphology has been essentially human for about two million years, the most refined neurological and physical attributes are perhaps but a few hundred thousand years old.

## SELECTION AND ADAPTATION

G. G. Simpson notes that those among our primate ancestors with faulty senses, who misjudged distances when jumping for a tree branch or who didn't hear the approach of predators, died. Only those with the agility and alertness that permitted survival in ruthless nature lived to contribute to our present-day gene pool. Such selection pressure continued with little modification until the rise of effective medical treatment and social reforms during the last five generations. In the modern artificial environment it is easy to forget the implications of selection and adaptation. George Schaller points out in "The Year of the Gorilla" that the gorilla behaves in the zoo as a dangerous and erratic brute. But in his natural environment in the tropical forests of Africa, he is shy, mild, alert and well-coordinated. Neither gorilla nor man can be fully investigated without considering the environments to which he is adapted.

Unique as we may think we are, it seems likely that we are genetically programmed to a natural habitat of clean air and a varied green landscape, like any other mammal. To be relaxed and feel healthy usually means simply allowing our bodies to react as evolution has equipped them to do for 100 million years. Physically and genetically we appear best adapted to a tropical savanna, but as a civilized animal we adapt culturally to cities and towns. For scores of centuries in the temperate zones we have tried to imitate in our houses not only the climate, but the setting of our evolutionary past: warm humid air, green plants, and even animal companions. Today those of us who can afford it may even build a greenhouse or swimming pool next to our living room, buy a place in the country, or at least take our children vacationing at the seashore. The specific physiological reactions to natural beauty and diversity, to the shapes and color of nature, especially to green, to the motions and sounds of other animals, we do not comprehend and are reluctant to include in studies of environmental quality. Yet it is evident that nature in our daily lives must be thought of, not as a luxury to be made available if possible, but as part of our inherent indispensable biological need. It must be included in studies of resource policies for man.

## DEPENDENCE ON NATURE

Studies in anthropology, psychology, ethology and environmental design have obvious implications for our attempts to structure a biologically sound human environment. Unfortunately, these results frequently are masked by the specifics of the studies themselves. Except for some pioneer work by Konrad Lorenz followed up at several symposia in Europe, nothing has been done to systematize these studies or extend their implications to modern social and economic planning. For example, Robert Ardrey's popular work, "The Territorial Imperative," explores territoriality as a basic animal attribute, and tries to extend it to man. But his evidence is somewhat limited, and we have no clear conception of what the thwarting of this instinct does to decrease human happiness. The more extensive studies on the nature of aggression explore the genetic roots of animal conflicts, roots that were slowly developed by natural selection over millions of generations. These studies suggest that the sources of drive, achievement, and even of conflict within the family and war among men are likely to be related to primitive animal responses as well as to culture.

Evidence exists that man is genetically adapted to a nomadic hunting life, living in small family groups and have only rare contact with larger groups. As such he led a precarious day-to-day existence, with strong selective removal due to competition with other animals, including other groups of humans. Such was the population structure to which man was ecologically restricted and adapted until as recently as 500 generations ago. Unless there has since been a shift in the major causes of human mortality before the breeding age (and except for resistance to specific diseases there is no such evidence), this period is far too short for any significant changes to have occurred in man's genetic makeup.

Studies of neuro-physiological responses to many characteristics of the environment are also an essential part of investigating genetic dependence on natural as opposed to artificial environment. The rapidly expanding work on electroencephalography in relation to stimuli is providing evidence of a need for frequent change in the environment for at least short periods, or, more specifically, for qualities of diversity in it. There is reason to believe that the electrical rhythms in the brain are highly responsive to changes in surroundings when these take the full attention of the subject. The rise of mechanisms for maintaining constant attention to the surroundings can be seen clearly as a product of long-term selection pressures in a "hunter and hunted" environment. Conversely, a monotonous environment produces wave patterns contributing to fatigue. One wanders what the stimuli of brick and asphalt jungles, or the monotony of corn fields, do to the nervous system.

Biotic as well as cultural diversity, from the neurological point of view, may well be fundamental to the general health that figures prominently in the discussions of environmental quality.

## RESULTS WITH PATIENTS

The interesting results of Maxwell Weismann in taking chronically hospitalized mental patients camping are also worth noting. Hiking through the woods was the most cherished activity. Some 35 of the 90 patients were returned to their communities within three months after the two-week camping experience. Other studies have shown similar results. Many considerations are involved, but it seems possible that in a person whose cultural load has twisted normal functioning into bizarre reactions, his innate genetic drives still continue to function. Responses attuned to natural adaptations would require no conscious effort. An equally plausible interpretation of Weismann's results is that the direct stimuli of the out-of-doors, of nature alone, produces a response toward the more normal. A definitive investigation of the bases for these responses is needed as guidance to urban planners and public health specialists.

These examples are concerned with the negative effects which many see as resulting from the unnatural qualities of man's present, mostly urban, environment. Aldous Huxley ventures a further opinion as he considers the abnormal adaptation of those hopeless victims of mental illness who appear most normal: "These millions of abnormally normal people, living without fuss in a society to which, if they were fully human beings, they ought not to be adjusted, still cherish 'the illusion of individuality,' but in fact they have been to a great extent deindividualized. Their conformity is developing into something like uniformity. But uniformity and freedom are incompatible. Uniformity and mental health are incompatible as well. . . . Man is not made to be an automaton, and if he becomes one, the basis for mental health is lost."

Clearly, a program of research could tell us more about man's subtle genetic dependence on the environment of his evolution. But of one thing we can be sure: only from study of human behavior in its evolutionary context can we investigate the influence of the environment on the life and fate of modern man. Even now we can see the bases by which to judge quality in our environment, if we are to maintain some semblance of one which is biologically optimum for humans.

We do not plead for a return to nature, but for re-examination of how to use science and technology to create environments for human living. While sociological betterment of the environment can do much to relieve poverty and misery, the argument that an expanding economy and increased material wealth alone would produce a Utopia is now substantially discounted. Instead, a natural concern for the quality of life in our affluent society is evident. But few economists or scientists have tried to identify the major elements of the quality we seek, and no one at all has attempted to use evolutionary principles in the search for quality. Solutions to the problems raised by attempts to evaluate quality will not be found before there is tentative agreement on the bases for judging an optimum human environment. A large body of evidence from studies in evolution, medicine, psychology, sociology, and anthropology suggests clearly that *such an environment will be a compromise between one in which humans have maximum contact with the properties of the environment to which they are innately adapted, and a more urban environment in which learned adaptations and social conventions are relied upon to overcome primitive needs.*

Our option to choose a balance between these two extremes runs out very soon. Awareness of the urgency to do something is national, and initial responses may be noted in several well-established but relatively narrow scientific disciplines. There has been the recent revival of eugenics. A balanced view has been proposed by Leonard Ornstein

*(Bulletin,* June 1967), who agrees with others that positive improvements in man's genetic make-up must wait until we are vastly more knowledgeable. He recommends control of degenerating effects from uncontrolled mutation (in the absence of high selection) until more positive measures can be taken.

## AN "IMPOSSIBLE" CHALLENGE

More extreme views have been expressed that man could be changed genetically to fit any future, but the means to do this and the moral justification of the aims sought are still far from being resolved. Many support the so-called evolutionary and technological optimists who, unlike their forefathers of little more than a generation ago, believe man can be changed radically when the time comes. They show a faith that science has proved its ability to draw on an expanding technology to do the impossible. The technologically impossible seems to have been accomplished time and time again during the past two or three generations, and may happen again. But some important scientific objectives have not been achieved, and we are likely to become more aware of the failures of science, of the truly impossible, as the irreversible disruptions of highly complex biological systems become more evident.

We suggest that the alternative to genetic modification of man is to select a course where the objectives only verge on the impossible. Let us regard the study and documentation of criteria for an environmental optimum as the "impossible" challenge for science and technology in the next two decades! Although considerable research in biology, sociology, and environmental design is already directed to this objective, there are several other types of study required that we outline briefly, simply to indicate the scope of the challenge.

First, a thorough examination must be undertaken of the extent to which man's evolutionary heritage dominates his activity both as an individual and in groups. The survival advantage of certain group activities has clearly figured in his evolutionary success and adaptive culture. Although cultural adaptation now dominates the biological in the evolution of man, his basic animal nature has not changed. Research leading to adequate understanding of the need to meet innate genetic demands lies in the field of biology, and more specifically in a combination of genetics, physical anthropology and ethology.

Second, we need to understand more of how cultural adaptations and social conventions of man permit him to succeed in an artificial environment. Cultural adaptation is the basis of his success as a gregarious social animal, and it will continue to be the basis by which he modifies evolutionarily imposed adaptations. Medical studies suggest there may be a limit to the magnitude of cultural adaptations, and that for some people this is nearly reached. Studies in sociology, cultural anthropology and psychology are all necessary to such research, in combination with environmental design and quantitative analysis of diversity in the native landscape.

Third, relationships between the health of individuals, both mental and physical, and the properties of the environment in which they live should be a fundamental area of research. It is easy to forget that we should expect as much genetic variability in the capacity of individuals to adjust to artificial environments as we find in the physical characteristics of man. Some portions of the population should be expected to have a greater inherent commitment to the natural environment, and will react strongly if deprived of it. Others may be much more neutral. Studies of the population as a whole must take into account the variability in reaction, and must therefore consider population genetics as well as psychiatry and environmental design.

Fourth, environmental qualities should be programmed so as to optimize for the maximal expression of evolutionary (i.e., human) capabilities at the weakest link in the ontogenic development of human needs. While there are many critical periods during our life, we believe the ties to natural environments to be most vital during youth. We have abundant evidence on our campuses and in our cities that the dislodgement of youth presents one— if not the most—serious obstacle to successful adoption of more complex social structures. The dislodgement of man in an artificial environment will vary throughout his ontogeny. Even the small child or infant cannot be expected to be indifferent to changes in the gross characteristics of his community, as he cannot within his own family.

Young men and women accept many of the modern social conventions, but retain the highly questioning mind that once led to new and better ways to hunt and forage. By early middle age, man's physical and mental agility has changed and he becomes a stronger adherent to the social conventions that make his own society possible. During the rise of modern man on the high African plains, and continuing into modern primitive societies, each community was very much dependent on its young men. They contributed to hunting and community protection through their strength and agility, commodities for which there is declining demand in modern society. Survival in the primitive groups was to some degree dependent on the willingness of youth to innovate and take risks, and this has become a fixed adaptation, requiring outlets of expression.

Over 30 years ago, sociologist W. F. Ogburn suggested that society in the future would require "prolonging infancy to, say, thirty or forty years or even longer." Is not our 20-year educational sequence a poorly-veiled attempt to do just that? From an evolutionary point of view will not this dislodgement of youth present the most serious obstacle to successful adoption of more complex social structures? We are compelled to acknowledge that our over-all technological environment for youth has not compensated for the loss of the challenges of the hunt and the freedom of the Veldt. The disruptions on our campuses

and in the cities indicates the need to plan environmental optima for this weakest link in the human need for expression of evolutionary capabilities.

Finally, systems ecology is developing the capacity for considering all of the relationships and their interactions simultaneously. The notion of fully describing the optimum for any organism may seem presumptuous. It requires measurement of every type of response, particularly behavioral responses, and their statement as a series of component equations. Synthesis in the form of a complex model permits mathematical examination of an optimum for the system as a whole. Until recently it seemed more reasonable to study such optimization for important resources such as fisheries, but the capability is available and relevant to the study of the environmental optimum of man, and its application must now be pursued vigorously.

These five approaches to the study of human environment provide an objective base for investigating the environmental optimum for man. We cannot close this discussion, however, without pointing out that the final decision, both as to the choice of the optimum and its implementation, is an ethical one. There is an optimum for the sick, and another for the well; there is an optimum for the maladjusted, and another for the well-adjusted. But in treating the problems of the poor and minority groups, in our preoccupation with their immediate relief, we may continue to overlook the ways in which cultural demands of the modern, sub-optimum environment go far beyond the capacity of learned adaptations.

## A COMPROMISE?

Considering our scientific effort to learn the functions and structure of the human body, and of the physical environment around us, the limited knowledge of man's relationships to his environment is appalling. Because of the very success of our scientific establishment we are faced with population densities and environmental contaminants that have left us no alternative but to undertake control of the environment itself. In this undertaking let us understand the need to choose a humane compromise—a balance between the evolutionary demands we cannot deny except with great emotional and physical misery, and the fruits of an unbelievably varied civilization we are loath to give up.

Yet are we even considering such a compromise? With rare exceptions are we not continuing to destroy much that remains of man's natural environment with little thought for the profit of the remote future? In the conflict between preservationists and industrialists (or agriculturalists) the latter have had it their way, standing as they do for "progress" and "modern living." While the balance between these conflicts is slowly changing, preservationists continue to be regarded as sentimentalists rather than realists.

Theodosius Dobzhansky says that "the preponderance of cultural over biological evolution will continue to increase in the foreseeable future." We could not wish this to be otherwise; adaptation to the environment by culture is more rapid and efficient than biological adaptation. But social structures cannot continue indefinitely to become more complex and further removed from evolutionary forces. At some stage a compromise must be reached with man's innate evolutionary adaptability.

## NEED FOR CONTINUING STUDY

We believe that the evidence of man's need for nature, particularly its diversity, is sufficient to justify a determined effort by the scientific community to obtain definitive answers to the questions we have posed. The techniques for studying the problems are to be found in separate disciplines, and there is a sufficient measure of willingness among scientists to undertake the new approaches. But the first steps will be faltering and financial support will be slow in coming.

Now that buttercups are rare, at least symbolically, and springs often silent, why study them? Have there not already been several generations for whom the fields and woods are nearly a closed book? We could encourage the book to close forever, and we might succeed, but in so doing we might fail disastrously. The desire to see and smell and know has not yet been suppressed and enthusiasm for natural history continues to bring vitality to millions. Let us recognize that we are a product of evolution, without apology for the close affinities with our primate forebears. We need only prepare consciously to make a compromise between our cultural and our genetic heritage by striking a balance of social structures with maintenance of natural environments. Most important, we must discover the mechanisms of environmental influence on man. There is no other satisfactory approach to an optimum environment.

# The Tragedy of the Commons

GARRETT HARDIN

At the end of a thoughtful article on the future of nuclear war, Wiesner and York[1] concluded that: "Both sides in the arms race are . . . confronted by the dilemma of steadily increasing military power and steadily decreasing national security. *It is our considered professional judgment that this dilemma has no technical solution.* If the great powers continue to look for solutions in the area of science and technology only, the result will be to worsen the situation."

I would like to focus your attention not on the subject of the article (national security in a nuclear world) but on the kind of conclusion they reached, namely that there is no technical solution to the problem. An implicit and almost universal assumption of discussions published in professional and semi-popular scientific journals is that the problem under discussion has a technical solution. A technical solution may be defined as one that requires a change only in the techniques of the natural sciences, demanding little or nothing in the way of change in human values or ideas of morality.

In our day (though not in earlier times) technical solutions are always welcome. Because of previous failures in prophecy, it takes courage to assert that a desired technical solution is not possible. Wiesner and York exhibited this courage; publishing in a science journal, they insisted that the solution to the problem was not to be found in the natural

The Tragedy of the Commons. From *Science*, Vol. 162, December 1968, pp. 1243–1248. Copyright 1968 by the American Association for the Advancement of Science. Reprinted by permission of the author and the publisher.

sciences. They cautiously qualified their statement with the phrase, "It is our considered professional judgment. . . ." Whether they were right or not is not the concern of the present article. Rather, the concern here is with the important concept of a class of human problems which can be called "no technical solution problems," and, more specifically, with the identification and discussion of one of these.

It is easy to show that the class is not a null class. Recall the game of tick-tack-toe. Consider the problem, "How can I win the game of tick-tack-toe?" It is well known that I cannot, if I assume (in keeping with the conventions of game theory) that my opponent understands the game perfectly. Put another way, there is no "technical solution" to the problem. I can win only by giving a radical meaning to the word "win." I can hit my opponent over the head; or I can drug him; or I can falsify the records. Every way in which I "win" involves, in some sense, an abandonment of the game, as we intuitively understand it. (I can also, of course, openly abandon the game—refuse to play it. This is what most adults do.)

The class of "No technical solution problems" has members. My thesis is that the "population problem," as conventionally conceived, is a member of this class. How it is conventionally conceived needs some comment. It is fair to say that most people who anguish over the population problem are trying to find a way to avoid the evils of overpopulation without relinquishing any of the privileges they now enjoy. They think that farming the seas or developing new strains of

...at will solve the problem—technologically. I try to show here that the solution they seek cannot be found. The population problem cannot be solved in a technical way, any more than can the problem of winning the game of tick-tack-toe.

## WHAT SHALL WE MAXIMIZE?

Population, as Malthus said, naturally tends to grow "geometrically," or, as we would now say, exponentially. In a finite world this means that the per capita share of the world's goods must steadily decrease. Is ours a finite world?

A fair defense can be put forward for the view that the world is infinite; or that we do not know that it is not. But, in terms of the practical problems that we must face in the next few generations with the foreseeable technology, it is clear that we will greatly increase human misery if we do not, during the immediate future, assume that the world available to the terrestrial human population is finite. "Space" is no escape.[2]

A finite world can support only a finite population; therefore, population growth must eventually equal zero. (The case of perpetual wide fluctuations above and below zero is a trivial variant that need not be discussed.) When this condition is met, what will be the situation of mankind? Specifically, can Bentham's goal of "the greatest good for the greatest number" be realized?

No—for two reasons, each sufficient by itself. The first is a theoretical one. It is not mathematically possible to maximize for two (or more) variables at the same time. This was clearly stated by von Neumann and Morgenstern,[3] but the principle is implicit in the theory of partial differential equations, dating back at least to D'Alembert (1717–1783).

The second reason springs directly from biological facts. To live, any organism must have a source of energy (for example, food). This energy is utilized for two purposes: mere maintenance and work. For man, maintenance of life requires about 1600 kilo-calories a day ("maintenance calories"). Anything that he does over and above merely staying alive will be defined as work, and is supported by "work calories" which he takes in. Work calories are used not only for what we call work in common speech; they are also required for all forms of enjoyment, from swimming and automobile racing to playing music and writing poetry. If our goal is to maximize population it is obvious what we must do: We must make the work calories per person approach as close to zero as possible. No gourmet meals, no vacations, no sports, no music, no literature, no art. . . . I think that everyone will grant, without argument or proof, that maximizing population does not maximize goods. Bentham's goal is impossible.

In reaching this conclusion I have made the usual assumption that it is the acquisition of energy that is the problem. The appearance of atomic energy has led some to question this assumption. However, given an infinite source of energy, population growth still produces an inescapable problem. The problem of the acquisition of energy is replaced by the problem of its dissipation, as J. H. Fremlin has so wittily shown.[4] The arithmetic signs in the analysis are, as it were, reversed; but Bentham's goal is still unobtainable.

The optimum population is, then, less than the maximum. The difficulty of defining the optimum is enormous; so far as I know, no one has seriously tackled this problem. Reaching an acceptable and stable solution will surely require more than one generation of hard analytical work—and much persuasion.

We want the maximum good per person; but what is good? To one person it is wilderness, to another it is ski lodges for thousands. To one it is estuaries to nourish ducks for hunters to shoot; to another it is factory land. Comparing one good with another is, we usually say, impossible because goods are incommensurable. Incommensurables cannot be compared.

Theoretically this may be true; but in real life incommensurables *are* commensurable.

Only a criterion of judgment and a system of weighting are needed. In nature the criterion is survival. Is it better for a species to be small and hideable, or large and powerful? Natural selection commensurates the incommensurables. The compromise achieved depends on a natural weighting of the values of the variables.

Man must imitate this process. There is no doubt that in fact he already does, but unconsciously. It is when the hidden decisions are made explicit that the arguments begin. The problem for the years ahead is to work out an acceptable theory of weighting. Synergistic effects, nonlinear variation, and difficulties in discounting the future make the intellectual problem difficult, but not (in principle) insoluble.

Has any cultural group solved this practical problem at the present time, even on an intuitive level? One simple fact proves that none has: there is no prosperous population in the world today that has, and has had for some time, a growth rate of zero. Any people that has intuitively identified its optimum point will soon reach it, after which its growth rate becomes and remains zero.

Of course, a positive growth rate might be taken as evidence that a population is below its optimum. However, by any reasonable standards, the most rapidly growing populations on earth today are (in general) the most miserable. This association (which need not be invariable) casts doubt on the optimistic assumption that the positive growth rate of a population is evidence that it has yet to reach its optimum.

We can make little progress in working toward optimum population size until we explicitly exorcize the spirit of Adam Smith in the field of practical demography. In economic affairs, *The Wealth of Nations* (1776) popularized the "invisible hand," the idea that an individual who "intends only his own gain," is, as it were, "led by an invisible hand to promote . . . the public interest."[5] Adam Smith did not assert that this was invariably true, and perhaps neither did any of his followers. But he contributed to a dominant tendency of thought that has ever since interfered with positive action based on rational analysis, namely, the tendency to assume that decisions reached individually will, in fact, be the best decisions for an entire society. If this assumption is correct it justifies the continuance of our present policy of laissez-faire in reproduction. If it is correct we can assume that men will control their individual fecundity so as to produce the optimum population. If the assumption is not correct, we need to reexamine our individual freedoms to see which ones are defensible.

## TRAGEDY OF FREEDOM IN A COMMONS

The rebuttal to the invisible hand in population control is to be found in a scenario first sketched in a little-known pamphlet[6] in 1833 by a mathematical amateur named William Forster Lloyd (1794–1852). We may well call it "the tragedy of the commons," using the word "tragedy" as the philosopher Whitehead used it:[7] "The essence of dramatic tragedy is not unhappiness. It resides in the solemnity of the remorseless working of things." He then goes on to say, "This inevitableness of destiny can only be illustrated in terms of human life by incidents which in fact involve unhappiness. For it is only by them that the futility of escape can be made evident in the drama."

The tragedy of the commons develops in this way. Picture a pasture open to all. It is to be expected that each herdsman will try to keep as many cattle as possible on the commons. Such an arrangement may work reasonably satisfactorily for centuries because tribal wars, poaching, and disease keep the numbers of both man and beast well below the carrying capacity of the land. Finally, however, comes the day of reckoning, that is, the day when the long-desired goal of social stability becomes a reality. At this point, the inherent logic of the commons remorselessly generates tragedy.

As a rational being, each herdsman seeks to maximize his gain. Explicitly or implicitly, more or less consciously, he asks, "What is the utility *to me* of adding one more animal to my herd?" This utility has one negative and one positive component.

1. The positive component is a function of the increment of one animal. Since the herdsman receives all the proceeds from the sale of the additional animal, the positive utility is nearly +1.

2. The negative component is a function of the additional overgrazing created by one more animal. Since, however, the effects of overgrazing are shared by all the herdsmen, the negative utility for any particular decision-making herdsman is only a fraction of −1.

Adding together the component partial utilities, the rational herdsman concludes that the only sensible course for him to pursue is to add another animal to his herd. And another; and another. . . . But this is the conclusion reached by each and every rational herdsman sharing a commons. Therein is the tragedy. Each man is locked into a system that compels him to increase his herd without limit —in a world that is limited. Ruin is the destination toward which all men rush, each pursuing his own best interest in a society that believes in the freedom of the commons. Freedom in a commons bring ruin to all.

Some would say that this is a platitude. Would that it were! In a sense, it was learned thousands of years ago, but natural selection favors the forces of psychological denial.[8] The individual benefits as an individual from his ability to deny the truth even though society as a whole, of which he is a part, suffers. Education can counteract the natural tendency to do the wrong thing, but the inexorable succession of generations requires that the basis for this knowledge be constantly refreshed.

A simple incident that occurred a few years ago in Leominster, Massachusetts, shows how perishable the knowledge is. During the Christmas shopping season the parking meters downtown were covered with plastic bags that bore tags reading: "Do not open until after Christmas. Free parking courtesy of the mayor and city council." In other words, facing the prospect of an increased demand for already scarce space, the city fathers reinstituted the system of the commons. (Cynically, we suspect that they gained more votes than they lost by this retrogressive act.)

In an approximate way, the logic of the commons has been understood for a long time, perhaps since the discovery of agriculture or the invention of private property in real estate. But it is understood mostly only in special cases which are not sufficiently generalized. Even at this late date, cattlemen leasing national land on the western ranges demonstrate no more than an ambivalent understanding, in constantly pressuring federal authorities to increase the head count to the point where overgrazing produces erosion and weed dominance. Likewise, the oceans of the world continue to suffer from the survival of the philosophy of the commons. Maritime nations still respond automatically to the shibboleth of the "freedom of the seas." Professing to believe in the "inexhaustible resources of the oceans," they bring species after species of fish and whales closer to extinction.[9]

The National Parks present another instance of the working out of the tragedy of the commons. At present, they are open to all, without limit. The parks themselves are limited in extent—there is only one Yosemite Valley—whereas population seems to grow without limit. The values that visitors seek in the parks are steadily eroded. Plainly, we must soon cease to treat the parks as commons or they will be of no value to anyone.

What shall we do? We have several options. We might sell them off as private property. We might keep them as public property, but allocate the right to enter them. The allocation might be on the basis of wealth, by the use of an auction system. It might be on the basis of merit, as defined by some agreed-upon standards. It might be by lottery. Or it might be on a first-come, first-served basis, administered to long queues. These, I think, are all the reasonable possibilities. They are all objectionable. But we must choose—or acquiesce in the destruction of the commons that we call our National Parks.

## POLLUTION

In a reverse way, the tragedy of the commons reappears in problems of pollution. Here it is not a question of taking something out of the commons, but of putting something in—sewage, or chemical, radioactive, and heat wastes into water; noxious and dangerous fumes into the air; and distracting and unpleasant advertising signs into the line of sight. The calculations of utility are much the same as before. The rational man finds that his share of the cost of the wastes he discharges into the commons is less than the cost of purifying his wastes before releasing them. Since this is true for everyone, we are locked into a system of "fouling our own nest," so long as we behave only as independent, rational, free-enterprisers.

The tragedy of the commons as a food basket is averted by private property, or something formally like it. But the air and waters surrounding us cannot readily be fenced, and so the tragedy of the commons as a cesspool must be prevented by different means, by coercive laws or taxing devices that make it cheaper for the polluter to treat his pollutants than to discharge them untreated. We have not progressed as far with the solution of this problem as we have with the first. Indeed, our particular concept of private property, which deters us from exhausting the positive resources of the earth, favors pollution. The owner of a factory on the bank of a stream—whose property extends to the middle of the stream—often has difficulty seeing why it is not his natural right to muddy the waters flowing past his door. The law, always behind the times, requires elaborate stitching and fitting to adapt it to this newly perceived aspect of the commons.

The pollution problem is a consequence of population. It did not much matter how a lonely American frontiersman disposed of his waste. "Flowing water purifies itself every 10 miles," my grandfather used to say, and the myth was near enough to the truth when he was a boy, for there were not too many people. But as population became denser, the natural chemical and biological recycling processes became overloaded, calling for a redefinition of property rights.

## HOW TO LEGISLATE TEMPERANCE?

Analysis of the pollution problem as a function of population density uncovers a not generally recognized principle of morality, namely: *the morality of an act is a function of the state of the system at the time it is performed.*[10] Using the commons as a cesspool does not harm the general public under frontier conditions, because there is no public; the same behavior in a metropolis is unbearable. A hundred and fifty years ago a plainsman could kill an American bison, cut out only the tongue for his dinner, and discard the rest of the animal. He was not in any important sense being wasteful. Today, with only a few thousand bison left, we would be appalled at such behavior.

In passing, it is worth noting that the morality of an act cannot be determined from a photograph. One does not know whether a man killing an elephant or setting fire to the grassland is harming others until one knows the total system in which his act appears. "One picture is worth a thousand words," said an ancient Chinese; but it may take 10,000 words to validate it. It is as tempting to ecologists as it is to reformers in general to try to persuade others by way of the photographic shortcut. But the essence of an argument cannot be photographed: it must be presented rationally—in words.

That morality is system-sensitive escaped the attention of most codifiers of ethics in the past. "Thou shalt not . . ." is the form of traditional ethical directives which make no allowance for particular circumstances. The laws of our society follow the pattern of ancient ethics, and therefore are poorly suited to governing a complex, crowded, changeable world. Our epicyclic solution is to augment statutory law with administrative law. Since it is practically impossible to spell out all the conditions under which it is safe to burn trash in the back yard or to run an automobile without smog-control, by law we delegate the details to bureaus. The result is administrative law, which is rightly feared for an ancient reason—*Quis custodiet ipsos custodes?* "Who shall watch the watchers themselves?" John Adams said that we must have "a government of laws and not men." Bureau administrators, trying to evaluate the morality of acts in the total system, are singularly liable to corruption, producing a government by men, not laws.

Prohibition is easy to legislate (though not necessarily to enforce); but how do we legislate temperance? Experience indicates that it can be accomplished best through the mediation of administrative law. We limit possibilities unnecessarily if we suppose that the sentiment of *Quis custodiet* denies us the use of administrative law. We should rather retain the phrase as a perpetual reminder of fearful dangers we cannot avoid. The great challenge facing us now is to invent the corrective feedbacks that are needed to keep custodians honest. We must find ways to legitimate the needed authority of both the custodians and the corrective feedbacks.

## FREEDOM TO BREED IS INTOLERABLE

The tragedy of the commons is involved in population problems in another way. In a world governed solely by the principle of "dog eat dog"—if indeed there ever was such a world—how many children a family had would not be a matter of public concern.

Parents who bred too exuberantly would leave fewer descendants, not more, because they would be unable to care adequately for their children. David Lack and others have found that such a negative feedback demonstrably controls the fecundity of birds.[11] But men are not birds, and have not acted like them for millenniums, at least.

*If* each human family were dependent only on its own resources; *if* the children of improvident parents starved to death; *if,* thus, overbreeding brought its own "punishment" to the germ line—*then* there would be no public interest in controlling the breeding of families. But our society is deeply committed to the welfare state,[12] and hence is confronted with another aspect of the tragedy of the commons.

In a welfare state, how shall we deal with the family, the religion, the race, or the class (or indeed any distinguishable and cohesive group) that adopts overbreeding as a policy to secure its own aggrandizement[13]? To couple the concept of freedom to breed with the belief that everyone born has an equal right to the commons is to lock the world into a tragic course of action.

Unfortunately this is just the course of action that is being pursued by the United Nations. In late 1967, some 30 nations agreed to the following:[14]

> The Universal Declaration of Human Rights describes the family as the natural and fundamental unit of society. It follows that any choice and decision with regard to the size of the family must irrevocably rest with the family itself, and cannot be made by someone else.

It is painful to have to deny categorically the validity of this right; denying it, one feels as uncomfortable as a resident of Salem, Massachusetts, who denied the reality of witches in the 17th century. At the present time, in liberal quarters, something like a taboo acts to inhibit criticism of the United Nations. There is a feeling that the United Nations is "our last and best hope," that we shouldn't find fault with it; we shouldn't play into the hands of the archconservatives. However, let us not forget what Robert Louis Stevenson said: "The truth that is suppressed by friends is the readiest weapon of the enemy." If we love the truth we must openly deny the validity of the Universal Declaration of Human Rights, even through it is promoted by the United Nations. We should also join with Kingsley Davis[15] in attempting to get Planned Parenthood-World Population to see error of its ways in embracing the same tragic ideal.

## CONSCIENCE IS SELF-ELIMINATING

It is a mistake to think that we can control the breeding of mankind in the long run by an appeal to conscience. Charles Galton Darwin made this point when he spoke on the centennial of the publication of his grandfather's great book. The argument is straightforward and Darwinian.

People vary. Confronted with appeals to limit breeding, some people will undoubtedly respond to the plea more than others. Those who have more children will produce a larger fraction of the next generation than those with more susceptible consciences. The difference will be accentuated, generation by generation.

In C. G. Darwin's words: "It may well be that it would take hundreds of generations for the progenitive instinct to develop in this way, but if it should do so, nature would have taken her revenge, and the variety *Homo contracipiens* would become extinct and would be replaced by the variety *Homo progenitivus*".[16]

The argument assumes that conscience or the desire for children (no matter which) is hereditary—but hereditary only in the most general formal sense. The result will be the same whether the attitude is transmitted through germ cells, or exosomatically, to use A. J. Lotka's term. (If one denies the latter possibility as well as the former, then what's the point of education?) The argument has here been stated in the context of the population problem, but it applies equally well to any instance in which society appeals to an individual exploiting a commons to restrain himself for the general good—by means of his conscience. To make such an appeal is to set up a selective system that works toward the elimination of conscience from the race.

## PATHOGENIC EFFECTS OF CONSCIENCE

The long-term disadvantage of an appeal to conscience should be enough to condemn it; but has serious short-term disadvantages as well. If we ask a man who is exploiting a commons to desist "in the name of conscience," what are we saying to him? What does he hear?—not only at the moment but also in the wee small hours of the night when, half asleep, he remembers not merely the words we used but also the nonverbal communication cues we gave him unawares? Sooner or later, consciously or subconsciously, he senses that he has received two communications, and that they are contradictory: (i) (intended communication) "If you don't do as we ask, we will openly condemn you for not acting like a responsible citizen"; (ii) (the unintended communication) "If you *do* behave as we ask, we will secretly condemn you for a simpleton who can be shamed into standing aside while the rest of us exploit the commons."

Everyman then is caught in what Bateson has called a "double bind." Bateson and his co-workers have made a plausible case for viewing the double bind as an important causative factor in the genesis of schizophrenia.[17] The double bind may not always be so damaging, but it always endangers the mental health of anyone to whom it is applied. "A bad conscience," said Nietzsche, "is a kind of illness."

To conjure up a conscience in others is tempting to anyone who wishes to extend his control beyond the legal limits. Leaders at the highest level succumb to this temptation. Has any President during the past generation failed to call on labor unions to moderate voluntarily their demands for higher wages, or to steel companies to honor voluntary guidelines on prices? I can recall none. The rhetoric used on such occasions is designed to produce feelings of guilt in noncooperators.

For centuries it was assumed without proof that guilt was a valuable, perhaps even an indispensible, ingredient of the civilized life. Now, in this post-Freudian world, we doubt it.

Paul Goodman speaks from the modern point of view when he says: "No good has ever come from feeling guilty, neither intelligence, policy, nor compassion. The guilty do not pay attention to the object but only to themselves, and not even to their own interests, which might make sense, but to their anxieties".[18]

One does not have to be a professional psychiatrist to see the consequences of anxiety. We in the Western world are just emerging from a dreadful two-centuries-long Dark Ages of Eros that was sustained partly by prohibition laws, but perhaps more effectively by the anxiety-generating mechanisms of education. Alex Comfort has told the story well in *The Anxiety Makers*;[19] it is not a pretty one.

Since proof is difficult, we may even concede that the results of anxiety may sometimes, from certain points of view, be desirable. The larger question we should ask is whether, as a matter of policy, we should ever encourage the use of a technique the tendency (if not the intention) of which is psychologically pathogenic. We hear much talk these days of responsible parenthood; the coupled words are incorporated into the titles of some organizations devoted to birth control. Some people have proposed massive propaganda campaigns to instill responsibility into the nation's (or the world's) breeders. But what is the meaning of the word responsibility in this context? It is not merely a synonym for the word conscience? When we use the word responsibility in the absence of substantial sanctions are we not trying to browbeat a free man in a commons into acting against his own interest? Responsibilty is a verbal counterfeit for a substantial *quid pro quo*. It is an attempt to get something for nothing.

If the word responsibility is to be used at all, I suggest that it be in the sense Charles Frankel uses it.[20] "Responsibility," says this philosopher, "is the product of definite social arrangements." Notice that Frankel calls for social arrangements—not propaganda.

## MUTUAL COERCION MUTUALLY AGREED UPON

The social arrangements that produce responsibility are arrangements that create coercion, of some sort. Consider bank-robbing. The man who takes money from a bank acts as if the bank were a commons. How do we prevent such action? Certainly not by trying to control his behavior solely by a verbal appeal to his sense of responsibility. Rather than rely on propaganda we follow Frankel's lead and insist that a bank is not a commons; we seek the definite social arrangements that will keep it from becoming a commons. That we thereby infringe on the freedom of would-be robbers we neither deny nor regret.

The morality of bank-robbing is particularly easy to understand because we accept complete prohibition of this activity. We are willing to say "Thou shalt not rob banks," without providing for exceptions. But temperance also can be created by coercion. Taxing is a good coercive device. To keep downtown shoppers temperate in their use of parking space we introduce parking meters for short periods, and traffic fines for longer ones. We need not actually forbid a citizen to park as long as he wants to; we need merely make it increasingly expensive for him to do so. Not prohibition, but carefully biased options are what we offer him. A Madison Avenue man might call this persuasion; I prefer the greater candor of the word coercion.

Coercion is a dirty word to most liberals now, but it need not forever be so. As with the four-letter words, its dirtiness can be cleansed away by exposure to the light, by saying it over and over without apology or embarrassment. To many, the word coercion implies arbitrary decisions of distant and irresponsible bureaucrats; but this is not a necessary part of its meaning. The only kind of coercion I recommend is mutual coercion, mutually agreed upon by the majority of the people affected.

To say that we mutually agree to coercion is not to say that we are required to enjoy it, or even to pretend we enjoy it. Who enjoys taxes? We all grumble about them. But we accept compulsory taxes because we recognize that voluntary taxes would favor the conscienceless. We institute and (grumblingly) support taxes and other coercive devices to escape the horror of the commons.

An alternative to the commons need not be perfectly just to be preferable. With real estate and other material goods, the alternative we have chosen is the institution of private property coupled with legal inheritance. Is this system perfectly just? As a genetically trained biologist I deny that it is. It seems to me that, if there are to be differences in individual inheritance, legal possession should be perfectly corrrelated with biological inheritance—that those who are biologically more fit to be the custodians of property and power should legally inherit more. But genetic recombination continually makes a mockery of the doctrine of "like father, like son" implicit in our laws of legal inheritance. An idiot can inherit millions, and a trust fund can keep his estate intact. We must admit that our legal system of private property plus inheritance is unjust—but we put up with it because we are not convinced, at the moment, that anyone has invented a better system. The alternative of the commons is too horrifying to contemplate. Injustice is preferable to total ruin.

It is one of the peculiarities of the warfare between reform and the status quo that it is thoughtlessly governed by a double standard. Whenever a reform measure is proposed it is often defeated when its opponents triumphantly discover a flaw in it. As Kingsley Davis has pointed out,[21] worshippers of the status quo sometimes imply that no reform is possible without unanimous agreement, an implication contrary to historical fact. As nearly as I can make out, automatic rejection of proposed reforms is based on one of two unconscious assumptions: (i) that the status quo is perfect; or (ii) that the choice we face is between reform and no action; if the proposed reform is imperfect, we presumably should take no action at all, while we wait for a perfect proposal.

But we can never do nothing. That which we have done for thousands of years is also action. It also produces evils. Once we are aware that the status quo is action, we can then compare its discoverable advantages and disadvantages with the predicted advantages and disadvantages of the proposed reform, discounting as best we can for our lack of experience. On the basis of such a comparison, we can make a rational decision which will not involve the unworkable assumption that only perfect systems are tolerable.

## RECOGNITION OF NECESSITY

Perhaps the simplest summary of this analysis of man's population problems is this: the commons, if justifiable at all, is justifiable only under conditions of low-population density. As the human population has increased, the commons has had to be abandoned in one aspect after another.

First we abandoned the commons in food gathering, enclosing farm land and restricting pastures and hunting and fishing areas. These restrictions are still not complete throughout the world.

Somewhat later we saw that the commons as a place for waste disposal would also have to be abandoned. Restrictions on the disposal of domestic sewage are widely accepted in the Western world; we are still struggling to close the commons to pollution by automobiles, factories, insecticide sprayers, fertilizing operations, and atomic energy installations.

In a still more embryonic state is our recognition of the evils of the commons in matters of pleasure. There is almost no restriction on the propagation of sound waves in the public medium. The shopping public is assaulted with mindless music, without its consent. Our government is paying out billions of dollars to create supersonic transport which will disturb 50,000 people for every one person who is whisked from coast to coast 3 hours faster. Advertisers muddy the airwaves of radio and television and pollute the view of travelers. We are a long way from outlawing the commons in matters of pleasure. Is this because our Puritan inheritance makes us view pleasure as something of a sin, and pain (that is, the pollution of advertising) as the sign of virtue?

Every new enclosure of the commons involves the infringement of somebody's personal liberty. Infringements made in the distant past are accepted because no contemporary complains of a loss. It is the newly proposed infringements that we vigorously oppose; cries of "rights" and "freedom" fill the air. But what does "freedom" mean? When men mutually agreed to pass laws against robbing, mankind became more free, not less so. Individuals locked into the logic of the commons are free only to bring on universal ruin; once they see the necessity of mutual coercion, they become free to pursue other goals. I believe it was Hegel who said, "Freedom is the recognition of necessity."

The most important aspect of necessity that we must now recognize, is the necessity of abandoning the commons in breeding. No technical solution can rescue us from the misery of overpopulation. Freedom to breed will bring ruin to all. At the moment, to avoid hard decisions many of us are tempted to propagandize for conscience and responsible parenthood. The temptation must be resisted, because an appeal to independently acting consciences selects for the disappearance of all conscience in the long run, and an increase in anxiety in the short.

The only way we can preserve and nurture other and more precious freedoms is by relinquishing the freedom to breed, and that very soon. "Freedom is the recognition of necessity"—and it is the role of education to reveal to all the necessity of abandoning the freedom to breed. Only so, can we put an end to this aspect of the tragedy of the commons.

## REFERENCES

1. J. B. Wiesner and H. F. York, *Sci. Amer.* **211** (No. 4), 27 (1964).
2. G. Hardin, *J. Hered.* **50,** 68 (1959); S. von Hoernor, *Science* **137,** 18 (1962).
3. J. von Neumann and O. Morgenstern. *Theory of Games and Economic Behavior* (Princeton Univ. Press, Princeton, N.J., 1947), p. 11.
4. J. H. Fremlin, *New Sci.,* No. 415 (1964), p. 285.
5. A. Smith, *The Wealth of Nations* (Modern Library, New York, 1937), p. 423.
6. W. F. Lloyd, *Two Lectures on the Checks to Population* (Oxford Univ. Press, Oxford, England, 1833), reprinted (in part) in *Population, Evolution, and Birth Control,* G. Hardin, Ed. (Freeman, San Francisco, 1964), p. 37.
7. A. N. Whitehead, *Science and the Modern World* (Mentor, New York, 1948), p. 17.
8. G. Hardin, Ed. *Population, Evolution, and Birth Control* (Freeman, San Francisco, 1964), p. 56.
9. S. McVay, *Sci. Amer.* **216** (No. 8), 13 (1966).
10. J. Fletcher, *Situation Ethics* (Westminster, Philadelphia, 1966).
11. D. Lack, *The Natural Regulation of Animal Numbers* (Clarendon Press, Oxford, 1954).
12. H. Girvetz, *From Wealth to Welfare* (Stanford Univ. Press, Stanford, Calif., 1950).
13. G. Hardin, *Perspec. Biol. Med.* **6,** 366 (1963).
14. U. Thant, *Int. Planned Parenthood News,* No. 168 (February 1968), p. 3.
15. K. Davis, *Science* **158,** 730 (1967).
16. S. Tax, Ed., *Evolution after Darwin* (Univ. of Chicago Press, Chicago, 1960), vol. 2, p. 469.
17. G. Bateson, D. D. Jackson, J. Haley, J. Weakland, *Behav. Sci.* **1,** 251 (1956).
18. P. Goodman, *New York Rev. Books* **10**(8), 22 (23 May 1968).
19. A. Comfort, *The Anxiety Makers* (Nelson, London, 1967).
20. C. Frankel, *The Case for Modern Man* (Harper, New York, 1955), p. 203.
21. J. D. Roslansky, *Genetics and the Future of Man* (Appleton-Century-Crofts, New York, 1966), p. 177.

# PART FIVE

# Prospects
# for a Sane Economics

*Economic development is the process by which the evil
day is brought closer when everything will be gone.**

Economists as a group have been guiltier than most in perpetuating the
most dangerous myths of this troubled age. Agricultural economists have
given us the fiction that seven billion mouths in the year 2000 can be easily
fed, in spite of the miserable failure of agriculture to feed half that number
today. Mineral economists rely on the cornucopian dream, in which advancing
technology conjures up ever cheaper minerals while consuming ever increasing amounts of energy and the earth's crust to do it. And economists of the
Presidential-advisor variety continue to assure our lawmakers that the "magic"
trillion dollar GNP is a milestone worth striving for. The fallacy in every case
lies in what has been left out of the accounting: the ecological costs of food
production; the facts of mineral distribution and diminishing returns; the
conversion of resources and amenities into pollutants and eyesores; the
massive expenditures for junk and planned obsolescence while social needs
go begging.

The jargon of the economist is itself a fascinating subject. If he speaks of
a "food surplus," read: "the starving are also broke; therefore supply exceeds
demand." If he says, "the Philippines are self-sufficient in rice," read: "politically motivated price supports have forced the peasants to switch to corn."
If he offers a "cost-benefit analysis," beware lest the group that pays the costs
is not the one which gets the benefits.

Fortunately, there has emerged from this wonderland of euphemism and
specious analysis a number of voices of reason. We present selections from
some (although by no means all) of them here. The reader will discover that
what is being advocated is no less than a revolution in economic philosophy.
Without it, the "ecological revolution" is foredoomed.

* Kenneth E. Boulding, in *Environmental Crisis*, H. W. Helfrich, Jr., Ed., Yale, 1970.

Our first author, Kenneth Boulding, has had a long and distinguished career as a heretic among economists. He has boldly ventured beyond supply and demand curves to ask the fundamental questions so many of his fellows have shunned: What limitations do the laws of biology and thermodynamics place on man's economic behavior, and how can they be brought into the balance sheet? How can we force economics to reflect the end of the expanding frontier? Is production a measure of success in a closed system, or is it a liability we must incur to replace our losses to deterioration and dissipation? These are profound issues, but we presume they are not yet reaching the ears of presidents, premiers and party chairmen. If they do, and the economic revolution they presage comes about—as it must if civilization long endures—it will be fair to record Professor Boulding as its prophet.

An enlightening essay on one aspect of our present, primitive economics is A. A. Berle's paper, "What GNP Doesn't Tell Us." The trouble with Gross National Product, Mr. Berle points out, is the "gross"—the final number does not discriminate between the useful and the frivolous, the constructive and the destructive, the humane and the malicious. We desperately need a more instructive measure of progress (or lack of it), and a serious attempt to calculate Berle's "gross national disproduct" would be a beginning. A comprehensive tabulation would be a staggering task, for it should include things *not* done (the neglect of cities, to use Mr. Berle's apt example), as well as the active blunders which erode quality of life today and undermine it for tomorrow. Obviously, the effort will involve assigning dollar values to these so-called "externalities"—including the ultimate economic costs of pollution, consumption and neglect which, now borne by no one, are mortgaging the future of everyone. This quantitative calculation of "disproduct" will be as unpopular as it is difficult, for it will surely show that industrialists are not the only guilty parties, nor the only ones who will have to pay. Among the great shocks awaiting a public now righteously indignant over the destruction of their environment is this one: we are all guilty, and the sane economics which must precede a solution will cost us all.

A related and long-neglected bit of economics is the study of benefits which accrue from not having children, or, rather, from not having large numbers of them. Stephen Enke has studied this question in the context of the "developing" nations, and his startling conclusions make it well worth struggling through the mathematics in his paper. For those who don't make it, we summarize the results of his calculations here: slower population growth favors economic welfare; money spent on birth control can be 100 times more effective in raising per capita income than money spent on traditional productive investments (factories, highways, etc.); the benefit to cost ratio of a major birth control program which halved fertility by the end of 30 years (in a hypothetical developing country) would be roughly 80 to 1. Thus Mr. Enke has quantified what thoughtful observers have long suspected: for underdeveloped nations struggling to raise their standard of living, population control is an economic imperative. (To those who argue that today's developed nations achieved that status without worrying about population growth, there is an obvious answer: *no* developed nation ever had to cope with growth rates as high as the 3 per cent and more prevalent in many UDC's today, because the death rates were higher then. Birth rates and death rates came down gradually with industrialization, while today in the UDC's, only the death rates have dropped.)

It is easy to become entangled in the percentages and rates of analyses like Mr. Enke's, however enlightening they may be, and overlook the absolute economic level which is being discussed. The reader is reminded, therefore, that Enke is talking about whether per capita income in a typical UDC will be $250 or $350 in the year 2000 (versus over $3500 in the U.S. in 1968). Realistically, even the higher figure must be regarded as a disaster. It is perfectly clear that anything remotely approaching even today's Eastern European material "standard of living" will be out of the question for most UDC's in the year 2000 under *any* set of economic assumptions. Why our statesmen strive so vigorously to conceal this elementary fact remains a partial mystery. Perhaps they believe the UDC's would not part so readily with the mineral wealth which sustains our consumption if they knew their own aspirations to homes, automobiles, and beefsteaks were delusions. Or perhaps they know our wealth would sit less comfortably without the myth that all men will soon share it.

The statesmen who deny the obvious and the economists and sociologists who embellish the hoax with regression analyses and intricate jargon have much to learn from Ivan Illich's radical statement, "Outwitting the 'developed' countries". In rejecting the economy and indeed the sanity of the development ethic and consumerism which the industrial nations brandish but cannot provide to the Third World, Illich offers some profound alternatives (for them and for us). He presents his case so well that it seems almost presumptuous to paraphrase or summarize him further here; we offer his essay as perhaps the most significant contribution in this volume.

# The Economics of the Coming Spaceship Earth

## KENNETH E. BOULDING

We are now in the middle of a long process of transition in the nature of the image which man has of himself and his environment. Primitive men, and to a large extent also men of the early civilizations, imagined themselves to be living on a virtually illimitable plane. There was almost always somewhere beyond the known limits of human habitation, and over a very large part of the time that man has been on earth, there has been something like a frontier. That is, there was always some place else to go when things got too difficult, either by reason of the deterioration of the natural environment or a deterioration of the social structure in places where people happened to live. The image of the frontier is probably one of the oldest images of mankind, and it is not surprising that we find it hard to get rid of.

Gradually, however, man has been accustoming himself to the notion of the spherical earth and a closed sphere of human activity. A few unusual spirits among the ancient Greeks perceived that the earth was a sphere. It was only with the circumnavigations and the geographical explorations of the fifteenth and sixteenth centuries, however, that the fact that the earth was a sphere became at all widely known and accepted. Even in the nineteenth century, the commonest map was Mercator's projection, which visualizes the earth as an illimitable cylinder, essentially a plane wrapped around the globe, and it was not until the Second World War and the development of the air age that the global nature of the planet really entered the popular imagination. Even now we are very far from having made the moral, political, and psychological adjustments which are implied in this transition from the illimitable plane to the closed sphere.

Economists in particular, for the most part, have failed to come to grips with the ultimate consequences of the transition from the open to the closed earth. One hesitates to use the terms "open" and "closed" in this connection, as they have been used with so many different shades of meaning. Nevertheless, it is hard to find equivalents. The open system, indeed, has some similarities to the open system of von Bertalanffy,[1] in that it implies that some kind of a structure is maintained in the midst of a throughput from inputs to outputs. In a closed system, the outputs of all parts of the system are linked to the inputs of other parts. There are no inputs from outside and no outputs to the outside; indeed, there is no outside at all. Closed systems, in fact, are very rare in human experience, in fact almost by definition unknowable, for if there are genuinely closed systems around us, we have no way of getting information into them or out of them; and hence if they are really closed, we would be quite unaware of their existence. We can only find out about a closed system if we partici-

The Economics of the Coming Spaceship Earth. From *Environmental Quality in a Growing Economy*, published by The John Hopkins Press for Resources for the Future, Inc. Reprinted by permission of the author and the publisher.

[1] Ludwig von Bertalanffy, *Problems of Life* (New York: John Wiley and Sons, 1952).

pate in it. Some isolated primitive societies may have approximated to this, but even these had to take inputs from the environment and give outputs to it. All living organisms, including man himself, are open systems. They have to receive inputs in the shape of air, food, water, and give off outputs in the form of effluvia and excrement. Deprivation of input of air, even for a few minutes, is fatal. Deprivation of the ability to obtain any input or to dispose of any output is fatal in a relatively short time. All human societies have likewise been open systems. They receive inputs from the earth, the atmosphere, and the waters, and they give outputs into these reservoirs; they also produce inputs internally in the shape of babies and outputs in the shape of corpses. Given a capacity to draw upon inputs and to get rid of outputs, an open system of this kind can persist indefinitely.

There are some systems—such as the biological phenotype, for instance the human body—which cannot maintain themselves indefinitely by inputs and outputs because of the phenomenon of aging. This process is very little understood. It occurs, evidently, because there are some outputs which cannot be replaced by any known input. There is not the same necessity for aging in organizations and in societies, although an analogous phenomenon may take place. The structure and composition of an organization or society, however, can be maintained by inputs of fresh personnel from birth and education as the existing personnel ages and eventually dies. Here we have an interesting example of a system which seems to maintain itself by the self-generation of inputs, and in this sense is moving towards closure. The input of people (that is, babies) is also an output of people (that is, parents).

Systems may be open or closed in respect to a number of classes of inputs and outputs. Three important classes are matter, energy, and information. The present world economy is open in regard to all three. We can think of the world economy or "econosphere" as a subset of the "world set," which is the set of all objects of possible discourse in the world.

We then think of the state of the econosphere at any one moment as being the total capital stock, that is, the set of all objects, people, organizations, and so on, which are interesting from the point of view of the system of exchange. This total stock of capital is clearly an open system in the sense that it has inputs and outputs, inputs being production which adds to the capital stock, outputs being consumption which subtracts from it. From a material point of view, we see objects passing from the noneconomic into the economic set in the process of production, and we similarly see products passing out of the economic set as their value becomes zero. Thus we see the econosphere as a material process involving the discovery and mining of fossil fuels, ores, etc., and at the other end a process by which the effluents of the system are passed out into noneconomic reservoirs—for instance, the atmosphere and the oceans—which are not appropriated and do not enter into the exchange system.

From the point of view of the energy system the econosphere involves inputs of available energy in the form, say, of water power, fossil fuels, or sunlight, which are necessary in order to create the material throughput and to move matter from the noneconomic set into the economic set or even out of it again; and energy itself is given off by the system in a less available form, mostly in the form of heat. These inputs of available energy must come either from the sun (the energy supplied by other stars being assumed to be negligible) or it may come from the earth itself, either through its internal heat or through its energy of rotation or other motions, which generate, for instance, the energy of the tides. Agriculture, a few solar machines, and water power use the current available energy income. In advanced societies this is supplemented very extensively by the use of fossil fuels, which represent as it were a capital stock of stored-up sunshine. Because of this capital stock of energy, we have been able to maintain an energy input into the system, particularly over the last two centuries, much larger than we would have been able to do with existing techniques if we had had to rely on the current input of available energy from the sun or the earth itself. This supplementary input, however, is by its very nature exhaustible.

The inputs and outputs of information are more subtle and harder to trace, but also represent an open system, related to, but not wholly dependent on, the transformations of matter and energy. By far the larger amount of information and knowledge is self-generated by the human society, though a certain amount of information comes into the sociosphere in the form of light from the universe outside. The information that comes from the universe has certainly affected man's image of himself and of his environment, as we can easily visualize if we suppose that we lived on a planet with a total cloud-cover that kept out all information from the exterior universe. It is only in very recent times, of course, that the information coming in from the universe has been captured and coded into the form of a complex image of what the universe is like outside the earth; but even in primitive times, man's perception of the heavenly bodies has always profoundly affected his image of earth and of himself. It is the information generated within the planet, however, and particularly that generated by man himself, which forms by far the larger part of the information system. We can think of the stock of knowledge, or as Teilhard de Chardin called it, the "noosphere," and consider this as an open system, losing knowledge through aging and death and gaining it through birth and education and the ordinary experience of life.

From the human point of view, knowledge or information is by far the most important of the three systems. Matter only acquires significance and only enters the sociosphere or the econosphere insofar as it becomes an object of human knowledge. We can think capital, indeed, as frozen knowledge or knowledge imposed on the material world in the form of improbable arrangements. A machine, for instance, originated in the mind of man, and both its construction and its use involve information processes imposed on

the material world by man himself. The cumulation of knowledge, that is, the excess of its production over its consumption, is the key to human development of all kinds, especially to economic development. We can see this pre-eminence of knowledge very clearly in the experiences of countries where the material capital has been destroyed by a war, as in Japan and Germany. The knowledge of the people was not destroyed, and it did not take long, therefore, certainly not more than ten years, for most of the material capital to be reestablished again. In a country such as Indonesia, however, where the knowledge did not exist, the material capital did not come into being either. By "knowledge" here I mean, of course, the whole cognitive structure, which includes valuations and motivations as well as images of the factual world.

The concept of entropy, used in a somewhat loose sense, can be applied to all three of these open systems. In the case of material systems, we can distinguish between entropic processes, which take concentrated materials and diffuse them through the oceans or over the earth's surface or into the atmosphere, and anti-entropic processes, which take diffuse materials and concentrate them. Material entropy can be taken as a measure of the uniformity of the distribution of elements and, more uncertainly, compounds and other structures on the earth's surface. There is, fortunately, no law of increasing material entropy, as there is in the corresponding case of energy, as it is quite possible to concentrate diffused materials if energy inputs are allowed. Thus the processes for fixation of nitrogen from the air, processes for the extraction of magnesium or other elements from the sea, and processes for the desalinization of sea water are anti-entropic in the material sense, though the reduction of material entropy has to be paid for by inputs of energy and also inputs of information, or at least a stock of information in the system. In regard to matter, therefore, a closed system is conceivable, that is, a system in which there is neither increase nor decrease in material entropy. In such a system all outputs from consumption would constantly be recycled to become inputs for production, as for instance, nitrogen in the nitrogen cycle of the natural ecosystem.

In regard to the energy system there is, unfortunately, no escape from the grim Second Law of Thermodynamics; and if there were no energy inputs into the earth, any evolutionary or developmental process would be impossible. The large energy inputs which we have obtained from fossil fuels are strictly temporary. Even the most optimistic predictions would expect the easily available supply of fossil fuels to be exhausted in a mere matter of centuries at present rates of use. If the rest of the world were to rise to American standards of power consumption, and still more if world population continues to increase, the exhaustion of fossil fuels would be even more rapid. The development of nuclear energy has improved this picture, but has not fundamentally altered it, at least in present technologies, for fissionable material is still relatively scarce. If we should achieve the economic use of energy through fusion, of course, a much larger source of energy materials would be available, which would expand the time horizons of supplementary energy input into an open social system by perhaps tens to hundreds of thousands of years. Failing this, however, the time is not very far distant, historically speaking, when man will once more have to retreat to his current energy input from the sun, even though this could be used much more effectively than in the past with increased knowledge. Up to now, certainly, we have not got very far with the technology of using current solar energy, but the possibility of substantial improvements in the future is certainly high. It may be, indeed, that the biological revolution which is just beginning will produce a solution to this problem, as we develop artificial organisms which are capable of much more efficient transformation of solar energy into easily available forms than any that we now have. As Richard Meier has suggested, we may run our machines in the future with methane-producing algae.[2]

[2] Richard L. Meier, *Science and Economic Development* (New York: John Wiley and Sons, 1956).

The question of whether there is anything corresponding to entropy in the information system is a puzzling one, though of great interest. There are certainly many examples of social systems and cultures which have lost knowledge, especially in transition from one generation to the next, and in which the culture has therefore degenerated. One only has to look at the folk culture of Appalachian migrants to American cities to see a culture which started out as a fairly rich European folk culture in Elizabethan times and which seems to have lost both skills, adaptability, folk tales, songs, and almost everything that goes up to make richness and complexity in a culture, in the course of about ten generations. The American Indians on reservations provide another example of such degradation of the information and knowledge system. On the other hand, over a great part of human history, the growth of knowledge in the earth as a whole seems to have been almost continuous, even though there have been times of relatively slow growth and times of rapid growth. As it is knowledge of certain kinds that produces the growth of knowledge in general, we have here a very subtle and complicated system, and it is hard to put one's finger on the particular elements in a culture which make knowledge grow more or less rapidly, or even which make it decline. One of the great puzzles in this connection, for instance, is why the take-off into science, which represents an "acceleration," or an increase in the rate of growth of knowledge in European society in the sixteenth century, did not take place in China, which at that time (about 1600) was unquestionably ahead of Europe, and one would think even more ready for the breakthrough. This is perhaps the most crucial question in the theory of social development, yet we must confess that it is very little understood. Perhaps the most significant factor in this connection is the existence of "slack" in the culture, which permits a divergence from established patterns and activity which is not merely devoted to reproducing the existing society but is devoted to changing it. China was perhaps too well-organized and had too little slack in its society to produce the kind of acceleration which we find in the somewhat poorer and less well-organized but more diverse societies of Europe.

The closed earth of the future requires economic principles which are somewhat different from those of the open earth of the past. For the sake of picturesqueness, I am tempted to call the open economy the "cowboy economy," the cowboy being symbolic of the illimitable plains and also associated with reckless, exploitative, romantic, and violent behavior, which is characteristic of open societies. The closed economy of the future might similarly be called the "spaceman" economy, in which the earth has become a single spaceship, without unlimited reservoirs of anything, either for extraction or for pollution, and in which, therefore, man must find his place in a cyclical ecological system which is capable of continuous reproduction of material form even though it cannot escape having inputs of energy. The difference between the two types of economy becomes most apparent in the attitude towards consumption. In the cowboy economy, consumption is regarded as a good thing and production likewise; and the success of the economy is measured by the amount of the throughput from the "factors of production," a part of which, at any rate, is extracted from the reservoirs of raw materials and noneconomic objects, and another part of which is output into the reservoirs of pollution. If there are infinite reservoirs from which material can be obtained and into which effluvia can be deposited, then the throughput is at least a plausible measure of the success of the economy. The gross national product is a rough measure of this total throughput. It should be possible, however, to distinguish that part of the GNP which is derived from exhaustible and that which is derived from reproducible resources, as well as that part of consumption which represents effluvia and that which represents input into the productive system again. Nobody, as far as I know, has ever attempted to break down the GNP in this way, although it would be an interesting and extremely im-

portant exercise, which is unfortunately beyond the scope of this paper.

By contrast, in the spaceman economy, throughput is by no means a desideratum, and is indeed to be regarded as something to be minimized rather than maximized. The essential measure of the success of the economy is not production and consumption at all, but the nature, extent, quality, and complexity of the total capital stock, including in this the state of the human bodies and minds included in the system. In the spaceman economy, what we are primarily concerned with is stock maintenance, and any technological change which results in the maintenance of a given total stock with a lessened throughput (that is, less production and consumption) is clearly a gain. This idea that both production and consumption are bad things rather than good things is very strange to economists, who have been obsessed with the income-flow concepts to the exclusion, almost, of capital-stock concepts.

There are actually some very tricky and unsolved problems involved in the questions as to whether human welfare or well-being is to be regarded as a stock or a flow. Something of both these elements seems actually to be involved in it, and as far as I know there have been practically no studies directed towards identifying these two dimensions of human satisfaction. Is it, for instance, eating that is a good thing, or is it being well fed? Does economic welfare involve having nice clothes, fine houses, good equipment, and so on, or is it to be measured by the depreciation and the wearing out of these things? I am inclined myself to regard the stock concept as most fundamental, that is, to think of being well fed as more important than eating, and to think even of so-called services as essentially involving the restoration of a depleting psychic capital. Thus I have argued that we go to a concert in order to restore a psychic condition which might be called "just having gone to a concert," which, once established, tends to depreciate. When it depreciates beyond a certain point, we go to another concert in order to restore it. If it depreciates rapidly, we go to a lot of concerts; if it depreciates slowly, we go to few. On this view, similarly, we eat primarily to restore bodily homeostasis, that is, to maintain a condition of being well fed, and so on. On this view, there is nothing desirable in consumption at all. The less consumption we can maintain a given state with, the better off we are. If we had clothes that did not wear out, houses that did not depreciate, and even if we could maintain our bodily condition without eating, we would clearly be much better off.

It is this last consideration, perhaps, which makes one pause. Would we, for instance, really want an operation that would enable us to restore all our bodily tissues by intravenous feeding while we slept? Is there not, that is to say, a certain virtue in throughput itself, in activity itself, in production and consumption itself, in raising food and in eating it? It would certainly be rash to exclude this possibility. Further interesting problems are raised by the demand for variety. We certainly do not want a constant state to be maintained; we want fluctuations in the state. Otherwise there would be no demand for variety in food, for variety in scene, as in travel, for variety in social contact, and so on. The demand for variety can, of course, be costly, and sometimes it seems to be too costly to be tolerated or at least legitimated, as in the case of marital partners, where the maintenance of a homeostatic state in the family is usually regarded as much more desirable than the variety and excessive throughput of the libertine. There are problems here which the economics profession has neglected with astonishing singlemindedness. My own attempts to call attention to some of them, for instance, in two articles,[3] as far as I can judge, produced no response whatever; and economists continue to think and act as if production, consumption, throughput, and the GNP were the sufficient and adequate measure of economic success.

It may be said, of course, why worry about all this when the spaceman economy is still a good way off (at least beyond the lifetimes of any now living), so let us eat, drink, spend, extract and pollute, and be as merry as we can, and let posterity worry about the spaceship earth. It is always a little hard to find a convincing answer to the man who says, "What has posterity ever done for me?" and the conservationist has always had to fall back on rather vague ethical principles postulating identity of the individual with some human community or society which extends not only back into the past but forward into the future. Unless the individual identifies with some community of this kind, conservation is obviously "irrational." Why should we not maximize the welfare of this generation at the cost of posterity? "*Après nous, le déluge*" has been the motto of not insignificant numbers of human societies. The only answer to this, as far as I can see, is to point out that the welfare of the individual depends on the extent to which he can identify himself with others, and that the most satisfactory individual identity is that which identifies not only with a community in space but also with a community extending over time from the past into the future. If this kind of identity is recognized as desirable, then posterity has a voice, even if it does not have a vote; and in a sense, if its voice can influence votes, it has votes too. This whole problem is linked up with the much larger one of the determinants of the morale, legitimacy, and "nerve" of a society, and there is a great deal of historical evidence to suggest that a society which loses its identity with posterity and which loses its positive image of the future loses also its capacity to deal with present problems, and soon falls apart.[4]

Even if we concede that posterity is relevant to our present problems, we still face the question of time-discounting and the closely related question of uncertainty-discounting. It is a well-known phenomenon that individu-

[3] K. E. Boulding, "The Consumption Concept in Economic Theory," *American Economic Review*, 35:2 (May 1945), pp. 1–14; and "Income or Welfare?," *Review of Economic Studies*, 17 (1949–50), pp. 77–86.

[4] Fred L. Polak, *The Image of the Future*, Vols. I and II, translated by Elise Boulding (New York: Sythoff, Leyden and Oceana, 1961).

als discount the future, even in their own lives. The very existence of a positive rate of interest may be taken as at least strong supporting evidence of this hypothesis. If we discount our own future, it is certainly not unreasonable to discount posterity's future even more, even if we do give posterity a vote. If we discount this at 5 per cent per annum, posterity's vote or dollar halves every fourteen years as we look into the future, and after even a mere hundred years it is pretty small—only about 1½ cents on the dollar. If we add another 5 per cent for uncertainty, even the vote of our grandchildren reduces almost to insignificance. We can argue, of course, that the ethical thing to do is not to discount the future at all, that time-discounting is mainly the result of myopia and perspective, and hence is an illusion which the moral man should not tolerate. It is a very popular illusion, however, and one that must certainly be taken into consideration in the formulation of policies. It explains, perhaps, why conservationist policies almost have to be sold under some other excuse which seems more urgent, and why, indeed, necessities which are visualized as urgent, such as defense, always seem to hold priority over those which involve the future.

All these considerations add some credence to the point of view which says that we should not worry about the spaceman economy at all, and that we should just go on increasing the GNP and indeed the gross world product, or GWP, in the expectation that the problems of the future can be left to the future, that when scarcities arise, whether this is of raw materials or of pollutable reservoirs, the needs of the then present will determine the solutions of the then present, and there is no use giving ourselves ulcers by worrying about problems that we really do not have to solve. There is even high ethical authority for this point of view in the New Testament, which advocates that we should take no thought for tomorrow and let the dead bury their dead. There has always been something rather refreshing in the view that we should live like the birds, and perhaps posterity is for the birds in more senses than

one; so perhaps we should all call it a day and go out and pollute something cheerfully. As an old taker of thought for the morrow, however, I cannot quite accept this solution; and I would argue, furthermore, that tomorrow is not only very close, but in many respects it is already here. The shadow of the future spaceship, indeed, is already falling over our spendthrift merriment. Oddly enough, it seems to be in pollution rather than in exhaustion that the problem is first becoming salient. Los Angeles has run out of air, Lake Erie has become a cesspool, the oceans are getting full of lead and DDT, and the atmosphere may become man's major problem in another generation, at the rate at which we are filling it up with gunk. It is, of course, true that at least on a microscale, things have been worse at times in the past. The cities of today, with all their foul air and polluted waterways, are probably not as bad as the filthy cities of the pretechnical age. Nevertheless, that fouling of the nest which has been typical of man's activity in the past on a local scale now seems to be extending to the whole world society; and one certainly cannot view with equanimity the present rate of pollution of any of the natural reservoirs, whether the atmosphere, the lakes, or even the oceans.

I would argue strongly also that our obsession with production and consumption to the exclusion of the "state" aspects of human welfare distorts the process of technological change in a most undesirable way. We are all familiar, of course, with the wastes involved in planned obsolescence, in competitive advertising, and in poor quality of consumer goods. These problems may not be so important as the "view with alarm" school indicates, and indeed the evidence at many points is conflicting. New materials especially seem to edge towards the side of improved durability, such as, for instance, neolite soles for footwear, nylon socks, wash and wear shirts, and so on. The case of household equipment and automobiles is a little less clear. Housing and building construction generally almost certainly has declined in durability since the Middle Ages, but this decline also reflects a change in tastes towards flexibility and fashion and a need for novelty, so that it is not easy to assess. What is clear is that no serious attempt has been made to assess the impact over the whole of economic life of changes in durability, that is, in the ratio of capital in the widest possible sense to income. I suspect that we have underestimated, even in our spendthrift society, the gains from increased durability, and that this might very well be one of the places where the price system needs correction through government-sponsored research and development. The problems which the spaceship earth is going to present, therefore, are not all in the future by any means, and a strong case can be made for paying much more attention to them in the present than we now do.

It may be complained that the considerations I have been putting forth relate only to the very long run, and they do not much concern our immediate problems. There may be some justice in this criticism, and my main excuse is that other writers have dealt adequately with the more immediate problems of deterioration in the quality of the environment. It is true, for instance, that many of the immediate problems of pollution of the atmosphere or of bodies of water arise because of the failure of the price system, and many of them could be solved by corrective taxation. If people had to pay the losses due to the nuisances which they create, a good deal more resources would go into the prevention of nuisances. These arguments involving external economies and diseconomies are familiar to economists, and there is no need to recapitulate them. The law of torts is quite inadequate to provide for the correction of the price system which is required, simply because where damages are widespread and their incidence on any particular person is small, the ordinary remedies of the civil law are quite inadequate and inappropriate. There

needs, therefore, to be special legislation to cover these cases, and though such legislation seems hard to get in practice, mainly because of the widespread and small personal incidence of the injuries, the technical problems involved are not insuperable. If we were to adopt in principle a law for tax penalties for social damages, with an apparatus for making assessments under it, a very large proportion of current pollution and deterioration of the environment would be prevented. There are tricky problems of equity involved, particularly where old established nuisances create a kind of "right by purchase" to perpetuate themselves, but these are problems again which a few rather arbitrary decisions can bring to some kind of solution.

The problems which I have been raising in this paper are of larger scale and perhaps much harder to solve than the more practical and immediate problems of the above paragraph. Our success in dealing with the larger problems, however, is not unrelated to the development of skill in the solution of the more immediate and perhaps less difficult problems. One can hope, therefore, that as a succession of mounting crises, especially in pollution, arouse public opinion and mobilize support for the solution of the immediate problems, a learning process will be set in motion which will eventually lead to an appreciation of and perhaps solutions for the larger ones. My neglect of the immediate problems, therefore, is in no way intended to deny their importance, for unless we at least make a beginning on a process for solving the immediate problems we will not have much chance of solving the larger ones. On the other hand, it may also be true that a long-run vision, as it were, of the deep crisis which faces mankind may predispose people to taking more interest in the immediate problems and to devote more effort for their solution. This may sound like a rather modest optimism, but perhaps a modest optimism is better than no optimism at all.

# What GNP Doesn't Tell Us

A. A. BERLE, JR.

It is nice to know that at current estimate the Gross National Product of the United States in 1968 will be above 850 billions of dollars. It would be still nicer to know if the United States will be better or worse off as a result. If better, in what respects? If worse, could not some of this production and effort be steered into providing more useful "goods and services"?

Unfortunately, whether the work was sham or useful, the goods noxious, evanescent, or of permanent value will have no place in the record. Individuals, corporations, or government want, buy, and pay for stuff and work—so it is "product." The labor of the Boston Symphony Orchestra is "product" along with that of the band in a honky-tonk. The compensated services of a quack fortune teller are "product" just as much as the work of developing Salk vaccine. Restyling automobiles or ice chests by adding tail fins or pink handles adds to "product" just as much as money paid for slum clearance or medical care. They are all "goods" or "services"—the only test is whether someone wanted them badly enough to pay the shot.

This blanket tabulation raises specific complaints against economists and their uncritical aggregated figures and their acceptance of production as "progress." The economists bridle. "We," they reply, "are economists, not priests. Economics deals with satisfaction of human wants by things or services. The want is sufficiently evidenced by the

What GNP Doesn't Tell Us. From *Saturday Review*, August 31, 1968. Copyright 1968 Saturday Review, Inc. Reprinted by permission of the author and the publisher.

fact that human beings, individually or collectively, paid for them. It is not for us to pass on what people ought to have wanted—that question is for St. Peter. A famous statistic in *America's Needs and Resources*—published by the Twentieth Century Fund in 1955—was that Americans in 1950 paid $8.1 billion for liquor and $10.5 billion for education. Maybe they ought to have cut out liquor and paid for more education instead—but they didn't, and value judgments are not our job. Get yourself a philosopher for that. We will go on recording what did happen."

What they are saying—and as far as it goes, they are quite right—is that nobody has given economists a mandate to set up a social-value system for the country. Fair enough—but one wonders. Closer thinking suggests that even on their own plane economists could perhaps contribute a little to the subject, although, as will presently appear, we must get ourselves some philosophy, too. One branch of social indicating may not be as far removed from cold economics as it would appear. Another branch is more difficult, though even it may yield to analysis.

Any audit of social result, any system of social indicators, requires solving two sets of problems. First, with all this Gross National Product reflecting payment to satisfy wants, did America get what it paid for? In getting it, did it not also bring into being a flock of unrecorded but offsetting frustrations it did not want? Essentially, this is economic critique. Second—and far more difficult—can a set of values be put forward, roughly expressing the essentials most Americans would agree their society ought to be, and be doing, against which the actual record of what it was and did can be checked? This second critique, as economists rightly contend, is basically philosophical.

As for the economic critique, let us take the existing economic record at face. Work was done, things were created, and both were paid for. The total price paid this year will be around $850 billion. But, unrecorded, not included, and rarely mentioned are some companion results. Undisposed-of junk piles, garbage, waste, air and water pollution come into being. God help us, we can see that all over the country. Unremedied decay of parts of the vast property we call "the United States" is evident in and around most American cities. No one paid for this rot and waste—they are not "product." Factually, these and other undesirable results are clear deductions from or offset items to the alleged "Gross National Product" we like so well.

The total of these may be called "disproduct." It will be a hard figure to calculate in dollar figures. Recorded as "product" is the amount Americans spent for television sets, stations, and broadcasts. Unrecorded is their companion disproductive effect in the form of violence, vandalism, and crime. Proudly reported as "product" are sums spent for medical care, public health, and disease prevention; unheralded is the counter-item, the "disproduct" of loss and misery as remediable malnutrition and preventable disease ravage poverty areas. Besides our annual calculation of "gross" national product, it is time we had some idea of Gross National Disproduct. Deducting it, we could know what the true, instead of the illusory, annual "net national product" might be. (Economists use "Net National Product" to mean Gross National Product less consumption of capital—but it is not a true picture.)

There is a difference, it will be noted, between "disproduct" and "cost." Everything made or manufactured, every service rendered by human beings, involves using up materials, if only the food and living necessities of labor. These are "costs." They need not enter into this calculation. Conventional statistics already set up a figure for "capital consumption," and

we deduct this from "Gross National Product." That is not what we have in mind here. We are trying to discover whether creation of "Gross National Product" does not also involve frustration of wants as well as their satisfaction. Pollution of air and water are obvious illustrations but there are "disproducts" more difficult to discern, let alone measure.

Scientists are increasing our knowledge of these right along. For example, cigarettes (to which I am addicted) satisfy a widespread want. They also, we are learning, engender a great deal of cancer. Now it is true that at some later time the service rendered in attempting to care for cancer (generated by cigarettes manufactured five years ago) will show up as "product"; so the work of attempted cure or caretaking will later appear as a positive product item. But that item will not be known until later. What we do know without benefit of figures is that against this year's output of tobacco products whose cash value is recorded we have also brought more cancer into being—an unrecorded "disproduct." We know at the end of any year how many more automobiles have been manufactured. We also know that each new car on the road means added injury and accident overall. Carry this process through our whole product list, and the aggregate of 'disproduct' items set against the aggregate of production will tell us an immense amount about our progress toward (or retrogression from) social welfare.

Once we learn to calculate disproduct along with product and discover a true "net," as well as a "gross," we shall have our first great "social" indicator. We shall know what the country accomplished.

It could be surprising and disillusioning. It might disclose that while satisfying human wants as indicated by the "gross" figure, in the process we had also violated, blocked, or frustrated many of these same wants and, worse, had done a great deal we did not want to do. Carrying the calculation further, we would probably find (among other things) that while satisfying immediate wants from today's productivity, we had been generating future wants (not to say needs) to repair the

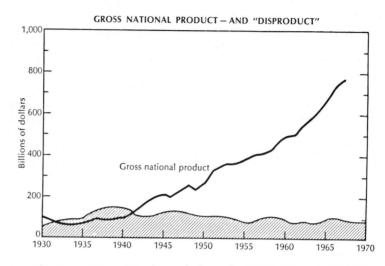

The Gross National Product, which reached $790 billion in 1967, includes all goods and services that someone is willing to pay for. GNP makes no discrimination between the useful and the frivolous.

damage, waste, and degeneration set up by current production.

Some of today's "gross" product carries with it a mortgage—it sets up brutal defensive requirements that must be met by tomorrow's work and things. Some forms of productivity may prove to generate more decay, damage, or waste annually than their total amount, while neglect of some production may annually place a usurious claim on future years. Failure to maintain cities at acceptable standards is a case in point: it sets up huge but unrecorded claims on the manpower and product of coming decades. It is entirely possible to score annual increases of Gross National Product as we presently figure it—and yet, after reckoning "disproduct," be little better off at the end of any year than at its beginning.

Calculation of "disproduct" is admittedly difficult. If seriously tackled, I think it at least partially possible. At first it would be far indeed from exact. All the same, "disproduct" is a plain fact of life—look out of your window and you can see some. Crude calculation of

the probable amounts needed to offset many items of "disproduct" is not insoluble; technicians in some lines have fairly concrete ideas along these lines already. Actuaries compute the "disproduct" resulting from automobile accidents, and your car insurance bill is calculated accordingly. Carry the process through and a crude though probably incomplete item could be developed. Using it, one could judge whether, materially at least, the country had moved forward or backward.

In this first bracket of critique, economists are not required to make value judgments of what is "good" or "bad." They, with the advice of the technical men in the various sectors, could merely be asked to tackle calculation of "disproduct" as well as of "product."

The second branch of the problem is harder. It raises the question of whether a good deal of Gross National Product should not be steered by social or political action toward creating a more satisfactory civilization. That, of course, requires some elementary assumptions as to what a satisfactory civilization ought to be and do. Can any such assumptions be made?

The question has not gone unnoticed. A philosopher, Sidney Hook (it would be Sidney Hook!), two years ago organized a combined conference of philosophical and economic pundits on the subject. Their proceedings were published in a book called *Human Values and Economic Policy*. They had themselves a fancy time. The opening gun was fired by Professor Kenneth J. Arrow of Stanford University, a mathematical economist. Consider, said Professor Arrow, a country that is not a dictatorship. In it, individuals have wide opportunity to find their own way to personal development and satisfaction. Then, he said, no picture can be drawn. Staffing it through equations, he evolved an "impossibility theorem," and thereupon tossed the ball to his fellow pundits. A colleague economist, Kenneth Boulding, rebutted, but it fell to a philosopher, Professor Paul Weiss of Yale, to counterattack. Professor Weiss forthrightly said that economists had been operating with an "unnecessary scarcity of ideas." The world, after all, is there—so they ought to add some conceptions of a "common-sense world and actual society, and a lived-through time."

Constructing enough of a value-system to use as critique of a Gross National Product indeed does seem not beyond common-sense possibility. The job does, without question, require setting out some values on which there is sufficient agreement to engage social opinion and, one hopes, social action. Production steered toward realizing these values can be described as "good." Production frustrating or tearing them down can be stigmatized as "bad." Let us try drawing up a list, tentative in the extreme. I think there would probably be considerable agreement that it is "good"; but if not, make a dinner table game of drawing a better one:

1. People are better alive than dead.
2. People are better healthy than sick.
3. People are better off literate than illiterate.

4. People are better off adequately than inadequately housed.
5. People are better off in beautiful than in ugly cities and towns.
6. People are better off if they have opportunity for enjoyment—music, literature, drama, and the arts.
7. Education above the elementary level should be as nearly universal as possible through secondary schools, and higher education as widely diffused as practicable.
8. Development of science and the arts should continue or possibly be expanded.
9. Minimum resources for living should be available to all.
10. Leisure and access to green country should be a human experience available to everyone.

Anyone can add to or change this list if he likes; my point is that at least a minimum set of values can be agreed on. We have done more here than draw up a list of pleasant objectives. We have set up criteria. By applying our list to the actual and recorded output of our Gross National Product, we begin to discern that some of these values are perhaps adequately pursued, some inadequately, some not served at all. Even now, the Gross National Product figure is broken down into many lines. It would have to be split up further or differently for purposes of criticism. The elementary value-system we have projected (or some better edition of it) could provide the basis for critique. It could permit discovery of whether the recorded outturn of our vast hubbub of activity, after subtracting "disproduct" from "product," tended toward producing social results more or less in accord with the objectives implied by our values. If Governor Nelson Rockefeller is right in believing that in a decade the Gross National Product of the United States will be a trillion and a half dollars, it should be possible to steer increasing amounts of it toward realization of this or any similar list of values, and the objectives it suggests.

I am aware that no American value-system can be real except as it expresses a common divisor of the thinking of 200 million Americans. Beyond that point, Professor Arrow's "impossibility theorem" probably was right enough. Only totalitarian police state dictatorships, denying their citizens choice of life and action, can lay down complete and all-inclusive value-systems, force their populations and their production into that mold, and audit the results in terms of their success in doing so. Free societies cannot. They must content themselves with common denomination of basic value judgments on which most of their people have substantial consensus—leaving them free to do as they please in other respects. When a free society attempts to impose value judgments going beyond consensus—as they did when the Prohibition Amendment was adopted in 1919—it fails. Yet because there is a wide measure of consensus on values, America does move along, does generate its enormous Gross National Product (and let us hope solid Net National Product) precisely because there is substantial agreement on what its people really want.

Also there is probably a high factor of agreement on priorities—that is, on what they want most. There are doubtful areas, of course. I will not risk a guess whether priority would be given to military preparedness over education were a Gallop Poll taken—more expenditures for defense and less for aid to education. But I am clear that both in values and in priorities a large enough measure of agreement does exist so that if we put our minds to it a critique of our outturn performance expressed in Gross National Product can be had.

And we ought not to be stopped or baffled or bogged down because philosophers cannot agree on the nature of "good," or because scientists cannot predict with certainty the social effects of value judgments carried into action. Wrong guesses about values show up in experience, as happened in the Prohibition experiment. In light of experience, they can be corrected. With even rudimentary social indicators, the current cascade of emo-

tional and sterile invective might be converted into rational dialogue. Constructive use of social-economic forces and even of currents of philosophical thinking might become possible.

I realize, of course, that up to now it has been assumed that social indicators, based on an expressed value-system, could not be achieved. Well, only a generation ago scholars assumed nothing could be done to alleviate the impact of assumedly blind economic forces let alone guide them. We know better today; rudimentary capacity to control and steer these forces already exists; the so-called New Economics increasingly guides their use. Similar thinking and similar tools can provide material on which social policy can be based. Combined with the economic tools currently being forged, social objectives might be brought out of dreamland into range of practical achievement.

Discussion and debate would inevitably result from comparison of actual operations with desired results. More intense and perhaps more fruitful controversy would be engendered in areas where there were items not appearing in our tentative list of values for lack of sufficient consensus. Protagonists would insist they be included; opponents would object. This could be healthy. It would be ballasted by realization that, were consensus achieved, constructive action could be possible. Any caterwaul that American society is "sick" could be qualified by emerging factual knowledge showing that either the accusation was untrue or, if true, that measures for cure could be taken. The debate might disadvantage some people; for one thing it might reduce the torrent of boring despair-literature presently drowning the reading public. Possibly even contrasting currents of new Puritanism might emerge perhaps providing a not unpleasant contrast, if not relief.

Knowing where American civilization is going is the first essential to saving it (if it is to be saved) or changing it (if it is to be altered).

# Birth Control
# for Economic Development

STEPHEN ENKE

There is a growing interest in the possibilities of lowering birth rates in order to raise per capita incomes in many of the less-developed countries. Described below is one economic-demographic method of assessing what reduced human fertility might contribute to increased economic development. Justifications of government programs to increase voluntary contraception are also considered.[1]

In less-developed countries, one-half or more of annual increases in national output is being "swallowed" by annual increases in population, with income per head rising very slowly. Most of these countries have natural increases of from 2 per cent to 3 per cent a year. Hence they are doubling their populations every 35 to 23 years. This results not from rising birthrates but from falling death rates during the past 25 to 40 years—mostly attributable to improved health measures.

Some of their governments have decided that they cannot afford to wait for a spontaneout decline in fertility, resulting perhaps from more education, greater urbanization, and improved living. Instead, a few governments are encouraging voluntary use of contraceptives. The objective is economic development.

Many questions remain. How effective in raising incomes per head is reducing fertility as compared with other investments of resources? Could and should governments of less-developed countries encourage voluntary contraception?

## INCOME PER HEAD

One measure of successful economic development is a rising income (output) per head of population.[2] It is ordinarily associated with other indicators of increasing welfare such as greater annual investment. Another measure is fewer people living in poverty.

Income (output) per head is a ratio. Governments have sought to raise this ratio by increasing its numerator—investing in factories, dams, and highways, and the like—in order to increase the annual national output of goods and services. However, where politically feasible, governments can also raise the ratio of output per head by decreasing the denominator. A comparison of economic effectiveness can be made of changing the denominator as well as the numerator.

In a very simple arithmetic calculation, an imaginary less-developed country may be expected, in 1980, to have a national output ($V$) of $2500 million and a population ($P$) of 12.5 million for a yearly output per head ($V/P$) of $200. The government may decide to spend an extra $2.5 million a year for 10 years starting in 1970 to raise $V/P$. It can use these funds to increase output ($\Delta V$) or to decrease population ($\Delta P$) from what they would otherwise be.[3] If the significant rate of return on traditional investments is 10 per cent annually,

Birth Control for Economic Development. From *Science*, Vol. 164, May 1969, pp. 798–801. Copyright 1969 by the American Association for the Advancement of Science. Reprinted by permission of the author and the publisher.

an investment of $25 million from 1970 to 1980 will yield a $\Delta V$ in 1980 of $2.5 million, so that $\Delta V/V$ is 0.1 per cent, or 1 in 1000.

Alternatively, the $2.5 million per year might have been spent on birth control. If the annual cost of an adult practicing contraception is $5[4] and the annual fertility of contraceptive users is otherwise typically 0.25 live births, then in 1980 the population (12.5 million) would be 1.25 million smaller than expected. Thus $\Delta P/P$ is 10 per cent or 1 in 10.

Apparently the amount of money spent each year on birth control can be 100 times more effective in raising output per head than the amount of money spent each year on traditional productive investments—for $V\Delta P/P\Delta V$ here equals 100. Had the rate of return on investments been 20 per cent annually instead of 10 per cent, had the annual cost of birth control been $10 instead of $5, or had the otherwise fertility of "contraceptors"[5] been 0.125 instead of 0.25, this superior effectiveness ratio would have been 50 to 1 instead of 100 to 1. Had all three parameters been altered by a factor of two to weaken the argument, the expenditures on birth control would still appear 12.5 times more effective.

The explanation is that it costs fewer resources to prevent a birth than to produce a person's share as a consumer in national output. Calculations of this kind do not convince everyone, however, for they exclude so many of the economic and demographic interactions that could be expected from reduced fertility.[6]

## DEVELOPA:
## A LESS-DEVELOPED COUNTRY

In order to assess the impacts of declining human fertility, a more complete economic-demographic model is needed as is applied here to a typical less-developed country named Developa. Any computer model should include at least the demographic and economic interactions shown in Fig. 1.

Specifically, the demographics involve projections of rates of mortality and fertility by age and sex, and data on the initial age and sex distribution of the less-developed country. Age and sex distributions can be calculated at 5-year intervals. Given the labor force participation coefficients by age and sex, the available labor force ($L$) can be computed.

The economics involve a national production function that relates number of employed workers ($N$), capital stock ($K$), and improving technology ($t$) to national output ($V$). Annual savings that increase $K$ are related positively to $V$ and negatively to $P$. An in-

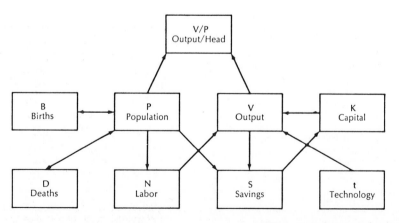

**FIG. 1.** Population and output per head

creasing *K* not only raises output per worker but reduces the surplus labor ratio *(L/N)*.

A frequently used national production function is of the type

$$\log V = \log z + n \log N + \\ k \log K + y \log (1 + t)$$

where *V*, *N*, and *K* are defined as above, *z* converts for units, *y* is years, and *n* and *k* are so-called output elasticities of labor and capital, respectively. Thus, if *n* is 0.5, a 10-per cent increase in *N* will occasion a 5-per cent increase in *V*. In this formulation *t* is an annually compounded shift factor that increases the productivity of labor and capital by the same multiplier.

In such a model the demographics affect the economics through a changing age distribution. Declining fertilities reduce the ratio of children (who consume but do not produce) to work-age adults (who do produce when employed with enough capital). Also more is saved and invested from a given *V* when *P* is smaller.[7]

Let us consider a nonexistent nation called Developa with the attributes typical of a less-developed country which has, in 1970, a population of 10 million and an income per head of $150. The crude birthrate is 44 per 1000 a year. When this model is used, what are the economic consequences of alternative fertility projections, given various parameters? Only two conditions are considered for fertility. When fertility is high the gross reproduction rate is 3.025 throughout.[8] When fertility is low the gross reproduction rate falls from 3.025 in 1970 to 1.95 in 1985 and 1.48 in A.D. 2000. (The crude birthrate falls from 44 to 31 and 26, respectively.) Life expectancy at birth increases slowly from 53.4 years in 1970 to 56.6 in 1985 and 59.0 in A.D. 2000.

The consequences of these contrasting projections for fertility over 30 years are shown in Table 1, starting with 1970 as a common base, for 1985 and A.D. 2000.[9] In both cases there is an improvement in output per head because of increasing capital per worker and contributions from improving technology—the latter compounding to 1.56 over the 30 years. However, when fertility is high, annual *V/P* increases only 1.63 times to $245, whereas when fertility is low it increases 2.36 times to $354 by A.D. 2000.

The number of persons living in "poverty"—defined arbitrarily as the state of being able to afford not more than $75 worth of goods and services a year—hardly changes

## TABLE 1

Declining fertility for economic development.

| Item | 1970 | 1985 High fertility | 1985 Low fertility | 2000 High fertility | 2000 Low fertility |
|---|---|---|---|---|---|
| *P*, population (10⁶) | 10.0 | 15.9 | 14.1 | 25.9 | 18.1 |
| *V*, output ($10⁹) | 1.50 | 2.92 | 2.99 | 6.33 | 6.43 |
| *V/P*, income per head ($) | 150 | 183 | 212 | 245 | 354 |
| *L*, available labor (10⁶) | 3.86 | 6.09 | 6.09 | 9.77 | 8.66 |
| *N*, employed labor (10⁶) | 3.28 | 5.41 | 5.49 | 9.01 | 8.26 |
| Unemployment rate (%) | 15.0 | 11.2 | 9.8 | 7.8 | 4.6 |
| *K*, capital stock ($10⁹) | 3.50 | 6.08 | 6.39 | 14.2 | 16.7 |
| *K/N*, capital per worker ($) | 1066 | 1126 | 1165 | 1572 | 2023 |
| *SV*, savings from income (%) | 6.60 | 10.3 | 12.3 | 14.5 | 18.1 |
| Earnings per worker ($) | 228 | 270 | 273 | 352 | 389 |
| Return on capital (%) | 15.0 | 16.8 | 16.4 | 15.7 | 13.5 |
| Children/population (%) | 40.4 | 44.5 | 37.4 | 51.9 | 30.6 |
| Dependency rate* (%) | 88.8 | 90.8 | 68.9 | 92.8 | 54.4 |
| Living in "poverty"† (10⁶) | 2.50 | 2.53 | 1.45 | 2.20 | 1.18 |

* Young and aged divided by work-age population.       † Personal income of less than $75 per year.

when fertility is high. Saving-from-income increases nationally from 6.6 per cent in 1970 to 18.1 per cent by A.D. 2000 when fertility is low. The capital per worker increases from $1066 to $2023. Hence in A.D. 2000 a worker earns $389 a year with low fertility as against $228 in 1970.

These various estimates are only suggestive. Their exact magnitudes are unimportant. What is significant is that combinations of alternative parameters indicate that declining fertility rates do contribute to economic welfare.[10] The absolute population size does not matter as much as the population growth rate. If a population doubles in 25 years, it does not mean that output will also double in that period. The labor force may double, but not all may be employed as productively if there is not a doubling of capital. Twice as much labor and capital will not double output if there is a scarcity of equally useful land. Were it not for a slow improvement in technology, most rapidly growing populations would be hard put to raise their per capita incomes.[11]

Conversely, a slowing rate of population growth accords more economic benefits than a slow growth rate, and hence part of the former's gains cannot last beyond a few decades. As fertility rates decline, the ratio of unproductive children to work-age population declines substantially. With low fertility in Developa, this ratio decreases from 0.83 in 1970 to 0.49 in A.D. 2000. With high fertility the ratio rises from 0.83 to 0.87. Fewer children per family give each family member more potential consumption from the same family income. But actual consumption should rise less than the potential consumption. The difference is "released" for investment.

With low fertility Developa can have a population of 18.1 million by A.D. 2000. Table 2 indicates what would happen if its leaders for some reason wanted this same population sooner, by 1989 instead, and so encouraged a continuation of the high-fertility rates of 1970. In 1989 $V/P$ is $197 instead of $354 in A.D. 2000 and $S/V$ is 11.5 per cent instead of 18.1 per cent. A worker's average annual earnings are $287 instead of $389. The ratio of the sum of the young and old dependents to the number in the work-age population is 0.914 instead of 0.554. Technology has had only 19 years instead of 30 years to make its contribution. This comparison at the same population size indicates that a slower population growth favors economic welfare.

## COSTS AND BENEFITS

The stipulated decline in fertility might be due entirely to increased use of contraceptives. It should then be possible to estimate very approximately, from the reduction in births, the number of women using contraceptives and the cost in resources of their doing so. How do these costs compare with the economic benefits?

It is hazardous to estimate the number of adults who must be using contraceptives in order to achieve a given birth decrement. And the cost per "contraceptor" a year is sensitive to the mix of methods used—a coil being cheaper than pills after several years, for example. Nevertheless very crude estimates of the cost for contraceptors in Developa, assuming conditions of low fertility, are that in A.D. 2000, for instance, there will be 2.8 million "contraceptors" whose use of contraceptives will cost $14 million.[12]

Estimating benefits is simpler if there is agreement on how to define them. Contraception results in a smaller population commanding more income per head because national output is little affected. It seems reasonable to ignore persons who would otherwise have been born, had it not been for contraception, and to consider only the living population. Thus Developa in A.D. 2000, with low fertility, has a population of 18.1 million and an income per head $109 higher than it would have been without contraception. The economic "benefit," defined as population times positive difference in income per head, in that year is $1.97 billion.

How can benefits and costs be compared? The ratio of benefit to cost in a particular year

## TABLE 2

Unfavorable, economic results of fast population growth (at same population).

| Item | 1989 (High fertility) | 2000 (Low fertility) |
|---|---|---|
| $P$, population ($10^6$) | 18.1 | 18.1 |
| $V$, output ($10^9$) | 3.57 | 6.43 |
| $V/P$, income per head ($) | 197 | 354 |
| $L$, available labor ($10^6$) | 6.89 | 8.66 |
| $N$, employed labor ($10^6$) | 6.22 | 8.26 |
| $L-N/L$, unemployment rate (%) | 9.8 | 4.6 |
| $K$, capital stock ($10^9$) | 7.44 | 16.7 |
| $K/N$, capital per worker ($) | 1196 | 2023 |
| $S/V$, savings from income (%) | 11.5 | 18.1 |
| Earnings per worker ($) | 287 | 389 |
| Return on capital (%) | 16.8 | 13.5 |
| Children/population (%) | 44.7 | 30.6 |
| Dependency rate* (%) | 91.4 | 54.4 |
| Living in "poverty"† ($10^6$) | 2.37 | 1.18 |

\* Young and aged divided by work-age population.

† Personal income of less than $75 per year.

has little meaning. In A.D. 2000 it happens to be 146, but the benefits enjoyed in that year were due to previous expenditures, whereas the costs of that same year will only bring benefits afterward. If benefits and costs are accumulated over the 30-year period, which makes a comparison more meaningful, the ratio is 82 to 1. This understates the case, for with no subsequent costs there will be benefits after A.D. 2000. Possibly significant to policy-makers with short time horizons is that the benefit-cost ratio is already 22 to 1 in the 5th year (1975).

## EXTENT OF PROGRAM

Still in Developa, the low-fertility policy requires widespread use of contraceptives, so much so that the practicality of such a birth control program must be questioned.[13]

The resource costs of the program are comparatively insignificant. From 1970 to A.D. 2000, the costs that yield $16.6 billion of benefits are $202 million, a figure about 0.2 per cent of the accumulated national income of the 30 years. These costs per head of population range from under 20 cents in the 5th year to slightly over 75 cents in the 30th year and average about 50 cents annually.

Hence, birth-control programs are not a serious rival for funds. Most less-developed countries annually use for economic development resources worth approximately $10 per capita. Even an extensive contraceptive program would leave about 95 per cent of development budgets available for traditional spending.[14]

The real question is not adequacy of funds, or even of specific resources such as paramedics and clinics eventually, but whether enough women and men will voluntarily practice effective contraception. Under a policy of low fertility the gross reproduction rate should decline steadily from 3.025 and is halved by A.D. 2000. In 1985 22 per cent of the population between 15 and 49 years of age would have to be practicing birth control. In A.D. 2000 this group would be about 30 per cent of the men and women of these ages. These percentages are considerably below comparable estimates for developed countries. But they are far above anything yet achieved in any less-developed country.

A less extreme and more attainable program would reduce the gross reproduction rate from 3.025 in 1970 to 2.60 in 1985 and 2.25 in A.D. 2000. With medium fertility $V/P$ by A.D. 2000 is $285, compared to $245 with high fertility and $354 with low fertility. Assuming medium fertility, among women and men 15 through 49 years old, necessary contraceptive users would be approximately 8 per cent in 1985 and 16 per cent in A.D. 2000.

How large a percentage of the relevant population will ever practice contraception voluntarily is unpredictable. Fortunately, no minimum participation is necessary to attain some benefits, with even 5 per cent practicing being better than none. And clearly this percentage can be influenced by government.

## OTHER WAYS
## TO HASTEN DEVELOPMENT

The economic-demographic model described above demonstrates that there are other ways of raising individuals' incomes than that of reducing human fertility. If families saved and invested slightly over twice the percentage of their incomes than was assumed, the same increases in income per head would be approximated with unchanged fertility. Or, if families would innovate technological improvements a little less than twice as rapidly as supposed, about the same economic gains could be realized without birth control.[15]

However, calculations of the proportionate increases in saving and technology that would give the same income increases per head as fertility reduction have no practical significance. Arithmetical equivalents are not real alternatives in this case. Families will not save and innovate more because they do not have fewer children.

If there is any association at all among progeny, savings, and innovation, it is more probably one that favors birth control. One could argue that the sort of family that chooses among alternatives, can discipline itself, and manages its affairs is likely to have fewer children, invest more savings, and innovate more improvements. The doing of one may indirectly even induce the others.

## GOVERNMENTAL ENCOURAGEMENT
## OF CONTRACEPTION

Could and should the government of a less-developed country encourage contraceptive use? Any such government could do many things to increase contraceptive practice. A government can at least have information and devices available at clinics. But it can also subsidize the retail sale of contraceptives and pay doctors to insert coils and perform vasectomies. It can pay bonuses to married women who remain nonpregnant, to "finders" who bring women to clinics for a coil insertion, and to fertile men or women who volunteer for sterilization. It can also educate and exhort through various advertising media.

A given expenditure that reduces fertility contributes so many times more to raising personal incomes than conventional development investments that a government can afford many activities if it increases the number of "contraceptors." If the percentage of adults using contraceptives remains small, despite government encouragement, at least something will have been gained. Government must then resort more exclusively to traditional investments for dams, and the like.

Many people raise the objection that promoting birth control is not a proper activity of government, arguing that whether adults do or do not have more children is their affair alone. Yet many governments encourage larger families. Some almost seem to have a policy of compulsory pregnancy and birth, with laws not only against abortion but also against furnishing contraceptive information or devices. Governments also have many programs that incidentally favor larger families—programs such as free schooling, public housing, and military conscription (which takes away the labor of sons).

A government that really wished to be neutral with regard to family size would often have not only to legalize contraceptive distribution but also to offset the incidental encouragement of fertility by social welfare programs through subsidizing birth control to some extent. Finally, if governments wish to give people more control over their lives, public health programs should not only reduce the risks of premature death but also the risks of unwanted progeny.[16]

## SUMMARY

Most less-developed countries have population increases approaching 3 per cent a year. Death rates have fallen dramatically in the past several decades, but annual birth-rates remain at around 4 per cent of population. Income per head is rising slowly.

Enough is known about the main parameters that a demographic-economic computer model can be used to assess the effects of declining fertility rates on various indices of economic welfare in a typical less-developed country. Thus halving in 30 years a 3.025 gross rate of reproduction results in income per head increasing 3.0 per cent a year instead of 1.7 per cent a year with no fertility change. Halving fertility also results in a third more capital per worker after 30 years.

A large birth-control program might directly cost about $5 a year per "acceptor." About 25 per cent of the population aged 15 through 49 would have to practice contraception on an average to halve the gross reproduction rate in 30 years. During this period the total cost might be roughly $200 million for a less-developed country that started with a population of 10 million. Accumulated benefits could be $16 billion. The benefit to cost ratio is roughly 80 to 1.

## REFERENCES AND NOTES

1. Many of the ideas and calculations presented here stem from research under contract and on overhead at TEMPO, General Electric's Center for Advanced Studies, in Santa Barbara, California, where my colleagues A. De Vany, W. E. McFarland, and R. A. Zind furnished valuable assistance.
2. National income is national output except for international debt service.
3. This 10-per cent rate of return is not compounded for two reasons. First, such compounding would imply that income from capital is entirely saved and invested, although it is otherwise assumed that only a small and varying fraction of income in general is saved and invested. Second, investments have a so-called "gestation period" in reality, the increment in output not commencing sometimes for several years after the investment of funds begins (for example, construction of factories). For simplicity, and because these two considerations are countervailing, they have been ignored. Their net effect if included would have favored the argument.
4. Contraceptive pills, wrapped and packaged, are now available to governments for about 25 cents a monthly cycle; distribution probably doubles this cost. Latex condoms wrapped in aluminum foil are available to governments at about $2.50 in the United States and $1.25 in Japan per gross. The new plastic condoms may be cheaper. Distribution costs through regular commercial channels could be around $0.60 per dozen. The intrauterine device costs about a penny to make and from $5 to $10 to insert (by public health doctors). In India, vasectomies are being performed at a direct cost less than $10. Direct costs per acceptor-year are sensitive to the mix of methods used and the number of years that a person uses each method. If half of all acceptors use condoms or pills and the other half take intrauterine devices or vasectomies, over a 5-year period the direct acceptor-year cost is less than $4.
5. A "contraceptor" is a person who voluntarily accepts (uses) contraceptives.
6. The above numerical example was the basis for President Johnson's statement to the United Nations General Assembly in San Francisco that $5 spent on birth control was worth $100 used for economic development.
7. The original precursor of the model used here was described by S. Enke [*Raising Per Capita Income Through Fewer Births,* General Electric-TEMPO, Santa Barbara, Calif., 1968)].
8. The gross rate of reproduction is the number of female live births a representative woman would be expected to have if she survived to age 50.
9. In these calculations $t$ is 0.015, $n$ is 0.5, and $k$ is 0.35. That $n$ and $k$ sum to less than unity implies diminishing returns to workers and capital because of land-resource scarcity. Annual savings for investment equal 0.25 $V$ minus $35 $P$ approximately.
10. Income per head of population slightly exaggerates improvements in economic welfare when it rises because of shifts in age distribution from children to work-age adults. In equivalent consumer units a child is here 0.75 of a work-age adult. In the low-fertility case the increase in income per equivalent consumer is from $171 in 1970 to $394 in A.D. 2000.
11. S. Enke, *Quart. J. Econ.* 77, 55 (1963).
12. Suppose the birth decrement is $X$ and the fertility rate is $y$. Then a first crude approximation of the number of "contraceptors" is $X/y$. However, there may have to be three fewer conceptions for each two births, because of abortions and miscarriages. And of every three women of fertile age, only two may be at risk of pregnancy, with the other one being either not exposed to intercourse, sterile, or already pregnant at the time. Given these ratios, these two effects cancel, leaving the $X/y$ relation. Few contraceptive methods are perfectly reliable in practice, and this may raise $X/y$ by 1.1 times. Thus, if $y$ is 0.2, for every one birth less there must be 5.5 women attempting contraception. At $5 per contraceptor a year, the cost of preventing a birth is then $27.50.
13. K. Davis, *Science* 158, 730 (1967).
14. See S. Enke, *Econ. J.* 76, 44 (1966).
15. S. Kuznets stressed savings and innovation as substitutes for contraception [*Proc. Amer. Philosoph. Soc.* 3 (No. 3), 170 (1967).
16. Useful readings include B. Berelson *et al., Family Planning and Population Programs* (Univ. of Chicago Press, Chicago, 1966); P. Demeny, *Demography* 2, 203 (1965); P. M. Hauser, *The Population Dilemma* (Prentice-Hall, Englewood Cliffs, N.J.,

1963); E. M. Hoover and M. Perlman, *Pakistan Develop. Rev.* **6,** 545–566 (Winter 1966); G. Ohlin, *Population Control and Economic Development* (Organisation for Economic Cooperation and Development, Paris, 1967); C. Tietze, "Effectiveness,

Acceptability and Safety of Modern Contraceptive Methods," *Paper No. 205* (World Population Conference, Belgrade, 1965) and *Studies in Family Planning* (occasional papers published by the Population Council, New York).

# Outwitting the "Developed" Countries

## IVAN ILLICH

It is now common to demand that the rich nations convert their war machine into a program for the development of the Third World. The poorer four fifths of humanity multiply unchecked while their per capita consumption actually declines. This population expansion and decrease of consumption threaten the industrialized nations, who may still, as a result, convert their defense budgets to the economic pacification of poor nations. And this in turn could produce irreversible despair, because the plows of the rich can do as much harm as their swords. US trucks can do more lasting damage than US tanks. It is easier to create mass demand for the former than for the latter. Only a minority needs heavy weapons, while a majority can become dependent on unrealistic levels of supply for such productive machines as modern trucks. Once the Third World has become a mass market for the goods, products, and processes which are designed by the rich for themselves,

the discrepancy between demand for these Western artifacts and the supply will increase indefinitely. The family car cannot drive the poor into the jet age, nor can a school system provide the poor with education, nor can the family icebox insure healthy food for them.

It is evident that only one man in a thousand in Latin America can afford a Cadillac, a heart operation, or a Ph.D. This restriction on the goals of development does not make us despair of the fate of the Third World, and the reason is simple. We have not yet come to conceive of a Cadillac as necessary for good transportation, or of a heart operation as normal healthy care, or of a Ph.D. as the prerequisite of an acceptable education. In fact, we recognize at once that the importation of Cadillacs should be heavily taxed in Peru, that an organ transplant clinic is a scandalous plaything to justify the concentration of more doctors in Bogota, and that a Betatron is beyond the teaching facilities of the University of Sao Paolo.

Unfortunately, it is not held to be universally evident that the majority of Latin Americans—not only of our generation, but also of the next and the next again—cannot afford any kind of automobile, or any kind of hospitalization, or for that matter an elementary school education. We suppress our consciousness of this obvious reality because we hate to recognize the corner into which our imagination has been pushed. So persuasive is the power of the institutions we have created that they shape not only our preferences, but actually our sense of possibilities. We have forgotten how to speak about modern transportation that does not rely on automobiles and airplanes. Our conceptions of modern health care emphasize our ability to prolong the lives of the desperately ill. We have become unable to think of better education except in terms of more complex schools and of teachers trained for ever longer periods. Huge institutions producing costly services dominate the horizons of our inventiveness.

We have embodied our world view into our institutions and are now their prisoners. Factories, news media, hospitals, governments, and schools produce goods and services packaged to contain our view of the world. We—the rich—conceive of progress as the expansion of these establishments. We conceive of heightened mobility as luxury and safety packaged by General Motors or Boeing. We conceive of improving the general well-being as increasing the supply of doctors and hospitals, which package health along with protracted suffering. We have come to identify our need for further learning with the demand for ever longer confinement to classrooms. In other words, we have packaged education with custodial care, certification for jobs, and the right to vote, and wrapped them all together with indoctrination in the Christian, liberal, or communist virtues.

In less than a hundred years industrial society has molded patent solutions to basic human needs and converted us to the belief that man's needs were shaped by the Creator as demands for the products we have invented. This is as true for Russia and Japan as for the North Atlantic community. The consumer is trained for obsolescence, which means continuing loyalty toward the same producers who will give him the same basic

packages in different quality or new wrappings.

Industrialized societies can provide such packages for personal consumption for most of their citizens, but this is no proof that these societies are sane, or economical, or that they promote life. The contrary is true. The more the citizen is trained in the consumption of packaged goods and services, the less effective he seems to become in shaping his environment. His energies and finances are consumed in procuring ever new models of his staples, and the environment becomes a by-product of his own consumption habits.

The design of the "package deals" of which I speak is the main cause of the high cost of satisfying basic needs. So long as every man "needs" his car, our cities must endure longer traffic jams and absurdly expensive remedies to relieve them. So long as health means maximum length of survival, our sick will get ever more extraordinary surgical interventions and the drugs required to deaden their consequent pain. So long as we want to use school to get children out of their parents' hair or to keep them off the street and out of the labor force, our young will be retained in endless schooling and will need ever-increasing incentives to endure the ordeal.

Rich nations now benevolently impose a straightjacket of traffic jams, hospital confinements, and classrooms on the poor nations, and by international agreement call this "development." The rich and schooled and old of the world try to share their dubious blessings by foisting their pre-packaged solutions on to the Third World. Traffic jams develop in Sao Paolo, while almost a million northeastern Brazilians flee the drought by walking 500 miles. Latin American doctors get training at the New York Hospital for Special Surgery, which they apply to only a few, while amoebic dysentery remains endemic in slums where 90 per cent of the population live. A tiny minority gets advanced education in basic science in North America—not infrequently paid for by their own governments. If they return at all to Bolivia, they become second-rate teachers of pretentious subjects at La Paz or Cochibamba.

The rich export outdated versions of their standard models.

The Alliance for Progress is a good example of benevolent production for underdevelopment. Contrary to its slogans, it did succeed—as an alliance for the progress of the consuming classes, and for the domestication of the Latin American masses. The Alliance has been a major step in modernizing the consumption patterns of the middle classes in South America by integrating them with the dominant culture of the North American metropolis. At the same time, the Alliance has modernized the aspirations of the majority of citizens and fixed their demands on unavailable products.

Each car which Brazil puts on the road denies fifty people good transportation by bus. Each merchandised refrigerator reduces the chance of building a community freezer. Every dollar spent in Latin America on doctors and hospitals costs a hundred lives, to adopt a phrase of Jorge de Ahumada, the brilliant Chilean economist. Had each dollar been spent on providing safe drinking water, a hundred lives could have been saved. Each dollar spent on schooling means more privileges for the few at the cost of the many; at best it increases the number of those who, before dropping out, have been taught that those who stay longer have earned the right to more power, wealth, and prestige. What such schooling does is to teach the schooled the superiority of the better schooled.

All Latin American countries are frantically intent on expanding their school systems. No country now spends less than the equivalent of 18 percent of tax-derived public income on education—which means schooling—and many countries spend almost double that. But even with these huge investments, no country yet succeeds in giving five full years of education to more than one third of its population; supply and demand for schooling grow geometrically apart. And what is true about schooling is equally true about the products of most institutions in the process of modernization in the Third World.

Continued technological refinements of products which are already established on the market frequently benefit the producer far more than the consumer. The more complex production processes tend to enable only the largest producer to continually replace outmoded models, and to focus the demand of the consumer on the marginal improvement of what he buys, no matter what the concomitant side effects: higher prices, diminished life span, less general usefulness, higher cost of repairs. Think of the multiple uses for a simple can opener, whereas an electric one, if it works at all, opens only some kinds of cans, and costs one hundred times as much.

This is equally true for a piece of agricultural machinery and for an academic degree. The midwestern farmer can become convinced of his need for a four-axle vehicle which can go 70 m.p.h. on the highways, has an electric windshield wiper and upholstered seats, and can be turned in for a new one within a year or two. Most of the world's farmers don't need such speed, nor have they ever met with such comfort, nor are they interested in obsolescence. They need low-priced transport, in a world where time is not money, where manual wipers suffice, and where a piece of heavy equipment should outlast a generation. Such a mechanical donkey requires entirely different engineering and design than one produced for the US market. This vehicle is not in production.

Most of South America needs paramedical workers who can function for indefinite periods without the supervision of an MD. Instead of establishing a process to train midwives and visiting healers who know how to use a very limited arsenal of medicines while working independently, Latin American universities establish every year a new school of specialized nursing or nursing administration to prepare professionals who can function only in a hospital, and pharmacists who know how to sell increasingly more dangerous drugs.

The world is reaching an impasse where two processes converge: ever more men have have fewer basic choices. The increase in population is widely publicized and creates panic. The decrease in fundamental choice causes anguish and is consistently overlooked. The population explosion overwhelms the imagination, but the progressive atrophy of social imagination is rationalized as an increase of choice between brands. The two processes converge in a dead end: the population explosion provides more consumers for everything from food to contraceptives, while our shrinking imagination can conceive of no other ways of satisfying their demands except through the packages now on sale in the admired societies.

I will focus successively on these two factors, since, in my opinion, they form the two coordinates which together permit us to define underdevelopment.

In most Third World countries, the population grows, and so does the middle class. Income, consumption, and the well-being of the middle class are all growing while the gap between this class and the mass of people widens. Even where per capita consumption is rising, the majority of men have less food now than in 1945, less actual care in sickness, less meaningful work, less protection. This is partly a consequence of polarized consumption and partly caused by the breakdown of traditional family and culture. More people suffer from hunger, pain, and exposure in 1969 than they did at the end of World War II, not only numerically, but also as a percentage of the world population.

These concrete consequences of underdevelopment are rampant; but underdevelopment is also a state of mind, and understanding it as a state of mind, or as a form of consciousness, is the critical problem. Underdevelopment as a state of mind occurs when mass needs are converted to the demand for new brands of packaged solutions which are forever beyond the reach of the majority. Underdevelopment in this sense is rising rapidly even in countries where the supply of classrooms, calories, cars, and clinics is also rising. The ruling groups in these countries build up services which have been designed

for an affluent culture; once they have monopolized demand in this way, they can never satisfy majority needs.

Underdevelopment as a form of consciousness is an extreme result of what we can call in the language of both Marx and Freud *"Verdinglichung"* or reification. By reification I mean the hardening of the perception of real needs into the demand for mass manufactured products. I mean the translation of thirst into the need for a Coke. This kind of reification occurs in the manipulation of primary human needs by vast bureaucratic organizations which have succeeded in dominating the imaginations of potential consumers.

Let me return to my example taken from the field of education. The intense promotion of schooling leads to so close an identification of school attendance and education that in everyday language the two terms are interchangeable. Once the imagination of an entire population has been "schooled," or indoctrinated to believe that school has a monopoly on formal education, then the illiterate can be taxed to provide free high school and university education for the children of the rich.

Underdevelopment is the result of rising levels of aspiration achieved through the intensive marketing of "patent" products. In this sense, the dynamic underdevelopment that is now taking place is the exact opposite of what I believe education to be: namely, the awakening awareness of new levels of human potential and the use of one's creative powers to foster human life. Underdevelopment, however, implies the surrender of social consciousness to pre-packaged solutions.

The process by which the marketing of "foreign" products increases underdevelopment is frequently understood in the most superficial ways. The same man who feels indignation at the sight of a Coca-Cola plant in a Latin American slum often feels pride at the sight of a new normal school growing up alongside. He resents the evidence of a foreign "license" attached to a soft drink which he would like to see replaced by

"Cola-Mex." But the same man is willing to impose schooling—at all costs—on his fellow citizens, and is unaware of the invisible license by which this institution is deeply enmeshed in the world market.

Some years ago I watched workmen putting up a sixty-foot Coca-Cola sign on a desert plain in the Mexquital. A serious drought and famine had just swept over the Mexican highland. My host, a poor Indian in Ixmiquilpan, had just offered his visitors a tiny tequila glass of the costly black sugar-water. When I recall this scene I still feel anger; but I feel much more incensed when I remember UNESCO meetings at which well-meaning and well-paid bureaucrats seriously discussed Latin American school curricula, and when I think of the speeches of enthusiastic liberals advocating the need for more schools.

The fraud perpetrated by the salesmen of schools is less obvious but much more fundamental than the self-satisfied salesmanship of the Coca-Cola or Ford representative, because the schoolman hooks his people on a much more demanding drug. Elementary school attendance is not a harmless luxury, but more like the coca chewing of the Andean Indian, which harnesses the worker to the boss.

The higher the dose of schooling an individual has received, the more depressing his experience of withdrawal. The seventh-grade dropout feels his inferiority much more acutely than the dropout from the third grade. The schools of the Third World administer their opium with much more effect than the churches of other epochs. As the mind of a society is progressively schooled, step by step its individuals lose their sense that it might be possible to live without being inferior to others. As the majority shifts from the land into the city, the hereditary inferiority of the peon is replaced by the inferiority of the school dropout who is held personally responsible for his failure. Schools rationalize the divine origin of social stratification with much more rigor than churches have ever done.

Until this day no Latin American country has declared youthful underconsumers of Coca-Cola or cars as lawbreakers, while all Latin American countries have passed laws which define the early dropout as a citizen who has not fulfilled his legal obligations. The Brazilian government recently almost doubled the number of years during which schooling is legally compulsory and free. From now on any Brazilian dropout under the age of sixteen will be faced during his lifetime with the reproach that he did not take advantage of a legally obligatory privilege. This law was passed in a country where not even the most optimistic could forsee the day when such levels of schooling would be provided for only 25 percent of the young. The adoption of international standards of schooling forever condemns most Latin Americans to marginality or exclusion from social life—in a word, underdevelopment.

The translation of social goals into levels of consumption is not limited to only a few countries. Across all frontiers of culture, ideology, and geography today, nations are moving toward the establishment of their own car factories, their own medical and normal schools—and most of these are, at best, poor imitations of foreign and largely North American models.

The Third World is in need of a profound revolution of its institutions. The revolutions of the last generation were overwhelmingly political. A new group of men with a new set of ideological justifications assumed power to administer fundamentally the same scholastic, medical, and market institutions in the interest of a new group of clients. Since the institutions have not radically changed, the new group of clients remain approximately the same size as that previously served. This appears clearly in the case of education. Per pupil costs of schooling are today comparable everywhere since the standards used to evaluate the quality of schooling tend to be internationally shared. Access to publicly financed education, considered as access to school, everywhere depends on per capita income. (Places like China and North Vietnam might be meaningful exceptions.)

Everywhere in the Third World modern institutions are grossly unproductive, with respect to the egalitarian purposes for which they are being reproduced. But so long as the social imagination of the majority has not been destroyed by its fixation on these institutions, there is more hope of planning an institutional revolution in the Third World than among the rich. Hence the urgency of the task of developing workable alternatives to "modern" solutions.

Underdevelopment is at the point of becoming chronic in many countries. The revolution of which I speak must begin to take place before this happens. Education again offers a good example: chronic educational underdevelopment occurs when the demand for schooling becomes so widespread that the total concentration of educational resources on the school system becomes a unanimous political demand. At this point the separation of education from schooling becomes impossible.

The only feasible answer to ever-increasing underdevelopment is a response to basic needs that is planned as a long-range goal for areas which will always have a different capital structure. It is easier to speak about alternatives to existing institutions, services, and products than to define them with precision. It is not my purpose either to paint a Utopia or to engage in scripting scenarios for an alternate future. We must be satisfied with examples indicating simple directions that research should take.

Some such examples have already been given. Buses are alternatives to a multitude of private cars. Vehicles designed for slow transportation on rough terrain are alternatives to standard trucks. Safe water is an alternative to high-priced surgery. Medical workers are an alternative to doctors and nurses. Community food storage is an alternative to expensive kitchen equipment. Other alternatives could be discussed by the dozen. Why not, for example, consider walking as a long-range alternative for locomotion by machine, and explore the demands which this would im-

pose on the city planner? And why can't the building of shelters be standardized, elements be pre-cast, and each citizen be obliged to learn in a year of public service how to construct his own sanitary housing?

It is harder to speak about alternatives in education, partly because schools have recently so completely pre-empted the available educational resources of good will, imagination, and money. But even here we can indicate the direction in which research must be conducted.

At present, schooling is conceived as graded, curricular, class attendance by children, for about 1000 hours yearly during an uninterrupted succession of years. On the average, Latin American countries can provide each citizen with between eight and thirty months of this service. Why not, instead, make one or two months a year obligatory for all citizens below the age of thirty?

Money is now spent largely on children, but an adult can be taught to read in one tenth the time and for one tenth the cost it takes to teach a child. In the case of the adult there is an immediate return on the investment, whether the main importance of his learning is seen in his new insight, political awareness, and willingness to assume responsibility for his family's size and future, or whether the emphasis is placed on increased productivity. There is a double return in the case of the adult, because not only can he contribute to the education of his children, but to that of other adults as well. In spite of these advantages, basic literacy programs have little or no support in Latin America, where schools have a first call on all public resources. Worse, these programs are actually ruthlessly suppressed in Brazil and elsewhere, where military support of the feudal or industrial oligarchy has thrown off its former benevolent disguise.

Another possibility is harder to define, because there is as yet no example to point to. We must therefore imagine the use of public resources for education distributed in such a way as to give every citizen a minimum chance. Education will become a political concern of the majority of voters only when each individual has a precise sense of the educational resources that are owing to him—and some idea of how to sue for them. Something like a universal G.I. Bill of Rights could be imagined, dividing the public resources assigned to education by the number of children who are legally of school age, and making sure that a child who did not take advantage of his credit at the age of seven, eight, or nine would have the accumulated benefits at his disposal at age ten.

What could the pitiful education credit which a Latin American Republic could offer to its children provide? Almost all of the basic supply of books, pictures, blocks, games, and toys that are totally absent from the homes of the really poor, but enable a middle-class child to learn the alphabet, the colors, shapes, and other classes of objects and experiences which insure his educational progress. The choice between these things and schools is obvious. Unfortunately, the poor, for whom alone the chioce is real, never get to exercise this choice.

Defining alternatives to the products and institutions which now pre-empt the field is difficult, not only, as I have been trying to show, because these products and institutions shape our conception of reality itself, but also because the construction of new possibilities requires a concentration of will and intelligence in a higher degree than ordinarily occurs by chance. This concentration of will and intelligence on the solution of particular problems regardless of their nature we have become accustomed over the last century to call research.

I must make clear, however, what kind of research I am talking about. I am not talking about basic research either in physics, engineering, genetics, medicine, or learning. The work of such men as Crick, Piaget, and Gell-Mann must continue to enlarge our horizons in other fields of science. The labs and libraries and specially trained collaborators these men need cause them to congregate in the few research capitals of the world. Their research can provide the basis for new work on practically any product.

I am not speaking here of the billions of dollars annually spent on applied research, for this money is largely spent by existing institutions on the perfection and marketing of their own products. Applied research is money spent on making planes faster and airports safer; on making medicines more specific and powerful and doctors capable of handling their deadly side-effects; on packaging more learning into classrooms; on methods to administer large bureaucracies. This is the kind of research for which some kind of counterfoil must somehow be developed if we are to have any chance to come up with basic alternatives to the automobile, the hospital, and the school, and any of the many other so-called "evidently necessary implements for modern life."

I have in mind a different, and peculiarly difficult, kind of research, which has been largely neglected up to now, for obvious reasons. I am calling for research on alternatives to the products which now dominate the market; to hospitals and the profession dedicated to keeping the sick alive; to schools and the packaging process which refuses education to those who are not of the right age, who have not gone through the right curriculum, who have not sat in a classroom a sufficient number of successive hours, who will not pay for their learning with submission to custodial care, screening, and certification or with indoctrination in the values of the dominant elite.

This counter-research on fundamental alternatives to current pre-packaged solutions is the element most critically needed if the poor nations are to have a livable future. Such counter-research is distinct from most of the work done in the name of the "year 2000," because most of that work seeks radical changes in social patterns through adjustments in the organization of an already advanced technology. The counter-research of which I speak must take as one of its assumptions the continued lack of capital in the Third World.

The difficulties of such research are obvious. The researcher must first of all doubt what is obvious to every eye. Second, he must persuade those who have the power of decision to act against their own short-run interests or bring pressure on them to do so. And, finally, he must survive as an individual in a world he is attempting to change fundamentally so that his fellows among the privileged minority see him as a destroyer of the very ground on which all of us stand. He knows that if he should succeed in the interest of the poor, technologically advanced societies still might envy the "poor" who adopt this vision.

There is a normal course for those who make development policies, whether they live in North or South America, in Russia or Israel. It is to define development and to set its goals in ways with which they are familiar, which they are accustomed to use in order to satisfy their own needs, and which permit them to work through the institutions over which they have power or control. This formula has failed, and must fail. There is not enough money in the world for development to succeed along these lines, not even in the combined arms and space budgets of the super-powers.

An analogous course is followed by those who are trying to make political revolutions, especially in the Third World. Usually they promise to make the familiar privileges of the present elites, such as schooling, hospital care, etc., accessible to all citizens; and they base this vain promise on the belief that a change in political regime will permit them to sufficiently enlarge the institutions which produce these privileges. The promise and appeal of the revolutionary are therefore just as threatened by the counter-research I propose as is the market of the now dominant producers.

In Vietnam a people on bicycles and armed with sharpened bamboo sticks have brought to a standstill the most advanced machinery for research and production ever devised. We must seek survival in a Third World in which human ingenuity can peacefully outwit machined might. The only way to reverse the disastrous trend to increasing underdevelopment, hard as it is, is to learn to laugh at accepted solutions in order to change the demands which make them necessary. Only free men can change their minds and be surprised; and while no men are completely free, some are freer than others.

# PART SIX

# Toward a Population Policy

*Family planning means if we are going to breed like rabbits, we should do it on purpose.\**

This section opens with the already classic paper on family planning by Kingsley Davis. It should surely be reread annually by members of the family planning establishment, for the persistence of certain myths long after this paper demolished them indicates that it contains more wisdom than can be absorbed in one sitting. As the reader will soon discover, family planning is not the same thing as population control, and the delusion that it is can only postpone effective action. (It is not that family planning is a *bad* idea, it is simply far from enough.) Equally significant in Prof. Davis' exposition is his admonishment that the industrial nations make a miserable model for anyone's population policy: their present growth rates of one to two per cent per year (called "low" by less perceptive members of the demographic community) are unprecedentedly high in historical terms, and the associated ill effects are already apparent. The remainder of Dr. Davis' paper is a forceful and eloquent analysis of the record of family-planning accomplishments, its extensive limitations in theory and practice, and some guidelines toward more effective policies. We recommend this paper as one of the most significant in this collection.

It is followed by another blow to the conventional wisdom of the family planners, in the form of Judith Blake's paper on population policy for Americans. She argues persuasively that the present emphasis on providing family planning services to the poor is misdirected: it is bad population policy (the great bulk of America's population growth is occurring in the affluent middle class), and it is tinged with class chauvinism ("is the government responding to a mandate from the poor or to an ill-concealed mandate from the well-to-do?"). Having identified the source of population growth as people in all social classes who *want* too many children, Professor Blake argues that fundamental sociological changes (as opposed to the mere provi-

* Justin Blackwelder, quoted in *The Subversive Science.*

sion of contraceptives) will be required to stop it. Her discussion of the present institutional mechanisms (family structure, sex roles, tax and abortion laws) which serve as pronatalist "policies" is most instructive.

There is much to be learned from Bernard Berelson's paper, "Beyond Family Planning." Dr. Berelson is president of the Population Council—a non-profit foundation whose principal efforts are family planning programs for the underdeveloped countries—and this position has understandably colored the views he presents. Specifically, he evaluates a very comprehensive compilation of fertility-control proposals against six criteria which seem calculated to preordain the result—namely that "family planning" or its extensions (as promoted by the Population Council) surpass all the alternatives in overall effectiveness. For example, three of his criteria are political viability, administrative feasibility, and ethical acceptability. Virtually every proposal which would represent a significant step beyond family planning is rated low in these three areas. Since the highly "feasible" family planning is audaciously rated "moderately high" in the crucial sixth category, presumed effectiveness, the outcome of the comparison is guaranteed to please the family planning establishment. We would counter as follows: unless we are willing at least to *bend* existing institutions and concepts, the battle to control population is surely lost. In this context, we are not impressed with the continuing use of that magical word, "feasibility," as a club to beat down novel and constructive approaches to civilization's problems. Finally, it must be emphasized that society's willingness to undertake radical action is proportional to the perceived consequences of not doing so. The moral, ethical, and philosophical decisions to which Dr. Berelson refers must be made in the context of the alternatives—and what, we ask, is the moral acceptability of famine, war, epidemic, or the loss of habitability of this planet? Obviously, Dr. Berelson does not share our view of the potential for such disasters. Indeed, he does not seem to believe that the developed countries have a serious population problem at all. We still hope to persuade him.

Joseph Spengler's essay displays an understanding of the costs of population growth which should be the envy of most of his fellow economists. But the paper is included in this section rather than the last because it trims the sociology of the population problem down to the essentials, and then says a great deal about how to solve it. The presently missing requirement for success at population stabilization, Prof. Spengler argues, is a general will, institutionalized and supported by sanctions. The general will is of course still nonexistent (indeed, this book and many of the papers in it are attempts to contribute to the groundwork for such a consensus). But the availability of acceptable means to implement a general will may have a great deal to do with bringing one about in time, and widespread discussion of concrete incentives and penalty programs such as Dr. Spengler proposes is therefore appropriate. There will of course be those who label his ideas infeasible—this suggests to us that they may have some chance for success.

Judith Blake and Kingsley Davis make it plain that the availability of cheap and effective contraceptives does not constitute a population control program. As Joseph Spengler reminds us in his last sentence, the converse is also true: sociological and economic measures which might otherwise control population will fail if suitable contraceptive technology is absent. A fitting conclusion to this section is therefore Carl Djerassi's discussion of this necessary but not sufficient ingredient, the birth control agent. As a developer of the steroid contraceptive and a chemist of long experience in the drug industry, Prof. Djerassi is uniquely qualified to discuss this subject. The stature of the source makes the conclusions all the more dismal: No revolution in chemical contraception (such as a "one-time" drug which would produce infertility until consciously reversed with an antidote) is imminent. The drug industry is hobbled in the search by the unrealistic public expectation of *no* side effects (even aspirin has them), institutionalized in an overcautious and often irrelevant regulatory bureaucracy. Dr. Djerassi does not minimize the need for adequate research and responsible precautions, but he reminds us that the inevitable side effects of contraceptive drugs must be balanced against the very considerable personal health hazards associated with pregnancy, and the disastrous societal consequences of overpopulation itself.

It has often been argued that a revolutionary contraceptive could at least partly compensate for the lack of education and motivation particularly (but not exclusively) prevalent in the UDCs. While the earlier papers in this section shed considerable doubt on this hypothesis, Dr. Djerassi's dismal prognosis makes it almost irrelevant. Such a technological "solution" in contraception is not likely in this century; we infer that, as with so many aspects of the problems we face, a revolution in *attitudes* is absolutely necessary. We can only hope it will also be sufficient.

# Population Policy:
# Will Current Programs Succeed?

KINGSLEY DAVIS

Throughout history the growth of population has been identified with prosperity and strength. If today an increasing number of nations are seeking to curb rapid population growth by reducing their birth rates, they must

Population Policy: Will Current Programs Succeed? From *Science*, Vol. 158, November 10, 1967, pp. 730–739. Copyright 1967 by the American Association for the Advancement of Science. Reprinted by permission of the author and the publisher.

be driven to do by an urgent crisis. My purpose here is not to discuss the crisis itself but rather to assess the present and prospective measures used to meet it. Most observers are surprised by the swiftness with which concern over the population problem has turned from intellectual analysis and debate to policy and action. Such action is a welcome relief from the long opposition, or timidity, which seemed to block forever any governmental attempt to restrain population growth, but relief that "at last something is being done" is no guarantee that what is being done is adequate. On the face of it, one could hardly expect such a fundamental reorientation to be quickly and successfully implemented. I therefore propose to review the nature and (as I see them) limitations of the present policies and to suggest lines of possible improvement.

## THE NATURE OF CURRENT POLICIES

With more than 30 nations now trying or planning to reduce population growth and with numerous private and international organizations helping, the degree of unanimity as to the kind of measures needed is impressive. The consensus can be summed up in the phrase "family planning." President Johnson declared in 1965 that the United States will "assist family planning programs in nations which request such help." The Prime Minister of India said a year later, "We must press forward with family planning. This is a programme of the highest importance." The Republic of Singapore created in 1966 the Singapore Family Planning and Population Board "to initiate and undertake population control programmes" (1).

As is well known, "family planning" is a euphemism for contraception. The family-planning approach to population limitation, therefore, concentrates on providing new and efficient contraceptives on a national basis through mass programs under public health auspices. The nature of these programs is shown by the following enthusiastic report from the Population Council (2):

No single year has seen so many forward steps in population control as 1965. Effective national programs have at last emerged, international organizations have decided to become engaged, a new contraceptive has proved its value in mass application, ... and surveys have confirmed a popular desire for family limitation ...

An accounting of notable events must begin with Korea and Taiwan ... Taiwan's program is not yet two years old, and already it has inserted one IUD [intrauterine device] for every 4-6 target women (those who are not pregnant, lactating, already sterile, already using contraceptives effectively, or desirous of more children). Korea has done almost as well ... has put 2,200 full-time workers into the field, ... has reached operational levels for a network of IUD quotas, supply lines, local manufacture of contraceptives, training of hundreds of M.D.'s and nurses, and mass propaganda ...

Here one can see the implication that "population control" is being achieved through the dissemination of new contraceptives, and the fact that the "target women" exclude those who want more children. One can also note the technological emphasis and the medical orientation.

What is wrong with such programs? The answer is, "Nothing at all, if they work." Whether or not they work depends on what they are expected to do as well as on how they try to do it. Let us discuss the goal first, then the means.

## GOALS

Curiously, it is hard to find in the population-policy movement any explicit discussion of long-range goals. By implication the policies seem to promise a great deal. This is shown by the use of expressions like *population control* and *population planning* (as in the passages quoted above). It is also shown by the characteristic style of reasoning. Expositions of current policy usually start off by lamenting the speed and the consequences of runaway population growth. This growth, it is then stated, must be curbed—by pursuing a vigorous family-planning program. That family planning can solve the problem of population growth seems to be taken as self-evident.

For instance, the much-heralded statement by 12 heads of state, issued by Secretary-General U Thant on 10 December 1966 (a statement initiated by John D. Rockefeller III, Chairman of the Board of the Population Council), devotes half its space to discussing the harmfulness of population growth and the other half to recommending family planning *(3)*. A more succinct example of the typical reasoning is given in the Provisional Scheme for a Nationwide Family Planning Programme in Ceylon *(4)*:

The population of Ceylon is fast increasing.... [The] figures reveal that a serious situation will be created within a few years. In order to cope with it a Family Planning programme on a nationwide scale should be launched by the Government.

The promised goal—to limit population growth so as to solve population problems—is a large order. One would expect it to be carefully analyzed, but it is left imprecise and taken for granted, as is the way in which family planning will achieve it.

When the terms *population control* and *population planning* are used, as they frequently are, as synonyms for current family-planning programs, they are misleading. Technically, they would mean deliberate influence over all attributes of a population, including its age-sex structure, geographical distribution, racial composition, genetic quality, and total size. No government attempts such full control. By tacit understanding, current population policies are concerned with only the *growth* and *size* of populations. These attributes, however, result from the death rate and migration as well as from the birth rate; their control would require deliberate influence over the factors giving rise to all three determinants. Actually, current policies labeled population control do not deal with mortality and migration, but deal only with the birth input. This is why another term, *fertility control,* is frequently used to describe current policies. But, as I show below, family planning (and hence current policy) does not undertake to influence most of the determinants of human reproduction. Thus the programs should not be referred to as population control or planning, because they do not attempt to influence the factors

responsible for the attributes of human populations, taken generally; nor should they be called fertility control, because they do not try to affect most of the determinants of reproductive performance.

The ambiguity does not stop here, however. When one speaks of controlling population size, any inquiring person naturally asks, What is "control"? Who is to control whom? Precisely what population size, or what rate of population growth, is to be achieved? Do the policies aim to produce a growth rate that is nil, one that is very slight, or one that is like that of the industrial nations? Unless such questions are dealt with and clarified, it is impossible to evaluate current population policies.

The actual programs seem to be aiming simply to achieve a reduction in the birth rate. Success is therefore interpreted as the accomplishment of such a reduction, on the assumption that the reduction will lessen population growth. In those rare cases where a specific demographic aim is stated, the goal is said to be a short-run decline within a given period. The Pakistan plan adopted in 1966 *(5,* p. 889) aims to reduce the birth rate from 50 to 40 per thousand by 1970; the Indian plan *(6)* aims to reduce the rate from 40 to 25 "as soon as possible"; and the Korean aim *(7)* is to cut population growth from 2.9 to 1.2 percent by 1980. A significant feature of such stated aims is the rapid population growth they would permit. Under conditions of modern mortality, a crude birth rate of 25 to 30 per thousand will represent such a multiplication of people as to make use of the term *population control* ironic. A rate of increase of 1.2 per cent per year would allow South Korea's already dense population to double in less than 60 years.

One can of course defend the programs by saying that the present goals and measures are merely interim ones. A start must be made somewhere. But we do not find this answer in the population-policy literature. Such a defense, if convincing, would require a presentation of the *next* steps, and these are not considered. One suspects that the entire question of goals is instinctively left vague because thorough limitation of population growth would run counter to national and group aspirations. A consideration of hypothetical goals throws further light on the matter.

*Industrialized nations as the model.* Since current policies are confined to family planning, their maximum demographic effect would be to give the underdeveloped countries the same level of reproductive performance that the industrial nations now have. The latter, long oriented toward family planning, provide a good yardstick for determining what the availability of contraceptives can do to population growth. Indeed, they provide more than a yardstick; they are actually the model which inspired the present population policies.

What does this goal mean in practice? Among the advanced nations there is considerable diversity in the level of fertility *(8)*. At one extreme are countries such as New Zealand, with an average gross reproduction rate (GRR) of 1.91 during the period 1960–64; at the other extreme are countries such as Hungary, with a rate of 0.91 during the same period. To a considerable extent, however, such divergencies are matters of timing. The birth rates of most industrial nations have shown, since about 1940, a wave-like movement, with no secular trend. The average level of reproduction during this long period has been high enough to give these countries, with their low mortality, an extremely rapid population growth. If this level is maintained, their population will double in just over 50 years— a rate higher than that of world population growth at any time prior to 1950, at which time the growth in numbers of human beings was already considered fantastic. The advanced nations are suffering acutely from the effects of rapid population growth in combination with the production of ever more goods per person *(9)*. A rising share of their supposedly high per capita income, which itself draws increasingly upon the resources of the underdeveloped countries (who fall farther behind in relative economic position), is spent simply to meet the costs, and alleviate the nuisances,

of the unrelenting production of more and more goods by more people. Such facts indicate that the industrial nations provide neither a suitable demographic model for the nonindustrial peoples to follow nor the leadership to plan and organize effective population-control policies for them.

*Zero population growth as a goal.* Most discussions of the population crisis lead logically to zero population growth as the ultimate goal, because *any* growth rate, if continued, will eventually use up the earth. Yet hardly ever do arguments for population policy consider such a goal, and current policies do not dream of it. Why not? The answer is evidently that zero population growth is unacceptable to most nations and to most religious and ethnic communities. To argue for this goal would be to alienate possible support for action programs.

*Goal peculiarities inherent in family planning.* Turning to the actual measures taken, we see that the very use of family planning as the means for implementing population policy poses serious but unacknowledged limits on the intended reduction in fertility. The family-planning movement, clearly devoted to the improvement and dissemination of contraceptive devices, states again and again that its purpose is that of enabling couples to have the number of children they want. "The opportunity to decide the number and spacing of children is a basic human right," say the 12 heads of state in the United Nations declaration. The 1965 Turkish Law Concerning Population Planning declares *(10)*:

*Article 1.* Population Planning means that individuals can have as many children as they wish, whenever they want to. This can be ensured through preventive measures taken against pregnancy. . . .

Logically, it does not make sense to use *family* planning to provide *national* population control or planning. The "planning" in family planning is that of each separate couple. The only control they exercise is control over the size of *their* family. Obviously, couples do not plan the size of the nation's population, any more than they plan the growth of the national income or the form of the highway network. There is no reason to expect that the millions of decisions about family size made by couples in their own interest will automatically control population for the benefit of society. On the contrary, there are good reasons to think they will not do so. At most, family planning can reduce reproduction to the extent that unwanted births exceed wanted births. In industrial countries the balance is often negative—that is, people have fewer children as a rule than they would like to have. In underdeveloped countries the reverse is normally true, but the elimination of unwanted births would still leave an extremely high rate of multiplication.

Actually, the family-planning movement does not pursue even the limited goals it professes. It does not fully empower couples to have only the number of offspring they want because it either condemns or disregards certain tabooed but nevertheless effective means to this goal. One of its tenets is that "there shall be freedom of choice of method so that individuals can choose in accordance with the dictates of their consciences" (11), but in practice this amounts to limiting the individual's choice, because the "conscience" dictating the method is usually not his but that of religious and governmental officials. Moreover, not every individual may choose: even the so-called recommended methods are ordinarily not offered to single women, or not all offered to women professing a given religious faith.

Thus, despite its emphasis on technology, current policy does not utilize all available means of contraception, much less all birth-control measures. The Indian government wasted valuable years in the early stages of its population-control program by experimenting exclusively with the "rhythm" method, long after this technique had been demonstrated to be one of the least effective. A greater limitation on means is the exclusive emphasis on contraception itself. Induced abortion, for example, is one of the surest means of controlling reproduction, and one that has been proved capable of reducing birth rates rapidly. It seems peculiarly suited to the threshold stage of a population-control program—the stage when new conditions of life first make large families disadvantageous. It was the principal factor in the halving of the Japanese birth rate, a major factor in the declines in birth rate of East-European satellite countries after legalization of abortions in the early 1950's, and an important factor in the reduction of fertility in industrializing nations from 1870 to the 1930's (12). Today, according to *Studies in Family Planning (13)*, "abortion is probably the foremost method of birth control throughout Latin America." Yet this method is rejected in nearly all national and international population-control programs. American foreign aid is used to help *stop* abortion (14). The United Nations excludes abortion from family planning, and in fact justifies the latter by presenting it as a means of combating abortion (15). Studies of abortion are being made in Latin America under the presumed auspices of population-control groups, not with the intention of legalizing it and thus making it safe, cheap, available, and hence more effective for population control, but with the avowed purpose of reducing it (16).

Although few would prefer abortion to efficient contraception (other things being equal), the fact is that both permit a woman to control the size of her family. The main drawbacks to abortion arise from its illegality. When performed, as a legal procedure, by a skilled physician, it is safer than childbirth. It does not compete with contraception but serves as a backstop when the latter fails or when contraceptive devices or information are not available. As contraception becomes customary, the incidence of abortion recedes even without its being banned. If, therefore, abortions enable women to have only the number of children they want, and if family planners do not advocate—in fact decry—legalization of abortion, they are to that extent denying the central tenet of their own movement. The irony of anti-abortionism in family-planning circles is seen particularly in hair-splitting arguments over whether or not some contraceptive agent (for example, the IUD) is in reality an abortifacient. A Mexican leader in family planning writes (17):

One of the chief objectives of our program in Mexico is to prevent abortions. If we could be sure that the mode of action [of the IUD] was not interference with nidation, we could easily use the method in Mexico.

The questions of sterilization and unnatural forms of sexual intercourse usually meet with similar silent treatment or disapproval, although nobody doubts the effectiveness of these measures in avoiding conception. Sterilization has proved popular in Puerto Rico and has had some vogue in India (where the new health minister hopes to make it compulsory for those with a certain number of children), but in both these areas it has been for the most part ignored or condemned by the family-planning movement.

On the side of goals, then, we see that a family-planning orientation limits the aims of current population policy. Despite reference to "population control" and "fertility control," which presumably mean determination of demographic results by and for the nation as a whole, the movement gives control only to couples, and does this only if they use "respectable" contraceptives.

## THE NEGLECT OF MOTIVATION

By sanctifying the doctrine that each woman should have the number of children she wants, and by assuming that if she has only that number this will automatically curb population growth to the necessary degree, the leaders of current policies escape the necessity of asking why women desire so many children and how this desire can be influenced (18, p. 41; 19). Instead, they claim that satisfactory motivation is shown by the popular desire (shown by opinion surveys in all countries) to have the means of family limitation, and that therefore the problem is one of inventing and distributing the best possible contraceptive devices. Overlooked is the fact that a desire for availability of contraceptives is compatible with high fertility.

Given the best of means, there remain the questions of how many children couples want and of whether this is the requisite number from the standpoint of population size. That it is not is indicated by continued rapid population growth in industrial countries, and by the very surveys showing that people want contraception—for these show, too, that people also want numerous children.

The family planners do not ignore motivation. They are forever talking about "attitudes" and "needs." But they pose the issue in terms of the "acceptance" of birth control devices. At the most naive level, they assume that lack of acceptance is a function of the contraceptive device itself. This reduces the motive problem to a technological question. The task of population control then becomes simply the invention of a device that will be acceptable (20). The plastic IUD is acclaimed because, once in place, it does not depend on repeated acceptance by the woman, and thus it "solves" the problem of motivation (21).

But suppose a woman does not want to use any contraceptive until after she has had four children. This is the type of question that is seldom raised in the family-planning literature. In that literature, wanting a specific number of children is taken as complete motivation, for it implies a wish to control the size of one's family. The problem woman, from the standpoint of family planners, is the one who wants "as many as come," or "as many as God sends." Her attitude is construed as due to ignorance and "cultural values," and the policy deemed necessary to change it is "education." No compulsion can be used, because the movement is committed to free choice, but movie strips, posters, comic books, public lectures, interviews, and discussions are in order. These supply information and supposedly change values by discounting superstitions and showing that unrestrained procreation is harmful to both mother and children. The effort is considered successful when the woman decides she wants only a certain number of children and uses an effective contraceptive.

In viewing negative attitudes toward birth control as due to ignorance, apathy, and outworn tradition, and "mass-communication" as the solution to the motivation problem *(22)*, family planners tend to ignore the power and complexity of social life. If it were admitted that the creation and care of new human beings is socially motivated, like other forms of behavior, by being a part of the system of rewards and punishments that is built into human relationships, and thus is bound up with the individual's economic and personal interests, it would be apparent that the social structure and economy must be changed before a deliberate reduction in the birth rate can be achieved. As it is, reliance on family planning allows people to feel that "something is being done about the population problem" without the need for painful social changes.

Designation of population control as a medical or public health task leads to a similar evasion. This categorization assures popular support because it puts population policy in the hands of respected medical personnel, but, by the same token, it gives responsibility for leadership to people who think in terms of clinics and patients, of pills and IUD's, and who bring to the handling of economic and social phenomena a self-confident naiveté. The study of social organization is a technical field; an action program based on intuition is no more apt to succeed in the control of human beings than it is in the area of bacterial or viral control. Moreover, to alter a social system, by deliberate policy, so as to regulate births in accord with the demands of the collective welfare would require political power, and this is not likely to inhere in public health officials, nurses, midwives, and social workers. To entrust population policy to them is "to take action," but not dangerous "effective action."

Similarly, the Janus-faced position on birth-control technology represents an escape from the necessity, and onus, of grappling with the social and economic determinants of reproductive behavior. On the one side, the rejection or avoidance of religiously tabooed but otherwise effective means of birth prevention enables the family-planning movement to avoid official condemnation. On the other side, an intense preoccupation with contraceptive technology (apart from the tabooed means) also helps the family planners to avoid censure. By implying that the only need is the invention and distribution of effective contraceptive devices, they allay fears, on the part of religious and governmental officials, that fundamental changes in social organization are contemplated. Changes basic enough to affect motivation for having children would be changes in the structure of the family, in the position of women, and in the sexual mores. Far from proposing such radicalism, spokesmen for family planning frequently state their purpose as "protection" of the family—that is, closer observance of family norms. In addition, by concentrating on *new* and *scientific* contraceptives, the movement escapes taboos attached to old ones (the Pope will hardly authorize the condom, but may sanction the pill) and allows family planning to be regarded as a branch of medicine: overpopulation becomes a disease, to be treated by a pill or a coil.

We thus see that the inadequacy of current population policies with respect to motivation is inherent in their overwhelmingly family-planning character. Since family planning is by definition private planning, it eschews any societal control over motivation. It merely furnishes the means, and, among possible means, only the most respectable. Its leaders, in avoiding social complexities and seeking official favor, are obviously activated not solely by expediency but also by their own sentiments as members of society and by their background as persons attracted to the family-planning movement. Unacquainted for the most part with technical economics, sociology, and demography, they tend honestly and instinctively to believe that something they vaguely call population control can be achieved by making better contraceptives available.

## THE EVIDENCE OF INEFFECTIVENESS

If this characterization is accurate, we can conclude that current programs will not enable a government to control population size. In countries where couples have numerous offspring that they do not want, such programs may possibly accelerate a birth-rate decline that would occur anyway, but the conditions that cause births to be wanted or unwanted are beyond the control of family planning, hence beyond the control of any nation which relies on family planning alone as its population policy.

This conclusion is confirmed by demographic facts. As I have noted above, the widespread use of family planning in industrial countries has not given their governments control over the birth rate. In backward countries today, taken as a whole, birth rates are rising, not falling; in those with population policies, there is no indication that the government is controlling the rate of reproduction. The main "successes" cited in the well-publicized policy literature are cases where a large number of contraceptives have been distributed or where the program has been accompanied by some decline in the birth rate. Popular enthusiasm for family planning is found mainly in the cities, or in advanced countries such as Japan and Taiwan, where the people would adopt contraception in any case, program or no program. It is difficult to prove that present population policies have even speeded up a lowering of the birth rate (the least that could have been expected), much less that they have provided national "fertility control."

Let us next briefly review the facts concerning the level and trend of population in underdeveloped nations generally, in order to understand the magnitude of the task of genuine control.

## RISING BIRTH RATES IN UNDERDEVELOPED COUNTRIES

In ten Latin-American countries, between 1940 and 1959 (23), the average birth rates (age-standardized), as estimated by our research office at the University of California, rose as follows: 1940–44, 43.4 annual births per 1000 population; 1945–49, 44.6; 1950–54, 46.4; 1955–59, 47.7.

In another study made in our office, in which estimating methods derived from the theory of quasi-stable populations were used, the recent trend was found to be upward in 27 underdeveloped countries, downward in six, and unchanged in one (24). Some of the rises have been substantial, and most have occurred where the birth rate was already extremely high. For instance, the gross reproduction rate rose in Jamaica from 1.8 per thousand in 1947 to 2.7 in 1960; among the natives of Fiji, from 2.0 in 1951 to 2.4 in 1964; and in Albania, from 3.0 in the period 1950–54 to 3.4 in 1960.

The general rise in fertility in backward regions is evidently not due to failure of population-control efforts, because most of the countries either have no such effort or have programs too new to show much effect. Instead, the rise is due, ironically, to the very circumstance that brought on the population crisis in the first place—to improved health and lowered mortality. Better health increases the probability that a woman will conceive and retain the fetus to term; lowered mortality raises the proportion of babies who survive to the age of reproduction and reduces the probability of widowhood during that age (25). The significance of the general rise in fertility, in the context of this discussion, is that it is giving would-be population planners a harder task than many of them realize. Some of the upward pressure on birth rates is independent of what couples do about family planning, for it arises from the fact that, with lowered mortality, there are simply more couples.

## UNDERDEVELOPED COUNTRIES WITH POPULATION POLICIES

In discussions of population policy there is often confusion as to which cases are relevant. Japan, for instance, has been widely praised for the effectiveness of its measures, but it is a very advanced industrial nation and, besides, its government policy had little or nothing to do with the decline in the birth rate, except unintentionally. It therefore offers no test of population policy under peasant-agrarian conditions. Another case of question-able relevance is that of Taiwan, because Taiwan is sufficiently developed to be placed in the urban-industrial class of nations. How-ever, since Taiwan is offered as the main show-piece by the sponsors of current policies in underdeveloped areas, and since the data are excellent, it merits examination.

Taiwan is acclaimed as a showpiece be-cause it has responded favorably to a highly organized program for distributing up-to-date contraceptives and has also had a rapidly drop-ping birth rate. Some observers have carelessly attributed the decline in the birth rate—from 50.0 in 1951 to 32.7 in 1965—to the family-planning campaign *(26)*, but the campaign began only in 1963 and could have affected only the end of the trend. Rather, the decline represents a response to modernization similar to that made by all countries that have become industrialized *(27)*. By 1950 over half of Tai-wan's population was urban, and by 1964 nearly two-thirds were urban, with 29 percent of the population living in cities of 100,000 or more. The pace of economic development has been extremely rapid. Between 1951 and 1963, per capita income increased by 4.05 percent per year. Yet the island is closely packed, having 870 persons per square mile (a popu-lation density higher than that of Belgium). The combination of fast economic growth and rapid population increase in limited space has put parents of large families at a relative dis-advantage and has created a brisk demand for abortions and contraceptives. Thus the favora-ble response to the current campaign to en-courage use of the IUD is not a good example of what birth-control technology can do for a genuinely backward country. In fact, when the program was started, one reason for expecting receptivity was that the island was already on its way to modernization and family plan-ning *(28)*.

**TABLE 1**

Decline in Taiwan's fertility rate, 1951 through 1966.

| Year | Registered births per 1000 women aged 15–49 | Change in rate (per cent)* |
|---|---|---|
| 1951 | 211 | |
| 1952 | 198 | −5.6 |
| 1953 | 194 | −2.2 |
| 1954 | 193 | −0.5 |
| 1955 | 197 | +2.1 |
| 1956 | 196 | −0.4 |
| 1957 | 182 | −7.1 |
| 1958 | 185 | +1.3 |
| 1959 | 184 | −0.1 |
| 1960 | 180 | −2.5 |
| 1961 | 177 | −1.5 |
| 1962 | 174 | −1.5 |
| 1963 | 170 | −2.6 |
| 1964 | 162 | −4.9 |
| 1965 | 152 | −6.0 |
| 1966 | 149 | −2.1 |

* The percentages were calculated on unrounded fig-ures. Source of data through 1965, *Taiwan Demo-graphic Fact Book* (1964, 1965); for 1966, *Monthly Bulletin of Population Registration Statistics of Taiwan* (1966, 1967).

At most, the recent family-planning cam-paign—which reached significant proportions only in 1964, when some 46,000 IUD's were inserted (in 1965 the number was 99,253, and in 1966, 111,242) *(29; 30,* p. 45)—could have caused the increase observable after 1963 in the rate of decline. Between 1951 and 1963 the average drop in the birth rate per 1000 women (see Table 1) was 1.73 percent per year; in the period 1964–66 it was 4.35 percent. But one hesitates to assign all of the accel-eration in decline since 1963 to the family-planning campaign. The rapid economic development has been precisely of a type likely to accelerate a drop in reproduction. The rise in manufacturing has been much greater than the rise in either agriculture or construction. The agricultural labor force has thus been squeezed, and migration to the cities has skyrocketed *(31)*. Since housing has not kept pace, urban families have had to restrict reproduction in order to take advan-tage of career opportunities and avoid domestic inconvenience. Such conditions have historically tended to accelerate a decline in birth rate. The most rapid decline came late in the United States (1921–33) and in Japan (1947–55). A plot of the Japanese and Taiwanese birth rates (Fig. 1) shows marked similarity of the two curves, despite a difference in level. All told, one should not attribute all of the post-1963 acceleration in the decline of Taiwan's birth rate to the family-planning campaign.

The main evidence that *some* of this acceleration is due to the campaign comes from the fact that Taichung, the city in which the family-planning effort was first concentrated, showed subsequently a much faster drop in fertility than other cities (*30*, p. 69; *32*). But the campaign has not reached throughout the island. By the end of 1966, only 260,745 women had been fitted with an IUD under auspices of the campaign, whereas the women of reproductive age on the island numbered 2.86 million. Most of the reduction in fertility has therefore been a matter of individual initiative. To some extent the campaign may be simply substituting sponsored (and cheaper) services for those that would otherwise come through private and commercial channels. An island-wide survey in 1964 showed that over 150,000 women were already using the traditional Ota ring (a metallic intrauterine device popular in Japan); almost as many had been sterilized; about 40,000 were using foam tablets; some 50,000 admitted to having had at least one abortion; and many were using other methods of birth control (*30*, pp. 18, 31).

The important question, however, is not whether the present campaign is somewhat hastening the downward trend in the birth rate but whether, even if it is, it will provide population control for the nation. Actually, the campaign is not designed to provide such control and shows no sign of doing so. It takes for granted existing reproductive goals. Its aim is "to integrate, through education and information, the idea of family limitation *within the existing attitudes, values, and goals* of the people" [*30*, p. 8 (italics mine)]. Its target is *married* women who do not want any more children; it ignores girls not yet married, and women married and wanting more children.

With such an approach, what is the maximum impact possible? It is the difference between the number of children women have been having and the number they want to have. A study in 1957 found a median figure of 3.75 for the number of children wanted by women aged 15 to 29 in Taipei, Taiwan's largest city; the corresponding figure for women from a satellite town was 3.93; for women from a fishing village, 4.90; and for women from a farming village, 5.03. Over 60 percent of the women in Taipei and over 90 percent of those in the farming village wanted 4 or more children (*33*). In a sample of wives aged 25 to 29 in Taichung, a city of over 300,000, Freedman and his co-workers found the average number of children wanted was 4; only 9 percent wanted less than 3, 20 percent wanted 5 or more (*34*). If, therefore, Taiwanese women used contraceptives that were 100-percent effective and had the number of children they desire, they would have about 4.5 each. The goal of the family-planning effort would be achieved. In the past the Taiwanese

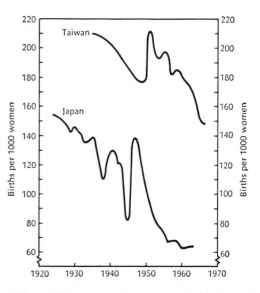

**FIG. 1.** Births per 1000 women aged 15 through 49 in Japan and Taiwan.

woman who married and lived through the reproductive period had, on the average, approximately 6.5 children; thus a figure of 4.5 would represent a substantial decline in fertility. Since mortality would continue to decline, the population growth rate would decline somewhat less than individual reproduction would. With 4.5 births per woman and a life expectancy of 70 years, the rate of natural increase would be close to 3 percent per year *(35)*.

In the future, Taiwanese views concerning reproduction will doubtless change, in response to social change and economic modernization. But how far will they change? A good indication is the number of children desired by couples in an already modernized country long oriented toward family planning. In the United States in 1966, an average of 3.4 children was considered ideal by white women aged 21 or over *(36)*. This average number of births would give Taiwan, with only a slight decrease in mortality, a long-run rate of natural increase of 1.7 percent per year and a doubling of population in 41 years.

Detailed data confirm the interpretation that Taiwanese women are in the process of shifting from a "peasant-agrarian" to an "industrial" level of reproduction. They are, in typical fashion, cutting off higher-order births at age 30 and beyond *(37)*. Among young wives, fertility has risen, not fallen. In sum, the widely acclaimed family-planning program in Taiwan may, at most, have somewhat speeded the later phase of fertility decline which would have occurred anyway because of modernization.

Moving down the scale of modernization, to countries most in need of population control, one finds the family-planning approach even more inadequate. In South Korea, second only to Taiwan in the frequency with which it is cited as a model of current policy, a recent birth-rate decline of unknown extent is assumed by leaders to be due overwhelmingly to the government's family-planning program. However, it is just as plausible to say that the net effect of government involvement in population control has been, so far, to delay rather than hasten a decline in reproduction made inevitable by social and economic changes. Although the government is advocating vasectomies and providing IUD's and pills, it refuses to legalize abortions, despite the rapid rise in the rate of illegal abortions and despite the fact that, in a recent survey, 72 percent of the people who stated an opinion favored legalization. Also, the program is presented in the context of maternal and child health; it thus emphasizes motherhood and the family rather than alternative roles for women. Much is made of the fact that opinion surveys show an overwhelming majority of Koreans (89 percent in 1965) favoring contraception *(38,* p. 27), but this means only that Koreans are like other people in wishing to have the means to get what they want. Unfortunately, they want sizable families: "The records indicate that the program appeals mainly to women in the 30–39 year age bracket who have four or more children, including at least two sons . . ." *(38,* p. 25).

In areas less developed than Korea the degree of acceptance of contraception tends to be disappointing, especially among the rural majority. Faced with this discouragement, the leaders of current policy, instead of reexamining their assumptions, tend to redouble their effort to find a contraceptive that will appeal to the most illiterate peasant, forgetting that he wants a good-sized family. In the rural Punjab, for example, "a disturbing feature . . . is that the females start to seek advice and adopt family planning techniques at the fag end of their reproductive period" *(39)*. Among 5196 women coming to rural Punjabi family-planning centers, 38 percent were over 35 years old, 67 percent over 30. These women had married early, nearly a third of them before the age of 15 *(40);* some 14 per cent had eight or more *living* children when they reached the clinic, 51 percent six or more.

A survey in Tunisia showed that 68 per cent of the married couples were willing to use birth-control measures, but the average number of children they considered ideal was 4.3 *(41)*. The corresponding averages for a village in eastern Java, a village near New Delhi, and a village in Mysore were 4.3, 4.0, and 4.2, respectively *(42, 43)*. In the cities of these regions women are more ready to accept birth control and they want fewer children than village women do, but the number they consider desirable is still wholly unsatisfactory from the standpoint of population control. In an urban family-planning center in Tunisia, more than 600 of 900 women accepting contraceptives had four living children already *(44)*. In Bangalore, a city of nearly a million at the time (1952), the number of offspring desired by married women was 3.7 on the average; by married men, 4.1 *(43)*. In the metropolitan area of San Salvador (350,000 inhabitants) a 1964 survey *(45)* showed the number desired by women of reproductive age to be 3.9, and in seven other capital cities of Latin America the number ranged from 2.7 to 4.2. If women in the cities of underdeveloped countries used birth-control measures with 100-percent efficiency, they still would have enough babies to expand city populations senselessly, quite apart from the added contribution of rural-urban migration. In many of the cities the difference between actual and ideal number of children is not great; for instance, in the seven Latin-American capitals mentioned above, the ideal was 3.4 whereas the actual births per women in the age range 35 to 39 was 3.7 *(46)*. Bombay City has had birth-control clinics for many years, yet its birth rate (standardized for age, sex, and marital distribution) is still 34 per 1000 inhabitants and is tending to rise rather than fall. Although this rate is about 13 percent lower than that for India generally, it has been about that much lower since at least 1951 *(47)*.

## IS FAMILY PLANNING THE "FIRST STEP" IN POPULATION CONTROL?

To acknowledge that family planning does not achieve population control is not to impugn its value for other purposes. Freeing women from the need to have more children than they want is of great benefit to them and their children and to society at large. My argument is therefore directed not against family-planning programs as such but against the assumption that they are an effective means of controlling population growth.

But what difference does it make? Why not go along for awhile with family planning as an initial approach to the problem of population control? The answer is that any policy on which millions of dollars are being spent should be designed to achieve the goal it purports to achieve. If it is only a first step, it should be so labeled, and its connection with the next step (and the nature of that next step) should be carefully examined. In the present case, since no "next step" seems ever to be mentioned, the question arises, Is reliance on family planning in fact a basis for dangerous postponement of effective steps? To continue to offer a remedy as a cure long after it has been shown merely to ameliorate the disease is either quackery or wishful thinking, and it thrives most where the need is greatest. Today the desire to solve the population problem is so intense that we are all ready to embrace any "action program" that promises relief. But postponement of effective measures allows the situation to worsen.

Unfortunately, the issue is confused by a matter of semantics. "Family *planning*" and "fertility *control*" suggest that reproduction is being regulated according to some rational plan. And so it is, but only from the standpoint of the individual couple, not from that of the community. What is rational in the light of a couple's situation may be totally irrational from the standpoint of society's welfare.

The need for societal regulation of individual behavior is readily recognized in other spheres—those of explosives, dangerous drugs, public property, natural resources. But in the sphere of reproduction, complete individual initiative is generally favored even by those liberal intellectuals who, in other spheres, most favor economic and social planning. Social reformers who would not hesitate to force all owners of rental property to rent to anyone who can pay, or to force all workers in an industry to join a union, balk at any suggestion that couples be permitted to have only a certain number of offspring. Invariably they interpret societal control of reproduction as meaning direct police supervision of individual behavior. Put the word *compulsory* in front of any term describing a means of limiting births —*compulsory sterilization, compulsory abortion, compulsory contraception*—and you guarantee violent opposition. Fortunately, such direct controls need not be invoked, but conservatives and radicals alike overlook this in their blind opposition to the idea of collective determination of a society's birth rate.

That the exclusive emphasis on family planning in current population policies is not a "first step" but an escape from the real issues is suggested by two facts. (i) No country has taken the "next step." The industrialized countries have had family planning for half a century without acquiring control over either the birth rate or population increase. (ii) Support and encouragement of research on population policy other than family planning is negligible. It is precisely this blocking of alternative thinking and experimentation that makes the emphasis on family planning a major obstacle to population control. The need is not to abandon family-planning programs but to put equal or greater resources into other approaches.

## NEW DIRECTIONS
## IN POPULATION POLICY

In thinking about other approaches, one can start with known facts. In the past, all surviving societies had institutional incentives for marriage, procreation, and child care which were powerful enough to keep the birth rate equal to or in excess of a high death rate. Despite the drop in death rates during the last century and a half, the incentives tended to remain intact because the social structure (especially in regard to the family) changed little. At most, particularly in industrial societies, children became less productive and more expensive *(48)*. In present-day agrarian socie-

ties, where the drop in death rate has been more recent, precipitate, and independent of social change *(49)*, motivation for having children has changed little. Here, even more than in industrialized nations, the family has kept on producing abundant offspring, even though only a fraction of these children are now needed.

If excessive population growth is to be prevented, the obvious requirement is somehow to impose restraints on the family. However, because family roles are reinforced by society's system of rewards, punishments, sentiments, and norms, any proposal to demote the family is viewed as a threat by conservatives and liberals alike, and certainly by people with enough social responsibility to work for population control. One is charged with trying to "abolish" the family, but what is required is selective restructuring of the family in relation to the rest of society.

The lines of such restructuring are suggested by two existing limitations on fertility. (i) Nearly all societies succeed in drastically discouraging reproduction among unmarried women. (ii) Advanced societies unintentionally reduce reproduction among married women when conditions worsen in such a way as to penalize childbearing more severely than it was penalized before. In both cases the causes are motivational and economic rather than technological.

It follows that population-control policy can de-emphasize the family in two ways: (i) by keeping present controls over illegitimate childbirth yet making the most of factors that lead people to postpone or avoid marriage, and (ii) by instituting conditions that motivate those who do marry to keep their families small.

## POSTPONEMENT OF MARRIAGE

Since the female reproductive span is short and generally more fecund in its first than in its second half, postponement of marriage to ages beyond 20 tends biologically to reduce births. Sociologically, it gives women time to get a better education, acquire interests unrelated to the family, and develop a cautious attitude toward pregnancy (50). Individuals who have not married by the time they are in their late twenties often do not marry at all. For these reasons, for the world as a whole, the average age at marriage for women is negatively associated with the birth rate: a rising age at marriage is a frequent cause of declining fertility during the middle phase of the demographic transition; and, in the late phase, the "baby boom" is usually associated with a return to younger marriages.

Any suggestion that age at marriage be raised as a part of population policy is usually met with the argument that "even if a law were passed, it would not be obeyed." Interestingly, this objection implies that the only way to control the age at marriage is by direct legislation, but other factors govern the actual age. Roman Catholic countries generally follow canon law in stipulating 12 years as the minimum *legal* age at which girls may marry, but the actual average age at marriage in these countries (at least in Europe) is characteristically more like 25 to 28 years. The actual age is determined, not by law, but by social and economic conditions. In agrarian societies, postponement of marriage (when postponement occurs) is apparently caused by difficulties in meeting the economic prerequisites for matrimony, as stipulated by custom and opinion. In industrial societies it is caused by housing shortages, unemployment, the requirement for overseas military service, high costs of education, and inadequacy of consumer services. Since almost no research has been devoted to the subject, it is difficult to assess the relative weight of the factors that govern the age at marriage.

## ENCOURAGING LIMITATION OF BIRTHS WITHIN MARRIAGE

As a mean of encouraging the limitation of reproduction within marriage, as well as postponement of marriage, a greater rewarding of nonfamilial than of familial roles would probably help. A simple way of accomplishing this would be to allow economic advantages to accrue to the single as opposed to the married individual, and to the small as opposed to the large family. For instance, the government could pay people to permit themselves to be sterilized (51); all costs of abortion could be paid by the government; a substantial fee could be charged for a marriage license; a "child-tax" (52) could be levied; and there could be a requirement that illegitimate pregnancies be aborted. Less sensationally, governments could simply reverse some existing policies that encourage childbearing. They could, for example, cease taxing single persons more than married ones; stop giving parents special tax exemptions; abandon income-tax policy that discriminates against couples when the wife works; reduce paid maternity leaves; reduce family allowances (53); stop awarding public housing on the basis of family size; stop granting fellowships and other educational aids (including special allowances for wives and children) to married students; cease outlawing abortions and sterilizations; and relax rules that allow use of harmless contraceptives only with medical permission. Some of these policy reversals would be beneficial in other than demographic respects and some would be harmful unless special precautions were taken. The aim would be to reduce the number, not the quality, of the next generation.

A closely related method of deemphasizing the family would be modification of the complementarity of the roles of men and women. Men are now able to participate in the wider world yet enjoy the satisfaction of having several children because the housework and childcare fall mainly on their wives. Women are impelled to seek this role by their idealized view of marriage and motherhood and by either the scarcity of alternative roles or the difficulty of combining them with family roles. To change this situation women could be required to work outside the home, or compelled by circumstances to do so. If, at the same time, women were paid as well as men and

given equal educational and occupational opportunities, and if social life were organized
around the place of work rather than around
the home or neighborhood, many women
would develop interests that would compete
with family interests. Approximately this policy
is now followed in several Communist countries, and even the less developed of these
currently have extremely low birth rates *(54)*.

That inclusion of women in the labor force
has a negative effect on reproduction is indicated by regional comparisons *(18*, p. 1195; *55)*.
But in most countries the wife's employment is
subordinate, economically and emotionally, to
her family role, and is readily sacrificed for the
latter. No society has restructured both the
occupational system and the domestic establishment to the point of permanently modifying the old division of labor by sex.

In any deliberate effort to control the
birth rate along these lines, a government has
two powerful instruments—its command over
economic planning and its authority (real or
potential) over education. The first determines
(as far as policy can) the economic conditions
and circumstances affecting the lives of all
citizens; the second provides the knowledge
and attitudes necessary to implement the
plans. The economic system largely determines
who shall work, what can be bought, what
rearing children will cost, how much individuals can spend. The schools define family roles
and develop vocational and recreational interests; they could, if it were desired, redefine
the sex roles, develop interests that transcend
the home, and transmit realistic (as opposed
to moralistic) knowledge concerning marriage,
sexual behavior, and population problems.
When the problem is viewed in this light, it
is clear that the ministries of economics and
education, not the ministry of health, should
be the source of population policy.

## THE DILEMMA
## OF POPULATION POLICY

It should now be apparent why, despite
strong anxiety over runaway population

growth, the actual programs purporting to
control it are limited to family planning and
are therefore ineffective. (i) The goal of zero,
or even slight, population growth is one that
nations and groups find difficult to accept.
(ii) The measures that would be required to
implement such a goal, though not so revolutionary as a Brave New World or a Communist
Utopia, nevertheless tend to offend most people reared in existing societies. As a consequence, the goal of so-called population control is implicit and vague; the method is only
family planning. This method, far from deemphasizing the family, is familistic. One of
its stated goals is that of helping sterile couples
to *have* children. It stresses parental aspirations and responsibilities. It goes along with
most aspects of conventional morality, such as
condemnation of abortion, disapproval of premarital intercourse, respect for religious teachings and cultural taboos, and obeisance to
medical and clerical authority. It deflects hos-
tility by refusing to recommend any change
other than the one it stands for: availability of
contraceptives.

The things that make family planning acceptable are the very things that make it ineffective for population control. By stressing the
right of parents to have the number of children
they want, it evades the basic question of population policy, which is how to give societies
the number of children they need. By offering
only the means for *couples* to control fertility,
it neglects the means for societies to do so.

Because of the predominantly pro-family
character of existing societies, individual interest ordinarily leads to the production of
enough offspring to constitute rapid population growth under conditions of low mortality.
Childless or single-child homes are considered
indicative of personal failure, whereas having
three to five living children gives a family a
sense of continuity and substantiality *(56)*.

Given the existing desire to have moderate-
sized rather than small families, the only
countries in which fertility has been reduced
to match reduction in mortality are advanced
ones temporarily experiencing worsened economic conditions. In Sweden, for instance, the

net reproduction rate (NRR) has been below replacement for 34 years (1930–63), if the period is taken as a whole, but this is because of the economic depression. The average replacement rate was below unity (NRR = 0.81) for the period 1930–42, but from 1942 through 1963 it was above unity (NRR = 1.08). Hardships that seem particularly conducive to deliberate lowering of the birth rate are (in managed economies) scarcity of housing and other consumer goods despite full employment, and required high participation of women in the labor force, or (in freer economies) a great deal of unemployment and economic insecurity. When conditions are good, any nation tends to have a growing population.

It follows that, in countries where contraception is used, a realistic proposal for a government policy of lowering the birth rate reads like a catalogue of horrors: squeeze consumers through taxation and inflation; make housing very scarce by limiting construction; force wives and mothers to work outside the home to offset the inadequacy of male wages, yet provide few childcare facilities; encourage migration to the city by paying low wages in the country and providing few rural jobs; increase congestion in cities by starving the transit system; increase personal insecurity by encouraging conditions that produce unemployment and by haphazard political arrests. No government will institute such hardships simply for the purpose of controlling population growth. Clearly, therefore, the task of contemporary population policy is to develop attractive substitutes for family interests, so as to avoid having to turn to hardship as a corrective. The specific measures required for developing such substitutes are not easy to determine in the absence of research on the question.

In short, the world's population problem cannot be solved by pretense and wishful thinking. The unthinking identification of family planning with population control is an ostrich-like approach in that it permits people to hide from themselves the enormity and unconventionality of the task. There is no reason to abandon family-planning programs; contraception is a valuable technological in-

strument. But such programs must be supplemented with equal or greater investments in research and experimentation to determine the required socioeconomic measures.

## REFERENCES AND NOTES

1. *Studies in Family Planning*, No. 16 (1967).
2. *Ibid.*, No. 9 (1966), p. 1.
3. The statement is given in *Studies in Family Planning* (1, p. 1), and in *Population Bull.* **23**, 6 (1967).
4. The statement is quoted in *Studies in Family Planning* (1, p. 2).
5. *Hearings on S. 1676, U.S. Senate, Subcommittee on Foreign Aid Expenditures, 89th Congress, Second Session, April 7, 8. 11* (1966), pt. 4.
6. B. L. Raina, in *Family Planning and Population Programs*, B. Berelson, R. K. Anderson, O. Harkavy, G. Maier, W. P. Mauldin, S. G. Segal, Eds. (Univ. of Chicago Press, Chicago, 1966).
7. D. Kirk, *Ann. Amer. Acad. Polit. Soc. Sci.* **369**, 53 (1967).
8. As used by English-speaking demographers, the word *fertility* designates actual reproductive performance, not a theoretical capacity.
9. K. Davis, *Rotarian* **94**, 10 (1959); *Health Educ. Monographs* **9**, 2 (1960); L. Day and A. Day, *Too Many Americans* (Houghton Mifflin, Boston, 1964); R. A. Piddington, *Limits of Mankind* (Wright, Bristol, England, 1956).
10. *Official Gazette* (15 Apr. 1965); quoted in *Studies in Family Planning* (1, p. 7).
11. J. W. Gardner, Secretary of Health, Education, and Welfare, "Memorandum to Heads of Operating Agencies" (Jan. 1966), reproduced in *Hearings on S. 1676* (5), p. 783.
12. C. Tietze, *Demography* **1**, 119 (1964); J. *Chronic Diseases* **18**, 1161 (1964); M. Muramatsu, *Milbank Mem. Fund Quart.* **38**, 153 (1960); K. Davis, *Population Index* **29**, 345 (1963); R. Armijo and T. Monreal, *J. Sex Res.* **1964**, 143 (1964); Proceedings World Population Conference, Belgrade, 1965; Proceedings International Planned Parenthood Federation.
13. *Studies in Family Planning*, No. 4 (1964), p. 3.
14. D. Bell (then administrator for Agency for International Development), in *Hearings on S. 1676 (5)*, p. 862.
15. *Asian Population Conference* (United Nations, New York, 1964), p. 30.
16. R. Armijo and T. Monreal, in *Components of Population Change in Latin America* (Milbank Fund, New York, 1965), p. 272; E. Rice-Wray, *Amer. J. Public Health* **54**, 313 (1964).
17. E. Rice-Wray, in "Intra-Uterine Contraceptive Devices," *Excerpta Med. Intern. Congr. Ser. No. 54* (1962), p. 135.
18. J. Blake, in *Public Health and Population Change*, M. C. Sheps and J. C. Ridley, Eds. (Univ. of Pittsburgh Press, Pittsburgh, 1965).
19. J. Blake and K. Davis, *Amer. Behavioral Scientist* **5**, 24 (1963).
20. See "Panel discussion on comparative acceptability of different methods of contraception," in *Re-*

search in *Family Planning,* C. V. Kiser, Ed. (Princeton Univ. Press, Princeton, 1962), pp. 373–86.

21. "From the point of view of the woman concerned, the whole problem of continuing motivation disappears,..." [D. Kirk, in *Population Dynamics,* M. Muramatsu and P. A. Harper, Eds. (Johns Hopkins Press, Baltimore, 1965)].

22. "For influencing family size norms, certainly the examples and statements of public figures are of great significance ... also ... use of mass-communication methods which help to legitimize the small-family style, to provoke conversation, and to establish a vocabulary for discussion of family planning." [M. W. Freymann, in *Population Dynamics,* M. Muramatsu and P. A. Harper, Eds. (Johns Hopkins Press, Baltimore, 1965)].

23. O. A. Collver, *Birth Rates in Latin America* (International Population and Urban Research, Berkeley, Calif., 1965), pp. 27–28; the ten countries were Colombia, Costa Rica, El Salvador, Ecuador, Guatemala, Honduras, Mexico, Panama, Peru, and Venezuela.

24. J. R. Rele, *Fertility Analysis through Extension of Stable Population Concepts.* (International Population and Urban Research, Berkeley, Calif., 1967).

25. J. C. Ridley, M. C. Sheps, J. W. Lingner, J. A. Menken, *Milbank Mem. Fund Quart.* **45,** 77 (1967), E. Arriaga, unpublished paper.

26. "South Korea and Taiwan appear successfully to have checked population growth by the use of intrauterine contraceptive devices" [U. Borell, *Hearings on S. 1676 (5),* p. 556].

27. K. Davis, *Population Index* **29,** 345 (1963).

28. R. Freedman, *ibid.* **31,** 421 (1965).

29. Before 1964 the Family Planning Association had given advice to fewer than 60,000 wives in 10 years and a Pre-Pregnancy Health Program had reached some 10,000, and, in the current campaign, 3650 IUD's were inserted in 1965, in a total population of 2½ million women of reproductive age. See *Studies in Family Planning, No. 19* (1967), p. 4, and R. Freedman *et al., Population Studies* **16,** 231 (1963).

30. R. W. Gillespie, *Family Planning on Taiwan* (Population Council, Taichung, 1965).

31. During the period 1950–60 the ratio of growth of the city to growth of the noncity population was 5:3; during the period 1960–64 the ratio was 5:2; these ratios are based on data of Shaohsing Chen, *J. Sociol. Taiwan* **1,** 74 (1963) and data in the United Nations *Demographic Yearbooks.*

32. R. Freedman, *Population Index* **31,** 434 (1965). Taichung's rate of decline in 1963–64 was roughly double the average in four other cities, whereas just prior to the campaign its rate of decline had been much less than theirs.

33. S. H. Chen, *J. Soc. Sci. Taipei* **13,** 72 (1963).

34. R. Freedman *et al., Population Studies* **16,** 227 (1963); *ibid.,* p. 232.

35. In 1964 the life expectancy at birth was already 66 years in Taiwan, as compared to 70 for the United States.

36. J. Blake, *Eugenics Quart.* **14,** 68 (1967).

37. Women accepting IUD's in the family-planning program are typically 30 to 34 years old and have already had four children. [*Studies in Family Planning No. 19* (1967), p. 5].

38. Y. K. Cha, in *Family Planning and Population Programs,* B. Berelson *et al.,* Eds. (Univ. of Chicago Press, Chicago, 1966).

39. H. S. Ayalvi and S. S. Johl, *J. Family Welfare* **12,** 60 (1965).

40. Sixty per cent of the women had borne their first child before age 19. Early marriage is strongly supported by public opinion. Of couples polled in the Punjab, 48 per cent said that girls *should* marry before age 16, and 94 per cent said they should marry before age 20 (H. S. Ayalvi and S. S. Johl, *ibid.,* p. 57). A study of 2380 couples in 60 villages of Uttar Pradesh found that the women had consummated their marriage at an average age of 14.6 years [J. R. Rele, *Population Studies* **15,** 268 (1962)].

41. J. Morsa, in *Family Planning and Population Programs,* B. Berelson *et al.,* Eds. (Univ. of Chicago Press, Chicago, 1966).

42. H. Gille and R. J. Pardoko, *ibid.,* p. 515; S. N. Agarwala, *Med. Dig. Bombay* **4,** 653 (1961).

43. *Mysore Population Study* (United Nations, New York, 1961), p. 140.

44. A. Daly, in *Family Planning and Population Programs,* B. Berelson *et al.,* Eds. (Univ. of Chicago Press, Chicago, 1966).

45. C. J. Goméz, paper presented at the World Population Conference, Belgrade, 1965.

46. C. Miro, in *Family Planning and Population Programs,* B. Berelson *et al.,* Eds. (Univ. of Chicago Press, Chicago, 1966).

47. *Demographic Training and Research Centre (India) Newsletter* **20,** 4 (Aug. 1966).

48. K. Davis, *Population Index* **29,** 345 (1963). For economic and sociological theory of motivation for having children, see J. Blake [Univ. of California (Berkeley)], in preparation.

49. K. Davis, *Amer. Economic Rev.* **46,** 305 (1956); *Sci. Amer.* **209,** 68 (1963).

50. J. Blake, *World Population Conference* [*Belgrade, 1965*] (United Nations, New York, 1967), vol. 2, pp. 132–36.

51. S. Enke, *Rev. Economics Statistics* **42,** 175 (1960); _____, *Econ. Develop. Cult. Change* **8,** 339 (1960); _____, *ibid.* **10,** 427 (1962); A. O. Krueger and L. A. Sjaastad, *ibid.,* p. 423.

52. T. J. Samuel, *J. Family Welfare India* **13,** 12 (1966).

53. Sixty-two countries, including 27 in Europe, give cash payments to people for having children [U.S. Social Security Administration, *Social Security Programs Throughout the World, 1967* (Government Printing Office, Washington, D.C., 1967), pp. xxvii-xxviii].

54. Average gross reproduction rates in the early 1960's were as follows: Hungary, 0.91; Bulgaria, 1.09; Romania, 1.15; Yugoslavia, 1.32.

55. O. A. Collver and E. Langlois, *Econ. Develop. Cult. Change* **10,** 367 (1962); J. Weeks, [Univ. of California (Berkeley)], unpublished paper.

56. Roman Catholic textbooks condemn the "small" family (one with fewer than four children) as being abnormal [J. Blake, *Population Studies* **20,** 27 (1966)].

57. Judith Blake's critical readings and discussions have greatly helped in the preparation of this article.

# Population Policy for Americans:
# Is the Government Being Misled?

JUDITH BLAKE

Pressure on the federal government for "action" to limit population growth in the United States has intensified greatly during the past 10 years, and at present such action is virtually unchallenged as an official national goal. Given the goal, the question of means becomes crucial. Here I first evaluate the particular means being advocated and pursued in public policy, then I present alternative ways of possibly achieving the goal.

The prevailing view as to the best means is remarkably unanimous and abundantly documented. It is set forth in the 17 volumes of congressional hearings so far published on the "population crisis" (1); in "The Growth of U.S. Population," a report by the Committee on Population of the National Academy of Sciences (2); in a statement made by an officer of the Ford Foundation who was asked by the Department of Health, Education, and Welfare to make suggestions (3); and, finally, in the "Report of the President's Committee on Population and Family Planning," which was officially released this past January (4). The essential recommendation throughout is that the government should give highest priority to ghetto-oriented family-planning programs designed to "deliver" birth-control services to the poor and uneducated, among whom, it is claimed, there are at least 5 mil-

Population Policy for Americans: Is the Government Being Misled? From *Science,* Vol. 164, May 2, 1969, pp. 522–529. Copyright 1969 by the American Association for the Advancement of Science. Reprinted by permission of the author and the publisher.

lion women who are "in need' 'of such federally sponsored birth-control assistance.

By what logic have the proponents of control moved from a concern with population growth to a recommendation favoring highest priority for poverty-oriented birth-control programs? First, they has assumed that fertility is the only component of population growth worthy of government attention. Second, they have taken it for granted that, to reduce fertility, one sponsors birth-control programs ("family planning"). Just why they made this assumption is not clear, but its logical implication is that population growth is due to births that couples would have preferred to avoid. Furthermore, the reasoning confuses couple control over births with societal control over them (5). Third, the proponents of the new policy have seized on the poor and uneducated as the "target" group for birth-control action because they see this group as the only remaining target for a program of voluntary family planning. The rest of the population is handling its family planning pretty well on its own: over 95 percent of fecund U.S. couples already either use birth-control methods or intend to do so. The poor, on the other hand—at least those who are fecund—have larger families than the advantaged; they not only use birth-control methods less but they use them less effectively. The family-planning movement's notion of "responsible parenthood" carries the implication that family size should be directly, not inversely, related to social and economic advantage, and the poor are seen as constituting the residual slack to be taken up by the movement's efforts. Why are the poor not conforming to the dictates of responsible parenthood? Given the movement's basic assumptions, there are only two answers: the poor are irresponsible, or they have not had the opportunity. Since present-day leaders would abhor labeling the poor irresponsible, they have chosen to blame lack of opportunity as the cause. Opportunity has been lacking, in their eyes, either because the poor have not been "educated" in family planning or because they have not been "reached" by family-planning services. In either case, as they see it, the poor have been deprived of their "rights" (2, p. 22; 6). This deprivation has allegedly been due to the prudery and hypocrisy of the affluent, who have overtly tabooed discussion of birth control and dissemination of birth-control materials while, themselves, covertly enjoying the benefits of family planning (7).

So much for the logic underlying recent proposals for controlling population growth in the United States. But what is the evidence on which this argument is based? On what empirical grounds is the government being asked to embark on a high-priority program of providing contraceptive services to the poor? Moreover, what, if any, are some of the important public issues that the suggested policy raises—what are its social and political side effects? And, finally, is such a policy, even if appropriate for the poor and even if relatively unencumbered by public disapproval, relevant to the problem of population growth in America? If demographic curtailment is really the objective, must alternative policies be considered and possibly given highest priority?

Turning to the alleged need for government-sponsored birth-control services, one may ask whether birth control has in fact been a tabooed topic among the middle and upper classes, so that the less advantaged could be said to have suffered "deprivation" and consequently now to require government help. One may then question whether

there is a mandate from the poor for the type of federally sponsored service that is now being urged, and whether as many as 5 million women are "in need" of such family-planning assistance.

## HAS BIRTH CONTROL BEEN A TABOOED TOPIC?

The notion that the American public has only recently become willing to tolerate open discussion of birth control has been assiduously cultivated by congressmen and others concerned with government policy on population. For example, Senator Tydings credited Senators Gruening and Clark and President Johnson with having almost singlehandedly changed American public attitudes toward birth control. In 1966 he read the following statement into the 28 February *Congressional Record* (8).

The time is ripe for positive action. Ten years ago, this was a politically delicate subject. Today the Nation has awakened to the need for Government action.

This change in public attitude has come about through the efforts of men who had the courage to brook the tides of public opinion. Senator Clark is such a man. Senator Gruening is such a man. So is President Johnson. Because of their leadership it is no longer necessary for an elected official to speak with trepidation on this subject.

A year later, Senator Tydings reduced his estimate of the time required for the shift in public opinion to "3 or 4 years" (9, p. 12; 10). Senator Gruening maintained (11) that the "ninety-eight distinguished men and women" who testified at the public hearing on S. 1676 were "pioneers" whose "names comprise an important honor roll which historically bears an analogy to other famous lists: the signers of the Declaration of Independence, those who ratified the Constitution of the United States and others whose names were appended to and made possible some of the great turning points in history." Reasoning from the continued existence of old, and typically unenforced, laws concerning birth control (together with President Eisenhower's famous antibirth-control statement), Stycos, in a recent article *(12)*, stated:

The public reaction to family planning in the United States has varied between disgust and silent resignation to a necessary evil. At best it was viewed as so delicate and risky that it was a matter of "individual conscience." As such, it was a matter so totally private, so sacred (or profane), that no external agents, and certainly not the state, should have anything to do with it.

Does the evidence support such impressionistic claims? How did the general public regard government sponsorship of birth control long before it became a subject of congressional hearings, a National Academy report, and a Presidential Committee report? Fortunately, a question on this topic appeared in no less than 13 national polls and surveys conducted between 1937 and 1966. As part of a larger project concerned with public knowledge and opinions about demographic topics, I have gathered together the original data cards from these polls, prepared them for computer processing, and analyzed the results. The data are all from Gallup polls and are all from national samples of the white, adult population. Here I concentrate on adults under 45—that is, on adults in the childbearing age group.

The data of Table 1 contradict the notion that Americans have only recently ceased to regard birth control as a tabooed topic. As far back as 30 years ago, almost three-quarters of the women questioned in these surveys actively approved having the *government* make birth-control information available to the married. By the early 1960's, 80 per cent or more of women approved overcoming legal barriers and allowing "anyone who wants it" to have birth-control information. The figures for men are similar. The question asked in 1964—the one question in recent years that did not mention illegality—brought 86 per cent of the women and 89 per cent of the men into the category of those who approved availability

## TABLE 1

Percentages of white U.S. men and women between the ages of 21 and 44 who, in various national polls and surveys made between 1937 and 1964*, expressed the opinion that birth-control information should be made available to individuals who desired it.

| Year | Men % | Men N | Women % | Women N |
|---|---|---|---|---|
| 1937 | 66 | 1038 | 70 | 734 |
| 1938 | 67 | 1111 | 72 | 548 |
| 1939 | 74 | 1101 | 73 | 630 |
| 1940 | 72 | 1127 | 75 | 618 |
| 1943 | 67 | 628 | 73 | 866 |
| 1945 | 64 | 714 | 70 | 879 |
| 1947 | 76 | 353 | 75 | 405 |
| 1959 | 78 | 301 | 79 | 394 |
| 1961 | 82 | 336 | 81 | 394 |
| 1962 | 85 | 288 | 80 | 381 |
| 1963 | 78 | 323 | 79 | 373 |
| 1964 | 89 | 324 | 86 | 410 |

* The questions asked of respondents concerning birth control were as follows. In 1937: Do you favor the birth control movement? In 1938, 1939, 1940, 1943, 1945, and 1947: Would you like to see a government agency (or "government health clinics") furnish birth-control information to married people who want it? In 1959, 1961, 1962, and 1963: In some places in the United States it is not legal to supply birth-control information. How do you feel about this—do you think birth-control information should be available to anyone who wants it, or not? In 1964: Do you think birth-control information should be available to anyone who wants it, or not?

of birth-control information for "anyone who wants it." Furthermore, in judging the level of disapproval, one should bear in mind that the remainder of the respondents, in all of these years, includes from 7 to 15 per cent who claim that they have "no opinion" on the subject, not that they "disapprove."

An important difference of opinion corresponds to a difference in religious affiliation. Among non-Catholics (including those who have "no religion" and do not attend church) approval has been considerably higher than it has been among Catholics. Among non-Catholic women, over 80 per cent approved as early as 1939, and among non-Catholic men the percentages were approximately the same. The 1964 poll showed that 90 per cent of each sex approved. Among Catholics, in recent years about 60 per cent have approved, and, in 1964, the question that mentioned neither the government nor legality brought opinions of approval from 77 per cent of the women and 83 per cent of the men.

Clearly, if birth-control information has in fact been unavailable to the poor, the cause has been a generalized and pervasive attitude of prudery on the part of the American public. Although public officials may have misjudged American opinion (and may have mistakenly assumed that the Catholic Church "spoke for" a majority of Americans, or even for a majority of Catholics), most Americans of an age to be having children did not regard birth control as a subject that should be under a blanket of secrecy and, as far back as the 1930's, evinced a marked willingness to have their government make such information widely available. It seems unlikely, therefore, that poorer sectors of our population were "cut off" from birth-control knowledge primarily because informal channels of communication (the channels through which most people learn about birth control) were blocked by an upper- and middle-class conspiracy of silence.

What has happened, however, is that pressure groups for family planning, like the Catholic hierarchy they have been opposing, have been acting as self-designated spokesmen for "public opinion." By developing a cause as righteous as that of the Catholics (the "rights" of the poor as against the "rights" of a religious group), the family planners have used the American way of influencing official opinion. Now public officials appear to believe that publicly supported birth-control services are what the poor have always wanted and needed, just as, in the past, official opinion acceded to the notion that such services would have been "offensive" to certain groups. Nonetheless, the question remains of whether or not publicly supported services are actually appropriate to the attitudes and objectives of the poor and uneducated in matters of reproduction. Is the government responding to a mandate from the poor or to an ill-concealed mandate from the well-to-do? If there is no mandate from the poor, the provision of birth-control services may prove a convenience for certain women but is likely to have little effect on the reproductive performance of the poor in general. Let us look at the evidence.

## IS THERE A MANDATE FROM THE POOR?

The notion that the poor have larger families than the affluent only because they have less access to birth-control information implies that the poor *desire* families as small as, or smaller than, those of the well-to-do. The poor are simply unable to realize this desire, the argument goes, because of lack of access to birth-control information. The National Academy of Sciences Committee on Population stated the argument very well (2, p. 10).

The available evidence indicates that low-income families do not want more children than do families with higher incomes, but they have more because they do not have the information or the resources to plan their families effectively according to their own desires.

The committee, however, presents none of the "available evidence" that "low-income families do not want more children than do families with higher incomes." Actually, my data supply evidence that runs counter to the statement quoted above, both with respect to the desired or ideal number of children and with respect to attitudes toward birth control.

I shall begin with the preferred size of family. A number of national polls, conducted over some 25 years, provide data concerning opinions on ideal family size. In addition, I include tabulations of data from two national surveys on fertility (the "Growth of American Families Studies"), conducted in 1955 and 1960 *(13, 14)*. My detailed analyses of the

## TABLE 2

Mean number of children considered ideal by non-Catholic women, according to education and economic status, for selected years between 1943 and 1968.

| Date | Age range | Level of education* | | | Income or economic status† | | | | Total respondents | |
|------|-----------|---------|----------------|-----------------|------|------|------|------|------|------|
| | | College | High school | Grade school | 1 | 2 | 3 | 4 | X | N |
| 1943 | 20–34 | 2.8 | 2.6 | 2.6 | 2.9 | 2.7 | 2.7 | 2.5 | 2.7 | 1893 |
| 1952 | 21+ | 3.3 | 3.1 | 3.6 | 3.3 | | 3.3 | 3.3 | 3.3 | 723 |
| 1955‡ | 18–39 | 3.1 | 3.2 | 3.7 | 3.2 | 3.1 | 3.2 | 3.5 | 3.3 | 1905 |
| 1955§ | 18–39 | 3.3 | 3.4 | 3.9 | 3.4 | 3.3 | 3.4 | 3.7 | 3.4 | 1905 |
| 1957 | 21+ | 3.4 | 3.2 | 3.6 | 3.3 | | 3.2 | 3.5 | 3.3 | 448 |
| 1959 | 21+ | 3.5 | 3.4 | 3.9 | 3.5 | | 3.5 | 3.6 | 3.5 | 472 |
| 1960‡ | 18–39 | 3.1 | 3.2 | 3.5 | 3.1 | 3.2 | 3.3 | 3.2 | 3.2 | 1728 |
| 1960§ | 18–39 | 3.2 | 3.4 | 3.6 | 3.2 | 3.3 | 3.5 | 3.4 | 3.4 | 1728 |
| 1963 | 21+ | 3.2 | 3.4 | 3.5 | 3.3 | 3.3 | 3.5 | 3.5 | 3.4 | 483 |
| 1966 | 21+ | 3.1 | 3.3 | 3.7 | 3.2 | 3.2 | 3.4 | 3.7 | 3.3 | 374 |
| 1967 | 21+ | 3.1 | 3.3 | 3.4 | 3.3 | 3.2 | 3.1 | 3.4 | 3.3 | 488 |
| 1968 | 21+ | 3.2 | 3.3 | 3.7 | 3.2 | 3.0 | 3.4 | 3.6 | 3.3 | 539 |

* Level of education is measured by the highest grade completed.   † Levels 1 to 4 for economic range in order from "high" to "low."   ‡ Minimum ideal (results from coding range answers to the lowest figure).   § Maximum ideal (results from coding range answers to the highest figure).

results of these polls and surveys are given elsewhere *(15)* and are only briefly summarized here. Table 2 gives mean values for the family size considered ideal by white, non-Catholic women, according to education and economic status.

The data lend little support to the hypothesis that the poor desire families as small as those desired by the middle and upper classes. Within both the educational and the economic categories, those on the lower rungs not only have larger families than those on

## TABLE 3

Percentages of white U.S. men and women between the ages of 21 and 44 who, in various national polls taken between 1943 and 1964, expressed the opinion that birth-control information should be made available to individuals who desired it. The percentages are given by level of education*; the numbers in parentheses are total numbers of respondents in each category.

| Year | Men | | | Women | | |
|------|---------|----------------|-----------------|---------|----------------|-----------------|
| | College | High school | Grade school | College | High school | Grade school |
| 1943 | 75 (184) | 68 (284) | 56 (157) | 82 (216) | 74 (442) | 60 (207) |
| 1945 | 74 (202) | 62 (360) | 58 (140) | 83 (216) | 68 (434) | 56 (207) |
| 1947 | 91 (84) | 72 (199) | 67 (66) | 81 (89) | 74 (228) | 72 (81) |
| 1959 | 88 (89) | 76 (163) | 65 (49) | 91 (55) | 79 (279) | 68 (41) |
| 1961 | 88 (102) | 81 (188) | 67 (46) | 84 (81) | 81 (265) | 78 (50) |
| 1962 | 91 (93) | 85 (171) | 61 (23) | 84 (79) | 82 (258) | 66 (44) |
| 1963 | 86 (105) | 79 (178) | 53 (40) | 81 (80) | 78 (251) | 81 (42) |
| 1964 | 92 (107) | 88 (188) | 83 (29) | 94 (79) | 86 (293) | 74 (38) |

* The level of education is measured by the last grade completed.

the higher rungs (at least in the case of non-Catholics) but say they want larger families and consider them ideal. This differential has existed for as long as information on preferred family size in this country has been available, and it persists. It thus seems extremely hazardous to base a major governmental effort on the notion that, among individuals (white individuals, at least) at the lower social levels, there is a widespread and deeply held desire for families as small as, or smaller than, those desired by the well-to-do. No major survey shows this to be the case.

Not only do persons of lower socioeconomic status prefer larger families than the more affluent do, they also generally favor birth control less. Tables 3 and 4 show the percentages of white men and women who expressed approval of birth control in surveys made between 1937 and 1964, by educational level and economic status, respectively.

Looking at the educational differential (Table 3), one finds that, in general, the proportion of those who approve birth control drops precipitately between the college and grade school levels. As far back as the early 1940's, over 80 per cent of women and 75 per cent of men with some or more college education approved government action on birth control. By 1964, over 90 per cent of both sexes approved. By contrast, only 60 per cent of men and women with an elementary school education approved in the 1940's, and, despite a rise in approval, there is still a differential. When non-Catholics alone are considered, the educational difference is even more pronounced in many cases.

Turning to economic or income status (Table 4), one generally finds the same results. The high proportions (close to 100 per cent) of women in the highest and next-to-highest economic brackets who, in recent years, have approved birth-control efforts is noteworthy, as is the fact that approximately 80 per cent of women in these brackets approved such efforts as far back as the 1930's. On the other

## TABLE 4

Percentages of white U.S. men and women between the ages of 21 and 44 who, in various national polls taken between 1937 and 1964, expressed the opinion that birth-control information should be made available to individuals who desired it. The percentages are given by economic status (levels 1–4*); the numbers in parentheses are total numbers of respondents in each category.

| Year | Men | | | | Women | | | |
|------|-----|-----|-----|-----|-------|-----|-----|-----|
|      | 1   | 2   | 3   | 4   | 1     | 2   | 3   | 4   |
| 1937 | 78 (112) | 70 (406) | 61 (520) |          | 67 (69)  | 78 (293) | 64 (372) |          |
| 1938 | 65 (125) | 74 (453) | 62 (521) |          | 80 (51)  | 73 (232) | 70 (259) |          |
| 1939 | 78 (116) | 75 (432) | 73 (553) |          | 71 (68)  | 77 (260) | 71 (302) |          |
| 1940 | 79 (131) | 75 (443) | 68 (553) |          | 80 (49)  | 78 (258) | 71 (311) |          |
| 1943 | 76 (80)  | 72 (219) | 62 (330) |          | 80 (90)  | 79 (272) | 68 (500) |          |
| 1945 | 73 (67)  | 66 (286) | 62 (352) |          | 83 (75)  | 77 (264) | 64 (531) |          |
| 1947 | 86 (42)  | 77 (123) | 72 (188) |          | 92 (38)  | 71 (119) | 73 (237) |          |
| 1959 | 83 (101) | 76 (120) | 73 (79)  |          | 83 (139) | 82 (152) | 72 (95)  |          |
| 1961 | 93 (42)  | 85 (80)  | 87 (103) | 69 (111) | 88 (41)  | 80 (97)  | 80 (76)  | 81 (138) |
| 1962 | 82 (45)  | 89 (71)  | 86 (94)  | 80 (74)  | 82 (51)  | 80 (75)  | 84 (110) | 77 (140) |
| 1963 | 88 (60)  | 84 (79)  | 76 (96)  | 61 (97)  | 87 (67)  | 79 (107) | 79 (98)  | 75 (100) |
| 1964 | 90 (67)  | 87 (26)  | 93 (82)  | 85 (79)  | 96 (90)  | 90 (87)  | 85 (104) | 78 (120) |

* Levels 1 to 4 for the years 1961–64 range from income of $10,000 and over down to incomes under $5000. Prior to 1961, levels 1 to 3 represent "upper," "middle," and "lower" income brackets.

hand, men and women in lower income brackets have been slower to approve birth-control policies.

Despite the inverse relationship just described, I may have overemphasized the lesser approval of birth-control programs on the part of persons of lower economic and social status. After all, in recent years approval often has been high even among people at the lowest social levels. Among women with only a grade school education, the percentage of those favoring birth-control programs averaged 73 per cent in polls taken between 1959 and 1964; among men at the lowest educational level, the corresponding average was 66 per cent. Yet it is undeniably true that, throughout the period for which data are available, the people who needed birth-control information most, according to recent policy pronouncements, have been precisely the ones who were least in favor of a policy that would make it widely available.

The truth of this conclusion becomes more evident when we move to an analysis of a question asked on the 1966 Gallup poll: Do you think birth-control pills should be made available free to all women on relief

who are of childbearing age? This question presents the public with the specific issue that is the focus of current policy—namely, birth control especially for the poor. A summary of the replies to this question is given in Table 5, together with average percentages of people who, in the five surveys made between 1959 and 1964, replied that they approved birth control generally.

It is clear that the overall level of approval drops when specific reference to a poverty-oriented birth-control policy is introduced. The decline is from an average of approximately 80 per cent for each sex during the period 1959-64 to 65 per cent for men and 71 per cent for women in 1966. Of most significance, however, is the fact that the largest proportionate drop in approval occurs among members of the "target" groups themselves—the poor and uneducated. In particular, there is a remarkable drop in approval among men at this socioeconomic level. There is a 42-per cent decline in approval among men who have had only a grade school education and a 29-per cent drop among those with a high school education. Among the college-educated men the drop in approval is only

**TABLE 5**

Percentages of white U.S. men and women between the ages of 21 and 44 who, in a 1966 poll, expressed approval of free distribution of birth-control pills for women on relief, and average percentages of individuals in this age group who, in polls taken between 1959 and 1964, expressed approval of birth control. Percentages approving and numbers of individuals interviewed are given as totals and also by education and economic status of the respondents.

| | Men | | | | Women | | |
|---|---|---|---|---|---|---|---|
| | 1966 | | 1959–64 | | 1966 | | 1959–64 |
| Item | % | N | (av. %) | | % | N | (av. %) |
| Total | 65 | 264 | 82 | | 71 | 385 | 81 |
| Education | | | | | | | |
| College | 82 | 98 | 87 | | 75 | 197 | 87 |
| High school | 58 | 142 | 82 | | 70 | 392 | 81 |
| Grade school | 38 | 24 | 66 | | 59 | 32 | 73 |
| Economic status | | | | | | | |
| 1 | 79 | 80 | 89 | | 70 | 110 | 87 |
| 2 | 69 | 75 | 84 | | 76 | 99 | 82 |
| 3 | 59 | 65 | 83 | | 70 | 91 | 80 |
| 4 | 39 | 41 | 74 | | 67 | 76 | 78 |

6 per cent. The results, by income, parallel those by education: there is a 47-per cent drop for men in the lowest income group but only a 9-per cent drop for those in the highest income bracket. Even if the tabulations are restricted to non-Catholics (data that are not presented here), the results are essentially the same.

If the ghetto-oriented birth-control policy urged on the federal government meets with limited public enthusiasm, how does the public view extension of that policy to teen-age girls? This question is of some importance because a notable aspect of the pressure for government-sponsored family-planning programs is advocacy of making birth-control information and material available at the high school level.

The Committee on Population of the National Academy of Sciences urges early education in "family planning" in order to prevent illegitimacy (2, p. 13).

... government statistics show that the mothers of approximately 41 per cent of the 245,000 babies born illegitimately in the United States every year are women 19 years of age or younger. Thus a large proportion of all illegitimate children are progeny of teen-age mothers. To reduce the number of such children born to teen-age mothers, high-school education in family planning is essential.

Katherine B. Oettinger, Deputy Secretary for Family Planning of the Department of Health, Education, and Welfare, importunes us not to "demand the eligibility card of a first pregnancy before we admit vulnerable girls to family planning services" *(16)*. The Harkavy report states (3, p. 29):

Eligibility requirements should be liberal with respect to marital status. Such services should be made available to the unmarried as well as the married. . . . Eligibility requirements should be liberal with respect to the age of unmarried women seeking help. This will undoubtedly pose some problems, but they may not be insurmountable. Some publically supported programs are already facing them (for example, in Baltimore).

Representative Scheuer from New York has berated the federal government for not "bringing family planning into the schools." He has cited the "desperate need for family planning by unmarried 14-, 15-, and 16-year-old girls in school [which] is so transparently evident that it almost boggles the imagination to realize that nothing has been done. Virtually no leadership has come from the federal government" (9, p. 18).

Obviously there is little recognition in these statements that such a policy might engender a negative public response. Yet such a possibility cannot be discounted. The results of the 1966 question "Do you think they [the pills] should be made available to teen-age girls?" suggest that a policy of pill distribution to female adolescents may be viewed by the public as involving more complex issues than the mere democratization of "medical" services. These results, tabulated by social level, are shown in Table 6.

It may be seen that, in general, a proposal for distribution of pills to teen-age girls meets with very little approval. There is more disapproval among women than among men. Even among women under the age of 30, only 17 per cent approve; among men in this age group, 29 per cent approve. At no age does feminine approval reach 20 per cent, and in most cases it is below 15 per cent. Furthermore, restriction of the results to non-Catholics does not raise the percentages of those who approve the policy. Most noteworthy is the socioeconomic gradient among men. Whereas 32 per cent of college-educated men approve distribution of pills to young girls, only 13 percent of men with a grade school education do. Thirty-three per cent of men in the highest income bracket approve, but only 13 per cent in the lowest bracket do.

Clearly, the extension of "family planning" to poor, unmarried teen-agers is not regarded simply as "health care." Individuals may approve, in a general way, a wider availability of birth-control information without approving federal expenditure to facilitate a high level of sexual activity by teen-age girls. One suspects that explicit recognition and im-

**TABLE 6**

Percentages of white U.S. men and women who, in a 1966 poll, expressed approval of making birth-control pills available to teen-age girls. Percentages approving and numbers of individuals interviewed are given by age groups, by education, and by economic status.

| Item | All religions | | | | Non-Catholics | | | |
|---|---|---|---|---|---|---|---|---|
| | Men | | Women | | Men | | Women | |
| | % | N | % | N | % | N | % | N |
| Age | | | | | | | | |
| Under 30 | 29 | 86 | 17 | 149 | 34 | 65 | 19 | 102 |
| 30–44 | 19 | 172 | 8 | 238 | 20 | 133 | 7 | 169 |
| Education | | | | | | | | |
| College | 32 | 98 | 15 | 100 | 36 | 75 | 13 | 71 |
| High school | 18 | 142 | 9 | 264 | 19 | 110 | 9 | 180 |
| Grade school | 13 | 24 | 11 | 35 | 6 | 17 | 14 | 28 |
| Economic status | | | | | | | | |
| 1 | 33 | 80 | 11 | 113 | 35 | 58 | 11 | 75 |
| 2 | 20 | 75 | 13 | 105 | 24 | 58 | 14 | 72 |
| 3 | 19 | 65 | 7 | 94 | 18 | 50 | 5 | 64 |
| 4 | 13 | 41 | 16 | 82 | 15 | 33 | 14 | 66 |

plied approval of such activity still comes hard to our population, and that it comes hardest to the group most involved in the problems of illegitimacy and premarital conception—namely, the poor and uneducated themselves. The extreme disapproval of a policy of pill distribution to teen-age girls that is found in lower-class groups (particularly among lower-class men) suggests that a double standard of sexual behavior is operative in these groups—a standard that does not allow open toleration of the idea that the ordinary teen-age girl requires the pill, or that a part of her junior high school and high school education should include instruction in its use.

## CAN "FIVE MILLION WOMEN" BE WRONG?

The most widely publicized argument favoring federal birth-control programs, and apparently the one that elected officials find most persuasive, is the claim that there are approximately "five million" poor women "in need" of publicly subsidized birth-control help (17). I list below some of the principal assumptions upon which this estimate is based—all of which introduce serious upward biases into the evidence.

1. It is claimed that women at the poverty and near-poverty levels desire families of 3.0 children. While this may be true of nonwhite wives at this economic level, it is not true, as we have seen, of white women, who comprise a major share of the "target" group and who, on the average, desire a number of children closer to 4 (especially if Catholics are included, as they are in the "five million").

2. It is assumed by the estimators that 82 percent of all poor women aged 15 to 44 are at risk of conception (that is, exposed sexually), in spite of the fact that only 45 per cent of poor women in this age group are married and living with their husbands. In arriving at the figure of 82 per cent, the estimators assumed that all women in the "married" category (including those who were separated from their husbands and those whose husbands were absent) were sexually exposed regularly, and that half of the women in the "non-married" category—that is, single, widowed, and divorced women—were exposed regularly. Information is scarce concerning the sexual behavior of widows and divorced women, but Kinsey's data on premarital coitus

leads one to believe that the assumption of 50 per cent for single women may be high. Among the women with a grade school education in Kinsey's sample, 38 per cent had had coitus at some time between the ages of 16 and 20, and 26 per cent, at some time between the ages of 21 and 25. Moreover, as Kinsey emphasizes, these encounters were characteristically sporadic *(18)*.

3. The proportion of sterile women among the poor is assumed to be 13 per cent, although the Scripps 1960 "Growth of American Families Study" showed the proportion among white women of grade school education to be 22 percent *(14, p. 159)*.

4. No allowance is made for less-than-normal fecundity, although the Scripps 1960 study *(14, p. 159)* had indicated that, among women of grade school education, an additional 10 per cent (over and above the 22 per cent) were subnormal in their ability to reproduce.

5. It is taken for granted by the estimators that no Catholic women would object, on religious grounds, to the use of modern methods, and no allowance is made for objection by non-Catholics, on religious or other grounds. In other words, it is assumed that all women "want" the service. Yet, in response to a question concerning the desirability of limiting or spacing pregnancies, 29 per cent of the wives with grade school education who were interviewed in the Scripps 1960 study said they were "against" such limitation or spacing *(14, p. 177)*. Among the Catholic wives with grade school education, the proportion "against" was 48 per cent, although half of these objectors were "for" the rhythm method. Similar objections among the disadvantaged have been revealed by many polls over a long period.

6. Perhaps most important, the estimate of 5 million women "wanting" and "in need of" birth-control information includes not only objectors but women who are already practicing birth control. Hence, in addition to all the other biases, the estimate represents a blanket decision by the estimators that the women require medical attention regarding birth con-trol—particularly that they need the pill and the coil. In the words of the Harkavy report *(2, attachment A, p. 19)*:

This may be considered a high estimate of the number of women who need to have family planning services made available to them in public clinics, because some of the couples among the poor and near poor are able to exercise satisfactory control over their fertility. However, even these couples do not have the same access as the non-poor to the more effective and acceptable methods of contraception, particularly the pill and the loop. So, simply in order to equalize the access of the poor and the near-poor to modern methods of contraception under medical supervision, it is appropriate to try to make contraceptive services available to all who may need and want them.

Yet the 1960 Scripps study found that, among fecund women of grade school education, 79 per cent used contraceptives *(14, p. 159)*. The 21 per cent who did not included young women who were building families and said they wanted to get pregnant, as well as Catholics who objected to birth control on religious grounds. As for the methods that women currently are using, it seems gratuitous for the federal government to decide that only medically supervised methods—the pill and the coil—are suitable for lower-income couples, and that a mammoth "service" program is therefore required. In fact, the implications of such a decision border on the fantastic— the implications that we should substitute scarce medical and paramedical attention for all contraceptive methods now being used by poor couples.

In sum, the argument supporting a "need" for nationwide, publicly sustained birth-control programs does not stand up under empirical scrutiny. Most fecund lower-class couples now use birth-control methods when they want to prevent pregnancy; in the case of those who do not, the blame cannot simply be laid at the door of the affluent who have kept the subject of birth control under wraps, or of a government that has withheld services. As we have seen, opinion on birth control has been, and is, less favorable among the poor and the less well educated than among the well-to-do. In addition, the poor desire larger families. Although it may be argued that, at the public welfare level, birth control has, until recently, been taboo because of the "Catholic vote," most individuals at all social levels have learned about birth control *informally* and without medical attention. Furthermore, the most popular birth-control device, the condom, has long been as available as aspirin or cigarettes, and certainly has been used by men of all social classes. When one bears in mind the fact that the poor have no difficulty in gaining access to illegal narcotics (despite their obvious "unavailability"), and that the affluent had drastically reduced their fertility before present-day contraceptive methods were available, one must recognize and take into account a motivational component in nonuse and inefficient use of contraceptives. Indeed, were relative lack of demand on the part of the poor not a principal factor, it would be difficult to explain why such an important "market" for birth-control materials—legal or illegal—would have escaped the attention of enterprising businessmen or bootleggers. In any event, any estimate based on the assumption that all poor women in the reproductive group "want" birth-control information and materials and that virtually all "need" publicly supported services that will provide them—including women with impaired fecundity, women who have sexual intercourse rarely or not at all, women who object on religious grounds, and women who are already using birth-control methods—would seem to be seriously misleading as a guide for our government in its efforts to control population growth.

Moreover, the proposal for government sponsorship takes no account of the possible advantages of alternative means of reaching that part of the "market" that may not be optimally served at present. For example, competitive pricing, better marketing, and a program of advertising could make it possible for many groups in the population who are now being counted as "targets" for government efforts to purchase contraceptives of various

kinds. When one bears in mind the fact that an important reason for nonuse or lack of access to contraceptives may be some sort of conflict situation (between husband and wife, adolescent child and parent, and so on), it becomes apparent that the impersonal and responsive marketplace is a far better agency for effecting smooth social change than is a far-flung national bureaucracy loaded with well-meaning but often blundering "health workers." The government could doubtless play an initial stimulating and facilitating role in relation to private industry, without duplicating, on a welfare basis, functions that might be more efficiently handled in the marketplace.

## WOULD THE POLICY HAVE SIDE EFFECTS?

The possible inadvisability of having the government become a direct purveyor of birth-control materials to poverty groups becomes more clear when we consider some of the risks involved in such a course of action.

Even if the goal of reducing family size were completely and widely accepted by the poorer and less well educated sectors of the population, we should not assume that the general public would necessarily view a policy concerned with the means and practice of birth control (in any social group) as it views ordinary medical care—that is, as being morally neutral and obviously "desirable." Birth control is related to sexual behavior, and, in all viable societies, sexual behavior is regulated by social institutions. It is thus an oversimplification to think that people will be unmindful of what are, for them at least, the moral implications of changes in the conditions under which sexual intercourse is possible, permissible, or likely. An issue such as distribution of pills to teen-age girls runs a collision course with norms about premarital relations for young girls—norms that, in turn, relate to the saliency of marriage and motherhood as a woman's principal career and to the consequent need for socially created restrictions on free sexual access if an important inducement to marriage is not to be lost. Only if viable careers alternative to marriage existed for women would the lessening of controls over sexual behavior outside of marriage be unrelated to women's lifetime opportunities, for such opportunities would be independent of the marriage market and, a fortiori, independent of sexual bargaining. But such independence clearly does not exist. Hence, when the government is told that it will be resolving a "medical" problem if it makes birth-control pills available to teen-agers, it is being misled into becoming the protagonist in a sociologically based conflict between short-run feminine impulses and long-run feminine interests —a conflict that is expressed both in relations between parents and children and in relations between the sexes. This sociological conflict far transcends the "medical" issue of whether or not birth-control services should be made widely available.

Actually, the issue of sexual morality is only one among many potentially explosive aspects of direct federal involvement in family-planning programs for the poor. Others come readily to mind, such as the possibility that the pill and other physiological methods could have long-run, serious side effects, or that racial organizations could seize on the existence of these programs as a prime example of "genocide." Eager promoters of the suggested programs tend to brush such problems aside as trivial, but the problems, like the issue of sexual morality, cannot be wished away, for they are quite patently there (9, p. 62). There *are* risks involved in all drug-taking, and it is recognized that many of the specific ones involved in long-term ingestion of the pill may not be discovered for many years. No one today can say that these are less than, equal to, or greater than the normal risks of pregnancy and childbirth. Equally, a class-directed birth-control program, whatever its intent, is open to charges of genocide that are difficult to refute. Such a program cannot fail to appear to single out the disadvantaged as the "goat," all the while implying that the very considerable "planned" fertility of most Amer-

icans inexplicably requires no government attention at all.

## POPULATION POLICY FOR AMERICANS

It seems clear that the suggested policy of poverty-oriented birth-control programs does not make sense as a welfare measure. It is also true that, as an inhibitor of population growth, it is inconsequential and trivial. It does not touch the principal cause of such growth in the United States—namely, the reproductive behavior of the majority of Americans who, under present conditions, want families of more than three children and thereby generate a growth rate far in excess of that required for population stability. Indeed, for most Americans the "family planning" approach, concentrating as it does on the distribution of contraceptive materials and services, is irrelevant, because they already know about efficient contraception and are already "planning" their families. It is thus apparent that any policy designed to influence reproductive behavior must not only concern itself with all fecund Americans (rather than just the poor) but must, as well, relate to family-size goals (rather than just to contraceptive means). In addition, such a policy cannot be limited to matters affecting contraception (or even to matters affecting gestation and parturition, such as abortion), but must, additionally, take into account influences on the formation and dissolution of heterosexual unions (19).

What kinds of reproductive policies can be pursued in an effort to reduce long-term population growth? The most important step toward developing such new policies is to recognize and understand the existing ones, for we already have influential and coercive policies regarding reproductive behavior. Furthermore, these existing policies relate not merely to proscriptions (legal or informal) regarding certain means of birth control (like abortion) but also to a definition of reproduction as a primary societal end and to an organization of social roles that draws most of the population into reproductive unions.

The existence of such pronatalist policies becomes apparent when we recall that, among human beings, population replacement would not occur at all were it not for the complex social organization and system of incentives that encourage mating, pregnancy, and the care, support, and rearing of children. These institutional mechanisms are the pronatalist "policies" evolved unconsciously over millenia to give societies a fertility sufficient to offset high mortality. The formation and implementation of antinatalist policies must be based, therefore, on an analysis and modification of the existing pronatalist policies. It follows, as well, that antinatalist policies will not necessarily involve the introduction of coercive measures. In fact, just the opposite is the case. Many of these new policies will entail a *lifting* of pressures *to* reproduce, rather than an *imposition* of pressures *not* to do so. In order to understand this point let us consider briefly our present-day pronatalism.

It is convenient to start with the family, because pronatalism finds its most obvious expression in this social institution. The pronatalism of the family has many manifestations, but among the most influential and universal are two: the standardization of both the male and the female sexual roles in terms of reproductive functions, obligations, and activities, and the standardization of the occupational role of women—half of the population—in terms of child-bearing, child-rearing, and complementary activities. These two "policies" insure that just about everyone will be propelled into reproductive unions, and that half of the population will enter such unions as a "career"—a life's work. Each of the two "policies" is worth considering.

With regard to sex roles, it is generally recognized that potential human variability is greater than is normally permitted *within* each sex category. Existing societies have tended to suppress and extinguish such variability and to standardize sexual roles in ways that imply that all "normal" persons will attain the status of parents. This coercion takes many forms, including one-sided indoctrination in schools, legal barriers and penalties for deviation, and the threats of loneliness, ostracism, and ridicule that are implied in the unavailability of alternatives. Individuals who—by temperament, health, or constitution—do not fit the ideal sex-role pattern are nonetheless coerced into attempting to achieve it, and many of them do achieve it, at least to the extent of having demographic impact by becoming parents.

Therefore, a policy that sought out the ways in which coercion regarding sex roles is at present manifesting itself could find numerous avenues for relieving the coercion and for allowing life styles different from marriage and parenthood to find free and legitimized expression. Such a policy would have an effect on the content of expectations regarding sex roles as presented and enforced in schools, on laws concerning sexual activity between consenting adults, on taxation with respect to marital status and number of children, on residential building policies, and on just about every facet of existence that is now organized so as exclusively to favor and reward a pattern of sex roles based on marriage and parenthood.

As for the occupational roles of women, existing pressures still attempt to make the reproductive and occupational roles coterminus for all women who elect to marry and have children. This rigid structuring of the wife-mother position builds into the entire motivational pattern of women's lives a tendency to want at least a moderate-size family. To understand this point one must recognize that the desired number of children relates not simply to the wish for a family of a particular size but relates as well to a need for more than one or two children if one is going to enjoy "family life" over a significant portion of one's lifetime. This need is increased rather than lessened by improved life expectancy. Insofar as women focus their energies and emotions on their families, one cannot expect that they will be satisfied to play their only important role for a diminishing fraction of their lives, or that they will readily regard make-work and dead-end jobs as a substitute for "mothering." The notion that most women will "see the error of their ways" and decide to have two-child families is naive, since few healthy and energetic women will be so misguided as to deprive themselves of most of the rewards society has to offer them and choose a situation that allows them neither a life's work outside the home nor one within it. Those who do deprive themselves in this fashion are, in effect, taking the brunt of the still existing maladjustment between the roles of women and the reproductive needs of society. In a society oriented around achievement and accomplishment, such women are exceptionally vulnerable to depression, frustration, and a sense of futility, because they are being blocked from a sense of fulfillment both at home and abroad.

In sum, the problem of inhibiting population growth in the United States cannot be dealt with in terms of "family-planning needs" because this country is well beyond the point of "needing" birth control methods. Indeed, even the poor seem not to be a last outpost for family-planning attention. If we wish to limit our growth, such a desire implies basic changes in the social organization of reproduction that will make nonmarriage, childlessness, and small (two-child) families far more prevalent than they are now. A new policy, to achieve such ends, can take advantage of the antinatalist tendencies that our present institutions have suppressed. This will involve the listing of penalties for antinatalist behavior rather than the "creation" of new ways of life. This behavior already exists among us as part of our covert and deviant culture, on the one hand, and our elite and artistic culture, on the other. Such antinatalist tendencies have also found expression in feminism, which has been stifled in the United States by means of systematic legal, educational, and social pressures concerned with women's "obligations" to create and care for children. A fertility-control policy that does not take into account the need to alter the present structure of reproduction in these and other ways merely trivializes the problem of population control and

misleads those who have the power to guide our country toward completing the vital revolution.

## REFERENCES AND NOTES

1. *Hearings on S. 1676, U. S. Senate Subcommittee on Foreign Aid Expenditures* (the 1965 and 1966 Hearings each comprise seven volumes; the 1967–1968 Hearings, to date, comprise three volumes) (Government Printing Office, Washington, D.C.).
2. "The Growth of U.S. Population." *Nat. Acad. Sci.-Nat. Res. Council Pub. 1279* (1965).
3. O. Harkavy, F. S. Jaffe, S. S. Wishik. "Implementing DHEW Policy on Family Planning and Population" (mimeographed, 1967; available from the Ford Foundation, New York).
4. "Report of the President's Committee on Population and Family Planning: The Transition from Concern to Action" (Government Printing Office, Washington, D.C., 1968).
5. K. Davis, *Science* **158**, 730 (1967); J. Blake, in *Public Health and Population Change*, M. C. Sheps and J. C. Ridley, Eds. (Univ. of Pittsburgh Press, Pittsburgh, Pa., 1965).
6. In the words of the Committee on Population, "The freedom to limit family size to the number of children wanted when they are wanted is, in our view, a basic human right ... most Americans of higher income and better education exercise this right as a matter of course, but ... many of the poor and uneducated are in fact deprived of the right."
7. W. J. Cohen, *Family Planning: One Aspect of Freedom to Choose* (Government Printing Office, Washington, D.C., 1966), p. 2. Cohen, former Secretary of Health, Education, and Welfare, says: "Until a few years ago, family planning and population problems were considered "hush-hush" subjects. Public discussion was curtailed not only in polite society, but in the legislative and executive branches of the government as well."
8. *Hearings on S. 2993, U.S. Senate Subcommittee on Employment, Manpower, and Poverty, 89th Congress, Second Session, May 10* (Government Printing Office, Washington, D.C., 1966), p. 31.
9. *Hearings on S. 1676, U.S. Senate Subcommittee on Foreign Aid Expenditures, 90th Congress, First Session, November 2* (Government Printing Office, Washington, D.C., 1967), pt. 1.
10. Senator Tydings (D–Md.) said at the Hearings on S. 1676 (see 9): "As recently as 3 or 4 years ago, the idea that Federal, State or local governments should make available family planning information and services to families who could not otherwise afford them was extremely controversial. But in a brief period of time there has been a substantial shift of opinion among the moral leadership of our country, brought about in large measure by the vigorous efforts of the distinguished Senator from Alaska, Ernest Gruening, the chairman of this subcommittee."
11. E. Gruening, "What the Federal Government is

now Doing in the Field of Population Control and What is Needed," speech presented before the U.S. Senate, 3 May 1967.

12. J. M. Stycos, in *World Population and U.S. Government Policy and Programs*, F. T. Brayer, Ed. (Georgetown Univ. Press, Washington, D.C., 1968).
13. R. Freedman, P. K. Whelpton, A. A. Campbell, *Family Planning, Sterility and Population Growth* (McGraw-Hill, New York, 1959).
14. P. K. Whelpton, A. A. Campbell, J. E. Patterson, *Fertility and Family Planning in the United States* (Princeton Univ. Press, Princeton, N.J., 1966).
15. J. Blake, *Demography* **3**, 154 (1966); *Population Studies* **20**, 27 (1966); *ibid.* **21**, 159 (1967); *ibid.*, p. 185; *ibid.* **22**, 5 (1968).
16. *Family Planner* **2**, 3 (1968).
17. The estimate (by Arthur A. Campbell) under discussion here may be found in the Harkavy report (see *3*, attachment A, pp. 4–19). Another estimate has been circulated by the Planned Parenthood Federation in a brochure entitled *Five Million Women* (Planned Parenthood, New York).
18. A. C. Kinsey, W. B. Pomeroy, C. E. Martin, P. B. Gebhard, *Sexual Behavior in the Human Female* (Saunders, Philadelphia, 1953), pp. 291 and 337.
19. K. Davis and J. Blake, *Econ. Develop. Cult. Change* **4**, 211 (1956).
20. I make grateful acknowledgment to the Ford Foundation for support of the research presented in this article and to the National Institutes of Health (general research support grant 1501-TR-544104) for assistance to Statistical Services, School of Public Health, University of California, Berkeley. I am also indebted to Kingsley Davis, whose critical comments and helpful suggestions have greatly advanced my thinking. The Roper Center and the Gallup Poll kindly supplied me with polling data.

# Beyond Family Planning

BERNARD BERELSON

This article rests on four propositions: (i) among the great problems on the world agenda is the population problem; (ii) that problem is most urgent in the developing countries, where rapid population growth retards social and economic development; (iii) there is a time penalty on the problem in the sense that, other things being equal, anything not done sooner may be harder to do later, due to increased numbers; and accordingly (iv) everything that can properly be done to lower population growth rates should be done, now. The question is, what is to be done? There is a certain agreement on the general objective (that is, on the desirability of lowering birth rates, though not on how far and how fast), but there is disagreement as to means.

The first response to too high growth rates deriving from too high birth rates is to introduce voluntary contraception on a mass basis, or try to. Why is family planning the first step taken on the road to population control? Probably because, from a broad political standpoint, it is the most acceptable one; since it is closely tied to maternal and child care it can be perceived as a health measure beyond dispute, and since it is voluntary it can be justified as a contribution to the effective personal freedom of individual couples. On both scores, it ties into accepted values and thus achieves political viability. Moreover, it is a gradual effort and an inexpensive one, both of which features contribute to its political acceptability.

How effective have family-planning programs been as a means toward population

Beyond Family Planning. From *Science*, Vol. 163, February 7, 1969, pp. 533–534. Copyright 1969 by the American Association for the Advancement of Science. Reprinted by permission of the author and the publisher.

control? There is currently some controversy among qualified observers as to its efficacy (*1*), and this is not the place to review that issue. There is agreement, however, that the problem is of such magnitude and consequence that additional efforts are needed to reach a "solution," however that is responsibly defined.

For the purpose of this article, then, let us assume that today's national family-planning programs, mainly based on voluntary contraception, are not "enough"—where "enough" is defined not necessarily as achieving zero growth in some extended present but simply as lowering birth rates quickly and substantially. "Enough" begs the question of the ultimate goal and only asks that a faster decline in population growth rates be brought about than is presently being achieved or in prospect—and, within the range of the possible, the faster the better (*2, 3*). Just to indicate roughly the order of magnitude, let us say that the proximate goal is the halving of the birth rate in the developing countries in the next decade or two—from, say, over 40 births per thousand per year to 20 to 25 (*4*). For obvious reasons, both emigration and increased death rates are ruled out of consideration.

What is to be done to bring that reduction about, beyond present programs of voluntary family planning? I address that question in two ways: first, by listing the programs or policies more or less responsibly suggested in recent years for achieving this end; second, by reviewing the issues raised by the suggested approaches.

## PROPOSALS BEYOND FAMILY PLANNING

Here is a listing of the several proposals, arranged in descriptive categories. The list includes both proposals for consideration and proposals for action.

### A. Extensions of voluntary fertility control.

1. Institutionalization of maternal care in rural areas of developing countries: a feasibility study of what would be required in order to bring some degree of modern medical or paramedical attention to every pregnant woman in the rural areas of five developing countries, with professional backup for difficult cases and with family-planning education and services a central component of the program, aimed particularly at women of low parity (*5*).

2. Liberalization of induced abortion (*6; 7*, p. 139; *8*).

### B. Establishment of involuntary fertility control.

1. Mass use of a "fertility control agent" by the government to regulate births at an acceptable level. The "fertility control agent," designed to lower fertility in the society to a level 5 to 75 percent below the present birth rate, as needed, would be a substance now unknown but believed to be available for field testing after 5 to 15 years of research work. It would be included in the water supply in urban areas and administered by "other methods" elsewhere (*9*). A related suggestion is the "addition of temporary sterilants to water supplies or staple food" (*10*).

2. "Marketable licenses to have children," given to women and perhaps men in "whatever number would ensure a reproduction rate of one" (say, 2.2 children per couple). For example, "the unit certificate might be the 'deci-child,' and accumulation of ten of these units, by purchase, inheritance or gift, would permit a woman in maturity to have one legal child" (*11*).

3. Temporary sterilization of all girls by means of time-capsule contraceptives, and of girls and women after each delivery, with reversibility allowed only upon governmental approval. Certificates of approval would be distributed according to national popular vote on desired population growth, and saleable on the open market (*12*).

4. Compulsory sterilization of men with three or more living children (*13*); a requirement of induced abortion for all illegitimate pregnancies (*6*).

### C. Intensified educational campaigns.

1. Inclusion of educational materials on population in primary and secondary school systems (6, 14, 15).

2. Promotion of national satellite television systems for directly disseminating information on population and family planning and for indirectly promoting acceptance of modern attitudes and practices in general (7, p. 162; 16; 17, especially pp. 13–14; 18).

### D. Incentive programs.

As used here, the term *incentive programs* refers to payments, or their equivalent, made directly to couples who use contraceptives or to couples who do not have children for specified periods. It does *not* refer to payments to field workers, medical personnel, volunteers, and others, for securing acceptance of contraceptive practice.

1. Payment, or the equivalent (for example, the gift of a transistor radio), for accepting sterilization (6, 19–21) or for the effective practice of contraception (21–24).

2. A bonus for child spacing or nonpregnancy (25–28); a savings certificate to couples for each 12-month period in which no child is born (29); a lottery scheme for preventing illegitimate births among teenagers in a small country (30); "responsibility prizes" for each 5 years of childless marriage or for vasectomy before the birth of a third child, and special lotteries, with tickets available to the childless (7, p. 138).

### E. Tax and welfare benefits and penalties.

That is, a system of social services that would discourage childbearing rather than encourage it, as present systems tend to do.

1. Withdrawal of maternity benefits, perhaps after the birth of N (3?) children (6, 21, 26) or in cases where certain limiting conditions, such as adequate child spacing, knowledge of family planning, or attainment of a given level of income, have not been met (31, pp. 130–31).

2. Withdrawal of child or family allowances, perhaps after the birth of N children (6; 26; 31, pp. 131–36).

3. Levy of tax on births after the Nth child (21; 26; 28, p. 30).

4. Limitation of governmentally provided medical treatment, housing, scholarships, loans, subsidies, and so on, to families with fewer than N children (6, 26).

5. Reversal of tax benefits, to favor the unmarried and the parents of fewer rather than more children (6; 7, pp. 136–37; 21; 26; 31, p. 137; 32).

6. Provision by the state of N years of free schooling, at all levels, to each family, to be allocated among the children as desired (33).

7. Pensions for poor parents with fewer than N children, as social security for their old age (21, 34, 35).

### F. Shifts in social and economic institutions.

That is, broad changes in fundamental institutional arrangements that could have the effect of lowering fertility.

1. Raising the minimum age at marriage, through legislation or through imposition of a substantial fee for marriage licenses (6, 32); through direct payment of bonuses for delayed marriage (25); through payment of marriage benefits only to parents of brides over 21 years old (31, p. 130); through government loans for wedding ceremonies when the bride is over a given age, or with the interest rate inversely related to the bride's age (36); through a "governmental 'first marriage grant' . . . awarded each couple in which the age of both [sic] partners was 25 or more" (7, p. 138); or through establishment of a domestic "national service" program for all men for the appropriate 2-year period in order to develop social services, inculcate modern attitudes toward (among other matters) family planning and population control, and delay marriage (37).

2. Measures to promote or require the participation of women in the labor force (outside the home), in order to provide roles and interests for women that are alternative or supplementary to marriage (6, 32, 38).

3. "Direct manipulation of family structure itself—planned efforts at deflecting the family's socializing function . . . or introducing nonfamilial distractions . . . into people's lives," specifically through employment of women outside the house (39); "selective restructuring of the family in relation to the rest of society" (6).

4. Promotion of "two types of marriage, one of them childless and readily dissolved, and the other licensed for children and designed to be stable"; marriages of the first type would have to constitute 20 to 40 percent of the total in order to allow free choice of family size for marriages of the second type (16, 40).

5. Encouragement of long-range social trends leading toward lower fertility—for example, "improved and universal general education, or new roads facilitating communication, or improved agricultural methods, or a new industry that would increase productivity, or other types of innovation that may break the 'cake of custom' and produce social foment" (41); improvement in the status of women (42).

6. Efforts to lower death rates even further, particularly infant and child death rates, in the belief that lower birth rates will follow (43).

### G. Political channels and organizations.

1. U.S. insistence on "population control as the price of food aid," with highly selective assistance based thereon, and exertion of political pressures on governments or religious groups that impede "solution" of the population problem (7, pp. 161–66; 44).

2. Reorganization of national and international agencies to deal with the population problem: within the United States, "coordination by a powerful governmental agency, a Federal Department of Population and Environment . . . with the power to take whatever steps are necessary to establish a reasonable population size" (7, p. 138; 45); within India, creation of "a separate Ministry of Population Control" (46, p. 96); development of an "international specialized agency larger than WHO to operate programs for extending family limitation techniques to the world . . . charged with the responsibility of effecting the transfer to population equilibrium" (16).

3. Promotion of zero growth in population as the ultimate goal, and acceptance of this goal now in order to place intermediate goals of lowered fertility in proper context (6).

### H. Augmented research efforts.

1. More research on social means for achieving necessary fertility goals (6).

2. Focused research on practical methods of sex determination (47).

3. Increased research directed toward improvement of the contraceptive technology (48).

## PROPOSALS: REVIEW OF THE ISSUES

Here are 29 proposals beyond family planning for dealing with the problem of undue population growth in the developing world. Naturally I cannot claim that these are all the proposals that have been made more or less responsibly toward that end, but my guess is that there are not many more and that these proposals are a reasonably good sample of the total list.

Since several of the proposals tend in the same direction, it seems appropriate to review them against the criteria that any such proposals might be required to meet. What are such criteria? There are at least six: (i) scientific, medical, and technological readiness; (ii) political viability; (iii) administrative feasibility; (iv) economic capability; (v) moral, ethical, and philosophical acceptability; and (vi) presumed effectiveness. In other words, the key questions are: Is the scientific, medical, technological base available or likely? Will governments approve? Can the proposal be administered? Can the society afford the proposal? Is it morally acceptable? And, finally, will it work?

**Scientific, medical, technological readiness.** Two questions are involved: (i) is the needed technology available? and (ii) are the medical or paramedical personnel needed in order to assure medical administration and safety available or readily trainable?

With regard to temporary contraception, sterilization, and abortion, not only is the needed technology available now, but it is being steadily improved and expanded. The intrauterine device (IUD) and the oral pill have been major contraceptive developments of the past decade, and several promising leads are now being followed up (49), though it cannot be said with much confidence that any of the efforts will produce measures suitable for mass use within the next few years (50). Improved technologies for sterilization, both male and female, are being worked on, and there has been a recent development in abortion technique, the so-called suction device.

However, neither Ehrlich's "temporary sterilants" nor Ketchel's "fertility control agent" (B-1) is now available or on the technological horizon, though that does not mean that the research task ought not to be pursued against a subsequent need, especially since any such substance could be administered to individuals on a voluntary basis as well as to the population as a whole on an involuntary basis. In the latter case, if administered through the water supply or a similar source, the substance would have to be medically safe and free of side effects for men and women, young and old, well and ill, physiologically normal and physiologically marginal, as well as for animals and perhaps plants. As some people have remarked, the proposal that such a substance be added to a water supply would face far greater difficulties of acceptance, simply on medical grounds, than the far milder proposals with regard to fluoridation to prevent tooth decay.

Though a substantial technology in fertility control does exist, that does not necessarily mean that the techniques can be applied where they are most needed; this is true partly because of limitations in the number of trained personnel. In general, the more the technology requires the services of medical or paramedical personnel (or, what is much the same, is perceived as requiring them), the more difficult it is to administer in the developing countries. In the case of sterilization and abortion, the medical requirement becomes more severe. For example, when the policy of compulsory vasectomy of men with three or more children was first being considered in India (see 13), it was estimated that the policy would affect about 40 million males: "one thousand surgeons or parasurgeons each averaging 20 operations a day for five days a week would take eight years to cope with the existing candidates, and during this time of course a constant supply of new candidates would be coming along" (51)—at present birth rates, probably some 3.5 million a year. A program of large-scale abortion (provided such a program was legal and acceptable) might additionally require hospital beds, which are in particularly short supply in most developing countries. However, the newer abortion technique might not require hospitalization—theoretically, the abortion "camp" may be feasible, as the vasectomy "camp" was, though the problems are substantially greater.

In short, the technology is available for some but not for all current proposals, and the case is similar for properly trained personnel.

**Political viability.** The "population problem" has been increasingly recognized by national governments and international agencies over the past decade, and policies for dealing with it have been increasingly adopted: national family-planning programs in some 20 to 25 countries; positive resolutions and actions within the United Nations family; large programs of support by such developed countries as the United States and Sweden; the so-called World Leaders' Statement, in which 30 heads of governments endorsed efforts to limit population growth. There is no reason to think that the trend toward population limitation has run its course.

At the same time, the political picture is by no means unblemished. Some favorable policies are not strong enough to support a vigorous program, even one limited to family planning on health grounds; in national politics, "population control" can become a handy issue for a determined opposition; internal ethnic balances are sometimes delicately involved, with political ramifications; national size is often equated with national power, from the standpoint of international relations and regional military balances; the motives behind the support and encouragement of population control by the developed countries are sometimes perceived as neocolonialist or neoimperialist; and on the international front, as represented by the United Nations, there is still considerable reluctance based on both religious and political considerations. In short, ambivalence on the part of the elite and recognition of the issue as a political liability are not absent even in the countries that favor population limitation.

Any social policy adopted by government rests on some minimum consensus concerning goals and means. They need not be the ultimate goals or the final means; the socioeconomic plans of developing countries are typically 5-year plans, not 20- or 40- or 100-year plans. Indeed, the ultimate goal of population policy—that is, zero growth—need not be agreed upon or even considered by officials who *can* agree upon the immediate goal of lowering growth by a specified amount or by "as much as possible" within a period of years. And since there are always goals beyond goals, one does not even need to know what the ultimate goal is—only the direction in which it will be found (which is usually more readily agreed upon). Would insistence *now* on the acknowledgment of an *ultimate* goal of zero growth advance the effort or change its direction?

To start with, the proposal of compulsory controls in India in 1967 (B-4) precipitated "a storm of questions in Parliament" *(52)*; the

proposal was withdrawn, and the issue resulted in a high-level shift of personnel within the family-planning organization. No other country has seriously entertained the idea. Other considerations aside, in many countries political instability would make implementation virtually impossible.

Social measures designed to affect the birth rate indirectly—for example, tax benefits, social security arrangements, and so on—have been proposed from time to time. In India there have been several such proposals: for example, by the United Nations mission (53, chap. 11), by the Small Family Norm Committee (26), by the Central Family Planning Council (54), and in almost every issue of such publications as *Family Planning News, Centre Calling,* and *Planned Parenthood.*

As Samuel reports, with accompanying documentation (21), "the desirability of imposing a tax on births of fourth or higher order has been afloat for some time. However, time and again, the suggestion has been rejected by the Government of India." In some cases action has been taken either by the central government [for example, income tax "deductions for dependent children are given for the first and second child only" (53, p. 87)] or by certain states ["Maharashtra and Uttar Pradesh have decided to grant educational concessions and benefits only to those children whose parents restrict the size of their families" (55)]. Indicative of political sensitivity is the fact that an order withdrawing maternity leave for nonindustrial women employees with three or more living children—at best a tiny number of educated women—was revoked before it went into effect (56). There is a special political problem in many countries, in that economic constraints on fertility often turn out in practice to be selective on class, racial, or ethnic grounds, and thus exacerbate political tensions. Moreover, the promotion of female participtaion in the labor force runs up against the political problem that such employment would be competitive with men in situations of already high male unemployment and underemployment.

Whether programs for eliminating population growth are or are not politically accept-able appears to depend largely upon whether they are perceived as positive or negative; where "positive" means that they are seen as promoting not only population limitation but other social benefits as well, and where "neg-ative" means that they are seen as limited to population control. For example, family plan-ning programs, as noted above, are often ra-tionalized as contributing to both maternal and child health and to the effective freedom of the individual family; a pension for the elderly would have social welfare benefits as well as indirect impact upon family size, in countries where a large family has been the traditional "social security system"; contracep-tive programs in Latin America are promoted by the medical community as a medical and humanitarian answer not to the population problem but to the extensive illegal and dan-gerous practice of abortion. On the other hand, imposing tax liabilities or withdrawing benefits after the birth of the Nth child, not to mention involuntary measures, can be attacked as punitive means whose only purpose is that of limiting population.

It would thus require great political cour-age, joined to very firm demographic convic-tions, for a national leader to move toward an unpopular and severe prescription designed to cure his country's population ills. Indeed, it is difficult to envisage such a political move in an open society where a political opposition could present a counter view and perhaps prevail.

The governmental decisions about mea-sures to be taken to deal with undue popula-tion growth must be made mainly by the countries directly involved; after all, it is their people and their nation whose prospects are most centrally affected. But in an intercon-nected world, with peace and human welfare at issue, others are properly concerned, for reasons both of self-interest and of humani-tarianism—other governments from the devel-oped world, the international community, private groups. What of the political consider-ations in this connection?

A recommendation (G-1) that the United States exert strong political pressures to effect population control in developing countries seems more likely to generate political oppo-sition abroad than acceptance. It is conceivable that such measures might be adopted here, but it is hardly conceivable that they would be agreed to by the proposed recipients. Such a policy seems likely to boomerang against its own objective, quite aside from ethical or political considerations.

The proposal (G-2) to create an interna-tional superagency seems more likely of suc-cess, but is not without its difficulties. The World Health Organization, UNICEF, and UNESCO have moved some distance toward family planning, if not population control, but only slowly and in face of considerable polit-ical restraint on the international front (57). A new international agency would find the road easier only if its efforts were restricted to the convinced countries. Certainly the interna-tional organizations now concerned with this problem would not be expected to abdicate in favor of a new agency. If it could be brought into being and given a strong charter for ac-tion, then, almost by definition, the interna-tional political climate would be such as to favor action by the present agencies, and then efficiency and not political acceptability would be the issue.

**Administrative feasibility.**   Given techni-cal availability and political acceptability, what can actually be done? This is where several "good ideas" run into difficulties in the devel-oping world, in the translation of a theoretical idea into a practical program.

It is difficult to estimate the administrative feasibility of several of the proposals listed above, if for no other reason than that the proponents do not put forward the necessary organizational plans or details. How are "fer-tility control agents" or "sterilants" to be ad-ministered on an involuntary mass basis in the absence of a central water supply or a food-processing system? How are men with three or more children to be reliably identified in a peasant society and impelled to undergo ster-ilization against their will; and what is to be done if they decline, or if a fourth child is born? What is to be done with parents who evade the compulsory programs, or with the children born as a result of this evasion? How can an incentive system be honestly run in the absence of an organized network of offices positioned and staffed to carry out the regulatory activity? How can a system of social benefits and penalties, including incentives to postpone or forego marriage, be made to work in the absence of such a network?

These questions are meant only to suggest the kinds of difficulties that must be taken into account if proposals are to be translated into programs. It would seem desirable that every responsibly made proposal address itself to such administrative problems. Some proposals do move in that direction. The feasibility in administration, personnel, and costs of the plan (A-1) to institutionalize maternal care in rural areas, with family planning attached, is currently under study in several developing countries.

The plan (C-1) to include population as a subject in the school curriculum has been carried forward as far as the preparation of educational materials, and in a few cases beyond that (58). The plans for incentive programs sometimes come down to only the theoretical proposition that people will do anything for money (in this case refrain from having children), but in some cases the permissible payment is proposed on the basis of an economic analysis, and in a few cases an administrative means is also proposed (59). The plan for governmental wedding loans scaled to the bride's age recognizes that a birth-registration system might be needed to control against misreporting of age (6).

Thus the *why* of population control is easy, the *what* is not very hard, but the *how* is difficult. We may know that the extension of popular education or an increase in the number of women in the labor force or a later age at marriage would all contribute to population control in a significant way. But there remains the administrative question of how to bring those developments about. In short, several proposals assume workability of a com-plicated scheme in a country that cannot now collect its own vital statistics in a reliable manner. Moreover, there is a limit to how much administrative burden the typical developing country can carry: it cannot manage many large-scale developmental efforts at a time, either within the field of population or overall. After all, population is not the only effort; agriculture, industry, education, health, communications, the military—all are important claimants. And, within the field of population, a country that finds it difficult to organize and run a family-planning program will find that harder when other programs are added. So, difficult administrative choices must be made.

**Economic capability.** From the standpoint of economic capability there are two questions: (i) is the program worthwhile when measured against the criterion of economic return, and (ii) if worthwhile, can it be afforded from present budgets?

Most of the proposals probably pass the second screen. If a fertility-control agent suitable for mass administration becomes available and politically and administratively acceptable, such a program would probably not be prohibitively expensive; incorporation of population materials into the school curriculum is not unduly expensive; imposing of taxes or withdrawing of benefits or increasing fees for marriage licenses might even return a net gain after administrative cost.

But a few proposals are costly in absolute if not relative terms. For example, the institutionalization of maternal care (proposal A-1) might cost some $500 million for construction and $200 million for annual operation in India, or, respectively, $25 million and $10 million in a country with population of 25 million (5) (although recent estimates are substantially lower). The plan for a "youth corps" in India would cost upward of $450 million a year if the participants were paid only $50 annually. The plan for payment of pensions to elderly fathers without sons could cost from $400 million to $1 billion a year, plus administrative costs (35). The satellite television system for India would cost $50 million for capital costs only, on a restricted project (*17*, p. 23), with at least another $200 million needed for receiving sets, broadcast terminals, and programming costs if national coverage were to be secured. All of these proposals are intended to have beneficial consequences beyond population control and hence can be justified on multiple grounds, but they are still expensive in absolute amounts.

The broad social programs of popular education, improved methods of agriculture, and increased industrialization (F-5) already absorb even larger sums, and they could no doubt utilize even more. Here the question is a different one. At present, in such countries as India, Pakistan, South Korea, and Turkey, the funds allocated to family-planning programs constitute less than 1 per cent—in most cases, much less—of the total funds devoted to economic development. Would that tiny proportion make a greater contribution to population control, over some specified period, if given over to education or industrialization or road-building than it makes when utilized directly for family plannnig (*60*)? From what we now know, the answer is certainly "No."

Beyond family planning, the situation is still less clear. On the assumption that some level of incentive or benefit would have a demographic impact, what would the level have to be to cut the birth rate by, say, 20 per cent? We simply do not know: the necessary experiments on administration and effectiveness have not been carried out. Let us review what has been proposed with respect to incentives. On the ground that incentives for vasectomy are better than incentives for contraception—since vasectomy is a one-time procedure and is likely to be more effective in preventing births—Pohlman (*20*) proposes for India a range of money benefits depending upon parity and degree of acceptance—from $7 to a father of four or more children if half the villagers in that category enter the program up to $40 to a father of three children if 75 per cent enter. If the 50-per cent criterion were met in both categories throughout India, the current plan would cost on the order of $260 million in incentives alone, apart from administrative costs. The de-

cline in the birth rate would be slightly over a fourth, perhaps a third—roughly equivalent to $35 to $40 per prevented birth (*61*).

Simon proposes an incentive of half the per capita income "each year to each fertile woman who does not get pregnant" (*23*). Here a special problem arises. In a typical developing population of 1000, about 25 to 30 percent of the married women of reproductive age give birth each year: a population of 1000 means from 145 to 165 such women, and a birth rate of, say, 40. Thus, the incentives paid to about three-fourths of the married women of reproductive age would have no effect on the birth rate, since these women would not be having a child that year in any case; thus the cost could be three to four times the amount "needed" for a desired result. Even if the incentive were fully effective and really did prevent a birth, a cut of ten points in the Indian birth rate would cost on the order of $250 million (or 5 million prevented births at $50 each). The cost would be substantially larger if the women (including the nonfecund or the semi-fecund) who would not have had a child that year in any case, could not be screened out effectively.

But these and other possibilities are only speculations: to date we simply do not know whether incentives will lower a birth rate, or, rather, we do not know how large the incentives would have to be in order to do so. These illustrations show only that an incentive program could be expensive. In any case, incentive systems would require a good amount of supervision and record-keeping; and, presumably, the higher the incentive (and hence the greater the chance of impact), the greater the risk of false reporting and the greater the need of supervision—which is not only expensive but difficult administratively.

**Moral, ethical, and philosophical acceptability.** Next, is the proposal not only politically acceptable but considered right and proper—by the target population, government officials, professional or intellectual elites, and the outside agencies committed to aid in its administration?

Coale states (*3, 62*), "One reason the

policy of seeking to make voluntary fertility universal is appealing—whether adequate or not—is that it is a natural extension of traditional democratic values: of providing each individual with the information he needs to make wise choices, and allowing the greatest freedom for each to work out his own destiny. The underlying rationale is that if every individual knowledgeably pursues his self-interest, the social interest will best be served." But what if "stressing the right of parents to have the number of children they want . . . evades the basic question of population policy, which is how to give societies the number of children they need?" (6). The issue rests at the center of political philosophy: how best to reconcile individual and collective interests.

Today, most observers would acknowledge that having a child is theoretically a free choice of the individual couple. However, for many couples, particularly among the poor of the world, the choice is not effectively free in the sense that the individual couple does not have the information, services, and supplies needed to implement a free wish in this regard. Such couples are restrained by ignorance, not only of contraceptive practice but of the consequences of high fertility for themselves, their children, and their country; they are restrained by religious doctrine, even though they may not accept the doctrine; they are restrained legally, as in the case of people who would choose abortion if that course were open to them; they are restrained culturally, as in the case of women subject to a tradition that reserves for them only the childbearing and rearing roles. Hence effective freedom of choice in the matter of childbearing is by no means realized in the world today, as recent policy statements have remarked (63).

To what extent should a society be willing to compromise its ethical standards for the sake of solving a great social problem? Suppose a program for population control resulted in many more abortions in a society where abortion is morally repugnant and where, moreover, abortion by acceptable medical standards is widely unattainable; how much fertility decline would be "worth" the result? What of infanticide under the same

conditions? How many innocent or unknowing men may be vasectomized for a fee (for themselves or for others who obtained their consent) before the practice calls for a moral restraint? How large an increase in the regulatory bureaucracy, or in systematic corruption through incentives, or in differential effect by social class to the disadvantage of the poor *(64)* is worth how much decrease in the birth rate? How much association of childbearing with monetary incentive is warranted before "bribing people not to have children" becomes contaminating, with adverse long-run effects on parental responsibility (65)? How much "immorality," locally defined as extramarital sex, outweighs the benefits of contraceptive practice (assuming that there is an association)? How much withholding of food aid is ethical, judged against degree of fertility decline? If it were possible to legislate a later age at marriage, would it be right to do so against the will of young women, in a society in which they have nothing else to do? In countries, like our own, where urbanization is a serious population problem, is it right to tell people *where* to live, or to impose heavy economic constraints that in effect "force" the desired migration? Is it right to withdraw educational benefits from children in "too large" families? Such withdrawal would not only be repressive from the standpoint of free education but in the long run would be unfortunate from the standpoint of fertility control. In the balance—and this is a question of great but neglected importance—what weight should be given the opportunities of future generations as against the ignorance, the prejudices, or the preferences of the present one?

Guidance on such ethical questions is needed. For further consideration, these propositions are put forward. (i) "An ideal policy would permit a maximum of individual freedom and diversity. It would not prescribe a precise number of children for each category of married couple, nor lay down a universal norm to which all couples should conform" (3). (ii) "An ideal program designed to affect the number of children people want would help promote other goals that are worth supporting on their own merits, or at least not conflict with such goals" (3). (iii) An ideal program would not burden the innocent in an attempt to penalize the guilty—for example, would not burden the Nth child by denying him a free education simply because he was the Nth child of irresponsible parents. (iv) An ideal program would not weigh heavily upon the already disadvantaged—for example, by withdrawing maternal or medical benefits or free education from large families, policies that would tend to further deprive the poor. (v) An ideal program would be comprehensible to those directly affected and hence subject to their response. (vi) An ideal program would respect present values concerning family and children, values which some people may not be willing to bargain away in a cost-benefit analysis. (vii) An ideal program would not rest upon the designation of population control as the final value justifying all others; "preoccupation with population growth should not serve to justify measures more dangerous or of higher social cost than population growth itself" (3).

**Presumed effectiveness.** If proposals are scientifically ready to be implemented, politically and morally acceptable, and administratively and financially feasible, to what extent will they actually work in bringing population growth under control? That is the final question.

To begin with, the compulsory measures would probably be quite effective in lowering fertility. Inevitably in such schemes, strongly motivated people are ingenious enough to find ways "to beat the system"; if such people were numerous enough the system could not be enforced except under conditions of severe political repression (66). Otherwise, if the scheme was workable, compulsion could have its effect.

What about the proposals for the extension of voluntary contraception? Institutionalizing maternal care in the rural areas, with family planning attached, does promise to be effective within, say, 5 to 10 years, particularly in its potential for reaching younger women and women of lower parity. The International

Postpartum Program did have that effect in the urban areas (67), and presumably the impact would extend to the rural areas, though probably not to the same degree because of the somewhat greater sophistication and modernization of the cities.

A liberalized abortion system—again, if workable—could also be effective in preventing unwanted births, but it would probably have to be associated with a contraceptive effort; otherwise there might be too many abortions for the system, as well as for the individual woman (who might need three a year to remain without issue).

Free abortion in cases where contraception had failed would probably make for a decline in fertility, but how large a one would depend upon the quality of the contraceptive program. With modern contraception (the IUD and the pill) the failure rates are quite small, but women who only marginally tolerate these two methods could fall back on abortion. Free abortion has certainly lowered fertility in Japan and in certain countries of eastern Europe (68) and, where medically feasible, would do so elsewhere as well; as a colleague observes, in this field one should not underestimate the attraction of a certainty as compared to a probability.

The large question of the impact of the various incentive and benefit or liability plans (D and E) simply cannot be answered: we have too little experience to know much about the conditions under which financial factors will affect childbearing to any substantial degree. Perhaps everyone has his price for everything; if so, we do not know what would have to be paid, directly or indirectly, to make people decide not to bear children.

Such as it is, the evidence from the pronatalist side on the effectiveness of incentives is not encouraging. All the countries of Europe have family allowance programs of one kind or another (69), most of them legislated in the 1930's and 1940's to raise the birth rate; collectively Europe has the lowest birth rate of any continent. The consensus among demographers appears to be that such programs cannot be shown to have affected an upward trend in the birth rate where tried.

As in the case of abortion for illegitimate pregnancies, several of the benefit or liability proposals would affect only a trivial fraction of people in much of the developing world. However, because the impact of incentive and benefit or liability plans is uncertain and may become important, we need to become better informed on the possibilities and limitations, and this information can come only from experimentation under realistic circumstances and at realistic levels of payment.

A higher age at marriage and a greater participation of women in the labor force are generally credited with effecting fertility declines. In a recent Indian conference on raising the age at marriage, the specialists seemed to differ only on the magnitude of the fertility decline that would result: a decline of 30 per cent in the birth rate in a generation of 28 years if the minimum age of the woman at marriage were raised to 20 (70), or a decline of not more than 15 percent in 10 years (71). I say "seemed to differ" since these figures are not necessarily incompatible. In either case, the decline is a valuable one. But an increase in the age at marriage is not easy to achieve, and that must come before the fertility effect.

Similarly, an increase in the proportion of working women would have its demographic effect, but could probably come about only in conjunction with other broad social trends like education and industrialization, which themselves would powerfully affect fertility, just as a decline in fertility would assist importantly in bringing these trends about (72). Both compulsory education and restrictions on child labor would lower the economic value of children, hence tend to produce a decline in fertility. The question is, how are they to be brought about?

Finally, whether or not research would affect fertility trends depends of course upon its nature and outcome. Most observers believe that, under the typical conditions of the developing society, any improvement in contraceptive technology would lead toward the realization of present fertility goals and might help turn the spiral down. Indeed, several observers believe that this is the single most important desideratum, over the short run. Easy means of determining sex should have some effect upon the "need for sons" and thus cut family size to some extent. Research on the social-economic side would probably have to take effect through programs of the kinds discussed above.

The picture is not particularly encouraging. The measures that would work to sharply cut fertility are politically and morally unacceptable to the societies in question (as with coercion), and in any case unavailable; or they are difficult of attainment in any foreseeable future, as in the case of broad social trends or a shift in age at marriage. The measures that might possibly be tried in some settings, like some version of incentives or benefit or liability plans, give uncertain promise of results at the probable level of operation. Legalization of abortion, where the needed medical facilities are available, would almost certainly have a measurable effect, but acceptability is problematic.

## CONCLUSION

This review leaves us with some conclusions concerning proposals that go beyond family planning.

1. There is no easy way to achieve population control. If this review has indicated nothing else, it has shown how many obstacles stand in the way of a solution to the population problem. Table 1 shows, by way of recapitulation, how the various proposals seem to fit the several criteria (73). That is only one observer's judgment of the present situation, but, whatever appraisal is made of specific items, it would appear that the overall picture is mixed.

2. Family-planning programs do not compare unfavorably with other specific proposals, especially when one considers that

any *actual* operating program is at a disadvantage when compared with any competitive *ideal* policy. Indeed, on this showing, if family-planning programs did not exist, they would have to be invented; it appears that they would be among the first proposals to be made and the first programs to be tried, given their generally acceptable characteristics.

In fact, when such proposals are made, it turns out that many of them call for *more* family planning, not less, but in a somewhat different form. In the present case, at least a third of the proposals listed above put forward, in effect, simply another approach to family planning, often accepting the existing motivation as to family size. In any case, family-planning programs are established, have some momentum, and, importantly, would be useful as the direct instrument through which other proposals would take effect. So, as a major critic (74) acknowledges (6), "there is no reason to abandon family-planning programs."

What is needed is the energetic and full implementation of present experience. Much more could be done on the informational side, on encouraging commercial distribution of contraceptives, on the use of paramedical personnel, on logistics and supply, on the training and supervision of field workers, on approaches to special groups of individuals, ranging from women after childbirth to young men drafted into the armed forces. If workers in this field did well what they know how to do, that in itself would in all likelihood make a measurable difference, competitive in magnitude with the probable effects of other specific proposals—not to mention the further impetus of an improved contraceptive technology.

3. Most of the proposed ideas are not new; they have been around for some time. So, if they are not being tried, it is not because they have not been known but because they have not been accepted—presumably, for reasons like those discussed above. In India, for example, several of the social measures being proposed have been, it would seem, under almost constant review by one or another committee for the past 10 to 15 years.

So it is not correct to imply that it is only new ideas that are needed; the ideas are there, but their political, economic, or administrative feasibility are problematic.

4. All of the proposers are dissatisfied to some degree with present family-planning efforts, but that does not mean that they agree with one another's schemes for doing better. Thus, Ohlin believes that "the demographic significance of such measures [maternity benefits and tax deductions for children] would be limited" (34). Ketchel eloquently opposes several "possible alternatives to fertility control agents" (9). Meier argues against the tax on children on both humanitarian and political grounds (16). The U.N. Advisory Mission to India commets (53, p. 87), "it is realised that no major demographic effects can be expected from measures of this kind [maternity benefits], particularly as only a small proportion of families are covered . . . but they could contribute, together with the family planning programme, to a general change in the social climate relating to childbearing." Earlier, in supporting a family-planning effort in India, Davis noted that "the reaction to the Sarda Act [the Child Marriage Restraint Act of 1929] prohibiting female marriage [below age 14] shows the difficulty of trying to regulate the age of marriage by direct legislation" (75). Myrdal warns against cash payments to parents in this connection and supports social awards in kind to the children (76). Kirk believes that "it might prove to be the height of folly to undermine the existing family structure, which continues to be a crucial institution for stabiilty and socialization in an increasingly mobile and revolutionary society" (77). Finally, Ehrlich is contemptuous of the professors whose "idea of 'action' is to form a committee or to urge 'more research.' Both courses are actually substitutes for action" (7, p. 191).

5. In a rough way, there appears to be a progression in national efforts to deal with the problem of population control. The first step is the theoretical recognition that population growth may have something to do with the prospects for economic development. Then, typically, comes an expert mission from

abroad to make a survey and report to the government, as has occurred in India, Pakistan, South Korea, Turkey, Iran, Tunisia, Morocco, and Kenya, among others. The first action program is in family planning, and most of the efforts are still at that level. Beyond that, it apparently takes (i) some degree of discouragement about progress combined with (ii) some heightened awareness of the seriousness of the problem to move the effort forward. To date, those conditions have been most prominently present in India—and that is the country that has gone farthest in the use of incentives and in at least consideration of further steps along the lines mentioned above.

6. Proposals need to be specific—proposals both for action and for further research. It is perhaps too much to ask advocates to spell out all the administrative details of the way their plan is to operate in the face of obstacles and difficulties, or even to spell out how it is to get permission to operate; the situations, settings, opportunities, and personalities are too diverse for that. But it does seem proper to ask for the fullest possible specification of actual plans, under realistic conditions, in order to test out their feasibility and likely effectiveness. Similarly, advocates of further research ought to spell out not only what would be studied, and how, but also

## TABLE 1

Illustrative appraisal of proposals, by criteria.

| Proposal | Scientific readiness | Political viability | Administrative feasibility | Economic capability | Ethical acceptability | Presumed effectiveness |
|---|---|---|---|---|---|---|
| A. Extension of voluntary fertility control | High | High on maternal care, moderate-to-low on abortion | Uncertain in near future | Maternal care too costly for local budget, abortion feasible | High for maternal care, low for abortion | Moderately high |
| B. Establishment of involuntary fertility control | Low | Low | Low | High | Low | High |
| C. Intensified educational campaigns | High | Moderate-to-high | High | Probably high | Generally high | Moderate |
| D. Incentive programs | High | Moderately low | Low | Low-to-moderate | Low-to-high | Uncertain |
| E. Tax and welfare benefits and penalties | High | Moderately low | Low | Low-to-moderate | Low-to-moderate | Uncertain |
| F. Shifts in social and economic institutions | High | Generally high, but low on some specifics | Low | Generally low | Generally high, but uneven | High, over long run |
| G. Political channels and organizations | High | Low | Low | Moderate | Moderately low | Uncertain |
| H. Augmented research efforts | Moderate | High | Moderate-to-high | High | High | Uncertain |
| Family-planning programs | Generally high, but could use improved technology | Moderate-to-high | Moderate-to-high | High | Generally high, but uneven, on religious grounds | Moderately high |

how the results might be applied in action programs to affect fertility. Social research is not always readily translated into action, especially into administrative action; and the thrust of research is toward refinement, subtlety, precision, and qualification, whereas the administrator must act in the large. Short of such specification, the field remains confronted with potentially good ideas, such as "raise the age at marriage" or "use incentives" or "substitute pension systems for male children," without being able to move very far toward implementation.

7. Just as there is no easy way, there is no single way. Since population control will at best be difficult, it follows that every acceptable step that promises some measure of impact should be taken. The most likely prospect is that population control, to the degree it is realized, will be the result of a combination of efforts—economic, legal, social, medical—each of which has some effect but not an immediately overwhelming one (78). Accordingly, it is incumbent upon workers in the professional fields concerned to look hard at various approaches, including family planning itself, in order to screen out what is potentially useful for application. In doing so, it may be the path of wisdom to move with the "natural" progression. Some important proposals seem reasonably likely of adoption —institutionalization of maternal care, population study in the schools, the TV satellite system for disseminating information, a better contraceptive technology, perhaps even liberalization of abortion laws in some settings —and we need to know not only how effective such efforts will be but, beyond them, how large a money incentive would have to be to effect a given amount of fertility control and how effective those indirect social measures are that are morally acceptable and capable of realization. It may be that some of the measures would be both feasible and effective—many observers 15 years ago thought that family-planning programs were neither— and a genuine effort needs to be made. The "heavy" measures—involuntary measures and political pressures—may be put aside for the time being, if not forever.

8. In the last analysis, what will be scientifically available, politically acceptable, administratively feasible, economically justifiable, and morally tolerated depends upon people's perceptions of consequences. If "the population problem" is considered relatively unimportant or only moderately important, that judgment will not support much investment of effort. If it is considered urgent, much more can and will be done. The fact is that, despite the large forward strides taken in international recognition of the problem in the 1960's, there still does not exist an informed, firm, and constant conviction in high circles that this is a matter with truly great implications for human welfare (79). Such convictions must be based on sound knowledge. Here it would appear that the demographers and economists have not sufficiently made their case to the world elite—or that, if made, the case has not sufficiently commanded their attention and support. Population pressures are not sharply visible on a day-to-day or even year-to-year basis, nor, short of major famine, do they show themselves in dramatic events. Moreover, the warnings of demographers are often dismissed, albeit unfairly and wrongly, on the basis of past forecasts that were not borne out (80). After all, only a generation ago we were being warned about a decline in population in the West. Asking government leaders to take steps toward population control is asking them to take very substantial steps indeed— substantial for their people as well as for their own political careers—hence the case must be virtually incontrovertible. Accordingly, the scientific base must be carefully prepared (and perhaps with some sense of humility about the ease of predicting or urging great events, for the record is not without blemishes). Greater measures to meet the problem—measures which exclude social repression and needless limitation of human freedom—must rely on heightened awareness of what is at stake, on the part of leaders and masses alike.

What is beyond family planning? Even if

most of the specific plans are not particularly new, that in itself does not mean that they are to be disregarded. The questions are: Which plans can be effected, given such criteria? How can they be implemented? What will be the outcome?

This article is an effort to promote the discourse across the professional fields concerned with this important issue. Given the recent stress on family-planning programs as the "means of choice" in dealing with the problem, it is natural and desirable that counter-positions be put forward and reviewed. But that does not in itself settle the critical questions. What can we do now to advance the matter? Beyond family planning, what?

## REFERENCES AND NOTES

1. See, for example, K. Davis, *Science* **158,** 730 (1967); R. G. Potter, R. Freedman, L. P. Chow, *ibid.* **160,** 848 (1968); F. W. Notestein, "Population growth and its control," paper presented before the American Assembly on World Hunger, Fall 1968.
2. See, for example, the section on "Goals" in K. Davis, *Science* **158,** 730 (1967).
3. A. J. Coale, "Should the United States start a campaign for fewer births?," presidential address presented before the Population Association of America, 1968.
4. For current targets of some national family-planning programs, see B. Berelson, "National family planning programs: Where we stand," paper presented at the University of Michigan Sesquicentennial Celebration, November 1967; the paper concludes: "By and large, developing countries are now aiming at the birth rates of Western Europe 75 years ago or the United States 50 years ago."
5. H. C. Taylor, Jr., and B. Berelson, *Amer. J. Obstet. Gynecol.* **100,** 885 (1968).
6. K. Davis, *Science* **158,** 730 (1967).
7. P. R. Ehrlich, *The Population Bomb* (Ballantine, New York, 1968).
8. S. Chandrasekhar, *Population Rev.* **10,** 17 (1966).
9. M. M. Ketchel, *Perspect. Biol. Med.* **11,** 687 (1968); see also Ketchel's article in *Med. World News* (18 Oct. 1968), p. 66.
10. Ehrlich appears to dismiss the scheme as unworkable (7, p. 136), though two pages later he advocates "ample funds" to "promote intensive investigation of new techniques of birth control, possibly leading to the development of mass sterilizing agents such as were discussed above."
11. K. E. Boulding, *The Meaning of the Twentieth Century: The Great Transition* (Harper & Row, New York, 1964), pp. 135–36.
12. W. B. Shockley, in a lecture delivered at McMaster University, Hamilton, Ontario, December 1967.
13. S. Chandrasekhar, as reported in the New York *Times,* 24 July 1967. Just as the present article was being completed, Chandrasekhar proposed (*ibid.,* 21 Oct. 1968) "that every married couple in India deny themselves sexual intercourse for a year. . . . Abstinence for a year would do enormous good to the individual and the country." The reader may wish to consider this the 30th proposal and test it against the criteria that follow.
14. S. Wayland, in *Family Planning and Population Programs,* B. Berelson, R. K. Anderson, O. Harkavy, J. Maier, W. P. Mauldin, S. J. Segal, Eds. (Univ. of Chicago Press, Chicago, 1966), pp. 353–62; _____, in "Family Planning Programs: Administration, Education, Evaluation," J. Ross and J. Friesen, Eds., in preparation; "Teaching Population Dynamics: An Instructional Unit for Secondary School Students" (Columbia University, New York, 1965); "Critical Stages in Reproduction: Instruction Materials in General Science and Biology" (Columbia University, New York, 1965). The two last-named publications are pamphlets prepared under Wayland's direction at Teachers College.
15. P. Visaria, *Economic Weekly* (8 Aug., 1964), p. 1343.
16. R. L. Meier and G. Meier, "New Directions: A Population Policy for the Future," unpublished manuscript.
17. *Preparatory Study of a Pilot Project in the Use of Satellite Communication for National Development Purposes in India* (UNESCO Expert Mission, 1968).
18. W. Schramm and L. Nelson, *Communication Satellite for Education and Development—The Case of India* (Stanford Research Institute, Stanford, Calif., 1968), pp. 63–66.
19. S. Chandrasekhar, as reported in the New York *Times,* 19 July 1967.
20. E. Pohlman (Central Family Planning Institute, India), "Incentives for 'Non-Maternity' Cannot 'Compete' with Incentives for Vasectomy," unpublished manuscript.
21. T. J. Samuel, *J. Family Welfare* **13,** 11 (1966).
22. J. Simon, "Money Incentives to Reduce Birth Rates in Low-Income Countries: A Proposal to Determine the Effect Experimentally," unpublished manuscript; "The Role of Bonuses and Persuasive Propaganda in the Reduction of Birth Rates," unpublished manuscript.
23. _____, "Family Planning Prospects in Less-Developed Countries, and a Cost-Benefit Analysis of Various Alternatives," unpublished manuscript.
24. S. Enke, *Population Rev.* **4,** 47 (1960).
25. M. Young, "The Behavioral Sciences and Family Planning Programs: Report on a Conference," *Studies in Family Planning,* No. 23 (1967), p. 10.
26. D. Bhatia, "Government of India Small Family Norm Committee Questionnaire," *Indian J. Med. Educ.* **6,** 189 (1967). As the title indicates, this is not a proposal but a questionnaire soliciting opinions on various ideas put forward to promote "the small family norm."
27. S. Enke, "The Gains to India from Population Control," *Rev. Econ. Statist.* **42,** 179, 180 (1960).
27a. J. W. Leasure, *Milbank Mem. Fund. Quart.* **45,** 417 1967).
28. J. J. Spengler, "Agricultural development is not

enough," paper presented before the Conference on World Population Problems, Indiana University, May 1967.

29. M. C. Balfour, "A Scheme for Rewarding Successful Family Planners," *Population Council Mem.* (1962).

30. W. P. Mauldin, "Prevention of Illegitimate Births: A Bonus Scheme," *Population Council Mem.* (1967).

31. R. M. Titmuss and B. Abel-Smith, *Social Policies and Population Growth in Mauritius* (Methuen, London, 1960).

32. A. S. David, *National Development, Population and Family Planning in Nepal* (1968), pp. 53–54.

33. J. Fawcett, personal communication.

34. G. Ohlin, *Population Control and Economic Development* (Development Centre of the Organisation for Economic Co-operation and Development, New York, 1967), p. 104.

35. W. P. Davison, personal communication. Davison suggests a good pension (perhaps $400 a year) for men aged 60, married for at least 20 years, with no sons.

36. K. Davis, personal communication.

37. B. Berelson and A. Etzioni, brief formulations, 1962 and 1967, respectively.

38. P. M. Hauser, in "The Behavioral Sciences and Family Planning Programs: Report on a Conference," *Studies in Family Planning*, No. 23 (1967), p. 9.

39. J. Blake, in *Public Health and Population Change: Current Research Issues,* M. C. Sheps and J. C. Ridley, Eds. (Univ. of Pittsburgh Press, Pittsburgh, 1965), p. 62.

40. For the initial formulation of the proposal, see R. L. Meier, *Modern Science and the Human Fertility Problems* (Wiley, New York, 1959), chap. 7.

41. P. M. Hauser, *Demography* **4**, 412 (1967).

42. "Family Planning and the Status of Women: Interim Report of the Secretary-General" (United Nations Economic and Social Council, Commission on the Status of Women, New York, 1968), especially p. 17 ff.

43. R. Revelle, quoted by M. Viorst, *Horizon* (summer 1968), p. 35; D. M. Heer and D. O. Smith, "Mortality level and desired family size," paper presented before the Population Association of America, April 1967.

44. Ehrlich makes the same point in *New Scientist* (14 Dec. 1967), p. 655: "Refuse all foreign aid to any country with an increasing population which we believe is not making a maximum effort to limit its population.... The United States should use its power and prestige to bring extreme diplomatic and/or economic pressure on any country or organization (the Roman Catholic Church?) impeding a solution to the world's most pressing problem."

45. In an earlier article Ehrlich calls for a "Federal Population Commission with a large budget for propaganda," presumably limited to the United States.

46. S. Chandrasekhar, in *Asia's Population Problems,* S. Chandrasekhar, Ed. (Allen & Unwin, New York, 1967), p. 96; Chandrasekhar cites a suggestion made in 1961 by Julian Huxley.

47. S. Polgar, in "The Behavioral Sciences and Family Planning Programs: Report on a Conference," *Studies in Family Planning,* No. 23 (1967), p. 10.

48. *The Growth of World Population* (National Academy of Sciences, Committee on Science and Public Policy, Washington, D.C., 1963), pp. 5, 28–36. This recommendation has of course been made on several occasions by several people. For an imaginative account of the impact of biological developments, see P. C. Berry, appendix to *The Next Thirty-Four Years: A Context for Speculation* (Hudson Institute, Croton-on-Hudson, New York, 1966).

49. See, for example, S. J. Segal, "Biological aspects of fertility regulation," paper presented at the University of Michigan Sesquicentennial Celebration, November 1967.

50. It is worth noting that such expectations are not particularly reliable. For example, in 1952–53 a Working Group on Fertility Control was organized by the Conservation Foundation to review the most promising "leads to physiologic control of fertility," based on a survey conducted by Paul S. Henshaw and Kingsley Davis. This group did identify a "lead" that became the oral contraceptive (then already under investigation) but did not mention the intrauterine device. It was searching specifically for better ways to control fertility because of the population problem in the developing world, and considered the contraceptive approach essential to that end: "It thus appears imperative that an attempt be made to bring down fertility in overpopulated regions without waiting for a remote, hoped-for transformation of the entire society. . . . It seems plausible that acceptable birth control techniques might be found, and that the application of science to developing such techniques for peasant regions might yield revolutionary results" [*The Physiological Approach to Fertility Control, Report of the Working Group on Fertility Control* (Conservation Foundation, New York, 1953)].

51. A. S. Parkes, *New Scientist* **35,** 186 (1967).

52. New York *Times* (17 Nov. 1967). The then Minister had earlier suggested a substantial bonus (100 rupees) for vasectomy, the funds to be taken from U.S. counterpart funds, "but both Governments are extremely sensitive in this area. Yet in a problem this crucial perhaps we need more action and less sensitivity" [S. Chandrasekhar (*46*)].

53. *Report on the Family Planning Programme in India* (United Nations Advisory Mission, New York, 1966).

54. *Implications of Raising the Female Age at Marriage in India* (Demographic Training and Research Centre, Chembur, India, 1968), p. 109; *Centre Calling* (May 1968), p. 4.

55. *Planned Parenthood* (Mar. 1968), p. 3.

56. *Ibid.* (Apr. 1968), p. 2.

57. For a review of this development see R. Symonds and M. Carder, *International Organisations and Population Control (1947–67)* (Institute of Development Studies, Univ. of Sussex, Brighton, England, 1968).

58. At present, population materials are being included in school programs in Pakistan, Iran, Taiwan, and elsewhere.

59. See, for example, Balfour (*29*), Mauldin (*30*), and

Pohlman (*20*) and, for the economic analysis, Enke (*27*) and Simon (*22*).

60. For the negative answer, see Enke (*27*) and Simon (*22*). Data are from family-planning budgets and national development budgets contained in 5-year development plans.
61. E. Pohlman, "Incentives in birth planning," in preparation.
62. Coale, however, does point out that "it is clearly fallacious to accept as optimal a growth that continues until overcrowding makes additonal births intolerably expensive."
63. See, for example, the World Leaders' Statement [*Studies in Family Planning*, No. 26 (1968)] and the Resolution of the International Conference on Human Rights on "Human Rights Aspects of Family Planning," adopted 12 May 1968, reported in *Population Newsletter*. No. 2 (issued by the Population Division, United Nations) (1968). p. 21 ff. Incidentally, the issue of population policy was apparently a live one in classical times, and resolved by the great philosophers in ways not fully consonant with modern views. Plato, in the *Republic* (Modern Library edition, pp. 412, 414), says, "the number of weddings is a matter which must be left to the discretion of the rulers, whose aim will be to preserve the average of population and to prevent the State from becoming either too large or too small"—to which end certain marriages have "strict orders to prevent any embryo which may come into being from seeing the light; and if any force a way to the birth, the parents must understand that the offspring of such a union cannot be maintained, and arrange accordingly." Aristotle, in *Politics* (Modern Library edition, p. 316) says, "on the ground of an excess in the number of children, if the established customs of the state forbid this (for in our state population has a limit), no child is to be exposed, but when couples have children in excess, let abortion be procured before sense and life have begun. . . ."
64. After noting that economic constraints have not been adopted in South Asia, though often proposed, Gunnar Myrdal continues: "The reason is not difficult to understand. Since having many children is a main cause of poverty, such measures would penalize the relatively poor and subsidize the relatively well off. Such a result would not only violate rules of equity but would be detrimental to the health of the poor families, and so of the growing generation" [*Asian Drama: An Inquiry into the Poverty of Nations* (Pantheon, New York, 1968), vol. 2, pp. 1502–03].
65. F. W. Notestein, in *Family Planning and Population Programs*, Berelson et al., Eds. (Univ. of Chicago Press, Chicago, 1966), pp. 828–29: "There is a real danger that sanctions, for example through taxation, would affect adversely the welfare of the children. There is also danger that incentives through bonuses will put the whole matter of family planning in a grossly commercial light. It is quite possible that to poor and harassed people financial inducements will amount to coercion and not to an enlargement of their freedom of choice. Family planning must be, and must seem to be, an extension of personal and familial freedom of choice and thereby an enrichment of life, not

coercion toward its restriction."
66. In this connection see the novel by A. Burgess, *The Wanting Seed* (Ballantine, New York, 1963). At the same time, Myrdal, a long-time observer of social affairs, remarks that "the South Asian countries . . . can, to begin with, have no other principle than that of voluntary parenthood. . . . State direction by compulsion in these personal matters is not effective. . ." [G. Myrdal, *Asian Drama: An Inquiry into the Poverty of Nations* (Pantheon, New York, 1968), p. 1501].
67. G. I. Zatuchni, "International Postpartum Family Planning Program: Report on the First Year," *Studies in Family Planning*, No. 22 (1967), p. 14 ff.
68. For example, the repeal of the free abortion law in Rumania resulted in an increase in the birth rate from 14 in the third quarter of 1966 to 38 in the third quarter of 1967. For an early report, see R. Pressat. *Population* **22**, 1116 (1967).
69. See *Social Security Programs Throughout the World, 1964* (U.S. Department of Health, Education, and Welfare, Washington, D.C., 1964).
70. S. N. Agarwala in *Implications of Raising the Female Age at Marriage in India* (Demographic Training and Research Centre, Chembur, India, 1968), p. 21.
71. V. C. Chidambaram, *ibid.*, p. 47.
72. Actually, recent research is calling into question some of the received wisdom on the prior need of such broad institutional factors for fertility decline. If further study supports the new findings, that could have important implications for present strategy in the developing countries. See A. J. Coale, in *Proc. U.N. World Population Conf.* (1965), vol. 2, pp. 205–09, and ———, "The decline of fertility in Europe from the French Revolution to World War II," paper presented at the University of Michigan Sesquicentennial Celebration, 1967.
73. As the roughest sort of summary of Table 1, if one assigns values from 5 for "high" to 1 for "low," the various proposals rank as follows: family-planning programs, 25; intensified educational campaigns, 25; augmented research efforts, 24; extension of voluntary fertility control, 20; shifts in social and economic institutions, 20; incentive programs, 14; tax and welfare benefits and penalties, 14; political channels and organizations, 14; establishment of involuntary fertility control, 14.
74. Davis was a strong advocate of family planning in India, and quite optimistic about its prospects even in the pre-IUD or pre-pill era. See K. Davis, in *The Interrelations of Demographic, Economic, and Social Problems in Selected Underdeveloped Areas* (Milbank Memorial Fund, New York, 1954). Davis concludes (pp. 87–88): "Although India is already well-launched in the rapid-growth phase of the demographic transition, there is no inherent reason why she should long continue in this phase. She need not necessarily wait patiently while the forces of urbanization, class mobility, and industrial development gradually build up to the point where parents are forced to limit their offspring on their own initiative and without help, perhaps even in the face of official opposition. . . . Realistically appraising her situation, India has a chance to be the first country to achieve a major

revolution in human life—the planned diffusion of fertility control in a peasant population prior to, and for the benefit of, the urban-industrial transition."

75. K. Davis, in *The Interrelations of Demographic, Economic, and Social Problems in Selected Underdeveloped Areas* (Milbank Memorial Fund, New York, 1954), p. 86.
76. G. Myrdal, *Asian Drama: An Inquiry into the Poverty of Nations* (Pantheon, New York, 1968), p. 1503.
77. D. Kirk, "Population research in relation to population policy and national family planning programs," paper presented before the American Sociological Association, August 1968.
78. It begins to appear that the prospects for fertility control may be improving over the decades. Kirk, after reviewing several factors that "favor a much more rapid [demographic] transition than occurred in the West"—changed climate of opinion, religious doctrine, decline of infant mortality, modernization, fertility differentials, grass-roots concern, and improved contraceptive technology —shows, in a remarkable tabulation, that the later a country began the reduction of its birth rate from 35 to 20 births per thousand, the shorter the time it took to achieve this reduction: from 73 years (average) for the period 1831–60, for example, to 21 years after 1951; the trend has been consistently downward for over a century [D. Kirk, "Natality in the developing countries: recent trends and prospects," paper presented at the University of Michigan Sesquicentennial Celebration, 1967].
79. Nor, often, does such a conviction exist among the general public. For example, in midsummer of 1968 a national sample of adults was asked in a Gallup poll, "What do you think is the most important problem facing this country today?" Less than 1 percent mentioned population growth (Gallup release, 3 Aug. 1968, and personal communication).
80. For an old but enlightening review, see H. Dorn, *J. Amer. Statist. Ass.* **45,** 311 (1950).

# Population Problem:
# In Search of a Solution

JOSEPH J. SPENGLER

*There's little we can do about erroneous teachings, but do the taxpayers have to subsidize them?*
Nicholas Von Hoffman

*Misgivings are to be silenced. Rewards will come later.*
I Ching: The Book of Changes

No problem commands more attention in the world of discourse than the population problem. The solution consists in halting population growth promptly. Yet man's efforts to accomplish this are remindful of the efforts of an acrobat who bounds up and down on a trampoline in the vain hope that eventually a rebound will carry him up to the top of the Empire State Building.

Why has a solution not been forthcoming? The answer is very simple. Forgotten is the fact

Population Problem: In Search of a Solution. From *Science*, Vol. 166, December 5, 1969, pp. 1234–1238. Copyright 1969 by the American Association for the Advancement of Science. Reprinted by permission of the author and the publisher.

that positive repressants will halt population growth in a pressure-ridden world if preventive measures are not taken in time to preserve this world's potential for comfort. No society really wills a solution. A solution will nowhere be found until it is willed, Panglossian voices are stilled, and whatever needs to be done is done.

## THE PROBLEM

The population problem flows from the finiteness of the world in which man is multiplying. Excesses may assume two forms. No more growth may be indicated because a country's existing stock of population may be large enough. Or the rate of flow of additions to it may be too large even though the stock is of less than optimum size. Growth of components of man's average standard of life is limited by the growth of elements entering into each component, above all by those elements whose supply increases least rapidly. Of these elements, the food supply is only one, and not always as critical as Malthus assumed 171 years ago. Man's mobility is very much greater, however, with the result that consciousness of density is correspondingly greater.

Even Malthus's fears may at last be irremediably confirmed. Within little more than a century the world's population may have grown abreast of the world's food supply of that time, even if the latter should grow eightfold and near to the attainable maximum. So great an increase in the world food supply, while feasible under one-world conditions, is unlikely in a hostility-ridden divided world; it presupposes a doubling of world acreage under cultivation and a quadrupling of average yield per acre. A population octuples in just over 105 years, if it grows 2 percent per year; in about 140 years, if it grows 1.5 percent per year.

The rate of population growth has accelerated over the past three centuries. Of most concern is the acceleration in the present century. By the 1950's the world rate of population growth was about $3\frac{1}{3}$ times the 0.53 percent per year experienced in 1900–10. The rate is expected to be slightly higher in 1960–90; thereafter it may decline slightly.

The rate of population growth has progressed differently in the underdeveloped than in the developed world. In 1900–10 the annual rate in the developed world was 0.87 percent, nearly $2\frac{1}{2}$ times the 0.36 percent experienced in the underdeveloped world. By the close of this century the rate in the underdeveloped world will be double that in the developed world. The latter, usually responsive to the impact of war or economic depression, is expected to approximate 1 percent in 1960–2000, a rate about one-seventh above the 1900–10 level. Meanwhile, in the underdeveloped world, the annual rate, only 0.36 percent per year in 1900–10, is expected to average slightly over 2 percent (1).

It is not surprising, therefore, that population threatens to overtake the food supply as well as other slowly growing components of the budget of life. Suppose the current world food supply is increased eightfold; even then, should world population continue to grow at a rate falling within the range of rates projected by the United Nations Secretariat to the year 2000—1.5 to 2.2 percent—it also would octuple by the latter part of the next century or soon thereafter.

Population would continue to grow for some time even after the *true rate* of increase had descended to zero, because its age composition must become transformed into that associated with the fertility and mortality patterns destined to produce balance between births and deaths. In the United States, for example, an increase of 30 to 50 percent might still take place after net reproduction had settled to unity (2). Higher percentages might be found in some countries.

The dangers of population growth are not confined to the underdeveloped world. In the United States, for example, what Washington rhetors promised would be a "Great Society," could become a "Eudaemonically Puny Society." The population of the continental United

States will number 300 million or more by the close of this century. Should the American population continue to grow about 1 percent per year, it would number one billion early in the 21st century. Of these, 80 to 90 percent would be situated in cities, many of them elements of crowded and continuous "metropolitan" areas. Land of *all* sorts would be down to 2 acres (0.81 hectare) or less per person. Much of it would not be very accessible, and little of it would be suited to supply the amenities of finite nature, demand for which is rising with the rapid growth of *discretionary* time and income per capita.

## SOCIAL RESPONSE

The degree to which population growth is controlled, given a stable mortality pattern, depends upon the means of control available and the degree of pressure members of a population are under to employ these means. Up to now, few administrators or scholars have given much attention to the pressure or motivational aspect of population growth; among the exceptions are Stephen Enke and Leonard Bower *(3)*. Moralists, of course, have always indulged in what journalists call "jawbone control," urging the fecund either to reproduce, or to refrain from reproduction, for the good of state, cult, or private situation. Some technologists and publicists for money-hungry Mission Controls put forward as solutions for many of man's problems (among them the control and feeding of his numbers) the complicated gadgetry and superb organization which has put men on the moon. Septuagenarian ecclesiastical celibates, on the contrary, are still content to rule effective solutions off limits.

It is true, of course, that the population problem is of relatively recent vintage. The need to regulate fertility hardly existed before the 19th century, so high was mortality. In the Middle Ages, and perhaps at other times, young people were often advised not to marry until they could support children in keeping

with their own station in life. Voluntary and involuntary celibacy also served to curb fertility in Western Europe more than in Asia. In the 19th century, long before modern methods of control had been developed, general fertility was quite effectively regulated, in Ireland by deferment of marriage and nonmarriage, and in France by these and available contraceptive methods. One may say, therefore, that in these countries the General Will to regulate numbers was strong, well fortified by the universe of rewards and penalties operative in each country. In other Western countries fertility passed under partial control, greater in amount than had obtained earlier, but less than was to be found in Ireland and France. Outside the sphere of Western European civilization, however, fertility changed very little because it was counterbalanced, as a rule, by unchanging high mortality.

The need for greater population control was not considered acute until the present century, particularly after the 1930's, when the decline in mortality accelerated in various underdeveloped countries. With little or no decline in fertility, the decline in mortality more than tripled the annual rate of population growth between the first and the sixth decade of the present century. Meanwhile, the increment of population discharged into a finite world each decade rose from about 90 million in 1900–10 to about 482 million in 1950–60; it may approximate 942 million by the 1990's.

The recognition of the acute need to control numbers, together with the necessity of providing families with a means of limiting the number of children to three or four or less, stimulated research on the improvement of contraceptive methods. Intrauterine devices and the contraceptive pill were added to the methods in use, and some of the latter were improved. Even more satisfactory means are in the offing.

While effective research has been done on contraceptive means, little has been done on the motivation to make use of these means. Man seemingly has acted upon Samuel Johnson's dictum, "How small . . . that part which laws or kings can cause cure." Advocates of birth control *(4)* have counted on individual incentive and on private "conscience," oblivious of the fact that free rein is thus allowed to men without "conscience" whose number may be legion. Little account is taken of the fact that man lives in a universe of penalties and rewards and tends to pursue courses of action free of penalty and productive of reward. Even less account is taken of the fact, stressed by Hardin *(5)* and economists generally, that the birth of a child gives release to a stream of external effects, some adverse and costly, which are incident upon others than the parents. Indeed, in many countries, among them the United States, this incidence is accentuated by legislation and administrative practice. Hence much of the cost of producing children is shifted to others than the parents, with the result that reproduction is stimulated. Furthermore, in sanctionless "free-ride" societies such as our own, efforts to shift even more of the cost from responsible parents to others are quite powerful, supported as they are by ideology, strong organization, and an imperfect understanding of cost-shifting by its victims.

## FAILURE?

In view of what has been said, it is unlikely that population growth will be halted, either in the developed or in the underdeveloped world. Optimistic reports come from those engaged in pressing for fertility control, though they have little effect, in view of the magnitude of the problem. One senses an ex parte aura about these reports. Nor does one find strong grounds for optimism in the fine reports of the Population Council or in recent world reviews of the state and extent of contraceptive practice *(6)*.

There is little evidence of a General Will in any country to regulate numbers effectively. In no developed country has the so-called right to parenthood been transformed into a privilege to be earned before it may be exer-

cised. In no developed country has effective response been made to the fact that poverty is associated with excessive family size. In no underdeveloped country has a government undertaken, or been allowed to undertake, a really effective fertility-control policy.

Failure is writ large in *Population Bulletin No. 7* of the United Nations, issued in 1965. The countries of the world, it was found, fell into two categories: the developed, with gross reproduction rates below 2 and averaging about 1.4; and the underdeveloped, with gross reproduction rates above 2 and averaging 2.6 or more. Around 1960 crude birth rates averaged 22 per 1000 inhabitants in the developed world and 41 to 42 per 1000 in the underdeveloped world. The world as a whole, with a crude birth rate of 35 to 36 per 1000, produced 105 to 110 million births, close to four-fifths of which took place in the underdeveloped world. Three decades from now, only about one-fourth of the world's population will live in the present developed world; in 1960, as in 1900, about one-third lived there.

The muted conclusion of the United Nations Secretariat is quite pessimistic. "The launching of new countries upon the transition from high to low fertility seems to have been temporarily halted; with a few possible exceptions, there is little sign of decided downward trends having begun in the remaining countries of high fertility" *(7)*. Moreover, in some countries when fertility has declined, the decline has been at least partly offset by a decline in mortality much as happened in 19th- and early 20th-century Europe. Of course, the impact of further declines in mortality is small after expectation of life at birth moves into the 70's.

## STABILIZATION PROPOSALS

Population growth can be halted, but it will not be halted until a General Will to halt it develops and becomes effectively institutionalized and supported by adequate sanctions. It is preferable, of course, that institutionalization assume the form of controlling mechanisms which are economic and fairly automatic in character and as free as possible of cumbersome administrative intervention.

A clear-cut target needs to be established. This would consist in, for example, an average number of living children per family sufficient to replace a stable population, given the prevailing mortality pattern and the population's marital composition. This average in most countries would fall within a range of from just over two to somewhat over three children per married couple. This average would aggregate into an annual number of births sufficient, in the longer run, to balance the number of deaths. In the shorter run, as noted earlier, births would continue to exceed deaths until the stable age composition associated with a zero rate of growth had been achieved. Of primary importance, however, is not statistical nicety but the establishment of a target number of births and living children, to be followed by such modification of the universe of rewards and penalties as proves necessary to assure realization of this target.

A distinction needs to be made between the number of births $R$ required to replace a population and the excess $E$ when the total number of births $T > R$ (or whatever is the number of births needed to assure the target rate of population growth). The cost of births $R$ may be viewed as the overhead cost of replacing a population and therefore properly chargeable, at least in part, to the total community. It need not and should not be charged to the community entirely or even in major part, however, because the utility or satisfaction which parents expect to derive from their children is so great that they will bear much if not all of the cost of producing them. Halting population growth may then be crudely said to consist of preventing $E$ through reducing $T$ to $R$—mainly by raising the cost of $E$ to a level high enough to discourage births in excess of $R$ when population replacement is the objective. The births included under $E$ may be described as *demerit wants*, a penalizable category of wants that may, as Louis Gasper suggests in another connection, be treated as counterparts to *merit wants*, a

normative category of wants whose satisfaction the state is likely to finance (8).

The halting process is somewhat more complicated, of course, than has been suggested. Reduction of fertility to a replacement level gradually produces a change in a population's age composition, and this in turn modifies the number of births until they move into long-run balance with deaths. Of major importance from an economic point of view, besides the slowing down of the rate of population growth, is the increase in the relative number of persons of productive age. For purposes of illustration consider the transformation of a stable female population described by Coale (9) and characterized initially by an expectation of life at birth of 70 years and a gross reproduction rate of 2.25, as in some underdeveloped countries. We should then have an annual growth rate of about 2.64 percent, with a population of which 3.05 percent would be aged 70 or more years, and 48.83 percent would be aged less than 20. Suppose now that the gross reproduction rate declines to 1.25 and the population again assumes stable form with a growth rate of about 0.55 percent. The percentage of the population aged 70 years or more rises to 8.13 while that of persons under 20 declines to 31.77. The percentage of the population of working age—20 to 69—rises from 48.12 to 60.1, signifying an increase in average potential productivity of about 25 percent and a decline of about 39 percent in the ratio of persons of dependent age to those of working age.

Roughly similar changes would take place in the male population component, corresponding to those of the female component, and together they would constitute the total population. Male life expectancy is lower than female life expectancy and male age composition differs slightly from female age composition (9).

Of primary concern here are the potential economic benefits associated with the decline in fertility. These are the increase in the ratio of persons of productive age to the total population, the decline in the ratio of dependents to persons of productive age, and the virtual disappearance of increase in population pressure occasioned by population growth.

The transformation described, together with its beneficial effects, does not come about automatically, although it has been approximated in part in the developed world as a result of the long-run decline in natality. Even given general availability of cheap and effective means of contraception—a condition not present in perhaps two-thirds of the world—achievement and maintenance of the requisite gross reproduction rate would not result. There exists no socioeconomic mechanism adequate to bring this result about automatically, much as the price mechanism brings about balance between supply and demand. The existing universe of rewards and penalties is not currently constituted to eventuate in $R$ births and no more. Nor is there disposition to alter the incidence of carrot and stick suchwise as to improve the net impact of current rewards and penalties. Indeed, this universe is being made more rather than less favorable to reproduction in many countries, among them the United States, with the result that forces making for poverty and deprivation are accentuated.

In the past, as noted earlier, reliance has been placed almost entirely upon "private conscience" despite the fact that the reproductive behavior of a considerable fraction of any population is little influenced by conscience. Herein lies the inadequacy of planned parenthood programs, admirable as they are and pathbreaking as they have been. There is need in addition for suitable motivation for the carrot and the stick.

Motivation to reproduction assumes a variety of forms, several of which are overriding except in marginal cases. Control of fertility may therefore be achieved through replacing these motives in part by functionally equivalent motives which do not result in reproduction. This may be done suchwise as merely to reduce average family size from current levels to levels compatible with stabilization of the population if that is the objective.

It is highly desirable, of course, that children not be penalized by policies intended to discourage reproduction. Such a policy could in effect penalize both innocent children and society insofar as it denied children their due share of opportunity to develop their potentials. A case in point might be recourse to the imposition of taxes upon low-income parents with excessive numbers of children. As a result, means for the rearing and training of these children might be unduly reduced by such a tax.

Of the diverse motives for reproduction several have always been dominant. One is the expectation of filial affection throughout life and especially in old age. This need cannot, as a rule, be met adequately through collective arrangements designed to replace the services of children; but it can be met nicely so long as there are one or two children. The other and probably more important motive for reproduction in most countries is the parents' expectation of economic support in their old age at the hands of their children. This motive may not, of course, be so powerful any longer in advanced countries with pension and social security systems. It exists even there, however, since pecuniary provision for support in retirement years, even when well-planned, is apt to be eroded by modern governments which sometimes prove more inclined to unproductive expenditure (armament races, space and other potlatch, and war) and savings-eroding inflation than to maintenance of the purchasing power of retirement income.

A first step to the effective control of fertility in underdeveloped countries is the gradual introduction of a social security system for those over 65 years of age, for instance. Given this arrangement, potential parents will be less inclined to have a family in excess of replacement size in order to be reasonably assured of support in old age. For this system to work, however, its benefits must be limited to those with no more than $x$ children when the value of $x$ is in the neighborhood of the replacement number of births (some of which will be multiple) under existing mortality conditions. The system would need to be financed through something like proportional income taxation and to yield correspondingly variable retirement income. The system would have to be introduced gradually and initially limited to families with *x* or fewer children and susceptible of further increase. The social cost of this system would fall quite short of the cost of reproducing and rearing the additional children who would have been born had the system not existed, in part because support of the aged is an overhead societal cost, much of which will be borne by society in any event.

It is essential to the success of this program that those under the social security system expect to be decidedly better off in their old age than they otherwise would have been. This requirement is easily met, however, as was indicated above in "Stabilization Proposals." Not only will the decline in natality release a large amount of resources formerly absorbed by population growth, but also the decline in the relative number of young persons of unproductive age is only partially offset by increase in the relative number of persons aged over 69, with the result that potential output per capita is significantly increased. For these reasons, together with the fact that savings per older person will be higher absolutely and in relation to his preretirement income, the situation of those under the social security program will be decidedly better than it otherwise would have been.

Under this social security system the deterrent to excessive reproduction in underdeveloped countries adopting it is the threat to families of not sharing in retirement benefits upon reaching age 65 if the number of living children should be excessive. This system can be made part of the fertility-regulating institutional structure of underdeveloped countries, most of which are without retirement systems. Such a system might also be grafted onto social security systems current in advanced countries.

This conditional social security arrangement may need to be supplemented or replaced in countries where it cannot be made effective. Such additional arrangement must meet three needs: (i) make potential parents aware at marriage of the probable aggregate cost of caring properly for two or three children; (ii) help assure adequate material sup-

port for children subsequently born to these parents; (iii) provide these parents with incentive not to exceed what is for them the target number of children. At the time of marriage a couple might be required to pay into a combination insurance and interest-bearing fund, designed to support surviving children in the event of the household-head's death, and otherwise to supplement the support of the couple's children in their more expensive teens. Should a couple remain childless or have fewer than the target number of children, all or some of the cumulating proceeds would be restored. Some time—say 20 years—after the birth of a couple's first child, they would be awarded a bonus if they had not produced more than the target number of children. The bonus would amount to a partial reward for a couple's contribution to the collective cost of population replacement. The arrangement described may be modified to increase the number of births if it should fall below the replacement level, or below some other desired level, as may happen in the United States.

The joint incentive flowing from the prospect of a share in both retirement benefits under the social security system and the insurance-bonus arrangement should be sufficient to induce most families not to exceed the target number of live children. Moreover, should this joint incentive not prove powerful enough, it might be strengthened by increasing the financial advantages associated with compliance. Recourse to physical sanction (for example, sterilization) should not, therefore, prove necessary, even if social approval of its use were given with respect to physically or mentally submarginal individuals.

In what has gone before, no provision has been made for varying the distribution of the stipulated aggregate number of births and children among the families composing a population. Such a provision becomes necessary, however, in proportion as a society accepts the principle that parenthood is not a right but a *privilege* to be reserved to those financially and morally capable of meeting the responsibilities of parenthood. A considerable number of any nation's population is physically, mentally, or otherwise unfit to assume and support these responsibilities. This is especially true of modern urban societies, into whose economies very few submarginal persons are economically absorbable under modern governmental, trade-union, and related constraints. At the same time a considerable number of families are willing and able to rear four or five children. Hence arrangements need to be made for the distribution of responsibility for the aggregate desired number of births and children. While state agencies might accomplish such distribution, it would be preferable to use deferred incentives of the sort already described, and thus allow the incidence of costs and returns to govern interfamily distribution of births and children.

Compliance with postredistribution quotas or targets might be assured through adaptation of the social security and insurance fund arrangements described earlier. This would maximize the degree of freedom of choice compatible with realization of the target. Participation in retirement benefits would be limited to those who did not exceed their reduced or enlarged quotas. Right to receipt of of a bonus would be contingent upon an insuree's not exceeding his postdistribution quota. Required payment into the insurance fund would vary directly and proportionately with the number of children in the insuree's postdistribution quota. An arrangement of this sort would be preferable to the state's licensing the right to have one or more children and then distributing the licenses in some manner. This arrangement would call for sanctions against violation in much greater measure than the arrangements proposed above.

## CONCLUSION

A dilemma arising from a conflict of freedoms confronts the inhabitants of most countries. In any one country, there is little advantage and much disadvantage to be had either from any population growth (most of Europe, Asia, parts of Africa, and the Western Hemis-

phere), or from a population growth at a rate, for instance, in excess of 0.5 to 1.0 percent. Growth at an excessive rate arises largely either from ignorance of effective means of birth control, or from current arrangements which permit much of the cost of excessive population growth to be shunted from parents with excessive numbers of children to nondiscretionary members of society, or from both—in sum, *from unrestricted freedom to procreate.* Exercise of this freedom thus conflicts with a variety of freedoms of the remainder of the population.

Solution of the population problem consists in reconciling exercise of this freedom to procreate with exercise of other freedoms—in equilibrating the two in such a way as to prevent continuation of disadvantageous population growth. Thus, the underlying problem is not novel, although the form which it assumes is novel. New also is the fact that continuation of undesirable population growth gives rise to irremediable evils, whereas continuation of most other disequilibria among freedoms gives rise mainly to evils which are remediable. Cushioning of excessive population growth does, of course, reduce its *visible* costs, but at the expense of *less visible* resources—use which might otherwise contribute to the increase of average material income, leisure, access to amenities, and so on.

Reconciliation of the freedoms in conflict may be accomplished through administrative measures based on appropriate legislation and decrees. This approach is not to be recommended, however, except as a last resort. It is cumbersome. It could become another "brick" in an emerging police state. It generates antigovernmental response from persons affected, since they tend to believe themselves to be arbitrarily deprived of options from among which they should be free to choose. It violates the rule that, since a great deal of government necessarily consists either of administrative or police action, or both, additions should not be made to a government's total administrative and police load when alternative measures, especially economic measures, may be used to accomplish particular collective purposes. Avoidable administrative measures are particularly undesirable in present-day states, whether developed or underdeveloped, because competent bureaucrats are in very short supply and governments already undertake a great deal of activity which they are quite unfit to conduct efficiently.

It is extremely desirable that population growth be halted in most countries and slowed down in others. As yet, however, there exists no General Will to bring about these objectives. Furthermore, even if a General Will should develop, it might be weakened if recourse were left entirely to administrative and police measures. It is essential to reorient the composition of the universe of penalties and rewards in such a way as to induce men to replace in part the freedom to reproduce by other freedoms. Two arrangements have been outlined that are jointly utilizable and compatible with retention of a high degree of freedom of choice. They have not been described in detail, since detail would necessarily vary with country and situation.

The two arrangements proposed—arrangements which are susceptible of considerable improvement—entail as little interference as possible with individual freedom of choice. Emphasis is placed upon the composition of the options available and to which individuals respond. The advantage of the proposed arrangements consists in the fact that payment for compliance is deferred until noncompliance is no longer possible. The incentive to limit family size appropriately thus is continually present so long as the wife is of reproductive age. Payment need not be repeated as under programs designed to encourage use of intrauterine devices. The ultimate payment can be made large enough, however, to encourage strong efforts at compliance. Furthermore, compliance in most instances is compatible with a family's having two or three

children and therefore enjoying the utilities and advantages associated with having these children.

The arrangements proposed are designed to reduce the functional importance of more than two children in most instances. The weaknesses in these arrangements are three. First, among those whose discount of the future is very high, future monetary rewards may offer only limited incentive in the present when decisions respecting reproduction must be made. Second, confidence in the governmental apparatus of the state may be limited. It may be feared that when rewards come due 20 to 45 years hence, the state will refuse to pay or pay in full. A combination of this fear with a high discount rate could, therefore, greatly reduce the capacity of the joint incentives to diminish fertility. Finally, the arrangements cannot succeed unless the means to control family size are widely available and very cheap in relation to the incomes of the masses.

## REFERENCES AND NOTES

1. M. Macura, in *World Population—The View Ahead*. R. N. Farmer, J. D. Long, G. J. Stolnitz, Eds. (Bureau of Business Research, Indian Univ., Bloomington 1968), p. 27.
2. T. Frejka, *Population Stud.* **22**, 379 (1968).
3. S. Enke, *Science* **164**, 798 (1969); L. Bower, *Demography* **5** (1), 422 (1968).
4. K. Davis, *Science* **158**, 730 (1967).
5. G. Hardin, *ibid.* **162**, 1243 (1968).
6. *Family Planning and Population Programs*. International Conference on Family Planning Programs, edited by planning committee. B. Berelson, chairman (Univ. of Chicago Press, Chicago, 1966); *Demography* **5** (2), whole issue (1968) (this is a special issue devoted to the progress and problems of fertility control throughout the world).
7. *Population Bulletin of the United Nations, No. 7* (1965), pp. 1, 135, 150, and 151.
8. R. A. Musgrave. *The Theory of Public Finance* (McGraw-Hill, New York, 1959), p. 13.
9. A. J. Coale and P. G. Demeny. *Regional Model Life Tables and Stable Populations* (Princeton Univ. Press, Princeton, N.J., 1966), pp. 114 and 210.

# Prognosis for the Development
# of New Chemical Birth-Control Agents

CARL DJERASSI

The very rapid rate of increase in the world's population, notably in the developing countries, has become a matter of worldwide concern. Fifteen years ago this was virtually a taboo subject, whereas the term *population explosion* has now become a household phrase. Symptomatic of the international concern with this problem and its enormous economic, political, and human implications is the fact that the very first report by the Committee on Science and Public Policy of the National Academy of Sciences dealt with the population problem (1). A veritable flood of articles and books has appeared on this subject in recent years, and the general consensus is that effective family planning must play a key role in the solution of this world problem.

At first glance, the prognosis for improved family-planning methods appears promising. During the past 10 years a major breakthrough in birth-control techniques has been achieved: the development of orally administered contraceptive agents (2, 3) of virtually 100 per cent effectiveness, and greatly increased use of improved intrauterine devices (IUD) (4). Both approaches lend themselves much more readily than conventional earlier methods (for example, the diaphragm, the condom, and so on) to broad-scale family planning in developing countries, and it is not surprising, therefore, that the well-publicized large-scale pro-

grams in such diverse countries as Chile, Egypt, South Korea, and Taiwan are based virtually exclusively on steroid oral contraceptive agents (5) and IUD's. Abortion is another effective means of population control, as demonstrated during the past 20 years on a country wide basis in Japan and eastern Europe, but the general tendency in research has been to concentrate on improved chemical agents for birth control, the dramatic effectiveness of the steroid oral contraceptive agents having provided the main impetus. Thus, considerable effort is being expended on overcoming one of the major drawbacks of these chemical agents—the necessity of taking a pill daily or with short interruptions—by developing "once-a-month" pills, or sustained-action formulations (Silastic implants, pellets, and so on) effective for many months or conceivably even years. Philanthropic organizations such as the Ford Foundation and the Population Council have been dedicating increasing amounts of money to the support of such research, and, during the past year, the National Institute of Child Health and Human Development of the U.S. Public Health Service has organized a Center for Population Research whose annual multimillion-dollar budget will be devoted to "the development of a variety of new methods of fertility regulation."

When we consider that such research has become not only respectable but also very fashionable, that ample financial resources are being mobilized by government, industrial, and philanthropic sources, and that the urgency and magnitude of the world's population

Prognosis for the Development of New Chemical Birth-Control Agents. From *Science*, Vol. 166, October 24, 1969, pp. 468–473. Copyright 1969 by the American Association for the Advancement of Science. Reprinted by permission of the author and the publisher.

explosion is widely recognized, then the prospects for the development of new or improved chemical contraceptive agents appear rosy indeed. My purpose in this article is to demonstrate that one factor, which has generally been overlooked and which is of rather recent origin, makes the prognosis for the introduction of new agents a progressively more dismal one. The Pugwash Conference, with its wide representation from developed and developing countries, appears to be a particularly suitable arena for airing this sensitive problem, especially since the topic "problems of population growth" has been put on the agenda of the 19th Conference in the context of "modern science and developing countries." As I intend to demonstrate in what follows, it is precisely this juxtaposition of "modern science and developing countries" which is creating an increasingly inhibiting atmosphere in the area of practical birth-control research if we equate "modern science" with "scientifically advanced nations."

While many of my comments also apply to newer work on improved IUD's, notably those containing metal or other chemical ingredients, I restrict my presentation to the development of newer *chemical* contraceptive agents *(6)*, since this is a research field in which I have been personally involved, directly or indirectly, for nearly 20 years *(7)*. All of the currently used orally or parenterally administered contraceptive agents are steroids, but it is reasonable to assume that clinically effective nonsteroidal organic chemicals (especially in the area of abortifacients) will also be developed. Irrespective of their chemical structure, there are at least six special or even unique factors that must be taken into consideration.

**1. Scientific complexity**  To judge from past experience, the development of an orally effective or parenterally administered sustained-action contraceptive from the chemical laboratory to final clinical use is one of the most complex sequences in medicinal research. Chemical investigations on steroids are performed in comparatively few laboratories (most of them large drug firms), and the large-scale synthesis of steroids is one of the most difficult of industrial chemical operations. The biological screening of potential candidates requires a very high level of sophistication, since the reproductive processes of the female and male are so complicated and involve so many endocrine as well as target organs. Examination for possible toxicity has to be of a long-term nature [the most recent U.S. Food and Drug Administration (FDA) requirements for animal tests establishing safety for chemical *(6)* contraceptives require testing for 10 years in monkeys], and not only must clinical trials be performed with large numbers of human subjects for long periods but they must also be accompanied by batteries of chemical laboratory tests in order to evaluate the effect of such contraceptive agents on many physiological parameters. The obvious conclusion is that such research, especially if it is of a pioneering nature leading to development of new contraceptive agents or approaches, can and will be done only by scientists from highly developed, scientifically advanced countries. Therefore, the fact that virtually all such work has so far been performed in North America and Europe is not surprising. In other words, the research and development work is being performed in those countries in which the population increase is the lowest, in which conventional birth-control measures have already been used for a long time, and—most importantly—in which it is possible to dispense with new birth-control measures without concomitant disastrous economic consequenecs.

**2. Time scale.**  By definition, if a contraceptive agent is to be used for family planning rather than as an adjunct to occasional sexual intercourse (for which, incidentally, "post-coital pills" are currently under investigation), it will be employed by an individual for long periods, frequently over many years. The statement is frequently made, notably in the lay press, that agents such as the female oral contraceptive pills will be taken by a woman for periods exceeding 20 years and that nothing is known about possible side effects resulting from such prolonged usage. While it is perfectly true that experiments on several thousand women would have to be conducted for 20 years in order to yield an unambiguous answer to such a question, our accumulated experience during the past 10 years shows that, given a receptive climate for the development of new agents, very few women would in fact remain on the same contraceptive pill for even 10 years. Nevertheless, every responsible investigator will grant that unusual caution must be exercised in the toxicological and clinical evaluation of such agents, and that statistically meaningful experiments on large numbers of women for reasonably long periods must be conducted before such drugs are released to the general public. In a recent private conference in our laboratory with several experts in biology and clinical medicine from the United States and Europe, it was concluded that more than 8 years would be required to satisfy all current U.S. FDA requirements for introduction of a new agent to the public—once the chemical and initial biological work had been completed. These initial studies are by no means trivial and would themselves entail 1 or more years; thus a new contraceptive agent, in order to be introduced in 1977 as an effective means of population control, must already, in 1969, have passed through the chemical and biological laboratories of its discoverer. The demographic implications of this statement are rather shocking for a developing country that may still be waiting for the ideal contraceptive agent (instead of using existing ones) while its population doubles every 20 years, as is now the case in many areas of the world.

The apparent need for new contraceptive methods is exemplified by the following quotation from an editorial in the *New York Times* (6 July 1969) on the world's population proliferation:

Although recent advances in contraceptive technology—notably the pill and the loop—have made possible dramatic reductions in the birth rate in a few small countries, efforts at population control have been disappointing so far in most of the developing world. Many demographers believe that if significant reductions in population growth are to be achieved there must be a technological breakthrough in contraception similar to that in food production.

This desire for new contraceptive agents seems to stem from the observation that, in large-scale studies in developing countries, the 2-year dropout figure with IUD's or with the steroid oral contraceptives exceeds 50 per cent. Personally, I am not convinced that any better results can be obtained with any method which requires a conscious act of conception control. For the populations of these developing countries it will be necessary to develop a procedure which produces, by a single administration of a birth-control agent, indefinite (but reversible) sterility, which could then be overcome temporarily by administration of a second, "fertility-producing" drug. The general state of the adult human population under these circumstances would be one of infertility which could be changed only by a conscious act, rather than the reverse state of affairs existing now. In the light of my subsequent remarks about the increasingly negative climate and conditions for clinical testing of new contraceptive agents, it seems exceedingly improbable that such a new approach can be brought to practical fruition in this century.

The *New York Times* editorial statement that "there must be a technological breakthrough in contraception similar to that in food production" must be viewed against this realistic background. Such remarks are frequently made in scientific as well as lay circles, but they are superficial. Improvement in food production (notably the recent dramatic results in wheat and rice production) is a technological matter which does not affect the palatability, acceptability, or biological properties of the food. A more appropriate analogy with respect to new contraception technology would be one between recently achieved improvements in food technology and improved chemical methods of manufacturing contraceptive pills, which would lower their price but would hardly affect population growth. Conversely, an appropriate counterpart in the food technology field to the required technological breakthrough in contraception would be the development of a completely new food (for instance, a synthetic food), whose acceptability to different populations would first have to be established, and whose mode of administration (for example, in pill form) would be quite novel. If solution of the world's food problems depended on such a basic technological development, then the prospects for solving them in this century would be rather dismal.

**3. Side effects and healthy population.** Items 1 and 2 are basically logistical ones, and we can now turn to some of the more sensitive issues emanating from the fact that the contraceptive approaches to be utilized in the underdeveloped parts of the world are in fact being discovered and developed in the most advanced nations. We are faced with the ironic situation that, in these advanced nations, in which sales of tobacco and alcohol are not restricted in spite of the serious "side effects" of these agents, new candidates for contraceptive agents must meet more rigorous standards than most other drugs. One of the reasons is the assumption that the use of contraceptive agents involves healthy individuals and that only absolutely minimum side effects can, and should, be tolerated. Such a position is illogical on several grounds. First, our society does not take such a position with much more dangerous agents such as alcohol and tobacco, in spite of the fact that no socially redeeming effects (for example, birth control) are associated with their use. Second, there really are no drugs that have no side effects; even aspirin has known gastric effects and causes occasional deaths (8). Third and most relevant to our topic is the fact that pregnancy itself, which the contraceptive agents prevent, is a condition (some women might even call it an illness) that is accompanied by side effects ranging from nausea to death (see Table 1). My thesis is that we cannot afford the luxury of such rigorous standards, which are probably unrealizable (it seems unlikely that a drug lacking side effects in a few individuals can ever be developed) and unrealistic (requirements of 10 to 20 years' clinical experience with human subjects prior to general use have been proposed by some circles, though not yet by government regulatory agencies), unless we are prepared to accept the reality that no new chemical birth-control agent that meets these standards will ever be developed.

**4. International role of the Food and Drug Administration.** The protocols for, and the conduct of, clinical trials in the United States have to be submitted to the FDA, which can disapprove them. This is the agency which subsequently approves or disapproves a drug for marketing. Except for export of

## TABLE 1

Risk of death with various contraceptive methods.
[From *Int. Planned Parenthood Fed. Med. Bull. 2*, No. 4 (1968)]

| Method | Pregnancies (No.) | Women aged 20–34 years (10⁶ users per year) | | Women aged 35–44 years (10⁶ users per year) | |
|---|---|---|---|---|---|
| | | Deaths due to pregnancy | Deaths due to method | Deaths due to pregnancy | Deaths due to method |
| IUD | 30,000 | 7 | Not known | 17 | Not known |
| Oral contraceptives | 5,000 | 1 | 13 | 3 | 34 |
| Diaphragm | 120,000 | 27 | 0 | 69 | 0 |
| Safe period | 240,000 | 55 | 0 | 135 | 0 |
| Pregnancy | 1,000,000 | 228 | | 576 | |

drugs, its mandate ends with the geographical boundaries of this country. Yet in actual fact its dominant role is now noted over most of the world (especially in Europe) and even recognized by the FDA itself through the establishment in 1966 of an Office of International Affairs *(9)*. Irrespective of the reasons, a drug that is formally disapproved in the United States has little chance to be marketed in Europe, and in the field of the steroid oral contraceptives the FDA has a *de facto* veto power in most European countries. The consequences of this situation are particularly serious in the field of birth control.

The FDA is a government regulatory body which is subject to tremendous political, journalistic, and legislative pressures. In a way, it is remarkable that the FDA has managed to maintain a considerable amount of independence even though many of the pressures exerted upon it have nothing to do with scientific facts. As stated above, the FDA's policies and standards for final approval of new contraceptive agents affect the possibility of even conducting initial clinical trials in the United States, and even abroad. For understandable reasons, FDA personnel have no incentive for expediting approval of new drugs, because their primary mandate is to protect the public from harm and fraud, rather than to stimulate medical advances. Consequently, the more novel the drug or mode of administration, the more extensive the data the agency requires for approval. The expense involved in conducting drug trials and in obtaining FDA approval in the United States generally runs now to millions of dollars and thus leads to the inevitable, albeit unfortunate, result that only very large commercial organizations have the financial and technical resources needed for carrying a new drug all the way to final, clinical use by the public. Expeditious FDA approval of a new drug, were it possible, would be looked upon by the press and the public today as kowtowing to a profit-hungry enterprise. And there have been unsavory examples that encourage caution. Unfortunately, this atmosphere has a particularly devastating effect on the development of new contraceptive agents.

These drugs, it should be noted, are really the first medicinal agents to be administered for very long periods to essentially healthy individuals, and neither the FDA nor the medical community has as yet solved satisfactorily the problem of what the standards should be in evaluating a drug used in such a population group for such purposes. This question must be answered eventually, because the trend in modern medicinal research is toward preventive medication, and in many conditions of aging and deterioration—for instance in atherosclerosis—the ideal preventive will have to be given to "healthy" individuals many years in advance of the actual occurrence of the disease.

Approval by the FDA (or occasionally by some European equivalent) is a virtual *sine qua non* before any contraceptive agent is accepted for wide use in one of the developing countries that have no significant governmental drug-control agencies, and the standards and designs of the clinical and even biological experiments are adapted to the American milieu. This situation occasionally has very unfortunate consequences in the birth-control field. Let me cite three examples, all very different.

The first illustrates the fact that epidemiological factors tend to be ignored, since drug approval is sought within the context of the American, or Western European, population. Thus, in Egypt—a country in which most of the government-supported birth-control programs are based on oral contraceptives—there seems to be an abnormally high incidence of liver involvement *(10)* after the use of steroid oral contraceptives; this, on further reflection, is not too surprising in view of the prevalence of *Bilharzia* infection in that country. In Iran, galactorrhea as a consequence of administration of the oral contraceptive *(10)* has been reported relatively frequently, whereas such a complication is seen very rarely in Europe or the United States. Under the present circumstances, such epidemiological factors will be studied only after a drug has passed the 10-year screen of FDA approval, which, of course, is much too late.

A second example illustrates the combined effect of general legal restrictions and FDA requirements. For perfectly understandable reasons, the FDA requires evidence that new drugs do not have teratogenic effects. While some tentative conclusions can be derived from animal experiments, the ultimate answer must come from human experience. Even the layman will recognize that agents affecting the ovum or sperm may present risks in that regard, and that it would be highly desirable therefore if, in the event the contraceptive agent being tested failed to prevent pregnancy, the pregnancy could be terminated through abortion and the fetus examined. In the United States and many other countries, such a procedure is legally impossible, and, as a result, initial clinical experiments with really novel "once-a-month" pills, which require access to potential abortion, cannot be conducted in the United States. The consequences of conducting such clinical work abroad in countries where it is permitted are considered below.

The third example illustrates what is potentially the most dangerous consequence, one arising from the fact that there exists no independent scientific body to which FDA scientific decisions can be appealed. Under certain circumstances, the FDA may wish to appoint an ad hoc advisory body of experts, whose decisions are not binding on the FDA, but there exists no independent group to whom the experimenter can appeal if he (rather than the FDA) wishes to do so. The need for such national and international appeal bodies is great in the field of birth-control agents, for the following reason. The single biggest bottleneck in fertility-control research is the lack of a satisfactory test animal, other than man, for evaluating efficacy and safety. Despite this lack, the FDA has recently imposed very special requirements for animal testing of female contraceptive agents (requirements quite distinct from those of other drugs) —one of them being the stipulation that toxicity studies with very high daily doses be made in dogs for 7 years and in monkeys for 10 years before large-scale clinical trials are permitted (11). The motivation, on political and even humane grounds, is understandable, but the scientific rationale for selecting these animals, notably the dog (whose semi-annual heat cycle and notorious sensitivity to female sex hormones hardly allow meaningful extrapolation to the human female with her monthly menstrual cycle), is highly debatable. Thus the World Health Organization Scientific Group (3) reached the following conclusion about animal studies with steroid contraceptives:

> The extrapolation to women of data derived from dose and duration studies in experimental animals is of questionable validity and may be misleading, particularly when it is impossible to assess the comparability of dosages and lifespans. In the light of these considerations, the interpretation of such data is extremely difficult. *There is no evidence to justify recent emphasis on the presumed advantages of observations in subhuman primates and in canines* [italics mine].

In spite of this scientific uncertainty, requirements that long-term tests be made in dogs have, to my knowledge, resulted in the recent discontinuance of at least two clinical trials of promising compounds. Even more serious is the fact that, as a consequence, this experience with FDA's practical power to determine scientific protocol has led one of the largest of American drug companies (which does not market any contraceptive agent) to discontinue virtually all research on contraceptive agents chemically related to female steroids. This self-imposed restriction may not be regretted by competitive drug firms, but it is certainly unfortunate as far as general scientific advances in population control are concerned, because this company's research organization is internationally recognized as being among those at the very top. There is little doubt that if the present climate concerning clinical testing of contraceptive agents had existed 15 years ago, none of the steroid oral contraceptives now being used would ever have been developed.

My prediction is that, as the FDA-imposed requirements for clinical testing of contraceptive agents become more and more complicated, increase costs enormously, and are not appealable (except through the courts) to an independent body, new companies will not enter the field, and existing ones with a very heavy commercial stake in the field will do less research (most of it of the "me-too" variety because of the somewhat lower risks of failure to secure official approval), and the resulting vacuum will not be filled by anybody else. Under these circumstances, the newly organized NIH Center for Population Research may well stimulate interesting basic research in reproductive physiology, but this will hardly result in development of a practical birth-control agent before the next 3 billion human beings are added to the world's population.

A partial solution to this problem—one that could be easily implemented in the United States—would be the appointment by the National Academy of Sciences of a permanent body of independent experts to whom questionable scientific decisions of the FDA with respect to animal and clinical testing could be appealed, and whose conclusions would be binding on the FDA.

**5. Foreign clinical experimentation.** Irrespective of the justification for prohibition, once clinical trials with a drug have been prohibited in the United States, it is difficult to resume them elsewhere. As a result—and this is particularly true of contraceptive agents because of the additional testing requirements imposed by both the United States and Great Britain as compared with requirements in the testing of other drugs—more and more of the preliminary clinical trials, following the initial chemical and biological studies, are performed abroad, frequently in one of the developing countries. Regardless of the caliber of such work, it takes little imagination to predict what kind of major issue can develop from such a state of affairs, in which preliminary trials on human beings, under the auspices of technically advanced countries, are performed first in developing countries.

**6. Implications for population control in developing countries.** Regardless of the site of initial clinical experimentation, there is no doubt that, on moral and political grounds alone, a new chemical contraceptive agent to be used on a massive scale in a developing country must also be approved and used on a wide scale in the country of its origin (the United States or a European country). For all practical purposes this means that, in most instances, it must have passed scrutiny by the FDA or one of its European counterparts (for example, the Dunlop Committee in Great Britain), with all of its advantageous protective safeguards but, also, unfavorable bureaucratic delays. The moral and political justification for such a stand is fairly obvious. The advanced countries are not only the ones from which new contraceptive agents emanate technically: they are also the ones that supply motivation and even pressure, coupled with financial and technical assistance, to the developing countries for the introduction of family-planning programs in which such contraceptive agents are used. These advanced countries are placed in a virtually untenable position when they propose the use of agents and procedures which they, themselves, are not prepared to use on their own populations (*12*). On a smaller scale, this is the objection to conducting initial clinical trials abroad.

It should be remembered that, even under ideal circumstances, the motivation of technologically advanced countries (generally countries of white population) preaching the family-planning gospel to the developing countries (frequently of nonwhite population) is highly suspect. Even within the United States, some of the economically deprived black inhabitants of our urban ghettos attribute genocidal motives to family-planning programs in their areas.

With these factors in mind, it must be realized that any position taken in the United States or Europe on presently used or potentially interesting future contraceptive agents has repercussions which extend far beyond the borders of these countries, and has worldwide consequences as far as population control is concerned. Thus, in the United

States, the more recent reports on an apparent relationship between the use of certain oral contraceptive steroids and thromboembolism leading to deaths in a very small number of individuals appears in the press under headlines like "Pill Kills," with implied or specifically stated criticism of the fact that their use in the United States continues to be permitted. Even if one accepted all these deaths as an established consequence (13) of the use of steroid contraceptive agents, the data in Table 1 demonstrate that the number of deaths is still far fewer than those associated with pregnancy. Indeed, even if the number of associated deaths were ten times as great, a strong logical case could still be made for the continued use of these steroids as lifesaving agents.

Of particular relevance is the observation that a statistically meaningful causal relationship (13) between thromboembolism and steroid contraceptive agents could be suggested only after extensive use by several hundred thousand women, since the incidence is in any event so very low. It is probably quite impractical to anticipate or even demonstrate the occurrence of other side effects of such low incidence in clinical trials (as compared to actual clinical practice), because the scope of such an experimental project in terms of number of subjects as well as duration of experiment would simply be too vast and would make it exceedingly difficult to bring to practical fruition any really novel chemical approach to contraception, be it in the female or the male. If major advances in fertility control are to occur, we must realize—and so must the regulatory agencies of the technically advanced countries—that some risks should be willingly undertaken in promoting and facilitating widespread clinical trial and reasonably prompt practical use of such new agents, risks commensurate with scientific caution, but caution unencumbered by bureaucartic inertia. Otherwise, with every passing year, the accumulated burden and penalties associated with a bulging world population become more severe.

## CONCLUSION

In a thought-provoking article on the population problem, Berelson stated (14) that "what will be scientifically available, politically acceptable, administratively feasible, economically justifiable, and morally tolerated depends upon people's perceptions of consequences." Within the narrow scope of the present article—namely, the prognosis for the development of new chemical birth-control agents—no degree of politically acceptable, administratively feasible, and economically justifiable motivation on the part of the developing countries will lead to new advances in contraception unless the technically advanced countries, foremost of which is the United States, recognize that their virtual scientific monopoly in the field of reproductive physiology imposes upon them a moral and logical obligation to take a global rather than a parochial view of novel contraceptive approaches. The pivotal role for future developments anywhere in the world rests to a considerable extent on government agencies such as the U.S. Food and Drug Administration, whose legal mandate is the protection of the national, rather than the international, population within the confines of national rather than global problems. Such a parochial view may perhaps be tolerated in research dealing with specific diseases, but its consequences will be disastrous when applied to a problem like the world's population growth.

Indeed, it is not fair to place the entire onus for satisfactory scientific designs of clinical protocols, scientific evaluation of clinical data, permission for eventual use by the general public, and continuous subsequent monitoring of the drug (in the present case, the contraceptive agent) on one agency, which can hardly fulfill all these partially competing functions in an objective manner. As far as the prospects for the development of better birth-control agents are concerned, the Achilles heel seems to be the presently unassailable ultimate authority of government regulatory agencies to pass judgment on scientific matters. The more questionable the scientific fact is, the more questionable this single scientific authority becomes. In view of the extraordinary scientific complexity and the many unanswered scientific questions in the field of human reproductive physiology, which cannot await leisurely answers because of the enormity of the problem of population growth, the ultimate authority on such scientific matters (especially during the experimental preclinical and clinical phases) should rest on independent bodies of experts to whose scientific judgment the governmental regulatory agencies as well as the investigator are prepared to bow. Since the appointment of membership to such "final courts of scientific appeal" is such a delicate matter, my recommendation is that the national responsibility in the United States be delegated to the National Academy of Sciences, and that the international responsibility be delegated to the World Health Organization. In fact, the World Health Organization already has such groups *(3, 4)* consisting of experts from developed and developing countries. All that is needed is to bestow on them the necessary authority.

## REFERENCES AND NOTES

1. *The Growth of World Population* (National Acad. of Sciences, Washington, D.C., 1963).
2. C. Djerassi, *Science* **151,** 1055 (1966).
3. "Hormonal Steroids in Contraception." *World Health Organ. Tech. Rep. Ser. No. 386* (1968) (report of a WHO scientific group).
4. "Basic and Clinical Aspects of Intra-uterine Devices," *World Health Organ. Tech. Rep. Ser. Nos. 332* and *397* (1966; 1968) (report of a WHO scientific group).
5. The cost of the agents themselves is no longer a critical factor, since, in such large-scale government-sponsored projects, it has already reached the level of 10 cents per woman per month.
6. For the purposes of this article, the conventional foam tablets, jellies, and the like are not considered within the definition of "chemical contraceptive agents."
7. My association with this field has been through Syntex Corporation, a commercial organization of which I am a director and president of the research division, rather than in my capacity as professor of chemistry at Stanford University. This connection may raise some question, perhaps reasonably, as to the objectivity of my remarks. However, this has also given me a kind of practical experience that is not readily available to anyone who has not been directly involved in the commercial development of pharmaceuticals for wide public use. I would also add that my own strong feelings about the importance of finding practical solutions to the world population problem have been a primary incentive in my work and in my efforts to bring my views to public attention. Therefore, I hope that any criticism will be directed at the content, rather than the source, of this article.
8. See, for instance, J. J. Bonica and G. D. Allen, in *Drugs of Choice, 1966–1967,* W. Modell, Ed. (Mosby, St. Louis, 1966), pp. 199–232; "National Clearinghouse for Poison Control Center Bulletin," *U.S. Dep. Health, Educ. Welf. Annu. Rep.* (Government Printing Office, Washington, D.C., 1968).
9. K. E. Taylor and C. O. Miller, *FDA Pap.* (1968), p. 27.
10. E. Diczfalusy, Karolinska Institute, Stockholm, personal communication.
11. E. J. Goldenthal, *FDA Pap.* (1968), p. 13.
12. In retrospect, it is interesting for me to recall a series of lectures that I presented in Sweden in September 1962 under the auspices of the Swedish Chemical Society, dealing with the developments of steroidal oral contraceptives. Sweden had at that time not yet approved oral contraceptive steroids for domestic use, yet, as part of its impressive and intelligent foreign assistance program involving population control measures, it was already promoting with great vigor the use of such contraceptive agents in certain Asian countries. In my lectures I emphasized the moral and logical objections to such a position.
13. The medical community seems by no means to be unanimous on this question; see L. E. Moses, *J. Amer. Med. Ass.* **208,** 694 (1969) and references cited therein.
14. B. Berelson, *Science* **163,** 533 (1969).

# PART SEVEN

# What We Must Do, and the Cost of Failure

*Doubt, of whatever kind, can be ended by action alone.**

No book of this length could hope to explore in any depth the spectrum of crises which either confront man today or loom in the not distant future. It is therefore fitting to include at the end a masterful survey which enumerates and even ranks according to importance many crisis problems we have slighted, as well as those we have examined. In "What We Must Do," biophysicist John Platt goes on to suggest that the solution to this vast nexus of threats will require a mobilization of science similar to that carried out by American and British scientists during World War II.

Radicals tend to be very suspicious of science in all of its forms, but we are convinced, with Platt, that our problems are already so complex that only a massive application of systematic knowledge can help us to overcome them. We are not enamored of technological solutions to sociological and biological problems—indeed as we have already indicated we feel the most fundamental change must occur in the minds of men. But such a change, to be effective, must be followed by a drastic reordering of scientific priorities— one which can carry man toward a stable equilibrium with his environment and away from today's ill-considered drive to dominate it.

We are not, of course, optimistic about our chances of success. Some form of ecocatastrophe, if not thermonuclear war, seems almost certain to overtake us before the end of the century. (The inability to forecast exactly which one—whether plague, famine, the poisoning of the oceans, drastic climatic change, or some disaster entirely unforseen—is hardly grounds for complacency.) In the last selection in this book, Ehrlich speculates about some of the possibilities in the form of a scenario, "Looking Backward from the Year 2000." The reader who finds it frivolous should note that every aspect of the scenario has some basis in contemporary events or knowledge —indeed, a good part of the background material is to be found in this volume. Such a picture may seem a grim close, and indeed it is intended to convey the cost of continued complacency. In one sense—that civilization much as we know it survives with only a costly lesson—it may be too hopeful.

* Thomas Carlyle, *Past and Present.*

# What We Must Do

## JOHN PLATT

There is only one crisis in the world. It is the crisis of transformation. The trouble is that it is now coming upon us as a storm of crisis problems from every direction. But if we look quantitatively at the course of our changes in this century, we can see immediately why the problems are building up so rapidly at this time, and we will see that it has now become urgent for us to mobilize all our intelligence to solve these problems if we are to keep from killing ourselves in the next few years.

The essence of the matter is that the human race is on a steeply rising "S-curve" of change. We are undergoing a great historical transition to new levels of technological power all over the world. We all know about these changes, but we do not often stop to realize how large they are in orders of magnitude, or how rapid and enormous compared to all previous changes in history. In the last century, we have increased our speeds of communication by a factor of $10^7$; our speeds of travel by $10^2$; our speeds of data handling by $10^6$; our energy resources by $10^3$; our power of weapons by $10^6$; our ability to control diseases by something like $10^2$; and our rate of population growth to $10^3$ times what is was a few thousand years ago.

Could anyone suppose that human relations around the world would not be affected to their very roots by such changes? Within the last 25 years, the Western world has moved into an age of jet planes, missiles and satellites, nuclear power and nuclear terror. We have acquired computers and automation, a service and leisure economy, superhighways, superagriculture, supermedicine, mass higher education, universal TV, oral contraceptives, environmental pollution, and urban crises. The rest of the world is also moving rapidly and may catch up with all these powers and problems within a very short time. It is hardly surprising that young people under 30, who have grown up familiar with these things from childhood, have developed very different expectations and concerns from the older generation that grew up in another world.

What many people do not realize is that many of these technological changes are now approaching certain natural limits. The "S-curve" is beginning to level off. We may never have faster communication or more TV or larger weapons or a higher level of danger than we have now. This means that if we could learn how to manage these new powers and problems in the next few years without killing ourselves by our obsolete structures and behavior, we might be able to create new and more effective social structures that would last for many generations. We might be able to move into that new world of abundance and diversity and well-being for all mankind which technology has now made possible.

The trouble is that we may not survive these next few years. The human race today is like a rocket on a launching pad. We have been building up to this moment of takeoff for a long time, and if we can get safely through the takeoff period, we may fly on a new and exciting course for a long time to

What We Must Do. From *Science*, Vol. 166, May 16, 1969, pp. 1115–1121. Copyright 1969 by the American Association for the Advancement of Science. Reprinted by permission of the author and the publisher.

come. But at this moment, as the powerful new engines are fired, their thrust and roar shakes and stresses every part of the ship and may cause the whole thing to blow up before we can steer it on its way. Our problem today is to harness and direct these tremendous new forces through this dangerous transition period to the new world instead of to destruction. But unless we can do this, the rapidly increasing strains and crises of the next decade may kill us all. They will make the last 20 years look like a peaceful interlude.

## THE NEXT 10 YEARS

Several types of crisis may reach the point of explosion in the next 10 years: nuclear escalation, famine, participatory crises, racial crises, and what have been called the crises of administrative legitimacy. It is worth singling out two or three of these to see how imminent and dangerous they are, so that we can fully realize how very little time we have for preventing or controlling them.

Take the problem of nuclear war, for example. A few years ago, Leo Szilard estimated the "half-life" of the human race with respect to nuclear escalation as being between 10 and 20 years. His reasoning then is still valid now. As long as we continue to have no adequate stabilizing peace-keeping structures for the world, we continue to live under the daily threat not only of local wars but of nuclear escalation with overkill and megatonnage enough to destroy all life on earth. Every year or two there is a confrontation between nuclear powers—Korea, Laos, Berlin, Suez, Quemoy, Cuba, Vietnam, and the rest. MacArthur wanted to use nuclear weapons in Korea; and in the Cuban missile crisis, John Kennedy is said to have estimated the probability of a nuclear exchange as about 25 per cent.

The danger is not so much that of the unexpected, such as a radar error or even a new nuclear dictator, as it is that our present system will work exactly as planned!—from border testing, strategic gambles, threat and counter-threat, all the way up to that "second-strike capability" that is already aimed, armed, and triggered to wipe out hundreds of millions of people in a 3-hour duel!

What is the probability of this in the average incident? 10 per cent? 5 per cent? There is no average incident. But it is easy to see that five or ten more such confrontations in this game of "nuclear roulette" might indeed give us only a 50-50 chance of living until 1980 or 1990. This is a shorter life expectancy than people have ever had in the world before. All our medical increases in length of life are meaningless, as long as our nuclear lifetime is so short.

Many agricultural experts also think that within this next decade the great famines will begin, with deaths that may reach 100 million people in densely populated countries like India and China. Some contradict this, claiming that the remarkable new grains and new agricultural methods introduced in the last 3 years in Southeast Asia may now be able to keep the food supply ahead of population growth. But others think that the reeducation of farmers and consumers to use the new grains cannot proceed fast enough to make a difference.

But if famine does come, it is clear that it will be catastrophic. Besides the direct human suffering, it will further increase our international instabilities, with food riots, troops called out, governments falling, and international interventions that will change the whole political map of the world. It could make Vietnam look like a popgun.

In addition, the next decade is likely to see continued crises of legitimacy of all our overloaded administrations, from universities and unions to cities and national governments. Everywhere there is protest and refusal to accept the solutions handed down by some central elite. The student revolutions circle the globe. Suburbs protest as well as ghettoes, Right as well as Left. There are many new sources of collision and protest, but it is clear that the general problem is in large part structural rather than political. Our traditional methods of election and management no

longer give administrations the skill and capacity they need to handle their complex new
burdens and decisions. They become swollen,
unresponsive—and repudiated. Every day now
some distinguished administrator is pressured
out of office by protesting constituents.

In spite of the violence of some of these
confrontations, this may seem like a trivial
problem compared to war or famine—until
we realize the dangerous effects of these instabilities on the stability of the whole system.
In a nuclear crisis or in any of our other crises
today, administrators or negotiators may often
work out some basis of agreement between
conflicting groups or nations, only to find
themselves rejected by their people on one
or both sides, who are then left with no
mechanism except to escalate their battles
further.

## THE CRISIS OF CRISES

What finally makes all of our crises still
more dangerous is that they are now coming
on top of each other. Most administrations
are able to endure or even enjoy an occasional crisis, with everyone working late together and getting a new sense of importance
and unity. What they are not prepared to deal
with are multiple crises, a crisis of crises all at
one time. This is what happened in New York
City in 1968 when the Ocean Hill-Brownsville
teacher and race strike was combined with a
police strike, on top of a garbage strike, on
top of a longshoremen's strike, all within a
few days of each other.

When something like this happens, the
staffs get jumpy with smoke and coffee and
alcohol, the mediators become exhausted,
and the administrators find themselves running two crises behind. Every problem may
escalate because those involved no longer
have time to think stragiht. What would have
happened in the Cuban missile crisis if the
East Coast power blackout had occurred by
accident that same day? Or if the "hot line"
between Washington and Moscow had gone

dead? There might have been hours of misin-
terpretation, and some fatally different decisions.

I think this multiplication of domestic
and international crises today will shorten
that short half-life. In the continued absence
of better ways of heading off these multiple
crises, our half-life may no longer be 10 or
20 years, but more like 5 to 10 years, or less.
We may have even less than a 50-50 chance
of living until 1980.

This statement may seem uncertain and
excessively dramatic. But is there any scientist
who would make a much more optimistic
estimate after considering all the different
sources of danger and how they are increasing? The shortness of the time is due to the
exponential and multiplying character of our
problems and not to what particular numbers
or guesses we put in. Anyone who feels more
hopeful about getting past the nightmares of
the 1970's has only to look beyond them to
the monsters of pollution and population
rising up in the 1980's and 1990's. Whether
we have 10 years or more like 20 to 30, unless
we systematically find new large-scale solutions, we are in the gravest danger of destroying our society, our world, and ourselves in
any of a number of different ways well before
the end of this century. Many futurologists
who have predicted what the world will be
like in the year 2000 have neglected to tell
us that.

Nevertheless the real reason for trying to
make rational estimates of these deadlines is
not because of their shock value but because
they give us at least a rough idea of how
much time we may have for finding and
mounting some large-scale solutions. The time
is short but, as we shall see, it is not too
short to give us a chance that something can
be done, if we begin immediately.

From this point, there is no place to go
but up. Human predictions are always conditional. The future always depends on what
we do and can be made worse or better by
stupid or intelligent action. To change our
earlier analogy, today we are like men coming
out of a coal mine who suddenly begin to

hear the rock rumbling, but who have also begun to see a little square of light at the end of the tunnel. Against this background, I am an optimist—in that I want to insist that there is a square of light and that it is worth trying to get to. I think what we must do is to start running as fast as possible toward that light, working to increase the probability of our survival through the next decade by some measurable amount.

For the light at the end of the tunnel is very bright indeed. If we can only devise new mechanisms to help us survive this round of terrible crises, we have a chance of moving into a new world of incredible potentialities for all mankind. But if we cannot get through this next decade, we may never reach it.

## TASK FORCE FOR SOCIAL RESEARCH AND DEVELOPMENT

What can we do? I think that nothing less than the application of the full intelligence of our society is likely to be adequate. These problems will require the humane and constructive efforts of everyone involved. But I think they will also require something very similar to the mobilization of scientists for solving crisis problems in wartime. I believe we are going to need large numbers of scientists forming something like research teams or task forces for social research and development. We need full-time interdisciplinary teams combining men of different specialties, natural scientists, social scientists, doctors, engineers, teachers, lawyers, and many other trained and inventive minds, who can put together our stores of knowledge and powerful new ideas into improved technical methods, organizational designs, or "social inventions" that have a chance of being adopted soon enough and widely enough to be effective. Even a great mobilization of scientists may not be enough. There is no guarantee that these problems can be solved, or solved in time, no matter what we do. But for problems of this scale and urgency, this kind of

focusing of our brains and knowledge may be the only chance we have.

Scientists, of course, are not the only ones who can make contributions. Millions of citizens, business and labor leaders, city and government officials, and workers in existing agencies, are already doing all they can to solve these problems. No scientific innovation will be effective without extensive advice and help from these groups.

But it is the new science and technology that have made our problems so immense and intractable. Technology did not create human conflicts and inequities, but it has made them unendurable. And where science and technology have expanded the problems in this way, it may be only more scientific understanding and better technology that can carry us past them. The cure for the pollution of the rivers by detergents is the use of non-polluting detergents. The cure for bad management designs is better management designs.

Also, in many of these areas, there are few people outside the research community who have the basic knowledge necessary for radically new solutions. In our great biological problems, it is the new ideas from cell biology and ecology that may be crucial. In our social-organizational problems, it may be the new theories of organization and management and behavior theory and game theory that offer the only hope. Scientific research and development groups of some kind may be the only effective mechanism by which many of these new ideas can be converted into practical invention and action.

The time scale on which such task forces would have to operate is very different from what is usual in science. In the past, most scientists have tended to work on something like a 30-year time scale, hoping that their careful studies would fit into some great intellectual synthesis that might be years away. Of course when they become politically concerned, they begin to work on something more like a 3-month time scale, collecting signatures or trying to persuade the government to start or stop some program.

But 30 years is too long, and 3 months is too short, to cope with the major crises that might destroy us in the next 10 years. Our urgent problems now are more like wartime problems, where we need to work as rapidly as is consistent with large-scale effectiveness. We need to think rather in terms of a 3-year time scale—or more broadly, a 1- to 5-year time scale. In World War II, the ten thousand scientists who were mobilized for war research knew they did not have 30 years, or even 10 years, to come up with answers. But they did have time for the new research, design, and construction that brought sonar and radar and atomic energy to operational effectiveness within 1 to 4 years. Today we need the same large-scale mobilization for innovation and action and the same sense of constructive urgency.

## PRIORITIES:
## A CRISIS INTENSITY CHART

In any such enterprise, it is most important to be clear about which problems are the real priority problems. To get this straight, it is valuable to try to separate the different problem areas according to some measures of their magnitude and urgency. A possible classification of this kind is shown in Tables 1 and 2. In these tables, I have tried to rank a number of present or potential problems or crises, vertically, according to an estimate of their order of intensity or "seriousness," and horizontally, by a rough estimate of their time to reach climactic importance. Table 1 is such a classification for the United States for the next 1 to 5 years, the next 5 to 20 years, and the next 20 to 50 years. Table 2 is a similar classification for world problems and crises.

The successive rows indicate something like order-of-magnitude differences in the intensity of the crises, as estimated by a rough product of the size of population that might be hurt or affected, multiplied by some estimated average effect in the disruption of their lives. Thus the first row corresponds to total or near-total annihilation; the second row, to great destruction or change affecting everybody; the third row, to a lower tension affecting a smaller part of the population or a smaller part of everyone's life, and so on.

Informed men might easily disagree about one row up or down in intensity, or one column left or right in the time scales, but these order-of-magnitude differences are already so great that it would be surprising to find much larger disagreements. Clearly, an important initial step in any serious problem study would be to refine such estimates.

In both tables, the one crisis that must be ranked at the top in total danger and imminence is, of course, the danger of large-scale or total annihilation by nuclear escalation or by radiological-chemical-biological-warfare (RCBW). This kind of crisis will continue through both the 1- to 5-year time period and the 5- to 20-year period as Crisis Number 1, unless and until we get a safer peace-keeping arrangement. But in the 20- to 50-year column, following the reasoning already given, I think we must simply put a big "✖" at this level, on the grounds that the peace-keeping stabilization problem will either be solved by that time or we will probably be dead.

At the second level, the 1- to 5-year period may not be a period of great destruction (except nuclear) in either the United States or the world. But the problems at this level are building up, and within the 5- to 20-year period, many scientists fear the destruction of our whole biological and ecological balance in the United States by mismanagement or pollution. Others fear political catastrophe within this period, as a result of participatory confrontations or backlash or even dictatorship, if our divisive social and structural problems are not solved before that time.

On a world scale in this period, famine and ecological catastrophe head the list of destructive problems. We will come back later to the items in the 20- to 50-year column.

The third level of crisis problems in the United States includes those that are already upon us: administrative management of com-

## TABLE 1

Classification of problems and crises by estimated time and intensity (United States).

| Grade | Estimated crisis intensity (number affected × degree of effect) | | Estimated time to crisis* | | |
|---|---|---|---|---|---|
| | | | 1 to 5 years | 5 to 20 years | 20 to 50 years |
| 1. | | Total annihilation | Nuclear or RCBW escalation | Nuclear or RCBW escalation | ⊠ (Solved or dead) |
| 2. | $10^8$ | Great destruction or change (physical, biological, or political) | (Too soon) | Participatory democracy Ecological balance | Political theory and economic structure Population planning Patterns of living Education Communications Integrative philosophy |
| 3. | $10^7$ | Widespread almost unbearable tension | Administrative management Slums Participatory democracy Racial conflict | Pollution Poverty Law and justice | ? |
| 4. | $10^6$ | Large-scale distress | Transportation Neighborhood ugliness Crime | Communications gap | ? |
| 5. | $10^5$ | Tension producing responsive change | Cancer and heart Smoking and drugs Artificial organs Accidents Sonic boom Water supply Marine resources Privacy on computers | Educational inadequacy | ? |
| 6. | | Other problems— important, but adequately researched | Military R & D New educational methods Mental illness Fusion power | Military R & D | |
| 7. | | Exaggerated dangers and hopes | Mind control Heart transplants Definition of death | Sperm banks Freezing bodies Unemployment from automation | Eugenics |
| 8. | | Noncrisis problems being "overstudied" | Man in space Most basic science | | |

* If no major effort is made at anticipatory solution.

## TABLE 2

Classification of problems and crises by estimated time and intensity (World).

| Grade | Estimated crisis intensity (number affected × degree of effect) | | Estimated time to crisis* | | |
|---|---|---|---|---|---|
| | | | 1 to 5 years | 5 to 20 years | 20 to 50 years |
| 1. | $10^{10}$ | Total annihilation | Nuclear or RCBW escalation | Nuclear or RCBW escalation | ✠ (Solved or dead) |
| 2. | $10^{9}$ | Great destruction or change (physical, biological, or political) | (Too soon) | Famines Ecological balance Development failures Local wars Rich-poor gap | Economic structure and political theory Population and ecological balance Patterns of living Universal education Communications-integration Management of world Integrative philosophy |
| 3. | $10^{8}$ | Widespread almost unbearable tension | Administrative management Need for participation Group and racial conflict Poverty-rising expectations Environmental degradation | Poverty Pollution Racial wars Political rigidity Strong dictatorships | ? |
| 4. | $10^{7}$ | Large-scale distress | Transportation Diseases Loss of old cultures | Housing Education Independence of big powers Communications gap | ? |
| 5. | $10^{6}$ | Tension producing responsive change | Regional organization Water supplies | ? | ? |
| 6. | | Other problems—important, but adequately researched | Technical development design Intelligent monetary design | | |
| 7. | | Exaggerated dangers and hopes | | | Eugenics Melting of ice caps |
| 8. | | Noncrisis problems being "overstudied" | Man in space Most basic science | | |

* If no major effort is made at anticipatory solution.

munities and cities, slums, participatory democracy, and racial conflict. In the 5- to 20-year period, the problems of pollution and poverty or major failures of law and justice could escalate to this level of tension if they are not solved. The last column is left blank because secondary events and second-order effects will interfere seriously with any attempt to make longer-range predictions at these lower levels.

The items in the lower part of the tables are not intended to be exhaustive. Some are common headline problems which are included simply to show how they might rank quantitatively in this kind of comparison. Anyone concerned with any of them will find it a useful exercise to estimate for himself their order of seriousness, in terms of the number of people they actually affect and the average distress they cause. Transportation problems and neighborhood ugliness, for example, are listed as grade 4 problems in the United States because they depress the lives of tens of millions for 1 or 2 hours every day. Violent crimes may affect a corresponding number every year or two. These evils are not negligible, and they are worth the efforts of enormous numbers of people to cure them and to keep them cured—but on the other hand, they will not destroy our society.

The grade 5 crises are those where the hue and cry has been raised and where responsive changes of some kind are already under way. Cancer goes here, along with problems like auto safety and an adequate water supply. This is not to say that we have solved the problem of cancer, but rather that good people are working on it and are making as much progress as we could expect from anyone. (At this level of social intensity, it should be kept in mind that there are also positive opportunities for research, such as the automation of clinical biochemistry or the invention of new channels of personal communication, which might affect the 20-year future as greatly as the new drugs and solid state devices of 20 years ago have begun to affect the present.)

## WHERE THE SCIENTISTS ARE

Below grade 5, three less quantitative categories are listed, where the scientists begin to outnumber the problems. Grade 6 consists of problems that many people believe to be important but that are adequately researched at the present time. Military R & D belongs in this category. Our huge military establishment creates many social problems, both of national priority and international stability, but even in its own terms, war research, which engrosses hundreds of thousands of scientists and engineers, is being taken care of generously. Likewise, fusion power is being studied at the $100-million level, though even if we had it tomorrow, it would scarcely change our rates of application of nuclear energy in generating more electric power for the world.

Grade 7 contains the exaggerated problems which are being talked about or worked on out of all proportion to their true importance, such as heart transplants, which can never affect more than a few thousands of people out of the billions in the world. It is sad to note that the symposia on "social implications of science" at many national scientific meetings are often on the problems of grade 7.

In the last category, grade 8, are two subjects which I am sorry to say I must call "overstudied," at least with respect to the real crisis problems today. The Man in Space flights to the moon and back are the most beautiful technical achievements of man, but they are not urgent except for national display, and they absorb tens of thousands of our most ingenious technical brains.

And in the "overstudied" list I have begun to think we must now put most of our basic science. This is a hard conclusion, because all of science is so important in the long run and because it is still so small compared, say, to advertising or the tobacco industry. But basic scientific thinking is a scarce resource. In a national emergency, we would suddenly find that a host of our scientific problems could be postponed for several years in favor of more urgent research. Should not our total human emergency make the same claims? Long-range science is useless unless we survive to use it. Tens of thousands of our best trained minds may now be needed for something more important than "science as usual."

The arrows at level 2 in the tables are intended to indicate that problems may escalate to a higher level of crisis in the next time period if they are not solved. The arrows toward level 2 in the last columns of both tables show the escalation of all our problems upward to some general reconstruction in the 20- to 50-year time period, if we survive. Probably no human institution will continue unchanged for another 50 years, because they will all be changed by the crises if they are not changed in advance to prevent them. There will surely be widespread rearrangements in all our ways of life everywhere, from our patterns of society to our whole philosophy of man. Will they be more humane, or less? Will the world come to resemble a diverse and open humanist democracy? Or Orwell's *1984*? Or a post-nuclear desert with its scientists hanged? It is our acts of commitment and leadership in the next few months and years that will decide.

## MOBILIZING SCIENTISTS

It is a unique experience for us to have peacetime problems, or technical problems which are not industrial problems, on such a scale. We do not know quite where to start, and there is no mechanism yet for generating ideas systematically or paying teams to turn them into successful solutions.

But the comparison with wartime research and development may not be inappropriate. Perhaps the antisubmarine warfare work or the atomic energy project of the 1940's provide the closest parallels to what we must do in terms of the novelty, scale, and urgency of the problems, the initiative

needed, and the kind of large success that has to be achieved. In the antisubmarine campaign, Blackett assembled a few scientists and other ingenious minds in his "back room," and within a few months they had worked out the "operations analysis" that made an order-of-magnitude difference in the success of the campaign. In the atomic energy work, scientists started off with extracurricular research, formed a central committee to channel their secret communications, and then studied the possible solutions for some time before they went to the government for large-scale support for the great development laboratories and production plants.

Fortunately, work on our crisis problems today would not require secrecy. Our great problems today are all beginning to be world problems, and scientists from many countries would have important insights to contribute.

Probably the first step in crisis studies now should be the organization of intense technical discussion and education groups in every laboratory. Promising lines of interest could then lead to the setting up of part-time or full-time studies and teams and coordinating committees. Administrators and boards of directors might find active crisis research important to their own organizations in many cases. Several foundations and federal agencies already have in-house research and make outside grants in many of these crisis areas, and they would be important initial sources of support.

But the step that will probably be required in a short time is the creation of whole new centers, perhaps comparable to Los Alamos or the RAND Corporation, where interdisciplinary groups can be assembled to work full-time on solutions to these crisis problems. Many different kinds of centers will eventually be necessary, including research centers, development centers, training centers, and even production centers for new sociotechincal inventions. The problems of our time—the $100-billion food problem or the $100-billion arms control problem—are no smaller than World War II in scale and importance, and it would be absurd to think that a few academic research teams or a few agency laboratories could do the job.

## SOCIAL INVENTIONS

The thing that discourages many scientists—even social scientists—from thinking in these research-and-development terms is their failure to realize that there are such things as social inventions and that they can have large-scale effects in a surprisingly short time. A recent study with Karl Deutsch has examined some 40 of the great achievements in social science in this century, to see where they were made and by whom and how long they took to become effective. They include developments such as the following:

Keynesian economics
Opinion polls and statistical sampling
Input-output economics
Operations analysis
Information theory and feedback theory
Theory of games and economic behavior
Operant conditioning and programmed learning
Planned programming and budgeting (PPB)
Non-zero-sum game theory

Many of these have made remarkable differences within just a few years in our ability to handle social problems or management problems. The opinion poll became a national necessity within a single election period. The theory of games, published in 1946, had become an important component of American strategic thinking by RAND and the Defense Department by 1953, in spite of the limitation of the theory at that time to zero-sum games, with their dangerous bluffing and "brinksmanship." Today, within less than a decade, the PPB management technique is sweeping through every large organization.

This list is particularly interesting because it shows how much can be done outside official government agencies when inventive

men put their brains together. Most of the achievements were the work of teams of two or more men, almost all of them located in intellectual centers such as Princeton or the two Cambridges.

The list might be extended by adding commercial social inventions with rapid and widespread effects, like credit cards. And sociotechnical inventions, like computers and automation or like oral contraceptives, which were in widespread use within 10 years after they were developed. In addition, there are political innovations like the New Deal, which made great changes in our economic life within 4 years, and the pay-as-you-go income tax, which transformed federal taxing power within 2 years.

On the international scene, the Peace Corps, the "hot line," the Test-Ban Treaty, the Antarctic Treaty, and the Nonproliferation Treaty were all implemented within 2 to 10 years after their initial proposal. These are only small contributions, a tiny patchwork part of the basic international stabilization system that is needed, but they show that the time to adopt new structural designs may be surprisingly short. Our cliches about "social lag" are very misleading. Over half of the major social innovations since 1940 were adopted or had widespread social effects within less than 12 years—a time as short as, or shorter than, the average time for adoption of technological innovations.

## AREAS FOR TASK FORCES

Is it possible to create more of these social inventions systematically to deal with our present crisis problems? I think it is. It may be worth listing a few specific areas where new task forces might start.

**1. Peace-keeping mechanisms and feedback stabilization.** Our various nuclear treaties are a beginning. But how about a technical group that sits down and thinks about the whole range of possible and impossible stabilization and peace-keeping mechanisms? Stabilization feedback-design might be a complex modern counterpart of the "checks and balances" used in designing the constitutional structure of the United States 200 years ago. With our new knowledge today about feedbacks, group behavior, and game theory, it ought to be possible to design more complex and even more successful structures.

Some peace-keeping mechanisms that might be hard to adopt today could still be worked out and tested and publicized, awaiting a more favorable moment. Sometimes the very existence of new possibilities can change the atmosphere. Sometimes, in a crisis, men may finally be willing to try out new ways and may find some previously prepared plan of enormous help.

**2. Biotechnology.** Humanity must feed and care for the children who are already in the world, even while we try to level off the further population explosion that makes this so difficult. Some novel proposals, such as food from coal, or genetic copying of champion animals, or still simpler contraceptive methods, could possibly have large-scale effects on human welfare within 10 to 15 years. New chemical, statistical, and management methods for measuring and maintaining the ecological balance could be of very great importance.

**3. Game theory.** As we have seen, zero-sum game theory has not been too academic to be used for national strategy and policy analysis. Unfortunately, in zero-sum games, what I win, you lose, and what you win, I lose. This may be the way poker works, but it is not the way the world works. We are collectively in a non-zero-sum game in which we will all lose together in nuclear holocaust or race conflict or economic nationalism, or all win together in survival and prosperity. Some of the many variations of non-zero-sum game theory, applied to group conflict and cooperation, might show us

profitable new approaches to replace our sterile and dangerous confrontation strategies.

**4. Psychological and social theories.** Many teams are needed to explore in detail and in practice how the powerful new ideas of behavior theory and the new ideas of responsive living might be used to improve family life or community and management structures. New ideas of information handling and management theory need to be turned into practical recipes for reducing the daily frustrations of small businesses, schools, hospitals, churches, and town meetings. New economic inventions are needed, such as urban development corporations. A deeper systems analysis is urgently needed to see if there is not some practical way to separate full employment from inflation. Inflation pinches the poor, increases labor-management disputes, and multiplies all our domestic conflicts and our sense of despair.

**5. Social indicators.** We need new social indicators, like the cost-of-living index, for measuring a thousand social goods and evils. Good indicators can have great "multiplier effects" in helping to maximize our welfare and minimize our ills. Engineers and physical scientists working with social scientists might come up with ingenious new methods of measuring many of these important but elusive parameters.

**6. Channels of effectiveness.** Detailed case studies of the reasons for success or failure of various social inventions could also have a large multiplier effect. Handbooks showing what channels or methods are now most effective for different small-scale and large-scale social problems would be of immense value.

The list could go on and on. In fact, each study group will have its own pet projects. Why not? Society is at least as complex as, say, an automobile with its several thousand parts. It will probably require as many research-and-development teams as the auto industry in order to explore all the inventions it needs to solve its problems. But it is clear that there are many areas of great potential crying out for brilliant minds and brilliant teams to get to work on them.

## FUTURE SATISFACTIONS AND PRESENT SOLUTIONS

This is an enormous program. But there is nothing impossible about mounting and financing it, if we, as concerned men, go into it with commitment and leadership. Yes, there will be a need for money and power to overcome organizational difficulties and vested interests. But it is worth remembering that the only real source of power in the world is the gap between what is and what might be. Why else do men work and save and plan? If there is some future increase in human satisfaction that we can point to and realistically anticipate, men will be willing to pay something for it and invest in it in the hope of that return. In economics, they pay with money; in politics, with their votes and time and sometimes with their jail sentences and their lives.

Social change, peaceful or turbulent, is powered by "what might be." This means that for peaceful change, to get over some impossible barrier of unresponsiveness or complexity or group conflict, what is needed is an inventive man or group—a "social entrepreneur"—who can connect the pieces and show how to turn the advantage of "what

might be" into some present advantage for every participating party. To get toll roads, when highways were hopeless, a legislative-corporation mechanism was invented that turned the future need into present profits for construction workers and bondholders and continuing profitability for the state and all the drivers.

This principle of broad-payoff anticipatory design has guided many successful social plans. Regular task forces using systems analysis to find payoffs over the barriers might give us such successful solutions much more often. The new world that could lie ahead, with its blocks and malfunctions removed, would be fantastically wealthy. It seems almost certain that there must be many systematic ways for intelligence to convert that large payoff into the profitable solution of our present problems.

The only possible conclusion is a call to action. Who will commit himself to this kind of search for more ingenious and fundamental solutions? Who will begin to assemble the research teams and the funds? Who will begin to create those full-time interdisciplinary centers that will be necessary for testing detailed designs and turning them into effective applications?

The task is clear. The task is huge. The time is horribly short. In the past, we have had science for intellectual pleasure, and science for the control of nature. We have had science for war. But today, the whole human experiment may hang on the question of how fast we now press the development of science for survival.

# Looking Backward from 2000 A.D.

Department of Population and Environment
Fifth Annual Report to the President
January 1, 2000

PAUL R. EHRLICH

## SUMMARY

**1. Population: Size.** The 1999 midyear population of the United States of North America was estimated to be 22.6 million, with a standard error of 3.2 million. The policy of special reproducer rations appears to have made significant inroads into the frequency of stillbirth, and child-health squads seem to be effectively reducing post-weaning child mortality. With the crude birth rate now standing at 30.7 and the death rate at 31.6, we are now clearly within striking distance of stabilizing our population. If present trends continue, the population will cease to decline early in 2001, and a slow rise in population size may be expected to commence thereafter. Approximately thirty-four per cent of the population now resides in SRU (Standard Reorganized Urban) Areas, and the redistribution program has returned to the inactive mode. The Division of Optimum Population is expected to recommend next year a program target of a stable population of thirty-two million by 2075.

**2. Population: Quality.** The consequences of the release of radioactivity in the 1981 reactor disaster at the Seaborg plant, combined with the overall increase in environmental radioactivity permitted before the Gofman-Tamplin Act of 1976 restricted emissions, are still causing serious repercussions in our population. The leukemia rate is still 740 per cent higher than the 1960 base rate, and that of chondrodystrophic dwarfism is now 890 per cent of base. Estimates of the degree to which radiation is responsible for the present levels of embryonic, neonatal, infant, and childhood deaths are difficult to obtain because of confounding with nutritional effects and the disorganization of our medical apparatus. Similarly, it is still impossible to sort out the causative factors for the present high level of carcinomas of all types in all age groups, but a substantial portion is thought to result from radiation damage.

It is encouraging that surviving molecular biologists and human geneticists are now relocated, and that research and training are proceeding as well as can be expected. Efforts are, of course, being heavily concentrated on the problem of repair of radiation damage in DNA (the genetic material).

The genetic variability inventory is nearing completion. Preliminary results indicate that the reduction of population size has not resulted in serious loss. The heterogeneity of the American population is considered by many specialists to have been responsible for its high survival rate relative to that of many other overdeveloped countries. It is suggested that in your State of the System address you emphasize, in layman's terms, the critical role played by "minorities" in our survival. The level of racial tension is now lower than at any previous date in our history, and positive efforts should be made to eliminate such tension entirely.

**3. Population: Health.** It is clear that lowered population density is a primary factor in preventing a resurgence of Marburgvirus B. Another factor is the recovery of the average diet to 2400 calories per day, and the increase of the high quality protein ration to almost forty grams daily. Famine has been estimated to have been directly or indirectly responsible for sixty-five million American deaths in the decade 1980-1989; the chances of a substantial hunger component in the next decade is now judged to be very small, unless another dramatic change in the climate occurs.

In addition, of course, the continual improvement of the quality of the atmosphere since the Great Die-Off has resulted in a population much less weakened by circulatory and respiratory diseases, and will thus lessen mortality due to interactions between malnutrition and cardiovascular and respiratory disorders. In the past eighteen years the turbidity of the atmosphere at all reporting points has shown almost continual decline except in areas affected locally by uncontrolled forest fires and dust from unattended farm land. (Even such local effects have been almost non-existent since 1992.) Finally, the restoration of relatively pure water supplies in many areas has further improved the epidemiological situation, although nitrate levels remain unacceptable in some areas where ground water was badly polluted.

Radiation still seems to be a factor in the continued susceptibility of some of the population to Marburgvirus B and in continued low resistance to some other diseases. However, the level of chlorinated hydrocarbons stored in human body tissues has dropped until this factor is now thought to be negligible in lowering resistance. Remember that although about 125 million American deaths were attributed to Marburgvirus B during the Great Die-Off, it is clear that as many as sixty million of these would not have occurred if the population had not been weakened by environmental deterioration. Therefore the estimate of ten million deaths due to environmental problems other than famine and disease is undoubtedly too low.

Rumors that Marburgvirus A (the strain which first infected 30 laboratory workers in 1967, killing seven, and which was only prevented from becoming epidemic by a stroke of luck) has been causing deaths in Central African populations are unconfirmed, but the Immigration and Carrier Act of 1996 will probably provide protection for the population of the United States, if the presence of that strain in the human population is confirmed.

**4. Resources: Food.** For the first time since these reports were initiated the Department can report progress on a broad front at restoring the productivity of American farms. The soil restoration program of the Department of Agriculture is now well out of the development stage, and trained extension workers are expected to be in contact with approximately twenty-five per cent of farmers working five acres or more during the next growing season. Acceptance of both humus building and integrated pest control techniques is extremely high in farmers who survived the disaster years of the mid-80's and, of course, it will be even higher among the graduates of the new Federal Agricultural University. Monitoring of all agricultural inputs by the Department of Population and Environment has completely eliminated the abuses of the agri-business swindles of the 1970s. With care it should be possible to return the American diet to the 1960 nutritional base level by 2010, as programs developing satisfactory substitutes for dairy products and sea foods are showing remarkable progress.

Food distribution is now considerably more equitable than in the base year 1960, and considering the broad support of the population redistribution program and the rapid recovery of the national railways it is confidently predicted that serious dietary inequities will not occur in the foreseeable future.

**5. Resources: Energy.** The Energy-Demand Control Act of 1998 has established the basis for rational utilization of the energy resources of the United States. In view of the great reduction in population size, fossil fuel supplies will be more than adequate (in combination with hydroelectric power) to sustain our economy over the next century. It is now estimated that Deuterium-He fusion will be operational, producing pollution-free power by 2050, which will allow about fifty years to complete the transition to all-electric power.

**6. Resources: Mineral.** Small population size, and continued availability of salvageable materials in Los Angeles and other cities which have not been reoccupied, have greatly eased the pressure on our reserves of non-renewable resources. The projected non-renewable resource crisis is now about 100 years into the future, although, if international trade is not firmly reestablished in the next decade, shortages of certain materials such as industrial diamonds may be serious. We must emphasize that national and international planning for resource husbandry and substitution must be organized as soon as possible. We must not let the lessons of the '70s and '80s go unheeded. Needless to say, the planning of the Stable Economy Commission must go ahead with all deliberate speed.

**7. Environment.** As indicated above, air and water quality have now both exceeded the 1960 base level by a considerable amount. Movement of chlorinated hydrocarbon residues into oceanic sinks is now estimated to have reached eighty-three per cent of completion. The Department concurs, however, with estimates of Eastbloc monitoring stations that the restoration of oceanic productivity is problematical. Fears of oxygen depletion are still present in certain segments of the population, and it is essential that they be reassured. Large terrestrial areas have reverted to green plants since the Die-Off, and even if oceanic ecosystems cannot be reestablished for several centuries no significant oxygen shortage is anticipated.

Whether or not weather patterns will eventually return to those of the early part of the Twentieth Century cannot be determined at this time. Those few atmospheric physicists who survived the Die-Off have not reached a consensus on the exact cause of the jet stream shifts of 1978-84. Much more basic research on turbulent flow will be necessary before any attempt to reestablish previous patterns by artificial means can be made, and any such program is clearly beyond our current capability. While a rapid spontaneous return is conceivable, it would clearly be foolish to plan on that basis. It is important to remember also that a *rapid* return now would cause serious disruption in the new agricultural programs which have been established, and might result in a return of famine.

## MAJOR RECOMMENDATIONS

1. The continuation of present pronatalist policies will be necessary for the foreseeable future. It is important, however, that the public be continually reminded that the fundamental role of this Department is not to encourage population growth, but to *regulate* the size of the population for the benefit of all our citizens. The public should be prepared for the institution of anti-natalist policies whenever conditions require them.

2. The Congress should immediately ratify the population convention of the United Nations World System Treaty.

3. Increased support of research in molecular biology, even in the face of extreme fiscal difficulties, is necessary in view of the severe genetic and metabolic difficulties faced by our population. The need to rebuild this area of science is made doubly urgent by the possible presence in the human population of Marburgvirus A and by the persistence of foci of Marburgvirus B in spite of the universal distribution of the Hsui vaccine. The reasons for the partial failure of the vaccine are as yet undetermined, but a larger cadre of trained scientists is clearly needed

to help with this and related problems. Some slowdown in training programs of the National Ecology Institute could be accepted and the funds shifted to molecular biology. Ecology is now recruiting more talented students than can be usefully employed.

4. Appeals for loosening of restrictions under the Immigration and Carrier Act should be ignored for at least one more year.

5. No changes in the activities of the Department of Agriculture are recommended except in the Wheatlands Holding Unit. In view of the small probability of weather changes permitting the Wheatlands Reserve to be cultivated in the near future, the funds expended on this unit would better be reallocated to the South Coastal unit.

6. The remaining restrictions on the use of internal combustion engines in agriculture may now be safely lifted, with of course the provision that pre-disaster leaded fuel stocks remain under bond.

7. As the climatic changes of the last quarter century appear to be more or less permanent, it is recommended that a new climatic base be established as of this date.

8. The Department recommends that the President's Human Survival Medal be awarded posthumously to Dr. John W. Gofman and Dr. Arthur R. Tamplin. These scientists, while employed by the Lawrence Radiation Laboratory, which was supported by Atomic Energy Commission (AEC) funds, challenged the AEC guidelines for permissible levels of radiation exposure. Their courage and determination in the face of ill-founded bureaucratic opposition from the AEC eventually led to the landmark Federal Radiation Emissions Act of 1976, popularly known as the Gofman-Tamplin Act. As you know, untold human suffering has been avoided because of the enforcement of the act. The Department feels that further recognition of Gofman and Tamplin at this time will drive home to our new government agencies the need both for extreme care in dealing with environmental problems, and your direct concern for the rights of individuals within those agencies to be heard.

## CONCLUSIONS

This is the first report of the Department in which the prognosis for the United States is mildly positive. In spite of this, a cautionary note must be added. In the national press there has been some comment to the effect that the environmental and public health disasters of the 1970s and 1980s were the result of "bad luck" or "Acts of God." As you know, Mr. President, if we had any luck it was good—for with bad luck the famines, disease, and competition for resources could have precipitated a thermonuclear war. It is only because most of the physical apparatus and records of our culture survived intact that recovery to the present point has been possible. We now can say with certainty that a major thermonuclear war in the 1970s or 1980s would have ended civilization permanently.

The Department urges you to remind our citizens that all of the trends leading to disaster were clear twenty years before the end came, and that we and the rest of mankind did nothing substantive to avert it. As a single example, the vulnerability of the world population to epidemic disease, due to large population size (overcrowding), hunger, and environmental deterioration was repeatedly pointed out by scientists. No substantial action was taken to correct the situation by a nation addicted to economic growth and ignorant of the limits of technology.

The cost of inaction, apathy, and unwarrented optimism has been the payment of nearly four billion human lives over a fifteen year period—and we are still paying. We cannot permit a repetition of such a disaster. Mr. President, it is imperative that this generation and those to follow be kept mindful of mankind's recent history.

Respectfully submitted,
(Signed)
*L. Page Kennedy*
Secretary